Broadcasting in the Arab World

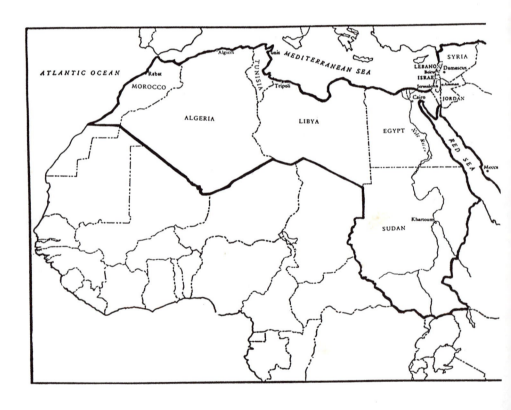

Broadcasting in the Arab World

A Survey of the Electronic Media in the Middle East

SECOND EDITION

Douglas A. Boyd

IOWA STATE UNIVERSITY PRESS / AMES

FOR CAROLE

who makes it all possible

Douglas A. Boyd is dean, College of Communications, and professor, Department of Communications and Department of Telecommunications, University of Kentucky, Lexington.

Authorization to photocopy items for internal or personal use, or the internal or personal use of specific clients, is granted by Iowa State University Press, provided that the base fee of $.10 per copy is paid directly to the Copyright Clearance Center, 27 Congress Street, Salem, MA 01970. For those organizations that have been granted a photocopy license by CCC, a separate system of payments has been arranged. The fee code for users of the Transactional Reporting Service is 0-8138-0468-X/93 $.10.

⊖ Printed on acid-free paper in the United States of America

First edition, 1993

Library of Congress Cataloging-in-Publication Data

Boyd, Douglas A.
      Broadcasting in the Arab world: a survey of the electronic media in the Middle East / Douglas A. Boyd.—2nd
            p.   cm.
      Includes bibliographical references and index.
      ISBN 0-8138-0468-X (acid-free paper)
      1. Broadcasting—Arab countries.   I. Title.
PN1990.6.A65B69   1993
384.54′09174927—dc20   92-39984

Contents

Preface, vii

Part 1 ARAB WORLD BROADCASTING

    Chapter 1   **Developments, Trends, Constraints,** 3

Part 2 NATIONAL SYSTEMS

    Chapter 2   **EGYPT,** 15

    Chapter 3   **THE SUDAN,** 55

    Chapter 4   **LEBANON,** 68

    Chapter 5   **SYRIA,** 84

    Chapter 6   **JORDAN,** 92

    Chapter 7   **YEMEN,** 107

Part 3 THE GULF STATES

    Chapter 8   **IRAQ,** 119

    Chapter 9   **KUWAIT,** 130

    Chapter 10   **SAUDI ARABIA,** 137

    Chapter 11   **BAHRAIN,** 172

    Chapter 12   **QATAR,** 177

    Chapter 13   **UNITED ARAB EMIRATES,** 182

    Chapter 14   **OMAN,** 190

    Chapter 15   **Conclusions,** 195

Part 4 NORTH AFRICA

    Chapter 16   **ALGERIA,** 203
                by Yahya Mahamdi

Chapter 17 **LIBYA,** 221
            by Drew O. McDaniel

Chapter 18 **MOROCCO,** 238
            by Claude-Jean Bertrand

Chapter 19 **TUNISIA,** 261
            by Donald R. Browne

Part 5 INTERNATIONAL RADIO BROADCASTING IN ARABIC

Chapter 20 **Broadcasting to the Arab World,** 281

Chapter 21 **International Radio Broadcasting
            in the Middle East,** 312

Chapter 22 **Arab Broadcasting: Problems,** 335

Notes, 343
Bibliography, 349
Index, 377

Preface

IN A STUDY OF THIS MAGNITUDE, one must depend on both official and unofficial contacts to provide information and to give access to facilities and documents. However, radio and television systems in the Arab world are operated directly by the government or indirectly through a government-sanctioned broadcasting organization. In some cases respondents provided information "off the record" because their jobs might be jeopardized by having their names associated with this study. Where possible, I provide references, and it is only in those cases where attribution is missing that I protected the source. I take complete responsibility for all of the information in the publication with the exception of the chapters on the Maghreb, the North African countries of Algeria (Yahya Mahamdi), Libya (Drew McDaniel), Morocco (Claude-Jean Bertrand), and Tunisia (Donald Browne).

Professors McDaniel, Bertrand, and Browne agreed to revise their earlier chapters for this, the second edition of the book. Michael Pilsworth was unable to participate in this project because of business commitments in the United Kingdom. Fortunately, Yahya Mahamdi, a native of Algeria who has worked with the electronic media in Algiers, was able to contribute a new Algerian chapter.

A large measure of thanks goes to my students of the second-year English class at the University of Riyadh, College of Engineering. It was in November 1963 that I learned from this class that Arab radio broadcasting was a great deal different from the American commercial system in which I had worked for several years. The Egyptian "Voice of the Arabs" was popular during this period and various programs on the Egyptian station were attractive to Saudi Arabian students. It became obvious to me that what was broadcast was taken as the "truth." During our conversational English exercises, the students expressed some interesting views about the assassination of President Kennedy—views held as a result of their radio experiences. It was these Saudi students who first inspired me to study Arab broadcasting. Several of the students had been to Cairo and had seen Egyptian television—a medium they were fascinated with because it seemed at the time to be the ultimate symbol of modernization. During that Saudi academic year, the government announced that the kingdom had decided to construct a television system, one with which I was later to work.

Thanks go to the Saudi Arabian government, which has been receptive to my research efforts over the years. Dr. Abdulrahman Shobaili, former Director General of Television and presently Deputy Minister of Higher Education, has provided encouragement since he first expedited the granting of permission for a three-month research trip to the kingdom in the spring of 1972. Professor and Mrs. John Y. Benzies have given continued support and made possible my three-month 1972 stay in Riyadh to complete my dissertation research. John Benzies was the manuscript editor for the first edition of this book.

It was at the invitation of Abdullah bin-Faisal bin-Turki al-Saud, President of the Royal Commission on Jubail and Yanbu, that I was able to be in Riyadh, Jubail, and Dhahran just prior to the January 16, 1991, Gulf War.

Without a grant from the Ford Foundation, the initial work would not have been possible. David Davis, formerly Officer-in-Charge, Office of Communication, and Chuck Robarts, Deputy Regional Representative for the Middle East and North Africa, were kind enough to approve funding. Ford offices in New York and Cairo were helpful with travel arrangements and visas. Financial support for the second edition of this book was provided by the Kaltenborn Foundation.

In March 1990 at an awards luncheon during the annual meeting of the Broadcast Education Association, Don Browne (author of Chapter 19) accurately noted after accepting a book award that even single-authored publications are, in fact, collaborative efforts. Additional thanks go to Ali Shummo, the Sudan; Salamah Abdul-Kadi, Jordan; Jawad Zada, Jordan; Professor Nabil Dajani, Lebanon; Mr. George Vasilliou, President of Cyprus; the late Terry Timmons, Saudi Arabia and the United Kingdom; Peter Hillger, United Arab Emirates; Anthony Ashworth, Oman; Adly, Mona, and Salim Bseiso, Kuwait and Canada; Shakib Al-Janabi, First Secretary, Embassy of India, Iraqi Interest Section, Washington, D.C.; Hamdy Kandil, formerly with UNESCO in Egypt and Paris; Mohammad Kamal, former Jordanian Ambassador to the United States and the founding Director of Jordanian Television;

Professor Hussein Amin of Helwan University in Cairo; Professor Jihan Rachty of Cairo University; J. P. Regnier, formerly with Radio Monte Carlo Middle East; and Alan Heil, Deputy Director for Programs, the Voice of America; and both Sherwood Demitz and David Gibson of the U.S. Information Agency Office of Media Research. The various offices of the U.S. Information Agency, the Voice of America, and the Foreign Broadcast Information Service provided various research reports and literature.

Thanks go to the British Broadcasting Corporation World Service Monitoring at Caversham Park, Reading, England, and to Peter Herrmann, formerly of the BBC External Broadcasting Research Department, London, now deputy director of research for Radio Liberty/Radio Free Europe. Richard Measham at BBC World Service Monitoring was especially helpful. Both Graham Mytton and Carol Forrester, BBC International Broadcasting and Audience Research (IBAR) Head and Librarian, respectively, have provided both friendship and assistance since 1985 when I was an IBAR Research Associate. Carol has been especially helpful with the international broadcasting sections of this and other projects.

The late Sydney W. Head, former editor of the Temple University Press International and Comparative Broadcasting series, spent long hours on the initial draft of the manuscript for the first edition of this book. Dr. Head had a keen interest in the Arab world, having lived in the Sudan in the 1960s. Until his untimely death on July 7, 1991, Syd continued to supply me with information about Middle East broadcasting from his vast international media database.

Professor John Benzies and Carole Boyd read every word of the 1982 manuscript. Their comments and suggestions were invaluable. For this new edition, Carole Boyd served as both critic and editor. One must have a strong marriage to do this twice!

Special thanks go to Carole, Kathie, and John Boyd, who understood the necessity of the lengthy trips to the Middle East and who cooperated during intense periods of writing. David Bartlett, Director, Temple University Press, was especially helpful with the first edition of this book, and agreed to release the copyright of the first edition for this version. Additional thanks go to the staff of Iowa State University Press for supporting and encouraging this project. Special thanks go to Gretchen Van Houten, acquisitions editor, and Carla Tollefson, editor.

Several years ago a student from an Arab country who was completing a doctorate at The Ohio State University asked me why in the first edition of this book some chapters were much longer than others. I replied that in the case of Saudi Arabia and Egypt, I knew these systems better than others because I had lived in both countries. In Saudi Arabia, I had helped establish the television system. There is another reason that I emphasize Saudi Arabia, Egypt, and transnational radio broadcasting. These two countries, for different reasons, continue to have a great deal of influence over the electronic media in the Middle East. The importance of transnational radio broadcasting—both within the region and from non-Arab states—emerges in the international section, Part 5.

There are two major exceptions to the American Psychological Association (APA, third edition) style followed in this book. First, in order to provide readers with a more complete list of references, some printed material is noted in the *Bibliography* that is not cited in the book itself. Second, rather than using the APA "personal communication" internal notation for interviews, personal letters, and similar types of unpublished information, they are listed in the text with the name of the correspondent and the word *interview, communication,* or *letter;* complete detailed information is in the *Bibliography* under *Personal Communications.* APA style does not require page numbers for references in the text unless they are direct quotations. However, I sometimes give page numbers in an attempt to guide the reader to specific information in a book, journal article, or other source of information.

Finally, a note about transliteration. Arabic terms and names have been transliterated in a standardized form throughout this publication. In most instances, the spelling is that preferred by the person or country involved. For example, I took the spelling for a country's major cities and landmarks from official maps rather than from a more scientific transliteration from Arabic used by Arabists. The former president of Egypt, Gamal Abdel Nasser, apparently preferred the spelling Abdel. However, in a book he wrote and published in the United States, the spelling appears as Abdul. In this publication, both spellings are used.

Regarding the various spellings of a Libyan leader's name used by Western journalists, Lamb (1988, p. 12) comments:

> Consider the trouble Westerners have in just agreeing on spelling the name of the Libyan leader, Moammar Kadafi. The *Los Angeles Times* spells it Kadafi; *Newsweek* doubles the *d* to spell Kaddafi; the *New York Times* and the *Christian Science Monitor* substitute *Q* for *K* to make it Qaddafi; the U.S. government exchanges a *d* for an *h* and slips in another *a* to get Qadhaafi; the *Washington Post* prefers Gadhafi, and the Associated Press, Khadafy.

For the reader who wishes a more interesting and knowledgeable comment on this subject, I suggest the preface to the Penguin Modern Classics edition of T. E. Lawrence's *Seven Pillars of Wisdom*: in reply to an editor's question as to whether Jedda and Jidda (Saudi Arabia) were spelled with deliberate inconsistency throughout the manuscript, Lawrence replied, "Rather!"

Part 1
Arab World Broadcasting

CHAPTER 1

Developments, Trends, Constraints

THIS STUDY ATTEMPTS to cover the subject of radio and television broadcasting in the Middle East, specifically the Arab world and North Africa. The term *Middle East* is subject to varying geographical interpretation by both scholars and those who have a general idea about the area from newspapers, magazines, and broadcast media news reports. The term *Middle East* appears to be British in origin (Koppes, 1976, pp. 95–98) and describes an area over which the British at one time had considerable influence. For the purposes of this undertaking the term *Arab world* is more appropriate because it provides some linguistic and ethnic boundaries and excludes such countries as Turkey, Iran, Israel, and Cyprus, which are often classified geographically as part of the Middle East. The study does include countries that are members of the Arab League—an association of Arab countries formed after World War II—with the exception of two countries, Somalia and Mauritania, which, while Islamic states, are not historically part of the Arab world. The definition of an Arab remains a topic of considerable discussion among those who are either Arabs, Arabists, or both. However, one criterion seems to apply to almost any definition—one who speaks Arabic as his or her primary language.

The countries discussed herein include Egypt, the Sudan, Lebanon, Syria, Jordan, Yemen, Iraq, Kuwait, Saudi Arabia, Bahrain, Qatar, the United Arab Emirates, Oman, Algeria, Libya, Morocco, and Tunisia. The sections that follow will discuss these countries as broadcasters, international broadcasting to and within the Arab countries, broadcasting cooperation among Arab countries, and problems of broadcasting in the Arab world. Egypt and Saudi Arabia are covered in more detail than other countries.

3

Egypt is an Arab world leader in the development of broadcasting and has influenced radio and television development in the region. Egypt is the primary television program producer in the area; Cairo is the Arab world film capital, the Hollywood of the Middle East. Saudi Arabia is a wealthy, large, and politically important country that has introduced broadcasting, as well as other Western technology and cultural forms, with great caution because of the conservative nature of its Islamic culture. Since the publication of the first edition of this book, Saudi Arabia, primarily because of its huge oil reserves, has become even more important to the West. No better evidence of this exists than the stationing of U.S. and other Western military forces in and near the eastern part of the kingdom.

Historical, religious, geographical, climatic, political, economic, and linguistic factors in this region make its broadcast media almost unique: each will be noted in the subsequent chapters as it impinges on the development of the electronic media. Before each country is discussed in detail, however, several general observations may be helpful.

Radio receivers are abundant in the Arab countries. Even when radio was a young medium there was a strong desire among Arabs in this oral culture to acquire sets. During the late 1950s and early 1960s, the availability of relatively inexpensive transistor receivers enabled lower-income people to purchase them. The sets, which could be operated on batteries, became popular in villages where electricity had not yet been provided. The "transistor revolution" coincided with political movements in areas such as North Africa, Egypt, and Iraq that overthrew ruling royal families or were successful in gaining independence from colonial powers.

The post–World War II leaders, such as Gamal Abdel Nasser and Anwar Sadat of Egypt, were interested in rapid social and economic change and saw broadcasting as a means of bypassing the print media that were primarily responsive to the literate elite who could both afford publications and read them. Throughout the 1980s, Iraqi President Saddam Hussein used the electronic media to perpetuate his carefully orchestrated personality cult.

In the Arab countries it is difficult to make a clear distinction between domestic and international radio broadcasting. Back in the 1950s, some Arab countries started building relatively powerful mediumwave (standard AM) transmitters in order to reach as far as possible. The mediumwave band at that time was not as cluttered with high-powered signals as it is today, and these domestically intended programs could be received in neighboring countries. Even now residents of Khartoum (the Sudan), Riyadh (Saudi Arabia), Amman (Jordan), and Baghdad (Iraq) can listen regularly to the domestic service of Radio Cairo. The service can be heard with particular clarity at night and in the past was often the only service available, as the countries in which listeners resided did not have a reliable national radio service that was capable of reaching all of the country. The Arab culture is traditionally an oral culture. With few competing forms of information and entertainment, radio listening was, and in some places still is, a major leisure activity. As we will see, in the wealthier states and in urban areas, television sets and video recorders are a major source of entertainment.

Those countries that were initially slow to develop radio services— Kuwait, Saudi Arabia, Qatar, and the United Arab Emirates—were also most vulnerable to radio propaganda from countries such as Syria, Iraq, and Egypt, which had political interests in deposing the Gulf ruling families. During the 1960s and, of course, the 1970s, these countries rapidly developed radio broadcasting facilities because they recognized the need for reliable communication with the indigenous population as well as with the Arab expatriates who came to work among them. The oil-rich countries could afford modern high-powered transmitters and impressive radio production studios. When the price of oil quadrupled after the 1973 Middle East War, the petroleum-exporting countries found themselves in potentially influential positions internationally and within the Arab world, and radio broadcasting became increasingly important to governments that attempted to disseminate a specific point of view. Increasingly since that time, then, governments and news-gathering organizations have monitored Middle East radio broadcasts to note both dramatic and subtle shifts in political policy, or to follow developments inside countries not easily covered by foreign journalists, such as the Mosque takeover in Mecca, Saudi Arabia, in November 1979 and the tunnel accident during the Hajj in Mecca during the summer of 1990 that killed 1,400 people.

Arabic is now second only to English as an international broadcasting language, with just under 50 international broadcasting organizations providing Arabic-language programming to the Arab world, several of them broadcasting on mediumwave. Thus, people in the Arab world can receive fairly reliably, even on inexpensive transistor radios, programs from the Voice of America, the British Broadcasting Corporation, Deutsche Welle (Germany), and Radio Monte Carlo Middle East (France). Surveys indicate that these and other services are avidly listened to in the Arab world by followers of Arab and international events. One explanation for the general receptivity to such non-Arab international radio broadcasts is the general organizational framework of Arab radio and television: with the exception of the unofficial radio and television stations operated in Lebanon by various political and religious groups, each country included in this study has a broadcasting system that is either directly operated by the government or is run by an organization that is funded and directly influenced by a government agency, generally a Ministry of Information.[1] Listeners understand that the government has its priorities and its points of view, and those who listen to non-Arab international broadcasts appear to be listening in order to gain another opinion about a local or international event. Listening during times of crisis is an almost standard procedure in the Middle East, particularly among the elite. There is no better example of such a crisis than the August 2, 1990, Iraqi invasion of Kuwait and subsequent Operation Desert Storm and Desert Shield. British Broadcasting Corporation and Voice of America survey data show just how much Arabs rely on foreign radio broadcasting during times of crisis. For example, the BBC reported that audiences in the United Arab Emirates (U.A.E.) increased from pre-invasion levels of 21.5 percent to 51.1 percent after August 2; in Cairo and Alexandria they increased from 18.1 percent to 46.3 percent (British Broadcasting Corporation, 1990b).

The term *international* or *transnational broadcasting*—or broadcasting across national boundaries—is usually associated with the radio medium. This is due, in part, to the technical limitations of television, a medium that is generally restricted to line-of-sight reception: with the exception of FM signals, radio transmissions travel much farther, and shortwave signals can be received very far from the location of the transmitter and antenna. But frequently in the Arab world, television from one country is viewed in other countries. Cairo television may be seen during the warm summer months in Israel, Lebanon, and even Syria. It is seen regularly along the western coast of Saudi Arabia as far south as Jidda. The tall antenna towers on apartment houses and private residences in Jidda are not necessary to receive Saudi Arabian television; they are to receive Egyptian television from across the Red Sea.

International television viewing is pervasive in the Arabian Gulf states, where the warm, humid weather during the long summer helps transmission conditions. Indeed, in some areas of the Gulf it is possible to receive as many as 12 different television signals. Furthermore, some countries have intentionally built transmitters to reach neighboring countries. When Kuwait television was being regularly, and enthusiastically, received in Saudi Arabia's Eastern Province in the late 1960s, Saudi Arabia constructed a powerful station in Dammam with the hope of reaching Kuwait. The station did not perform to expectations and was converted in the mid-1970s to the German Phase Alternate Line (PAL) color system so that Bahrain and the United Arab Emirates could receive color programming on their own standard. Saudi Arabia constructed a lower-power UHF transmitter to broadcast to its citizens on its own chosen color standard—the French Sequential Color and Memory (SECAM) system. The Saudi government has always had a strong desire to broadcast to others in addition to its own citizens.

Television service is a reality in all Arab countries—rich and poor alike, for even the poorer countries such as Egypt, the Sudan, and Yemen realize that this visual medium is an important political and developmental tool. Television equipment is expensive and must be paid for with hard currency.[2] Each time a poor country makes the decision to increase transmission power or to buy a new camera or videotape recorder, money is being diverted from other developmental projects. In the large, less affluent countries such as Oman and the Sudan, where it is necessary to utilize satellite ground stations and leased satellite transponders for internal distribution of television, the expense is often painful; but it is apparently seen by leaders as necessary. In the more affluent Arab countries in North Africa and the Arabian Gulf, television facilities are modern and extensive: television in the Gulf started slowly in the late 1960s but expanded rapidly in the 1970s and 1980s.

In the Gulf states, as in other parts of the Arab world, large sums of money are necessary for expensive radio and television broadcasting equipment. However, even in the early 1990s, the Gulf states still have the additional expense of importing almost all operation and maintenance personnel. These countries have a relatively small native-born population, and with numerous business and civil service opportunities available to able citizens, there are not enough people to undertake all the development schemes desirable. The result, for the broadcast media in the Gulf, is that many of the people who work at the stations are Arabs from other countries, usually Egypt, Jordan, or Lebanon. In a few Gulf countries, nonindigenous Arabs still hold important management positions.

In many Arab countries a radio receiver is a status symbol: the larger and more intricate the set, the higher the status. Expensive all-wave radios (shortwave and FM in addition to the standard broadcast band), with built-in cassette capability, are so popular as to have generated a whole new industry in many Arab countries—the pirate duplication of both Western and Middle Eastern music tapes. Pirate copies of professionally recorded, popular Arabic and Western music tapes can be purchased in most Gulf countries for as little as $1.25. But because of the availability in Arab countries of low-cost transistor radios from Japan, South Korea, Taiwan, and the People's Republic of China, and because of the low or nonexistent import tax on these radios, people lower on the income scale can also afford to purchase or to have access to a set.

New technologies and better economic conditions have, then, changed listening patterns since Brunner (1953, p. 149) noted that a substantial amount of Arab radio listening was done by groups of people—mostly men—in village coffee houses. Even so, it is not unusual for groups of people (mostly males) to listen to radio and view television and videotapes in commercial establishments or in private residences. The explanation for this is, in part, the Arab concept of friendliness and hospitality: when a person is in public, perhaps listening to music or news on a radio in the street, there is an implied invitation for others to join him.

Through individually owned sets or sets within families or clubs or in public places, the availability of television programs in Arab countries is probably much higher than readers not familiar with the Middle East may suspect—though again a distinction must be drawn between the affluent and the poor countries. In the Gulf states of Kuwait, Saudi Arabia, Qatar, and the United Arab Emirates, set ownership is very high for the native-born population. People can quite easily afford imported, mostly Japanese, color sets. In the late 1980s, large-screen projection sets were common among the wealthier families. In countries such as Syria, Egypt, and the Sudan, it is government policy to make television sets available to as many people as possible. There is very strong motivation among the poor to acquire a television receiver: in Egypt it is not unusual for a television set to be purchased by village leaders before electricity reaches their area. In a poor section of Cairo, an extended family may pool resources to purchase a used black-and-white or even color set from a neighborhood dealer. In that crowded, polluted city it is often necessary and cheaper to be entertained in the home; and parents moreover believe that television is a way in which their children's education, and possibly their view of the world, can be broadened.

In the Arabian Gulf states, television has relatively little competition. Few cinemas and nightclubs exist and, among those, few appeal to the home- and family-centered Arab culture. Videocassette recorders are therefore pervasive there: the Arabian Gulf, specifically in Kuwait, Saudi Arabia, Bahrain, Qatar, and the U.A.E., may be the largest videocassette market in the world. Tape libraries are thriving and the underground market for pirated Egyptian, American, and British television programs is now a major business.

Direct Broadcast Satellite (DBS) transmission is not yet a major factor in the Arab world. Most people in the poorer countries cannot afford a satellite dish and associated equipment to convert satellite signals to those that can be seen on a standard television receiver. The Gulf states have not permitted private dish ownership, even though some wealthy citizens in the U.A.E., Kuwait, and Saudi Arabia—usually members of the royal family or wealthy merchants—have erected television receive-only (TVRO) equipment. The future of DBS is, however, potentially promising, especially in the Gulf. Both Western and Arab broadcasters and private corporations have a financial interest in providing Arabs with entertainment-oriented programming. The French television networks are already available in many parts of North Africa. As satellite reception dishes become smaller in size, they become not only less expensive but also less physically obvious. Dishes now exist that are flat because they are electronically curved; they can be attached to windows that face the appropriate satellite.

Arab countries have created their own satellite system—ARABSAT. Originally suggested at a meeting of Gulf ministers of information during the oil-rich days of the 1970s as a means of linking the electronic media in the Gulf states, ARABSAT became a reality in 1985. Two satellites have been launched, one from a European Ariane 3 rocket launched from French Guiana on February 8, 1985 ("Finance gap short," 1985), the other from a U.S. space shuttle with a Saudi Arabian astronaut on board. The system has had many problems, the majority of which are financial and political. Primarily inspired and financed by Saudi Arabia, ARABSAT has its administrative headquarters in the Saudi capital, Riyadh; the technical headquarters is in Tunis.

Despite occasional suggestions to the contrary, the basic idea behind ARABSAT was Arab world satellite self-sufficiency, something the Gulf states could well afford until the international price of oil declined. Financially, other Arab states were burdened by the necessity of having to use hard currency to have Western companies construct down- and up-linking facilities to use ARABSAT. The result was that by 1987, only 7 of the 22 nations signing the ARABSAT agreement had ground facilities capable of using the system (Amt, 1987). Additionally, ARABSAT user charges are higher than those of INTELSAT. Clearly, since 1987, ARABSAT has become more of a communication force in the Middle East, but not necessarily as a means of connecting the electronic media. Rather, ARABSAT has become a telecommunications satellite that is sometimes used to connect Arab world broadcasters.

To a great extent, programming is basically entertainment oriented on Arab television stations and it is not unfair to say that both radio and television in the Arab world are believed by consumers to be primarily for entertainment. The director of Egyptian television observed during a May 1980 meeting that "a television set is usually bought with the intention of entertainment. Nobody thinks of television as a means of education when they go to buy a television set" (Tawffik, 1980). However, this does not mean that educational programs do not exist. And in some Arab countries a good deal of programming time is concerned with political information— though in general such nonentertainment programming, including news and commentary, merely extols the accomplishments of the political leaders.

Imported entertainment programs from Europe and the United States are used to some extent on all Arab television systems. The percentage of imported Western programs is higher in the Gulf states, where there is a limited artistic tradition and where, during the initial stages of television's development, emphasis was placed on construction of physical facilities to transmit rather than on production equipment for local programming. Western programming appears to be quite in keeping with the beliefs of the systems' administrators, whose respective countries look to the West for political support and economic ties; and the elite, who have had the funds to travel outside the Middle East, rather expect that Western programs will be provided as a matter of course. In multi-channel Gulf states such as Kuwait, Saudi Arabia, Bahrain, and the U.A.E., one channel is devoted exclusively, or nearly so, to non-Arab programming. The entirely English-language second Saudi television channel transmits both imported and locally produced material. The trend toward permissiveness in Western television programs has served, however, to narrow the choice of those available to Arab countries, as programs have to be edited for excessive sex, violence, and, in the case of Saudi Arabia, references to Christianity.

Television stations in the Arab Middle East have always telecast classic Egyptian cinema productions as a main category of Arabic-language programming, but it was not until after the 1967 Middle East War and the termination of the conflict in Yemen that the Gulf states started importing new Egyptian films and videotapes. By the mid-1970s such productions were an important source of hard currency for the Egyptian Radio-Television Federation, but their high prices and the move of former President Sadat toward the eventual signing of a peace treaty with Israel caused some states to reduce or altogether to stop Egyptian program purchases. At the same time, the Egyptian political and economic situation caused a new production system to appear: artists preferred to work outside the country to gain more money through payment in hard currency and to avoid some Egyptian personal income tax. Their new productions were essentially Egyptian written, produced, directed, and acted but were taped in London, Athens, Amman, or Dubai. Relatively high-quality Arabic-language programs have proliferated. Many are contemporary in that they deal with the problems of families attempting to cope with the clash of generations. Some are historical in nature and deal with traditional Islamic themes: these latter are particularly appropriate for sale to the Gulf states, which have attempted to make television somewhat more Islamic since events such as the Soviet invasion of Afghanistan, the Mecca Mosque occupation, the Iranian Revolution, and the Gulf War.

Television in the Arab Middle East has a predominantly Western style: television is itself, after all, a Western invention that has been molded by North American and European film and artistic traditions. Creativity in the television medium is moreover tied to electronic requirements and technological innovations: with each new innovation—special effects generators, videotape, chroma key, videotape editing, digital effects—comes a new creative use for it. Virtually all television stations in the Arab world were purchased from and installed by West European, American, and Japanese equipment manufacturers: usually the installation agreement called for production training of the buyers by Western experts, or for their training in the country where the equipment was manufactured. Furthermore, various programs sponsored by both Western and Middle Eastern governments as well as by private foundations have taken experts to the Arab countries to advise or have sent Middle Eastern nationals to the United States, Great Britain, France, or West Germany to train in television production. The natural result of all this is a Western-type television program in Arabic. With regard to production, there is very little that is uniquely Arab in Arab world television.

Three additional aspects of Arab broadcast media need attention. They are related but separate problems. First, almost no serious research has been done in the Arab world on radio and television. The systems in Jordan and pre–civil war Lebanon did undertake the study of listeners so that they would have information on which to base commercial rates; some social science research has been done to determine media use in villages. But almost no "effects" research has been done even by those systems, and they have not worked in cooperation with university investigators. However, during the 1980s some very interesting research was done by Arab graduate students at U.S. universities. The general research void is caused by a lack of funds for an activity that is not believed to be a priority, a general misunderstanding of research methodology, and a lack of qualified personnel to undertake and interpret research results. Although not unique to the Arab world, this situation points to a second concern related to Arab broadcasting: a lack of mechanisms or structures for citizen input to the system. This does not mean that phone calls and letters from listeners and viewers are ignored: little effort, however, is made to solicit citizen comment about radio and television programming on a regular basis. Many media managers believe that by themselves they have the ability and knowledge to provide a well-rounded broadcast schedule that includes news, entertainment, and educational programming: for them, the statement by former French broadcast official Arthur Conte—"I am the public"—applies (Thomas, 1972, p. 150). There is also an occasional fear voiced that citizen feedback would not be positive, and officials are not sure how to react to negative comments. To a certain extent, Arab television managers now know that some systematic citizen feedback is necessary if they are to attract viewers. Unlike the 1970s, many citizens no longer must rely on the government system for visual entertainment. Those with videocassette recorders have become their own television station program directors.

Although unevenly distributed, radio receivers, television sets, and videocassette recorders are abundant in the Arab world. The BBC estimates that Middle East and North African residents own 73.5 million radio receivers, 36.1 million television sets, and 10.2 million videocassette recorders (British Broadcasting Corporation, 1991b).

Finally, while there are exceptions in the Arab Middle East, broadcasting officials generally seem to have neither a philosophy nor goals for radio and television that are tied to the goals of the country and the appropriate central planning organization; the inevitable interagency conflicts have not worked to the advantage of the consumer.

The preceding overview of broadcasting in the Arab world is not intended to be comprehensive, but rather is provided as a start toward the discussion of individual systems of radio and television in a part of the world that increasingly dominates the political and economic concerns of many nations.

Part 2
National Systems

CHAPTER 2

EGYPT

THE ARAB REPUBLIC OF EGYPT is located in the northeastern corner of the African continent. An estimated 46 million people live within the country's 386,611 square miles. The majority of the population resides in the Nile Delta, in the Nile Valley, and along the Suez Canal—a relatively small arable area on which the country depends, for it still has essentially an agricultural economy. Migration from rural areas to cities has contributed to Cairo's traffic, pollution, and housing problems.

Egypt has a rich and well-publicized history. The country's modern historical period dates from 1805, when Mohammed Ali became ruler with Ottoman blessings. Descendants of Ali ruled the country until the revolution of July 23, 1952, which resulted in a military coup that exiled King Farouk and brought to power first Mohammed Neguib and then, very soon, Gamel Abdel Nasser, Egypt's president until his death in 1970. Anwar Sadat, another of the officers involved in the revolution, was vice-president when Nasser died and succeeded him as president. Anwar Sadat was assassinated while watching a military parade in Cairo in October 1981. He was succeeded by his vice-president, Hosni Mubarak. All four presidents have influenced the electronic media.

BBC statistics indicate that there are 18 million radio receivers, 8 million television sets, and 1.7 million videocassette recorders in Egypt (British Broadcasting Corporation, 1991b).

IT IS IMPORTANT to understand the development of radio and television in Egypt before broadcasting in other countries is discussed. Under Nasser's leadership, the country was the first to construct high-powered mediumwave and shortwave transmitters to reach the indigenous population as well as to carry the Nasserite Pan-Arab message to the remainder of the Arab world. Nasser started a foreign-language service that rivaled those of the major international broadcasters. Broadcast facilities were provided from which various African and Middle Eastern revolutionary groups might broadcast to their own countries. When Egypt started a television service, the country was able to undertake a massive artistic effort, its well-developed film industry and tradition of live theater providing what almost all other countries in the Arab world lacked—performers as well as personnel to operate the complicated equipment and to produce programs. Even after the March 1979 Egyptian-Israeli peace treaty that resulted in agreements by Arab ministers of information to boycott Egyptian media, ironically Egyptian films, videotapes, and artists still dominated Arab television.

Under Mubarak, Egypt has continued political policies promoted by former President Sadat. Known as a moderate Arab state, it has diplomatic relations with Israel and was a major supporter of the coalition military effort during the Gulf War.

RADIO

Radio broadcasting in Egypt began haphazardly in the 1920s, thereby following the pattern of some European countries as well as that of the United States. Reportedly, over 100 amateur wireless stations were operating during this period, mostly in the Cairo area (UNESCO, 1949, p. 217). Not all stations were operated by amateurs; merchants ran stations that disseminated commercial messages between songs (Metwally, n.d., p. 1), utilizing a format not unlike that of popular commercial stations in other parts of the world. But by 1930 most of these stations had closed because of decreased interest on the part of the operators: stations that operated as businesses had found that too few radio sets existed at the time and that economic conditions in Egypt were not conducive to commercial radio. Recent Egyptian perceptions of the early stations are interesting and have tended to vary with the political climate in the country. In the late 1960s, the pre-1931 stations were said to have had "no national objectives for the public interest. [A]ll they were interested in was material gains" ("The history of," 1970, p. 63). However, by the late 1970s they were seen as unacceptable because "competition . . . increased and this led to higher advertisement costs, together with a lot of inconvenience" (Metwally, n.d., p. 1).

One of the obvious problems that the Egyptians faced was how to organize the regulation of the new medium. The British were quite influential in the administration of the country at the time, but they appear to have been powerless to bring radio under any kind of formal government regulatory structure—or they were uninterested in doing so. A U.S. Department of Commerce report of 1930 describes the government's attitude: "[T]he identity of [the two Cairo stations] is known to the public, but officials are careful to avoid 'learning officially' of them since any cognizance would probably necessitate closing the station" (Batson, 1930, p. 103). In 1931 the government indeed decreed that all stations be closed, thereby leaving Egypt without a radio service for a time. But radio broadcasting was rapidly developing throughout the world, and sets were becoming more common in the large cities such as Cairo among upper-class families and among the large expatriate community of Britons, Greeks, and Italians. The government, no doubt influenced by British residents and by the British Broadcasting Corporation example, determined that radio broadcasting would be a government-sanctioned activity. A memorandum to this effect was sent to the Council of Ministers by the Ministry of Communications on July 15, 1932.

One week later the Ministry of Communications memorandum was adopted and a 10-year renewable contract was signed with the Marconi Company of the United Kingdom to provide a noncommercial broadcast service for Egypt. The system was financed by a license fee on receivers, 60 percent of which was paid to Marconi to operate the station and 40 percent of which was for the government to utilize in connection with actual construction and costs associated with the operation of transmitters (Metwally, n.d., p. 1). The official opening date of the Marconi-operated Egyptian radio service was May 31, 1934 ("The history of," 1970, p. 63).

This service proved to be a professionally operated and popular undertaking. The sale of radio sets and therefore income for both Marconi and the government steadily increased. By late 1939, the number of receivers in Egypt was estimated to be 86,477 at a yearly license fee of about four dollars each ("What do you," 1971, p. 63). While radio ownership was clearly beyond the means of the average Egyptian, radio receivers were acquired by enterprising merchants who understood that a receiver would be a popular attraction at a restaurant or coffeehouse, which in the Arab world is still an important gathering place for males in late afternoon and evening hours. When television was introduced in Egypt and other Arab countries, many coffeehouse owners tended to replace radios with television sets. Later videocassette recorders were added to the television receivers.

During the formative years of Egyptian radio, the service attracted many talented announcers, actors, musicians, and journalists from the established theater, film, music, and print media sectors of Cairo. Several of these early employees, most of whom worked at first on a free-lance basis, became influential in future Egyptian broadcasting and information undertakings; many of the more talented have since worked for systems in other Arab countries. The BBC Empire Service (later World Service) used Egyptian announcers when it started its Arabic service in January 1938.[1]

The physical facilities, if not the entire tone of Egyptian broadcasts under the Marconi contract, were unmistakably British. *Wireless World* ("England in Egypt," 1935, p. 15) described the first studio:

Egyptian broadcasting has gone "all British" in the matter of its new studio in Cairo, the architectural design of which follows the Tudor style. The studio is approached through a small soundproof lobby illuminated by an old English lantern. The specially treated walls of the studio are paneled and at one end is an old English fireplace on which stand three electric candles showing red, green, or white, as desired, for signaling from the control room.

The Marconi contract was renewed in 1943 with a stipulated expiration date of January 31, 1949. One important provision of the new government/Marconi contract called for more direct Egyptian participation in the management of broadcasting. The new contract even mandated the percentage of Egyptian salaried and hourly paid employees ("The history of," 1970, p. 63). However, the second contract did not last until 1949; and on March 4, 1947, the government canceled the Marconi contract and the radio service became Egyptian owned and operated ("What do you," 1971, p. 63). "National considerations" are generally given as the motivation to terminate the contract, but a more specific explanation was the increasing Egyptian resistance to British policy, particularly in something as sensitive as radio broadcasting, and the general decline of British influence in the Arab world following World War II.

GOVERNMENT BROADCAST ADMINISTRATION

The history of Egypt's government regulation or control of broadcasting is no different from that seen in other developing and some developed countries. One of the main difficulties these governments faced was deciding in whose care they would place the new medium—a problem that they did not completely understand and one whose resolution for political or developmental purposes they could not settle. The Ministry of Communication was responsible for radio until August 19, 1939, when it was moved to the Ministry of Social Affairs; on April 18, 1942, it was placed under the Ministry of Interior, where it remained until the end of World War II. After the termination of the second Marconi contract, and until the 1952 revolution, the broadcast service was moved at various times between Social Affairs and Interior. After the revolution, it was administered by the military officers in control, until a Ministry of Information was established. Even since the Ministry of Information was started and broadcasting has been given some autonomy by the formation of the Egyptian Radio-Television Federation, ultimate control over the electronic media has alternated—depending on political circumstances—between the Information Ministry and the Office of the President.

PRE-REVOLUTIONARY
BROADCASTING—EGYPTIANIZATION

Between the end of the second Marconi contract and the 1952 revolution, radio broadcasting underwent a period of administrative consolidation during which the government attempted to define the goals and philosophy that the medium should follow. The British Marconi management had established the basis for a well-run professional broadcast operation, but the foreign management was perceived by Egyptians to be no longer needed, since a cadre of Egyptian managers had been trained to take responsibility. Continued British management was considered to be particularly inappropriate in view of the anti-British feelings that started to surface after World War II.

In 1949, Egypt promulgated public law No. 98 in an attempt to make radio an independent organization under the Council of Ministers. The law provided another stipulation: it mandated that the language of the radio service be Arabic, the national language ("The history of," 1970, p. 65). However, the service has never broadcast domestically exclusively in Arabic. The first general program, started in 1934, broadcast in Arabic, French, and English, featuring a mixture of music, news, drama, and informational programs. When a second transmitter was constructed, a 4-hour European Program was added, broadcasting French and English to the foreign community and to those Egyptians who had acquired a second language. It would be inaccurate to say that the foreign program was imposed by Marconi management. The Egyptian elite has been relatively Western in orientation since the 1800s, and it is not unusual for upper-class Egyptian homes to use French or English as a language of convenience. One of the reasons that the American University in Cairo is an attractive place for the children of the elite to study is that some do not have a sufficient grasp of written Arabic to attend an Egyptian university.

RADIO BROADCASTING AFTER THE REVOLUTION

It is beyond the scope of this study to enumerate the motivations for the 1952 revolution. However, factors that contributed to the military takeover by the Free Officers included a general dislike for King Farouk, who was viewed by many leaders as inept and as possessing personal habits inappropriate for the leader of an Islamic society. Egypt also had serious political problems of its own making, and difficult relations with Great Britain, which had stationed troops in the country; important too was the Egyptian Army's basic failure to be an effective fighting force during the 1948 Palestine War.

Axiomatically, revolutionary governments assume control of the mass media. Neguib and then Nasser inherited a radio system that, while modest in size, immediately became the voice of the revolution—though even a revolution could not make Arabic the exclusive language of Egyptian radio. They did not have to nationalize it, as it was already a government-organized activity. Radio service employees were, in fact, government employees who supported the revolution and helped organize a broadcast service that articulated its goals and provided favorable coverage of Nasser's speeches and appearances. The Egyptian print media, on the other hand, had a long history of independence, both financial and editorial. While many journalists supported Nasser, some did not. As a result, Nasser slowly tightened control of the print media until 1960, when they were in effect nationalized.[2]

It will probably never be known why Nasser devoted Egyptian administrative energy and such extensive economic resources to the establishment of what is still the Arab world's largest and most influential broadcast service. However, two observations about this man may help to clarify his motivation for the expansion of radio and, later, for the construction of a television service. Nasser was different from most other Arab leaders who came to power in the 1950s. Like them, because of his army background, he was relatively sophisticated; but he also came from a modest rural environment and understood and was able to capitalize on his knowledge of the oral Arab culture and the power and emotionalism of the Arabic language. A gifted public speaker, Nasser was the first Arab leader to understand and utilize the power of the electronic media.

Secondly, Nasser had a wider vision of his leadership than most people initially thought. In his 1955 monograph, *Egypt's Liberation: The Philosophy of the Revolution*, Nasser notes three areas of influence in which he envisioned both himself and Egypt working, both militarily and diplomatically, against imperialism and nationalism. He called these areas "circles": the first, the Arab circle, "the most important, . . . the one with which we are most closely linked"; the second, the African continent on which Egypt is located, on which Nasser saw (and attempted to foment) struggle between whites and blacks; and the third, the Islamic circle, "which circumscribes continents and oceans and is the domain of our brothers in faith" (1955, pp. 85–111). It was after this publication was printed that Nasser became interested in the Third World movement. The three circles became the target areas for a powerful, well-financed radio broadcasting system.

RADIO STUDIO FACILITIES AND SERVICES

In the introduction to this study it was stated that the distinction between domestic and international broadcasts in the Arab world is not easily made. The following discussion of individual Egyptian radio services therefore does not emphasize where the broadcasts are received, but rather the intended audience.

Shortwave and mediumwave transmitters are scattered throughout the country and are provided with programs to broadcast by means of a network of both cable and microwave links: until the late 1980s, the only service that did not originate from the central broadcasting complex in Cairo was a local radio service in Alexandria. The Cairo broadcasting complex, completed in the early 1960s, houses production, engineering, and administration for both radio and television. Over 40 radio studios operate around the clock there, ranging in size from news reading rooms to studios that will accommodate symphony orchestras.

DOMESTIC AND REGIONAL BROADCASTS

The following discussion reviews the evolution of Egypt's radio services from the beginning of the 1952 revolution until the radio service's reorganization after Mubarak became president.

Main Program

The Main Program is a direct outgrowth of the original broadcasts from the Marconi station in 1934. In other Arab countries it is widely known as "Radio Cairo," as are some of the other Egyptian radio services. One of the problems that researchers have found in undertaking radio-listening survey research in the Arab world is that non-Egyptians cannot always distinguish among the numerous Egyptian radio services that they receive. The stations are clearly identified as distinct services; the confusion as to the name of the specific service appears to stem in part from the announcers' custom between programs of preceding the name of the service with the statement, "This is Cairo"—stating the location of the broadcast service's origin rather than its specific name. This custom probably comes from the BBC World Service practice in both English and Arabic of saying, "This is London."[3] At the time of the revolution, the Main Program broadcast 11 hours per day. The program was expanded immediately after July 1952; and by 1962 it was on the air for just under 20 hours per day, as it was in 1980 (Metwally, n.d., p. 6). Much of the initial increase in transmitting power after the revolution was given to the Main Program; and during the 1950s and 1960s, when Egypt wanted to reach other Arab countries, shortwave transmitters were brought on-line for added coverage. Another reason for adding shortwave transmitters for dissemination of what was essentially a domestic service was to allow the large Egyptian expatriate community working in the Gulf to receive this program.

The Main Program has something for everyone: a mixture of regularly scheduled newscasts, music, commentary, and various forms of entertainment, the most dominant of which is drama. Entertainment, not entirely devoid of an educational/development message, occupies a large portion—probably as much as one-half the total daily transmission schedule. The Main Program, along with another service, "Voice of the Arabs," was the most important means of reaching Egyptian supporters in other Arab countries prior to the 1967 war. The general tone of Egyptian broadcasts dramatically changed after the Arab defeat in that war (see also Chapter 21). It changed even more dramatically after Anwar Sadat became president in 1970. The following 1970 statement about the goals of the Main Program provides some insight into the importance that Egypt attached to it: "[T]he most important [of the goals] are the supportive maintenance of the morale of the audience to stay ready and alert for the battle [against Israel] and awareness of the facts, dimensions, goals, and means of psychological warfare, and strengthening of the relationship between the masses and the active army on the front" ("What do you," 1971, p. 68). The service is indeed important, both because it is a continuation of the first identifiably Egyptian program and because many of the other Egyptian services are spin-offs from its broadcasts.

This study does not include an extensive analysis of estimated audiences for international radio broadcasts. However, even limited information from available surveys can provide a basic idea about audience trends at the time the surveys were done. Provided that respondents did not confuse Radio Cairo (Main Program) with other services—Voice of the Arabs was identified separately—17.9 percent of respondents in the 1974 survey done in Kuwait listened to Radio Cairo once per week or more often. Among respondents to the same survey, 17.5 percent said that they listened to the Voice of the Arabs at least once per week; and approximately one-third said that they tuned that often to an Egyptian radio service.[4] A survey done in Jordan in September 1978 revealed that 16.3 percent and 18.4 percent of respondents tuned "once a week or more often" to Radio Cairo and the Voice of the Arabs respectively (USICA, 1978b, p. 11).

Regardless of the prevailing political climate in the Middle East, then, residents of other countries appear to be interested in what the Egyptian Main Program is saying. During the period when Iraq occupied Kuwait, a BBC study estimates that in Riyadh, Saudi Arabia, the Main Program (Radio Cairo) was the third most listened to station, following the BBC and Radio Monte Carlo Middle East (British Broadcasting Corporation, 1990b).

Sudan Program

Egypt and the Sudan have had a continuing close relationship since before 1956 when the two countries were administratively linked by the British. The Sudan Program had its origins in a weekly 30-minute feature, "Sudan Corner," broadcast on the Main Program. The weekly feature was lengthened after the revolution, apparently as a means of strengthening relations between Egypt and its neighbor to the south. In 1953 the program, still on the Main Program wavelength, was further expanded to 30 minutes per day. On March 17, 1954, the program became an entirely separate service with its own transmitter and assigned frequency (Metwally, n.d., p. 4), and an office was opened in Khartoum, Sudan, to help provide its program material ("What do you," 1971, p. 72).

Second Program

The Second Program was started "on May 5, 1957 to provide the elite with the developments of contemporary intellectual, cultural and artistic trends" (Metwally, n.d., p. 4). Similar in format to the BBC's Radio 3, the service is intended to cater to intellectual tastes in the urban areas of Cairo and Alexandria. Its mediumwave transmissions were extended to 3.5 hours per day in 1962 (Mohammed Shaban interview, 1974). Since then, they have varied, depending on Egypt's relationship with the Sudan.

Alexandria Local Service

Until the Egyptian government's Ministry of Information started experimenting with what amounts to local radio in the late 1980s, the only Egyptian radio service to originate outside of the broadcasting complex in Cairo, the Alexandria Local Service, was started on July 26, 1954,[5] and was intended to be the first of a series of local services that officials believed would serve to reflect the character of each major region. "Alex" was the ideal location for such a new service, as the city is Egypt's second largest and is an important Mediterranean port; its radio service is probably the only one in Egypt to request and later utilize research regarding listener attitudes and preferences (Mahrns interview, 1974). Transmission time has remained relatively constant since the service was started at 8 hours per day.

Scarce financial resources are an obvious factor in limiting local services that are not directly under Cairo's control. However, another reason local services were not added under Nasser and Sadat is that the government wanted to retain administrative control. The concentration of both engineering and production facilities in one building in downtown Cairo makes defense against dissident forces that might wish to use these stations easier.

People's Program

The People's Program was created on July 29, 1959, in order to combine the various special interest programs formerly included, even prior to the revolution, in the Main Program. These programs, known as "Corners," were targeted to farmers, women, youth, the armed forces, and the police (Metwally, n.d., p. 4). The People's Program transmissions are primarily intended for the group of people who make up the majority of Egypt's population—the *fellaheen*, or illiterate farmers, and those former *fellaheen* who have migrated to urban centers. The casual visitor to Cairo, who is mainly interested in major tourist attractions, may not realize the extent of subsistence-level living in Egypt: only a few miles from Cairo, people live in a manner not unlike that of their ancestors thousands of years ago. This group is, then, the main target audience for this service and for the special programming—carefully presented in the form of Arabic that is most easily understood by listeners—that it features. The People's Program has used most known forms of radio programming in order to promote national development: to promote farming advances, literacy training, population planning, and the concept of nationhood among a people who have tended to be distrustful of government.[6]

By the mid-1970s, the Program devoted 3 hours per day to educational programs, 1.75 hours to broadcasts tied to the national school curriculum, and .5 hour per day to literacy training. In 1970 the service embraced the Canadian Farm Forum concept, whereby programs about farming and other development topics are produced and transmitted to groups of listeners who then discuss the program after it has been broadcast. The program started with six "clubs" in one province and then gradually spread. For a short time, Egypt attempted an unusual twist to the project: on one evening the radio broadcast was followed by a discussion and then a television program on a subject similar to that of the radio broadcast (Al-Mowaled, 1974). This format has not been continued due to problems with television receiver maintenance and the fact that Egypt generally does not have the adminis-trative skill or the motivation to coordinate such undertakings.

Daily program time reached a peak of 9 hours in 1972 and has dropped slightly to 8.5 hours per day. Egyptian peasants listen to a variety of Egyptian and foreign radio services, but it is probably the People's Program on transistor radios that Xavier Delcourt (1978, p. 42) referred to as "part of the[ir] minimum daily requirement, beside the 'foul,' the traditional bean puree."

Middle East Program

The Middle East Program traces its beginnings to a 1959 Presidential Decree of Nasser's establishing the following new goals for Egyptian broadcasting:

1. Elevating the standards of the arts.
2. Strengthening national feeling and social cooperation, spreading solidarity

between social groups and supporting accepted traditions.
3. Participating in the spread of culture among the masses.
4. Discussing social problems and strengthening spiritual and moral values.
5. Reviving the Arabic literary, scientific and artistic heritage.
6. Informing the public about the best products of human civilization.
7. Enlightening the public about both internal and international news.
8. Informing foreign countries about the U.A.R. and the Arab world.
9. Encouraging talents in different areas of thought and creativity.
10. Strengthening relations between national residents and expatriates.
11. Providing public entertainment. ("What do you," 1971, p. 64)

The decree also—and most importantly here—gave the broadcasting organization "economic character." It allowed broadcast services to accept commercial advertising and to utilize, within certain limits, the "hard" international currency that might result from such advertising. This initial move on the part of Nasser has been helpful to the electronic media in Egypt because the commercial income can so readily be used for the purchase of spare parts and equipment: the broadcasting organization thus avoids the complex bureaucratic process of obtaining from the government economic and banking establishments permission to spend hard currency. Radio advertising was first allowed on the People's Program and later on the Alexandria Service.

The Middle East Program was intended to be a commercial regional service: programming began on May 31, 1964 (*A.R.E. broadcasting in brief*, n.d., p. 3), from a powerful mediumwave transmitter near Alexandria that helped send the commercial message as far as the Arabian Gulf and throughout North Africa. The service was immediately attractive to marketers of international products in the Middle East (e.g., cigarettes, cosmetics, aspirin, food products, automobiles, candy) who found that many national broadcast systems, particularly in the wealthier states, allowed no advertising at all. In fact, during the 1960s the Middle East Program had commercial competition only from the Jordanian Radio Service, whose low-powered transmitters covered only a restricted area. Strong competition appeared only in the 1970s when an increasing number of Gulf states allowed local radio advertising.

The Egyptian commercial service quickly became popular. Primarily a nighttime and early morning service, its format was "DJ" Top-40 style, with fast patter on the part of the announcer between commercial messages and popular songs—a format in which Egypt led the Arab world. On an international level, Radio Monte Carlo Middle East (see Chapter 20, Western Europe) took the basic Middle East Program format and, with the aid of Egyptian announcers, made it more professional (Regnier interview, 1980). In fact, Radio Monte Carlo Middle East still employs former Middle East Radio announcers (Taquet interview, 1989).

Egyptian broadcasting officials have always been reluctant to discuss income from commercial advertising. Most sales take place through large Cairo-based advertising agencies, the majority of which are affiliated with the large publishing houses. One of the obvious problems that a potential advertiser on the Middle East Program faces is a lack of research data that provide a basic profile of listeners. The research department of the Egyptian broadcasting organization restricts itself to program analyses and has not been asked to undertake research that would provide advertisers with an estimate of the number and demographic characteristics of its listeners. By contrast, survey research results are used heavily in the marketing strategy of the service's main competitor, Radio Monte Carlo Middle East.

Holy Koran Broadcast

Egypt's religious service, first transmitted on March 29, 1964 (*A.R.E. broadcasting in brief*, n.d., p. 3), features Koran readings, religious discussions, and commentary for 18.5 hours daily on both shortwave and mediumwave frequencies. It was started for sincere religious reasons: Egypt has long been an important Islamic nation that has made contributions to religious ethics. But such broadcasts helped Nasser in two respects. First, they provided high-profile evidence that the government realized the importance of the conservative Islamic factions of the Egyptian population, some of whom opposed Nasser. Second, the broadcasts were a reminder to those in Egypt and other countries—especially the conservative Gulf states—that Egypt was still a Moslem country despite the close ties that it had at the time with the Soviet Union and East European countries, that, at least until the U.S.S.R. lost its grip on Eastern Europe, were viewed by many of the more traditional states as having philosophies that were incompatible with Islam.

Youth Broadcast

Started in 1975, the Youth Broadcast is one of the newest of the Egyptian radio services. It broadcasts in the afternoon from 1500 to 1700 hours on the same frequency as the People's Program, and is intended to reach a school-age audience with an educational, political, and social message.

European Program

Begun like the Main Program in 1934, the European Program at the time of the revolution did not exceed 4 hours per day. These hours were rapidly expanded to 15 in 1962, cut back to 14 in 1978 (Metwally, n.d., p. 7), and later expanded to 17 hours per day. Although radio and television programming in European languages, primarily English, is done by almost every Arab country, Egypt has been a leader in European-language broadcasting among those states east of the North African countries. It has, as noted earlier, a large European expatriate community who speak English, French, German, Italian, and Greek; in addition there is an Armenian community that retains its culture and language. The European program starts, then, at 0700, with 15-minute broadcasts in Greek, German, Italian, and French. News broadcasts are spread throughout the day at specified intervals: French at 1400 and 2100, English at 1450 and 2000, German at 1800.[7] Programming between the news bulletins is heavily music-oriented with specific periods set aside for requests, popular music, and so forth. Some programming is supplied by embassies and by cultural centers that are supported by foundations or governments. The basic format appears to be quite flexible and depends on the number and sort of qualified people, most of whom work on a part-time basis, who are available to read news and produce programs.

Musical Program

The music service first started in March 1968 ("What do you," 1971, p. 73) during a difficult period of time after the Egyptian defeat in 1967, and it may have been meant to provide a diversion from what observers agree was, prior to June 1967, a steady diet of rather heavy-handed Nasserite rhetoric. There are occasional brief interruptions, but the music is basically continuous and actually constitutes two services on separate mediumwave frequencies—one for Arabic and another for popular European music. Total programming time is 9.5 hours per day.

Palestine Broadcast

Almost every Arab country provides time for a program that is devoted to discussion of the Palestinian problem. These radio services strive mainly to attract Palestinians who reside in the country where the broadcast originates, but they also seek to attract local non-Palestinian Arabs and Palestinians who reside in Israel, the Occupied West Bank, and other Arab countries. With the possible exception of non-government-financed, clandestine PLO broadcasts from Lebanon during and after the 1975 Civil War, those who operate the program production and transmission facilities are dependent on the ever-shifting political climate under the host government. The result everywhere is an erratic transmission schedule and constantly changing program formats.[8]

The Egyptian Palestine Program became an "independent" service on October 29, 1960, with a daily half-hour broadcast. The schedule was expanded gradually until it reached 6 hours per day in three transmission periods: 0800 to 1000, 1200 to 1300, and 1600 to 1900 (Metwally, n.d., p. 7). The programs use designated times on other national radio services: for example, the first 2-hour broadcast uses the Voice of the Arabs wavelength (see Chapter 21, Voice of the Arabs). But Egypt has also occasionally curtailed its Palestine broadcasts or stopped them altogether. The most serious interruptions appear to have occurred between 1975 and 1979—a period during which Egypt concluded several agreements with Israel, starting with the return of the Sinai and continuing with a formal Egyptian-Israeli peace treaty. After the September 1975 Egyptian-Israeli Sinai agreement, the Egyptian government temporarily stopped all Palestine broadcasts from Egyptian facilities because the broadcasts were criticizing the host government (Tanner, 1975, p. 3). Resumed broadcasts were again halted in the late 1970s during the preliminaries to the peace treaty between Egypt and Israel.

Voice of the Arabs

This service was officially inaugurated on July 4, 1953 (*A.R.E. broadcasting in brief*, n.d., p.3), one year after the revolution; it is covered in more detail later. Daniel Lerner (1958, pp. 255, 309, 310) was probably the first to examine the service within its Arab media milieu and to suggest some direct effects of the broadcasts. From a 30-minute per day beginning the program expanded rapidly, reaching 7 hours per day in 1954; by the 1967 Middle East War, the service stopped just short of 24-hour per day operation.

The Voice of the Arabs is probably the best known and most widely listened to regional Arabic radio service. It further provides the best example of how Nasser used radio to promote his own views on Pan-Arabism, which included, for a period of time, calls for assassinations and the overthrow of selected Arab governments. Nasser and his advisors realized that in order to bring the Nasserite message to the rest of the Arab Middle East—the "first circle"—radio was the ideal medium. The channel would be one that could utilize Arabic, a language that especially lends itself to an emotional rather than a logical appeal. Radio further bypassed the problem of illiteracy in the Arab world. Finally, the countries in which the Voice's message would be received were unable to defend themselves against the service because they lacked the facilities. Few Arab countries in the 1950s had a viable domestic broadcasting service to provide an alternative to the Egyptian broadcasts and virtually no jamming transmitters were available to stop them. More important, at the time the service started and experienced its greatest growth, the political leaders in other Arab countries neither understood nor appreciated how potentially disruptive the Voice would be.

Some of the Voice's strong rhetoric was markedly effective in aiding those in other countries, most notably Jordan, Iraq, and North Yemen, who wanted to instigate government change or to influence government policy—

especially when a Western power such as Great Britain was involved.

Until his dismissal after the 1967 Middle East War, Ahmed Said served as director and chief announcer of the Voice of the Arabs. Under his guidance its basic format was formulated: attacks on those Arab countries that did not agree with Nasser's policies were packaged between music of famous Egyptian singers, drama, "talks," and news. In the late 1950s, special programs were sent out to specific regions, singling out for attack a country such as Saudi Arabia—a favorite target—or in some cases even singling out specific people for vituperation. The 1967 war ended what might be called the "Ahmed Said Era." It had been Said who contributed most to the psychological defeat that Egyptians and other Arabs felt immediately after the war: it had been he, although not he alone, who had provided the prewar confidence in military victory—an optimism that continued into the second day of the Six-Day War. When the enormity of the defeat became known to Egyptians, they seemed to know that they had been misled both prior to and during the early stages of the war. It was surely the "Ahmed Said Era" to which Issawi (1963, p. 217) referred in his succinct characterization of the Voice of the Arabs: it "has to be heard to be believed: for sheer venom, vulgarity, and indifference to truth it has few equals in the world."

After 1967 the tone of the service changed dramatically, as though those who were then appointed to administer it were attempting to compensate for past excesses. One of the official Voice goals as of 1971 was to promote "adher[ence] to the scientific, interpretation of language [and] purif[ication of] that language [of] repetition, exaggeration, superficiality, and unpreparedness" ("What do you," 1971, p. 69). Senior employees of the Voice who worked for the service both before and since the 1967 war have stated that the transmissions have become so bland that they are indistinguishable from the Radio Cairo domestic service. The Voice of the Arabs was the first major propaganda radio station in the Middle East to have an impact on listeners. It provided the model for others, most notably transmissions from Iraq and Syria, that came later. Since the assassination of Sadat, the service has become Egypt's main regional service. Radio Cairo's Main Program, on the other hand, has increasingly become domestic in orientation.

FOREIGN-LANGUAGE AND BEAMED SERVICES

The expansion of foreign-language and special beamed broadcasts depended heavily on studio and transmitter facilities that were built after the 1952 revolution. Before 1952, Egypt did not have any shortwave transmission capability: installation of shortwave transmitters was immediately ordered. Their completion on July 3, 1953, marked the beginning of programs to Southeast Asia, India, and Pakistan. As new transmitters and studios were made available, more services were added, with the ultimate goal of reaching areas of the world that Egypt and Nasser wanted to address. The new services tended to concentrate on those "circles" that Nasser identified in his writings: the Islamic nations, Africa south of the Sahara, and later the Third World. One of the reasons that the numerous language services were possible is the nature of the program that the Egyptians pursued to attract Third World students to Egyptian educational institutions. Students, a few contract employees, and people who had requested residence in Egypt as part of various resistance movements became the backbone of the foreign-language services. The completion of the Cairo broadcasting complex in the early 1960s provided the studio and administrative space to house, coordinate, and expand the foreign broadcasts. The political and economic changes that followed the 1967 war have tended to stabilize transmission hours and to eliminate some languages. However, the exposure that the international broadcasts are perceived to bring remains attractive, and some officials speak of expanding English-language broadcasts to a worldwide service similar to the one now operated by Russia.

Table 2.1 indicates the chronology of Egyptian international broadcasts in hours and minutes per day, as of 1980.

The Hebrew service, one of the earlier foreign-language programs that Egypt categorized as international broadcasting, deserves special mention before the discussion of Egyptian radio is concluded. The majority of the broadcasts have been on mediumwave, as Israel is the intended target. The broadcast hours in Table 2.1 are somewhat misleading, since they reflect the post-1979 Egyptian-Israeli peace agreement transmission schedule. During the 1960s and until 1978, the Hebrew program ranged from 12 to 15 hours per day, operating mostly in the afternoon and evening. Programming until 1978 was very heavy-handed, with news, commentary, and interview programs designed to promote the Arab cause among Hebrew-speakers; most of the service's announcers are trained at Cairo University, where Hebrew is taught, and some further improved their speaking skills by talking with Israeli prisoners captured and interned in Egypt after the October 1973 war. The service, some of which is broadcast in English, has used Western popular music in generous amounts to attract listeners. Those who administer the Hebrew service point to a 1974 U.S. Information Agency survey indicating that the Hebrew Service did indeed attract listeners, about the same number as Radio Cairo's Main Program (USIA, 1975, pp. 2, 5, 11). However, Israelis who have listened note that many tune in only because of curiosity and the popular music. And the music featured on the Egyptian Hebrew service has apparently been less of an attraction since the

Table 2.1. Egyptian foreign-language services

Year Started	Language	Duration	Target Area
1953	Indonesian	1:45	Indonesia
	English	1:15	Indian Peninsula
	Urdu	1:50	Pakistan
	Arabic	1:00	South East Asia
1954	Turkish	1:00	Turkey
	Hebrew	5:00	Israel (post peace agreement)
	Persian	-	Iran (discontinued Dec. 10, 1977)
	Swahili	2:00	East Africa
	Malayan	45	Malaysia
1955	Portuguese	1:15	Portugal
	Spanish	1:15	Latin America
	Arabic	1:00	Latin America
	Amharic	1:00	Ethiopia
1956	English	1:30	Europe
	French	1:30	Europe
	Tigrigna	-	Eritrea (discontinued 1956)
1957	Somali	1:00	Somalia
1958	Kurdish	-	Syria, Iraq, Iran, in Surani and Karamanji dialects (operates intermittently)
	Bengali	1:00	Bangladesh and India
	German	1:00	Europe
1959	Italian	1:45	Europe
	Arabic	-	Europe (discontinued July 5, 1969)
	English	1:30	West Africa
	French	2:00	West Africa
	Hausa	2:00	Nigeria, Ghana, Sierra Leone, Niger, Dahomey, Togo, Ivory Coast, Chad, Liberia, Cameroon
1960	Lingala	45	Zaire
1961	Nyanja	-	Zambia and Malawi (discontinued Dec. 24, 1977)
	English	2:00	Central and South Africa
	Foulani	1:00	West Africa
	Siamese	30	Thailand
1962	Lesotho	-	Swaziland and South Africa (operates intermittently)
	Pushtu	1:00	Afghanistan
1963	Portuguese	-	Angola-Mozambique (discontinued Dec. 14, 1977)

Table 2.1. *(continued)*

Year Started	Language	Duration	Target Area
1964	Shona	45	Zimbabwe
	Sindebelle	45	Zimbabwe
1965	Zulu	45	Southern Africa
1966	Hindi	1:00	India
	Yoruba	1:00	Nigeria, Dahomey
	Ibo	-	West Nigeria (discontinued July 5, 1969)
	English	1:30	North America
	Arabic	-	West Africa (discontinued Dec. 10, 1977)
	Arabic	-	East, Central and South Africa (discontinued Jan. 11, 1969)
1967	Afari	1:00	Djibouti
1968	Russian	-	Soviet Union (discontinued Dec. 12, 1977)
	Bambara	1:00	Mali, Guinea, Ivory Coast
	Oulouf	1:00	Senegal and minorities in neighboring countries
	French	-	Canada (discontinued Dec. 10, 1977)
	Arabic	1:00	North America
	Arabic	-	Vietnam (discontinued July 1, 1976)
	Arabic	2:00	North America

Source: Metwally, n.d., pp. 9–12; *WRTH*, 1980, pp. 164–65; *A.R.E. broadcasting in brief*, n.d., p. 5.

Israeli domestic radio service started playing Western popular music. Egypt has decreased the service's hours for two reasons: first, the peace agreement implies a normalizing of relations that almost mandates some changes in the service. Second, since the peace agreement, Egypt has had to strive to explain its actions to the other Arab countries, many of whom attempted to isolate Sadat as a political leader. Part of the transmission time devoted to Hebrew prior to 1979 was later used to broadcast to the other Arab countries in Arabic (Rushty interview, 1979).

By 1973, 20 years of expansion in international radio broadcasting had made Egypt a major international radio force—the sixth largest international broadcaster, in terms of weekly program output. As Table 2.2 indicates, however, some shifts in transmission hours during the 1980s had moved Egypt by 1986 to seventh place.

In April 1981 (Egyptian Radio and Television Union, 1988) Egyptian radio was reorganized around a "network concept" wherein all of the above-noted services were grouped into seven general programming

Table 2.2. Weekly broadcast hours, 1950–1986

Country	1950	1960	1970	1980	1986
United States[a]	597	1495	1907	1901	2411
Soviet Union[b]	533	1015	1908	2094	2229
Chinese People's Republic	66	687	1267	1350	1446
German Federal Republic	-	315	779	804	821
United Kingdom	643	589	723	719	733
Albania	26	63	487	560	588
Egypt	-	301	540	546	560
North Korea	-	159	330	597	535

Source: British Broadcasting Corporation, *BBC handbook 1980,* 1980, p. 57; British Broadcasting Corporation, *BBC handbook 1987,* 1986, p. 180.
[a]Includes Voice of America (including Radio Marti), Radio Liberty, Radio Free Europe.
[b]Includes Radio Moscow, Radio Station Peace and Progress, and regional stations.

classifications. However, despite the name changes for some of the services, relatively few major program changes took place. The changes were not so much a departure from the extensive radio services that had evolved since the revolution. Rather, the Ministry of Information believed that changes were necessary in order to accommodate the increasing importance of videocassettes, popular radio programs from the West and other Arab countries, and changing radio-listening tastes. The following reflects the seven-network concept; within each network, there are specific targeted programs for specialized audiences.

The Main Network
A national service, similar to the old Main Program, the Main Network transmits 24 hours per day.

The Local Network
This is an outgrowth of the Alexandria Service. The nine local stations are, in fact, less autonomous than they might appear. However, they have some local programming origination capability, despite the fact that network control is located in Cairo.

The Quran Network
Officially, this radio service is designed to reinforce Islamic instruction and values. However, its wider political mission is noted above.

The Cultural Network
Directed at minority music tastes exhibited by the more well-educated members of the population, this service includes the Cairo-based European Service that continues to transmit news and information in English, French, German, and Greek.

The Voice of the Arabs
This service is described both above and extensively in Chapter 21.

The Communication Network
This is the same as the previously described Middle East Program. Its main task is to attract commercial advertising in order to bring hard currency to Egyptian radio.

The Overseas Network
Egypt's foreign-language services transmit under this heading (Egyptian Radio and Television Union, 1988).

RADIO TRANSMISSION FACILITIES

Until 1956, most of Egypt's radio transmitters were located at the Abu Zabal site on a hill near Cairo, the location of the original Marconi transmitter. Since that time transmitter sites have been spread throughout the country, with most facilities being located between Cairo and Alexandria in the Nile Delta. During the 1956 British-French-Israeli invasion of Egypt, the Royal Air Force bombed the Abu Zabal transmitter site with the hope of eliminating the transmission capability of both Radio Cairo (Main Program) and the Voice of the Arabs. The attack only temporarily interrupted their services (El-Kashlan interview, 1974), and a British plan to replace Cairo's services with an anti-Nasser station on Cyprus failed (see Chapter 21, Sharq al-Adna). The incident did teach the Egyptians a lesson: diversify transmitter locations and prepare stand-by transmitters and studios for possible future attacks. Engineers—a profession with a high standing within the broadcasting profession—have had little trouble convincing management that without efficient, well-maintained transmitters, programs will not reach domestic or international audiences.

The many aforementioned services required a system of high-powered medium- and shortwave transmitters that could be supplied with a broadcast signal from a master control area. The system could thus feed signals to selected transmitters and extend the reach of a specified service, should the decision be made to do so. The broadcasting complex completed in the early 1960s provided the switching capability. Transmitter construction throughout the Nasser years—the 1950s and 1960s, as Table 2.3 indicates—provided the power.

Transmitter and antenna construction is a particularly expensive undertaking for a country such as Egypt that not only must import the high technology but has so little money with which to pay for it. Between 1956 and 1974 some transmitters were supplied by the Soviet Union and the East

Table 2.3. Egyptian mediumwave and shortwave radio transmission powers, 1952–1970: Nasser's transmitter building program

Year	Mediumwave (kw)	Shortwave (kw)	Total
1952	72	-	72
1953	74	140	214
1954	176	270	446
1955	180	380	560
1956	180	380	560
1957	202	380	582
1958	544	530	1074
1959	834	500	1334
1960	834	540	1374
1961	834	740	1574
1962	834	790	1624
1968	2188	1700	3888
1969–1970	2188	1850	4038

Source: "What do you know?" 1971, p. 76; and El-Kashlan interview.

European countries with which Egypt had close ties at the time. Various military, trade, and cultural agreements during this period apparently helped secure loans and credits that were used to purchase transmission equipment. President Sadat later turned to the United States and Europe—especially to the United States—for military and economic assistance, and by the mid-1970s Western countries became transmission equipment suppliers again. Egypt felt that new transmitters were needed in order to defend itself against radio attacks by other Arab countries that objected to the move to normalize relations with Israel, and some of the older medium- and shortwave transmitters needed to be refurbished or replaced. The transmitters the Egyptians believed to be powerful in the 1950s and 1960s—for example, mediumwave transmitters of 500 kilowatts—were no longer very effective or reliable in reaching other parts of the Arab world, where many of the countries had installed transmitters of 1000 kilowatts. In 1978, then, the Egyptian Radio-Television Federation embarked on a transmitter expansion program that effectively doubled its shortwave and tripled its mediumwave transmission capability. This program was designed to provide additional high-powered transmitters for the Voice of the Arabs and the Koran Program and to place lower-powered transmitters in the Egyptian provinces in order to rebroadcast the already established national services.

The new high-powered mediumwave transmitters were built and installed by Continental Electronics of Dallas, Texas. To upgrade the Koran Program, a 500-kilowatt facility was ordered for Tanta, in the Delta. To increase the power of the Voice of the Arabs Program, a 1000-kilowatt mediumwave transmitter was ordered for the Nile Delta area: the Egyptians were later to order another so that the Voice would be broadcast by a 2000-kilowatt facility—two 1000-kilowatt transmitters operating in parallel (Abdu interview, 1979). Eighty low-power transmitters for 20 sites were ordered from the Harris Corporation Broadcast Products Division of Quincy, Illinois, under a $5.8 million contract awarded in March 1979 ("Harris wins $5.2," 1979). These transmitters have been intended primarily for the rebroadcast of domestic programs.

Modern Egypt has found itself in serious economic straits. With a rapidly expanding population, it has had to import food and market it at subsidized prices in order to feed its people. The large-scale American aid program that followed the Sinai disengagement agreements between Egypt and Israel appeared to be a partial solution to the country's serious economic situation. First negotiated by Kissinger under the Nixon and Ford administrations, the aid program was again expanded under President Carter and provided for assistance in all facets of development. Each ministry or major administrative unit in the Egyptian government could apply for assistance through a central aid-coordinating office that ranked projects in terms of importance and then passed them along to the mission of the Agency for International Development (AID) in Cairo. Under this arrangement, the Egyptian Radio-Television Federation requested loans through the Ministry of Information for both radio and television equipment. It was agreed however, that the purchase of television equipment—possibly because television was perceived by some American officials as a luxury—was not to be given the same priority as the purchase of that for radio. Thus, three loans were arranged for the eventual Continental and Harris radio-transmitter contracts.

A possible explanation for the U.S. government's interest in financing new Egyptian radio transmitters came to light in the summer of 1980. Apparently the Central Intelligence Agency had persuaded Egyptian authorities to use an undetermined number of its transmitters to broadcast an anti-Khomeini radio service known as "The Free Voice of Iran." Before the programs were identified as being broadcast by American intelligence personnel, entertainment programs were interspersed with news and commentary that called for the support of former Iranian Prime Minister Shahpur Bakhtiar. *The New York Times* quoted American officials as saying that "Egypt had been promised additional transmitter facilities by the United States through the Agency for International Development to compensate for the Egyptian facilities used by the C.I.A." (Binder, 1980, p. 3).

There apparently was special concern at both the American Embassy in Cairo and the State Department in Washington over the request for funds to order the second 1000-kilowatt transmitter for the new Voice of the Arabs facility. The more seasoned State Department officials may have remembered the strong anti-American propaganda broadcast by the Voice during the 1950s and 1960s. An even more vivid recollection, perhaps, was how the Voice of the Arabs and Cairo Radio's Main Program were used by Nasser during the opening hours of the 1967 war to broadcast to other countries the allegation that American and British planes were flying cover for Israeli fighters that neutralized the Egyptian Air Force. The immediate result of those broadcasts had been violent anti-American demonstrations throughout the Arab world, which led to the severing of diplomatic relations between many Arab countries and the United States. Also, State Department and International Communication Agency officials may have thought that the expenditure would simply be an inappropriate use of economic development funds. These American concerns were allayed and the additional funds for the second transmitter were allocated (Bang interview, 1979). Egypt is still willing to invest valuable economic resources—and to invest time in complicated negotiations—in order to maintain its stature as the Arab world's most influential broadcaster.

Table 2.4. U.S. AID loans to Egyptian Radio-Television Federation for radio transmitters

Loan Number	Amount
030	$10 million
036	$ 5 million
038	$ 5 million

Source: Loan figures were supplied by the Agency for International Development (Bang interview 1979).

EGYPTIAN TELEVISION

By the fourth anniversary of the Egyptian revolution, Nasser and his advisors had reason to believe that their efforts in radio were effective, both internationally and domestically. It appeared only natural to those close to radio that television broadcasting would be the next step. Egypt was not the first country to establish television in the Arab world. In 1956 the Iraqi government purchased a small station that was imported originally as part of a British trade fair, providing the beginnings of Arab world government-controlled television. Prior to the opening of the Baghdad station, the American armed forces had established low-power stations on the American standard for military personnel at Wheelus Air Force Base near Tripoli

(Libya) and Dhahran (Saudi Arabia). Moreover, the Arabian American Oil Company (ARAMCO) had begun a similarly low-powered station that still operates in Saudi Arabia's Eastern Province.

Despite Egypt's precarious economic situation during the last part of the 1950s, the decision was made to begin a television service. Studies were undertaken and international corporations submitted bids in 1956, but the joint British-French-Israeli Suez invasion stopped work on television until 1959 (Nassr, 1963, p. 86). In late 1959 a contract was signed between the United Arab Republic and the Radio Corporation of America (RCA) to provide a complete television service for Egypt and the beginnings of a service for Syria.

Little information is available from either the American or the Egyptian government concerning the origins of the RCA television contract. By 1959 the United States had an amiable, although not close, relationship with the Nasser government. The United States had refused to supply arms and help finance construction of the High Dam in Aswan in the mid-1950s, and Egypt had turned to the Soviet Union and Eastern European countries for military assistance and help with the dam project. It has been alleged that the United States helped financially with the introduction of television by lending money for or subsidizing the RCA contract. This has been denied by both governments, but observers believe that Egypt's hard currency holdings at the time were not sufficient for such an undertaking. If no U.S. assistance was offered, and Egypt used hard currency from its own small store, its commitment to a television service was serious indeed. One possible explanation for the selection of RCA for the large Egyptian installation and the more modest Syrian one is that the company was perhaps then the only one that could complete the task by the specified date. At the time, RCA was probably the only company that could supply cameras, antennas, videotape recorders, and audio, switching, and microwave equipment without sub-contracting to other firms. RCA also had the experience and personnel to provide a complete television system.

Immediately after the RCA contract was signed, the government started building the large Cairo broadcasting complex on the Nile; but television, it was decided, would be introduced before the completion of the new building. The first studios were located temporarily in an old building in downtown Cairo because television's initial broadcast was targeted for the eighth anniversary of the revolution. The first pictures appeared on July 21, 1960 (Nassr, 1963, p. 86), using the 625-line European standard.

Three separate channels were provided under the RCA contract. The Main Program was transmitted on Channel 5 from a 10-kilowatt transmitter. Channels 9 and 7, each with 2-kilowatt transmitters, were introduced as respectively the Second Program and the Cultural/Foreign Program. The Main Program was the first to be extended throughout the country through links to other transmitters, the first of which was in Egypt's second largest city, Alexandria. After the major population areas were linked, two channels—the Main by 1975 (Tawffik, 1980, p. 1) and the Second by 1979 (Abdu interview, 1979)—were available to most of Egypt's population from a chain of transmitters along the length of the Nile. This coverage was made possible by the fact that Egypt's population is largely distributed along the narrow agricultural area irrigated by the Nile. Although Egypt is the size of Texas and New Mexico geographically, the country's 46 million people are thus crowded into a relatively small area, the country's arable lands being among the most densely populated in the world. The country did not have to wait, then, to link distant villages by satellite ground stations, as did Saudi Arabia, Oman, and the Sudan, when such facilities became available: the construction of microwave stations along the river was coordinated with the telecommunications authority and the Egyptian railway system.

Nasser and his advisors were unique among Middle Eastern leaders at the time both because of the role they envisioned for both radio and television and because of their commitment of financial resources and personnel to the attainment of that vision. It was generally the practice in other Arab countries to start modest radio and television operations and then to determine whether they should be expanded in terms of programming capability and coverage area. Nasser inherited a limited radio service and rapidly expanded programming and transmission capability; television started as a multi-channel operation and (as we have seen) its extension to the major population centers of the country was begun as soon as microwave links could be created.

TELEVISION, 1960 TO 1967

Because of its well-financed radio service and film industry, Egypt had the talent to start a multi-channel operation without importing engineering or production staff from other countries. This talent also enabled Egypt to produce a relatively high percentage of its own programs—something no other Arab country was able to do.

The television channels were intended to parallel the spread and success of the three main kinds of program groupings found on radio: a Main Program (Channel 5) would provide a mixture of popular programming, news, and programs with developmental and educational themes; a Second Program (Channel 9), designed initially to be for the urban areas, would feature programs that would appeal to a sophisticated audience; and a Third Program (Channel 7) would cater mostly to the foreign community, featuring Egyptian-made programs in French and English as well as imported films and tapes. The third channel was closed after the 1967 war for financial reasons, as it was believed to be a luxury. Some of its programs were shifted to the other channels (Samiha Rahman interview, 1974).

From the beginning, Egyptian television has featured an abundance of Egyptian feature-length films: they are an important source of local programs. After the revolution, many films had maintained the traditional formats of Egyptian films—romance, music, and slapstick comedy—but they were now oriented toward the development of a new socialist nation where education, dedication, and hard work were to better the Arab world. Even so, the film industry and the television channels did not turn out mere political pap. The Egyptian character is essentially kind, fun-loving, and possessed of a sophisticated sense of humor: these traits are too ingrained in the population for bland programming to conquer.

A great deal of early television programming was done live and some was taped on the RCA machines supplied as part of the television contract. The television portion of the broadcasting complex was designed for 11 large studios plus small ones for interviews and news. Several were constructed so that the television drama could take place on a stage before a live audience of several hundred people. By Western television standards these productions, some of which were replayed into the mid-1970s, were not well done. Much of the action was improvisation. Camera shots consistently included hanging microphones and actors waiting offstage. The overall effect was that of a theater performance being recorded by television cameras. It was only when the export market for taped plays became lucrative that dramatic productions became more sophisticated, done without an audience in a large studio with the intention of editing the final product.[9]

Several mobile units were supplied as part of the RCA contract and these were used for sporting events, major public speeches by Nasser and other political leaders, and the often televised airport greetings of visiting heads of state. Film shot for television was, however, the main way of covering events in Egypt. Monochrome film stock was relatively inexpensive and the country had an abundance of people able to shoot, process, and edit it. In addition, the edited product could easily be duplicated and sent via air to other television stations.

News was a regular feature and was deemed important enough for more than one channel to show the same newscast in Arabic. Later, regularly scheduled newscasts in both French and English were started. After the revolution, Egypt developed the practice of having the state news agency provide guidance regarding the order of news items on both radio and television, and during periods of political crisis, Egypt's Middle East News Agency would actually supply the material. This practice, generally referred to by Arab journalists as "news protocol," has been adopted by virtually every Arab country. The term refers to a set of guidelines for each country's media that mandates that stories about the head of state and his family come first, generally to be followed by stories about those Arab countries with which the country has close relations. Stories about the rest of the Arab world and other foreign countries follow. The effect has been to give the head of state a great deal of visibility: he is almost always featured, if only in a still picture of his receiving visitors.

Dizard (1966, p. 150) notes that while Nasser and his themes appeared to be omnipresent, those who were controlling the medium used "relative restraint in [their] television propaganda." Egypt did not attempt to utilize what was seen as an entertainment medium to show executions, as did Syria, or to show endless televised revolutionary trials, as was done in Iraq. Dizard accurately observes that Nasser was careful to avoid appealing directly to the television audience; rather, his speeches to various groups on selected occasions were televised, thereby leaving the impression "of televised coverage of events in which [Nasser was] the leading orator addressing a meeting to which the television audience [was] invited as onlookers" (1966, p. 151).

During these early television years, foreign programming was also used. Older movies that had originally been subtitled for cinema were purchased by Egyptian television; American and British programs were televised. However, during this period, the new shows were relatively few, as it was so expensive to dub or to subtitle them. As additional Arab countries started television systems, it became feasible for program distributors to help finance those costly operations. Some of the work was undertaken in Egypt, but increasingly the subtitling and dubbing center of the Arab world became Beirut, Lebanon, where in the 1950s the ARAMCO television station in Saudi Arabia had had its programming subtitled.

TELEVISION, 1967 TO 1974

The June 1967 war resulted in an Egyptian defeat that was militarily, economically, and psychologically devastating. The Israelis captured the Sinai and the Egyptian Air Force was temporarily eliminated. The closing of the Suez Canal destroyed Egypt's main source of hard currency. As previously noted, the pre-war media campaign had implied that Egypt would be militarily successful against Israel, and when the extent of the defeat became known to the population, it was crushing. President Nasser, in a speech broadcast on television and virtually every radio transmitter in Egypt, assumed blame for the defeat and attempted to resign; but the population took to the streets and urged him to stay on as president.

Immediately after the war, there was a decrease in the amount of foreign programming that was shown on television. The third channel, over which much had been telecast, was eliminated, and the British and American programs that constituted the bulk of the imported programs were deemed unacceptable due to the break in diplomatic relations with Great Britain and the United States. Almost all forms of programming on television placed less emphasis on Egypt's military capability, tending instead toward the nationalistic, the educational, and the religious. When Egypt decided to assume a closer relationship with its military supplier, the Soviet Union, and to construct an air defense system against Israeli air attack, military personnel and hardware from the Soviet Union poured into the country—and cultural agreements between Egypt and the Soviet bloc countries brought increased programs from them. The broadcast system being financially hard-pressed, television started showing films about Soviet and East European life: there was no particular liking for such programs among television programmers, but they were either free of charge or inexpensive and pleased those whom Egypt at the time believed to be its friends. The general technical quality of Egyptian television declined between 1967 and 1974. There was less money for new equipment and the original RCA equipment began to show signs of deterioration because of lack of maintenance and the difficult Egyptian climatic conditions of heat and dust. Also, Egypt needed to purchase its spare parts from a company that had been banned from doing business in the Arab world: certain companies, including Coca-Cola, Ford, and RCA, had in 1967 been put on the Arab League boycott list[10] for alleged business dealings with Israel. That problem was solved, at least temporarily, by purchasing RCA parts through a supplier rather than directly.[11] The financial picture for television improved slightly between 1970 and 1974 because of program sales to other Arab countries—some of which, like Saudi Arabia, had refused to purchase Egyptian-made television programs until about 1970 because of the difficult relations between the two countries after Nasser sent troops to fight in North Yemen. The post-1970 program sales produced some hard currency that the Egyptian Radio-Television Federation could use to upgrade equipment by purchasing such things as Ampex videotape recorders and Marconi cameras. But the change in government after Nasser's death and Sadat's ascendancy to the presidency in 1970 does not appear to have had much effect on television programming or the structure of the Federation. Sadat was extensively covered by television in the same manner Nasser was, but Sadat was never so commanding an orator. Sadat's television appearances almost always occurred on the occasion of his addresses to the National Assembly or during functions such as national celebrations. Perhaps so few changes took place in television and radio after 1970 because of the manner in which the broadcast media operate as a government bureaucracy. On August 13, 1970, President Nasser signed a presidential decree ("Text of the," 1970, pp. 50–57) annulling the 1966 decrees that had established radio, television, and broadcast engineering as separate departments under the Ministry of Information. The new decree formally established the Egyptian Radio-Television Federation and created four distinct sectors—radio, television, engineering, and finance—each of which had a chairman who reported directly to the Minister of Information. All personnel connected with broadcasting in Egypt, including some Ministry of Information officials, were transferred to serve under the aegis of a section.

The exact number of employees now connected with the Federation is not known by the Egyptian government, but estimates range from 12,000 to 15,000. One reason for the wide disparity in the estimates is that many of the employees, including me at one time, are temporary and come only to do a specific announcing shift or to take a part in a play. The broadcasting organization in Egypt is indeed large, with too many permanent staff members; the various sectors could function effectively—some say a great deal more efficiently—with one-third to one-half the people.

But this situation is not unique within the Egyptian bureaucracy. A university education in Egypt is much sought after by the people on the lower end of the socioeconomic scale as a way of gaining entry into the middle class; those in the middle and upper classes want a university education in order to maintain their places in society. After the revolution, the government expanded opportunities for Egyptians to gain an education: new campuses were built and old ones were enlarged. When the number of graduates increased in the late 1950s, the government realized that few employment opportunities existed for educated men and women, thus rendering them a potentially disgruntled political force. The solution was to guarantee every university graduate a government job. Graduates are assigned to various departments almost on a random basis, although some attempt is made to utilize training in finance, languages, and the social sciences. The Federation, then, like virtually every other government organization, is flooded with people who have no other place to go. One often sees in government offices large numbers of people with little to do except invent ways to make the bureaucracy more cumbersome. In 1980 the gross monthly pay for a new graduate in his first government job was only 30 Egyptian pounds, or approximately $42.90 at the tourist exchange rate: the salary, low even by Egyptian standards, tends to discourage graduates from seeking government employment and rather functions, in effect, as a kind of unemployment compensation.

Whatever the perceived quality of Egyptian television after its initial stage of development, Egyptians were watching the medium. Lorimor and Dunn (1968–1969, p. 683) found that 73 percent of respondents in their study watched television; 1 percent of the sample watched between 7 and 8 hours, with more women than men viewing more than 3 hours each day.

TELEVISION, 1974 TO 1981

There are those who argue about which country won the October 1973 Egyptian-Israeli War. Egyptians know that they were at least the side that achieved a psychological victory—one that brought them out of a long period of depression and self-examination following the 1967 war. During the brief engagement itself and immediately afterward, the Egyptian media took a very different approach than they had during and after the 1967 war. Radio tended to be more honest about the military situation it reported from the front and to be less boastful about the apparent victory when the Suez Canal was crossed. Television programming, which took a little longer to produce and air and would presumably be seen only within Egypt, was a bit more upbeat, reflecting the confidence Egyptians were recovering as good news came in. The Egyptians also improved their approach to helping the international press by increasing liaison with reporters and facilitating the shooting, processing, editing, and exporting of newsfilm. Plans solidified for construction of a satellite ground station to transmit and to receive television signals.

After the 1973 war, it was not so much program philosophy or formats that changed as subject matter and mood. Nine months after the Egyptian-Israeli engagement, Egyptian television still showed taped dramas that dealt with some aspect of the military victory; dancers in fatigues reenacted the Suez crossing; and interviews with government officials, religious leaders, and university professors examined virtually every aspect of the military action. President Sadat continued to make public appearances and speeches that were covered extensively. News items and special programs about the United Nations, United States, and Israeli agreements regarding military disengagement received a high priority.

More than any other Egyptian mass medium, television has tended to reflect the changing international political orientation of the country. Before the 1973 war, Sadat dismissed his vice-president and other officials who were apparently plotting, with Soviet help, against him. This action, known as the "corrective revolution," led to, among other things, Sadat's order for all Soviet military advisors to leave the country. During the Nixon administration, Kissinger promoted the reestablishment of the U.S.-Egyptian diplomatic relations that had been severed in June 1967. These moves along with the general mood of the Sadat government gradually changed Egypt during the 1970s from a socialist orientation to one that was more hospitable to free enterprise and decidedly pro-West.

After 1974, the year when the door was formally opened to the West, the number of British and American programs on Egyptian television increased. The television sector decided to continue the development of color. The French government had been successful in persuading Egypt to adopt the SECAM system and had installed SECAM color equipment in one of the Egyptian studios before the 1973 war. After the war, the decision was made to convert both production and transmission facilities to color. This action helped the technical quality of television because in 1974 most of the monochrome equipment that had been installed by RCA in 1960, such as switchers and cameras, had been too long in use—and it was, after all, only monochrome. Color television was believed by some to be a luxury that Egypt could not afford, but the attitude among broadcasting officials prevailed: the new equipment was necessary for the production of programs to be sold to other countries that were converting to color and anyway monochrome television equipment was becoming increasingly difficult to purchase. In August 1974 Ahmed Abul-Magd, then Minister of Information, officially opened a new and impressive color television production studio ("LE 1.45 m," 1974, p. 1). Outfitted with sophisticated audio, lighting, and video equipment from Great Britain, it was used primarily for taping of drama.

After 1974, the revenue that television derived from advertising and from program sales to other Arab countries increased significantly. The aforementioned change in Egypt's political orientation had a great deal to do with the increase in advertising. Sadat's "Open Door Policy" encouraged foreign companies to invest and do business in Egypt and some currency restrictions on the importation of goods were lifted, resulting in a change in the variety and the amount of foreign goods in Egyptian shops. Disposable income among some middle-class and upper middle-class urban Egyptian families increased, due to both the open door policy and the high salaries of family members working in Gulf countries. Before 1974 there was little incentive for companies to advertise, and most advertising was restricted to Egyptian state industries that marketed petroleum products, soap, cigarettes, insect sprays, and electrical appliances such as hot water heaters, but advertising had always been permitted on Egyptian television. In 1976 the old products were still advertised: but they were joined by commercials for American and European cigarettes (later banned from broadcasting), American and Japanese automobiles, American air conditioners, food, and imported perfumes, cosmetics, and soft drinks.

Egyptian advertising rates are two tiered, providing a lower cost in Egyptian pounds for local advertising by businesses and state-owned industry. Commercials for imported products must be paid for in hard currency and are much more expensive than local advertising, often by as much as a factor of four (Egyptian Radio-Television Federation, 1979).

Since the early 1980s, Egyptian television has become a more important advertising outlet for those wishing to reach this large market with a variety of goods and services. In fact, Egypt follows the trend in many industrialized countries where advertising expenditures have shifted some from radio and the print media to television. Egyptian television reports a 799 percent increase in television advertising revenue between 1978 and 1988 (Egyptian Radio and Television Union, 1988).

The changing economic mood in Egypt and the increased economic fortunes of the Arabian Gulf states after the 1973 war combined to make the production of television programs for other countries a profitable business for Egyptian producers. As noted earlier, television organizations in other Arab countries have generally relied on Egypt as a source of Arab-produced material for television when politics would permit it. Egyptian talent (and therefore the Cairene dialect) are well known throughout the Arab world because of Egyptian films, videos, television, radio, and recorded music. Until the 1970s, tapes of programs made for Egyptian audiences were sold to other countries: during the 1970s, especially the late 1970s, more productions were undertaken with the express idea of marketing them in other countries, particularly those countries in the Gulf that could afford to purchase them at relatively high prices.

The potentially lucrative market in the Gulf provided an opportunity for independent producers, using Egyptian talent, to rent the Egyptian color television studios for the production of drama for export. This practice, of course, led to direct competition for the television operation itself. In 1976, the Egyptian studio rentals were curtailed; and at one point television-sector employees were banned from working in Egypt for private producers ("TV employees banned," 1976, p. 1). This move prompted the producers to rent studios in Great Britain, Germany, Greece, Jordan, Bahrain, and Dubai, to import Egyptian talent and to tape programs that they then sold directly to Arab world television stations. Once the producers and talent left Egypt for television series production, they were reluctant to return to tape programs in Cairo even when the television organization tried to entice them to do so: the Egyptian television studios and editing facilities were rented for relatively high prices, and producers had learned that they could travel abroad, import Egyptian talent, and produce programs more cheaply elsewhere than in Egypt. In other countries, the producers did not have to pay everyone from janitors to engineers for their "cooperation," and talent liked leaving the country to work because they were paid there in hard currency and could avoid the relatively heavy Egyptian income tax. Eventually, the Egyptian Radio-Television Federation created its own production company, the "Voice of Cairo," which used the Cairo television facilities but was organized along private sector lines so as to compete more effectively for material and talent. Competition has only increased—but the "Voice of Cairo" has been actively involved in both production and program sales in the Arab world. Certainly the competition has tended to stabilize rapidly increasing program prices.

Similar to the situation in the United States, where the export of feature films and television programs is an important business that helps the balance of payments, Egyptian media products—especially films and television programs—provide the country with valuable hard currency, and the government has started to make it easier to produce television programs in Egypt. Although not motivated by potential media exports, the government has changed many laws that now make it easier for Egyptians to have foreign bank accounts. This has helped alleviate the situation described earlier where tax laws had actually encouraged Egyptian actors, writers, and producers to do creative work in other countries.

The Ministry of Information has made it easier for independent producers to rent Egyptian Radio-Television Federation television studios. The "Voice of Cairo" project is an example of an attempt to keep Egyptian television productions, and hard currency, in Cairo. Also, in the late 1980s the government announced that it would build a new television production facility outside Cairo. The Sixth of October TV Center was to have been an entirely new studio and equipment facility near the Pyramids (Egyptian Radio and Television Union, 1988), thus helping to relieve the crowded conditions in the radio and television building on the Nile. However, the Sixth of October TV Center is now a distant possibility. The funds for the project were to come from Saudi Arabian investors. Several factors, including the downturn in the Saudi economy, Egyptian government concern over potential Saudi Arabian control over television production projects, and the 1990–1991 Gulf conflict have delayed the project.

Since Egypt's peace treaty with Israel, many Arab countries have joined the call by the more militant countries to isolate Egypt and boycott its exports. Many countries have broken diplomatic relations with Egypt or reduced the size of diplomatic missions in Cairo; Libya, Syria, and Iraq stopped all airline flights to Egypt. Countries that have supported the boycott vowed no longer to purchase Egyptian television programs, adding that they did not need to buy directly from Egypt because so much quality material, produced outside of Egypt, was available from Egyptian artists.[12] However, there has been no evidence to suggest that Egyptian program sales to the Arab world decreased as a result; they may actually have increased (Tawffik interview, 1980; Abdullah interview, 1979). The post-boycott marketing efforts of the television sales staff in Cairo became more aggressive, and the creation of a program-marketing company structured to give the impression of being independent from the Egyptian government helped those who still wanted to buy from Egypt. Finally, because so much Egyptian talent was used in both "Voice of Cairo" and independent productions taped outside Egypt, it was difficult for viewers to tell where programs were made. This situation has worked to the advantage of program purchasers in other countries who have felt that they should at least appear to abide by the boycott. A combination of advertising revenue and income from program sales helped Egypt begin to convert to SECAM color transmission in 1977; gradually, local production, including news, became color. All new transmitters, many of which were added between 1977 and 1980, were capable of color transmission: they brought the Second Program to locations previously served by the Main Program (Abdu interview, 1979).

In 1979, some countries decreased or stopped altogether the purchase of Egyptian television programs. Lebanon produces most of its own Arabic-language programming, and South Yemen and Libya have not purchased material for several years. Iraq stopped the purchase of programs after the decision to boycott was taken at a Baghdad (Iraq) meeting in 1979.

Because of the complex nature of the Egyptian Radio-Television Federation budget, the percentage of income from various sources is difficult to determine. Sources of income include advertising revenue, program sales, funds from the state budget, and revenue from a type of license on receivers. During the Nasser years the government attempted to encourage the availability of radio and television receivers: the radio license fee, which was the original means of financing Egyptian radio, was eliminated not only because the tax was difficult to collect after transistor radios became common, but because the government did not want to discourage radio ownership among those who could least afford the license fee. It was felt, however, that television would require some kind of contribution from set owners, who would initially be urban citizens able to afford to help finance the medium. The problem that Egypt faced along with many other developing countries was how to verify set ownership and to collect fees. Culturally both poor and financially well-off Egyptians function outside of government controls and tend to mistrust government officials and institutions. The government believed that cheating would be so widespread as to render ineffective a license fee system similar to that used in Japan and many West European countries. The Egyptian solution was one that guaranteed income for television but was not particularly fair, as it did not necessarily gain income directly from those who used the medium. An amount was added monthly to electricity bills, which were all handled through the national electricity authority: Egyptian homes have few electrical appliances and the belief was that those who were heavy consumers of electricity were heavy television users. Some such surcharge was probably the only way that revenue could be collected systematically, and Egypt was not alone in adopting the system. In the late 1970s Cyprus, following the example of Greece, changed to a television license fee system very similar to Egypt's.

An Egyptian viewer, having access to electricity and a television receiver and within range of transmitters, is provided with about 120 hours of television programming per week on two national channels. The Main

Program generally begins daily between 1500 and 1600 and runs continuously until approximately midnight. The Second Program begins about 1700 and also lasts until around midnight. Transmissions are extended on Friday and Sunday, respectively the Moslem and Christian days of rest; for important sporting events such as soccer matches; and during selected months throughout the school year, when instructional programs are broadcast in the morning. Although factors such as availability of programs, political events, national celebrations, and important religious months such as Ramadan and Hajj all alter the schedule, the basic daily schedule for the two national channels has remained about the same since the 1970s. The broadcasting authority publishes a weekly magazine, *Broadcasting*, which provides a detailed television and radio schedule; the publication also provides articles about broadcasting personalities and features about various aspects of the broadcast media.

There is something for everyone on Egyptian television. Both channels use the "continuity announcer" format in which someone—usually an attractive female who is striving to become a television or cinema star—introduces each program. Between programs, slides of Cairo or the Egyptian countryside are shown with background music; short taped popular songs and clustered commercials are seen. The transitions between programs are not always according to schedule because program times are only estimates. Foreign programs with no commercials inserted are considerably shorter than the standard 30 minutes or 1 hour. Also, there is a shortage of videotape recorders during transmission time because they are heavily utilized for the recording of satellite feeds for news and local production. This shortage sometimes presents viewers with awkward pauses between programs and commericals.

The medium is not without critics. *The Egyptian Gazette*, Cairo's daily English-language newspaper, has often led press criticism of various aspects of television. A 1977 editorial attacks television by noting that "television is a LE [Egyptian Pound] 12 million per year liability to the state and poses a mental hazard to 38 million people." It continues:

> There are two prominent schools of thought on the quality of TV programmes and both have very sharply defined views. One believes that the programmes are written "by the mentally retarded, for the mentally retarded, and in order to promote mental retardation growth rates" in the country. The other thinks that "taking into consideration the acute shortage of public lavatories in Cairo, the TV building, under the present circumstances, would be put to far better use by being converted into a giant public convenience."
>
> Talented Egyptians are nowhere to be seen. The vast majority have fled to other Arab states where the pay is good and where their talents are appreciated and put to good use. No one should be surprised if films made in the Gulf by Egyptians are sold to Egyptian TV and this will be the rule rather

than the exception if TV continues to be run like an agricultural co-op. ("Television's 12,000," 1977, p. 2)

Comments like the above are infrequent but deal perceptively with some of the major flaws both obvious and not so obvious to the viewer. But, in fact, most television viewers are apparently satisfied with what they see; and many feel fortunate to own or to have access to a receiver.

TELEVISION, 1981 TO 1992

Several factors contributed to both the maturation and expansion of Egyptian television. First, a third channel was added. Second, the sophistication of programming—especially drama and soap opera-like series— guided domestic and international financial success. Third was the assassination of Anwar Sadat and the political evolution of Egypt as part of the Arab world.

Readers are reminded that in the 1960s Egypt operated three television channels. The third, catering largely to more sophisticated audiences in and around Cairo, was discontinued in 1967. In October 1985 (*Egyptian Radio and T.V. Union yearbook*, 1986) the Third Channel was reborn, albeit with a different configuration and programming philosophy than the one that stopped just after the 1967 war. The Third Channel is, in fact, one that attempts to provide some programming of a local nature for two distinct areas: Greater Cairo, and the Suez Canal from transmitters in Ismailia.

With more modern television production equipment as well as access to updated studios, during the 1980s both independent and government-hired artists created more hours of programming that were more sophisticated in terms of production values and artistic content. Egyptian audiences and viewers in other Arab countries demanded better products and, for the most part, they got what they wanted. The Lebanese civil war that started in 1975 effectively eliminated the Lebanese as competitors for Egyptian program sales. Jordan exports programming to other countries, but its facilities are too limited and artistic base too thin to compete with Egypt. Thus, Egypt has become part of the regional television success story, joining India and Brazil, for example, in helping to stem the traditional flow of media products from the West—mostly from the United States—to the Third World.

Finally, another factor that has contributed to the confidence-building of Egyptian television and added to the attractiveness of Egyptian video products in other countries was the death in October 1982 of President Anwar Sadat. Although President Mubarak has largely continued the practices of the man he served as vice-president, Sadat's death effectively removed the man despised at the time in some Arab countries, and by some elements in Egypt, as the one who signed a peace treaty with Israel. In the process of consolidating government power and promoting popular support for his policies, President Mubarak has relaxed government guidance of news and even censorship of both films and television series. This does not mean, of course, that the government is not firmly in control of both print and electronic media. However, under Mubarak there is a tendency for artists and journalists to have more room for free expression.

VIDEOCASSETTE RECORDERS

Throughout this publication there are references to videocassette recorders. While it is true that the Gulf states have the highest VCR penetration in the world, there are several reasons that VCRs are both available and widely used in Egypt. Amin and Boyd (1991, pp. 10, 11) note some of the major reasons that Egyptians find videocassette recorders an attractive alternative to state-run television.

Controlled Television News and Entertainment: Where governments or public corporations present heavily controlled news and entertainment, viewers have acquired VCRs in an attempt to influence what they see.

Affluence: Countries with a high per capita GNP have high rates of VCR ownership. Egypt does, however, have an affluent upper class and a large number of citizens of modest economic means who have brought television sets and VCRs home from working in the Gulf states.

Suppression of Political Activity: In countries where political expression on television is limited, VCRs are a means of communicating political and religious points of view.

There is another reason that many, especially those better off financially, either rent or purchase videocassettes. Because virtually all tapes in Egypt are pirated, the larger video rental stores and the shops that sell soft drinks and food and also rent cassettes have first-run foreign and Egyptian films. During the summer of 1991, *Silence of the Lambs*, for example, was available for rental in Cairo for only 50 cents per night (Schmidt, 1991). Many Western films are available on tape before they are in local cinemas. I previewed in Cairo a rented tape of *Batman* that was shot with a hand-held video camera in a British theater.

REGIONAL EXPANSION OF
EGYPTIAN TELEVISION VIA SATELLITE

Throughout this and some other chapters, the pervasiveness of Egyptian film and video material in the Middle East has been documented. It is, in fact, quite accurate to say that Cairo is the Hollywood of the Arab world. It has been possible to see Egyptian television—especially during the hot, humid summer months—in parts of Saudi Arabia, Jordan, Lebanon, and Israel since the 1970s. Tapes of Egyptian television programming are a part of virtually every Middle East television system. Satellite distribution has presented Egypt with new opportunities. First, through the ARABSAT system, it is possible for television systems in the Middle East to rebroadcast Egyptian television live. Beginning in 1990, Egypt started offering via satellite connection rebroadcasts of the Egyptian main service. In late 1990 Bahrain permitted limited rebroadcasting of Egyptian television. For a time following the 1991 Gulf War, Egyptian television was used in place of the Kuwaiti television service. With Kuwait's studio facilities looted and destroyed by Iraq during the 1990–1991 invasion, satellite-fed rebroadcasts of Egyptian television were used extensively in Kuwait until some local production capability became possible (Amin interview, 1991).

Egypt hopes to be one of the major regional satellite-delivered services—the Arab world version of British Sky Broadcasting (BSkyB) in the United Kingdom or the Hong Kong-based StarTV Channel. Egypt's stock of films and television productions and ARABSAT-leased transponders make this technically possible, but Egyptian SpaceNet service faces competition from the London-based, Saudi-financed Middle East Broadcasting Centre (MBC) service (Waldman, 1992). Cable News Network International (CNNI) is a factor, although primarily in the Cairo area. Through an agreement with the Ministry of Information, CNNI is broadcast via an Egyptian UHF transmitter from service provided by a transponder on a Russian Gorizont satellite. The service is not widely available to the general population because it is expensive; the scrambled service requires a decoder that must be purchased plus a monthly fee. Thus, only a few thousand potentially influential people see the service—mostly government officials, those working in embassies, expatriates, and members of the Egyptian elite (Foote and Amin, 1992).

SET OWNERSHIP AND VIEWING PATTERNS

In 1969 the government claimed that there were 498,000 television sets in Egypt (Arab States Broadcasting Union, 1969). Since this estimate was given, the number of sets has probably more than doubled. Among the more affluent, a television set—a color set after 1977—has become a normal part of a household. Increasingly, expatriate Egyptian salaries from employment in the Gulf help low-income families acquire sets; many Egyptians bring them on the plane with them when they return to Egypt on leave, as sets in the Gulf states are easily available and relatively inexpensive because of the absence of import taxes.

Shops in Egypt carry a variety of television receivers. Both Japanese and European sets may be found, in addition to the monochrome receivers that are assembled in Egypt. The Nasser government started a state television receiver manufacturing company in Cairo shortly after television was begun. The first agreement was with RCA; but, with the Arab League boycott, other agreements were made. For a period of time, sets were assembled with parts from a Hungarian electronics firm. The locally made sets have a price advantage but the imported sets have a reputation of being more reliable.

Television is an ideal medium for a culture that is family-oriented and tends to center much of its entertainment around the home. Cairo and Alexandria are culturally rich, with live music, theater, cinemas, and sporting activities—mostly associated with private clubs. However, the majority of Egyptians are not in an economic or social position to take advantage of these opportunities and must stay closer to home. Even for those with the money and motivation to seek enjoyment outside the home, the over-population in Cairo makes it physically difficult:

> [T]he streets are crowded to explosion point. It is very hard, sometimes practically impossible to find a parking place for your car. That is why most Cairenes turn to television for their evening entertainment. This also applies to most other cities, not overlooking inflation which does not allow driving out or going to the movie with the economic means of the average Egyptian. (Tawffik, 1980, pp. 5–6)

During the period when television was new, the government subsidized and installed hundreds of sets in rural and urban cultural centers. This worked well until the sets started to deteriorate. Over the years, the number of villages that have been connected to the national electrical grid has increased. As this has happened, the villages—most of which are in proximity to the Nile and therefore in range of a television transmitter—have become television oriented. The usual pattern of set acquisition starts with a local businessman or political leader who purchases a set. As financial conditions permit, families follow. Sets are usually also available to those who visit the local coffee house, as the owners realize the attraction that a set has for customers. An American volunteer worker near Beni Sueif, a town south of Cairo, noted that as electrical poles that would carry electricity to her village were erected, a local leader and a businessman both purchased sets—prior to electricity's actually reaching the population (Corcoran interview, 1980).

In an urban setting such as Cairo, the problem is more a lack of money than electricity. Often more than one family shares a television set by having several members contribute to the purchase price. In the more crowded, lower-income sections of Cairo, such as Bulaq and Shubra, young couples as well as residents in their forties save for years to get a set. It is frequent that women sell pieces of gold jewelry, often representing family savings, in order to make the important purchase. Given a choice between a refrigerator and a television set, many lower-income people select the television set (Rugh interview, 1980). Many acquire their sets second-hand from dealers who occasionally help finance them. Among the lower classes, television set ownership is more than a status symbol: it is a means of family entertainment within what is essentially an urban subsistence-level existence and a way of providing what is believed to be a better education for children, if only by giving them a view of the world.

A characteristic of Arab broadcast organizations is that they do not support media research efforts. Egypt's is no exception. The research office of the Egyptian Radio-Television Federation does some content analysis studies, but it mainly counts transmission hours for both radio and television; the Egyptians are ready and able to provide the number of hours per week devoted to a specific type of program such as drama or music, but studies that attempt to assess how and under what conditions citizens utilize the electronic media are almost nonexistent. Even students at Cairo University and the American University have not been encouraged to undertake such studies. A possible explanation of this is the reluctance of a traditional people to respond to official questioning, and the fear among broadcasting officials of negative criticism.

In a 1977 study of the media habits of Egyptian editors, television was mentioned often as a source of entertainment rather than information (Boyd and Kushner, 1979, p. 109). I found that one grouping of Egyptians, most of them government officials who were entertainment oriented, both liked and trusted television (Boyd, 1978, p. 503).

Egypt may have a radio and television system that is too extensive and in many respects sophisticated for a country of its size and limited financial resources. For example, the addition of a Teletext service in both Arabic and English ("Egyptian teletext," 1992), while admittedly modern, is unnecessary in this developing country. It employs more people than are necessary for the efficient operation of its television and radio services. The system is the largest and the most influential in the Arab world and it is likely to remain so no matter what the political environment of the Middle East or the intentions of the political leadership in Egypt. Too much money has been invested in facilities—and too many people depend for a living on the electronic media—to change the system dramatically.

CHAPTER 3

THE SUDAN

THE DEMOCRATIC REPUBLIC OF THE SUDAN is the largest country in Africa, with an area of 967,500 square miles. The country shares frontiers with eight nations: Egypt, Libya, Chad, the Central African Republic, Zaire, Uganda, Kenya, and Ethiopia. Its estimated population of 24 million live in predominantly rural settings within nine provinces.

The Sudan gained independence from Great Britain in 1956. After independence, the country underwent a period of political adjustment during which military and elected officials alternately administered the country. In a May 1969 military coup, Jaafar Nimeri emerged as a respected leader and was later elected president. A major accomplishment of Nimeri's leadership was a 1972 treaty with the South Sudan Liberation Front that had been fighting to separate the southern and northern parts of the country. The Sudan is unlike most other Arab countries in that a sizable number of its citizens in the south are not Moslems and do not speak Arabic. The 1972 agreement recognized both the English language and Christianity in the south and granted some degree of autonomy to the three southern provinces.

In April 1985, while out of the country, Nimeri was overthrown by his Defense Minister. Since then there has been another coup, resulting in military rule that dissolved the constitution, parliament, and political parties.

Economic problems have troubled the country since independence. Primarily agricultural, the Sudan had hopes of becoming the "breadbasket of the Middle East"; but that has not happened. Instead, a severe drought for most of the 1980s, the civil war in the south, and a flood of refugees from countries to the south have left it one of the poorest countries in the world. The fact that the Sudan has no oil to help with development means that much of its valuable foreign exchange has increasingly had to be used for petroleum imports.

The BBC estimates that there are 4 million radio sets, 2.1 million television receivers, and 100,000 videocassette recorders in the Sudan (British Broadcasting Corporation, 1991b).

RADIO BROADCASTING

The Sudan has had serious problems with the development of a broadcasting system. The country is very large and its population scattered. Unlike Egypt's, its political leadership has not placed a high priority on the electronic media. Even during the intense military operations in the south prior to the 1972 treaty, a time when the government was trying to make the populated areas of the south feel that they were equal members of a united country, almost no attempt was made to communicate with the "rebels" either by enlarging broadcasting facilities or by creating a specifically directed program. Several factors have complicated broadcasting development: a lack of hard currency for equipment, a division of administrative responsibility for radio between two ministries, and technical problems with the construction of transmitters that could reach the population with a broadcasting signal. There were consequent problems in radio production and morale, its staff having to work so closely with others having different loyalties. The various strong personalities that have headed the two ministries stopped any progress on a working agreement until the early 1980s. As late as 1977, it was not unusual for then President Nimeri to call the Director General of Radio Broadcasting early in the morning to determine why the main Arabic service was not on the air at the designated sign-on time: the Director General once advised him to call authorities at the Ministry of Communication, as they were responsible for transmitter operation (Salheen, 1977). When television was started, the Ministry of Information, which directly operates both of the electronic media, stipulated that television be entirely operated by Ministry of Information engineers.

A great deal of help was offered to the Sudan's infant broadcasting effort by other nations, and many radio employees were sent for training in other countries such as the United States, Great Britain, West Germany, and Australia. For a period of time in the 1960s, the United States Agency for International Development helped with training by contracting with the National Association of Educational Broadcasters to bring American personnel such as Professor Sydney Head to the Sudan to advise on training. Radio officials still consistently state that lack of trained personnel is the biggest problem they face: those who become skilled technicians, producers, and announcers are attracted to high-paying jobs in the Arabian Gulf.

After the 1967 Middle East War, during the period that roughly coincided with Egypt's closeness with the communist bloc nations, the Sudan grew more dependent on the Soviet Union and East European countries for economic and military aid: thus, in 1971, it was the Sudan's Russian advisors who suggested the construction of a super-power 1500-kilowatt mediumwave transmitter. They as well as the Sudanese realized that the existing low-power shortwave and mediumwave transmitters—some of which had been supplied by the United States Agency for International Development (AID) (Head, 1974, p. 226)—were inadequate for national coverage even at night, when mediumwave signals travel their longest distances. Czechoslovakia then granted the Ministry of Communication a loan that the two ministries associated with radio broadcasting were "pressed" to use for a powerful transmitter (Shummo, 1979), and a contract was signed with the Czechoslovakian Tesla Company for a super-power transmitter and two smaller units. (The Tesla Company has supplied several powerful units to Arab world countries that had close relations with the Soviet Union, among them Egypt, Syria, and Iraq.) But problems developed shortly after the transmitter deal was concluded and the equipment shipped to the Sudan. At this time, President Nimeri grew increasingly dissatisfied with what was believed to be Soviet involvement in Sudanese internal affairs: military and trade agreements with the Soviet Union and East European countries were terminated, and relations between the Sudan and those countries grew cool. In effect, the United States and some European countries replaced the Soviet Union and the then Soviet-dominated East European countries as military and economic benefactors.

The result of the estrangement between the Sudan and the U.S.S.R. for both ministries associated with radio was a slowdown in work on the vitally important transmitter. First, the supplier said that it was having problems supplying specific parts for the facility; then personnel problems were blamed for the delay in installation. By 1976, the transmitter was tested, but unspecified design flaws emerged that kept it from operating at peak efficiency. An even more serious problem concerned the electrical power to operate the transmitter—actually two 750-kilowatt units designed to work in parallel for a total output of 1500 kilowatts. The transmitter site near a national hydroelectric project south of Khartoum had been selected with an eye to power access. However, the powerful transmitter required about 5 million watts to operate at peak power, and only about 9000 kilowatts were available from the hydroelectric generators: therefore, with not enough power available for the local population, agricultural operations, and the transmitters as well, only one of the transmitters has operated intermittently. The electrical power and design problems still have not been solved and many Sudanese must still, then, listen to foreign radio stations to receive news and entertainment; yet no additional transmission facilities are planned by the Sudanese government.

In the mid-1970s, Ministry of Information and Communication officials realized that studio space was not adequate for program production and transmission. A small studio complex was constructed adjacent to the existing studio building in Omdurman and new Philips audio equipment was installed and tested; but though broadcast installations almost always have strict security systems in developing countries, and in coup-prone Sudan security has been provided by the army, the equipment was destroyed before it had ever been used.[1] When President Nimeri returned from a trip to the United States and Europe on July 1, 1976, he found an attempted coup in progress, apparently backed by Libyan leader Kaddafi.[2] A small army unit guarding the radio studios succeeded in saving the older studios from destruction, but the new building was gutted by fighting. Work immediately commenced on reconstruction of the building, and new equipment was ordered and installed. By 1979, the studio addition was in use. The 1976 coup attempt has had a lasting effect on security around the complex, which also houses the television studios. It is now an army post with permanently stationed troops and each entrance is guarded with combat-ready troops in tanks. Even if a coup is successful in the future, employees who are loyal to the president will not be immediately helpful to those who may want to broadcast, since they have been ordered to return immediately to their native villages should something happen: that will make it difficult—according to Ministry of Information reasoning—for a new government to find them quickly and restore what might amount to normal programming.

RADIO SERVICES

National Program

Intended to reach the entire country with a mixture of news, music, commentary, and educational and cultural programs, the National Program—generally known as Radio Omdurman—is in Arabic. The ill-fated super-power transmitter was supposed to carry this program, which in 1980 operated for 18 hours per day (0600 to 2400) on mediumwave and shortwave. Several attempts have been made to produce a continuing series of educational programs; and programs about nutrition and medicine have received particular attention from the radio services, in cooperation with the Ministry of Health.

Those in charge of programs that are intended to promote national development are attempting to carry out the task assigned, and do even more than strictly required, but a shortage of both trained personnel and transmission power to reach a national audience has tended to discourage some officials.

The country's extreme poverty and political instability are reflected in the disorganized state of its attempts to transmit Radio Omdurman broadcasts via shortwave. One monitor reports hearing Radio Omdurman on five different frequencies during 1991 (Dexter, 1992).

Koranic Station

Most Arab world countries devote radio transmission time to Koran readings and religious discussions for their predominantly Moslem citizens. Egypt and Saudi Arabia have special services for this purpose; but the Sudan, not having similar facilities, limits such programming to a 2-hour, 1530 to 1730, block on both mediumwave and shortwave.

Voice of the Sudanese Nation

This service operates from 1730 to 2300 daily on one shortwave transmitter and is apparently receivable throughout the Sudan on short-wave; but the majority of Sudanese citizens lack radios with shortwave capability and shortwave listening is not popular among them. Most of the Voice's programs are in Arabic, but news in French and English is part of the daily schedule and constitutes the service's only non-Arabic programming.

National Unity Radio

Little is known about this intermittent radio service, except that it has been monitored in both Arabic and English on a shortwave frequency used by the government (Dexter, 1992).

Juba Local Service

Following the 1972 peace accords with the southern Sudan, the predominantly non-Arabic-speaking population in the area was given some degree of autonomy, and part of this restructuring was the appointment of regional ministers based in Juba to parallel ministers who headed the major governmental departments in Khartoum. The Minister of Information for the Southern Region has responsibility for a local broadcast service, which includes local programming in English and Arabic, but the majority of the time the Juba station rebroadcasts one of the Omdurman services. Perhaps the most obvious irony in the gestures that the national government has made to the south is a relative lack of attention to specialized broadcast coverage, although both radio and television transmitters have been installed to serve the area. The government insists on broadcasting in the recognized national language, Arabic, which most of the southerners do not speak. English is also used, but the language is not universally spoken. Leaders from the south are making efforts to convince the national government to introduce vernacular languages so that programming in Dinka, Zandi, and Nur can be started (Thiik interview, 1979). In 1991 Radio Juba programming was occasionally rebroadcast by Radio Omdurman (Dexter, 1992).

A lack of radio facilities to reach the entire country has serious implications when one considers political events in the Arab world. The

Sudan finds itself in a position similar to that of Saudi Arabia during the 1960s, when the kingdom did not have the transmitter power to reach citizens with information that would counter radio attacks by other countries. The Sudan's generally pro-Western orientation during the late 1970s, combined with its support of Egypt's President Sadat and its troop withdrawal from the Arab peacekeeping force in Lebanon, has caused it to be the target of radio propaganda from other Arab countries—notably from Libya, Syria, and Iraq. The Sudanese government is too shrewd and forthright to engage in a word-for-word radio battle with other Arab countries, a relative restraint that its lack of transmitters makes almost necessary, but its problem still persists in that the attacks are heard by a Sudanese population who might react as a result of their cumulative effect.

Lacking adequate domestic facilities, Sudanese radio and television have used available equipment plus the government-controlled print media to disseminate replies and denials through the Sudan News Agency (SUNA), which supplies almost all national news to the media. The example that follows not only provides an example of an early information war, it also illustrates the shifting political loyalties among nations. Readers are reminded that the Sudan supported the August 1990 Iraqi invasion of Kuwait.

In March 1979, both Libyan and Syrian radio services broadcast news about Sudanese strikes and arrests that the government claimed did not occur, the stories having been filed through SUNA facilities by Syrian and Libyan news agency representatives in Khartoum (Ministry of Information and Culture, 1979, p. 4); and Iraqi Radio reported in October 1979 that the Sudanese president was wounded while speaking to a gathering of Sudanese businessmen, his presidential palace having been stormed. A reply to the Iraqi allegations typifies the basic Sudanese reaction to all such attacks:

> We have never heard, except from the Tekriti Baath mass media that a coup could be accomplished by simply storming a Presidential Palace. The [Iraqi] News Agency could not tell us about the broadcasting station and other important utilities. Naturally it had nothing to say because on the same day and the following morning the President's voice was being heard on Radio Omdurman to the accompaniment [sic] ovation of enthusiastic masses. . . .
>
> Fabricated news about Sudan in the Iraqi mass media would have no effect on the Sudan and its people. The Sudanese President is always among the masses, a thing Iraqi leaders would never venture to do. (*SUNA-Daily Bulletin*, 1979, p. 7)

In the Arab world, only the Sudan lacks the transmission strength to make a domestic or an international impact on radio-conscious Arabs.

Data are not available on radio station preferences in rural areas of the Sudan. However, a May 1977 survey done for the International Communication Agency in Khartoum and Port Sudan provides information about urban preferences for foreign stations. Most survey respondents listened to foreign stations in Arabic; Radio Cairo was the station most often mentioned, with 20 percent of the respondents stating that they listened to it at least once per week. Percentages for Radio Voice of the Gospel (RVOG), the British Broadcasting Corporation, the Voice of America, and Radio Monte Carlo were respectively 16, 13, 12, and 9 percent: the survey was taken just after RVOG, a station operated by a religious organization in Ethiopia and respected for its newscasts, was taken over by the Ethiopian government (USICA, 1978a, p. 11). These figures are for urban areas where the Sudanese radio signal is strong; it is quite likely that the incidence of both medium- and shortwave foreign radio listening in rural areas is higher, due to reception problems with the Sudanese radio signal there. But factors of convenience aside, the popularity of foreign radio generally stems from the knowledge among listeners that government media almost always promote news items favorable to the government in power. Foreign radio is seen as a source of another point of view.

TELEVISION

Both the British and West Germans demonstrated television in the Sudan in 1962 (Ministry of Information and Culture, 1971, p. 106), but the development of the medium was undertaken almost entirely by the Federal Republic of Germany. The West German government's goal was to provide a basic system and to train personnel for program production that would be largely development oriented: but while educational programming is present on Sudanese television, the medium has emerged as entertainment oriented, featuring a high percentage of programs from the West and from Egypt.

In 1963 a low-power transmitter was installed in a makeshift studio in an old hotel adjacent to the Radio Omdurman studio complex. For the first eight years of the undertaking, German engineers and production specialists were in residence, installing equipment and training Sudanese in all facets of television, and some personnel were sent to Germany and other countries for training. During the early stages of television, transmission was restricted to a few hours each evening and served only an area around the capital—one that had few television sets, despite government efforts to put some receivers in public places. Sets were installed in clubs, coffeehouses, and restaurants in a manner similar to efforts in other Arab countries. Television viewing quickly became a communal activity.

The expansion of television facilities was hampered initially by government disinterest and a lack both of funds and of any means of interconnecting stations outside the capital; no telecommunications system then existed for networking. In the 1960s, the government realized that it must devise a national system for the dissemination of mass communication—for networking, telex, and telephone—in addition to providing reliable communication for the military and government. This was to be an expensive undertaking for a poor country that constitutes over 8 percent of the African continent. As a first step, microwave stations were built stretching from the Khartoum-Omdurman area to those centers that were most heavily populated; and in 1972 a second television station was opened in Wad Medani, a predominantly agricultural area about 180 kilometers south of the capital in El Gezira Province. A third station was opened about 300 kilometers north of the capital in Atbara in the Nile Province, a center of activity for the Sudanese Workers Trade Union, where the Sudan Railway is headquartered (Sudan Television, n.d., p. 3). These stations are part of the Sudan Rural Television Project, financed by various government departments with large shares of both financial help and inspiration from the West Germans, and they were constructed so that programs to serve the viewers in each area could be produced locally. (Programming includes features about occupational health, literacy, social problems, and agriculture.) These stations are linked by a microwave system to the Omdurman television complex and are used for rebroadcasting (Rahman interview, 1979b). Another part of the project is a kind of Tele-Club system: receivers powered by gasoline generators have been placed in one hundred villages with separate viewing centers for men and women.

As part of the same burst of expansion after the 1972 peace accord with the Southern Region was reached, plans were finalized with the usual West German assistance for a new, more powerful, PAL color-capable transmitter to be built in Omdurman, and for the construction of a new studio building to house equipment that would replace unreliable older equipment. Administrative offices and a studio complex were completed in 1974 in a building next to the original television facility: two large new studios provided more production space and served as the originating point for the color transmissions that started in 1974; live studio color news and interviews began in 1976 (Rahman interview, 1979a). In 1980 two studios to be used exclusively for news and interviews were completed in another adjoining building, thus allowing local production to take place during the evening transmissions. Most of the new color equipment is German and includes one-inch videotape recorders and a new remote truck with small ENG-type mini-cameras. All videotape equipment, except for the German one-inch Bosch machines, is Ampex and is relatively new. Inadequate videotape recording facilities have hampered the production of local programs, but Sudanese television greatly benefitted from a meeting of the Organization of African Unity in Khartoum in 1978. Television coverage of the gathering was important to the Sudan as well as to those attending the meeting. Each country in attendance wanted a taped daily transmission to be sent via the INTELSAT system to its own television system, showing its involvement in the pan-African conference; and President Nimeri, wanting the world and his countrymen to see the Sudan in the African spotlight, provided a special allocation of funds so that additional television equipment—specifically five Ampex recorders—could be purchased.

In 1978 the Sudan Domestic Satellite System (SUDOSAT) was inaugurated. The system, which also provides telephone and telex service, is operated by the Sudan Telecommunications Public Corporation and provides the national television signal to the provincial capitals of Nyala, El Fasher, Kadugli, El Damazin, Dongola, Karima, Wadi Halfa, Malakal, Bor, Juba, Yambio, and Wau (Sudan Television, n.d.; "Extension," p. 4). On the whole, the distribution of television by the national microwave and satellite system thus completed has worked quite well. Television service has been interrupted regularly, however, by ground station and transmitter failures caused by lack of not only spare parts, but also maintenance personnel and fuel to power generators—the last sometimes being created by thefts of fuel from the generator storage tanks. Since the early 1980s, this situation has grown much worse. Because of the civil war in the south, the drought and famine, a ruined economy, and a crippled government, technically sophisticated projects either have been neglected or have fallen into disarray because the responsible ministry lacks the ability to acquire spare parts.

TELEVISION PROGRAMMING

The one national color channel operates for about 52 hours per week, sending out a daily 7-hour evening transmission and broadcasting additional hours on Friday mornings and afternoons. The national service is a mixture, made up 60 percent of religious programs, locally produced dramatic shows, educational programs, interviews, news, and sports, and 40 percent of programs imported from the United States, Great Britain, Egypt, and other Arab countries. The Director General of Television has commented on the balance between locally produced and imported programs:

> We can't broadcast only local programmes because it would be very expensive. For instance, the price of a 60 minute, hired film is about $100. If we wanted to produce the same programme here, it would cost $700. So we have to keep this ratio. (Akol, 1979, p. 43)

Officials also give political reasons for importing programs:

> If we just broadcast our own programmes, our viewers wouldn't be in a position to see whether we were progressing or not. Take the Egyptian series for example: people look at them from different angles—the subject, the quality and the technique. By showing them, we give our viewers the chance to evaluate our own work. (Akol, 1979, p. 43)

Among the American programs televised have been 13-week segments of almost every American popular action/adventure series that has not been completely adult oriented, since both sex and excessive violence must be edited from the programs. The Director General defends American programs such as *Kojak* because they are easily edited for sex ("We don't show legs—no kissing, no sex") and because "we're teaching our people that crime is advancing and it will reach us one day—if it's not here already." The television authority attempts to be responsive to viewer reactions to the imported foreign programs. For example, *Six Million Dollar Man* was removed from the air because viewers complained that their children were jumping from roofs like Steve Austin (Akol, 1979, p. 43).

An important part of daily programming is the 2100 news. The newscast is in color, usually lasts for 20 to 30 minutes, and closely resembles an American small- to medium-market television newscast alternating two news readers on camera. Accounts of presidential activities are important in the newscast, but other stories of national origin on tape or film are shown among items on international news and local sports and weather. The Sudan has the capability of receiving the European Broadcasting Union's two daily news summaries by satellite; but for several weeks in late 1979, Sudanese television could not use the material because the Ministry of Communication had not paid the down-leg satellite costs. International news came on a delayed basis via air shipments of news film from VISNEWS and UPITN from London. Almost all locally done newsfilm in 1980 was black and white because of a lack of raw color film stock and the chemicals to process footage. This situation serves to highlight the financial problems of Sudanese television. Those who are responsible for the overall operation of the television network must constantly watch hard currency expenditures so that, for example, enough lighting instruments and replacement lamps are available.

The Sudanese television viewer receives a varied program diet from the one national channel. Those who receive the signal from the Wad Medani and Atbara stations may additionally see the development-oriented programs designed specifically for their respective areas: occasionally, such locally produced programs are telecast nationally from the Omdurman headquarters. During October 1979 Sudanese television broadcast what has been termed the most popular imported program ever to be shown, *Roots*, subtitled in Arabic.

BROADCAST FINANCING

Financing for Sudanese radio has traditionally been from receiver licenses imposed under British rule. Since independence, military and civilian governments have not enforced the license fee that is supposedly collected by the postal authority because of problems of collection after the introduction of the small, relatively inexpensive transistor radio and the government's eagerness for the population to acquire radio and television receivers. The government has had to assume the responsibility for most broadcast financing, particularly the expense of ground stations and transmitters for the completion of the national television network. Both radio and television are financed partially by advertising; and an organization that is independent of the radio and the television programming departments is responsible for all aspects of that effort, including the taping of the commercial announcements themselves. Commercials were first allowed on Radio Omdurman in April 1961 (Head, 1962, p. 51), and on Sudanese television in June 1965 (*Sudan Echo*, 1965).

Products sold in the Middle East are promoted by 30- and 60-second filmed commercials that are usually made in Egypt and Lebanon: advertised products include Aspro (aspirin), Halls Cough Drops, Rothman Cigarettes, Dr. Scholl Shoes, Signal Tooth Paste, and some food products such as processed cheese. Local television advertising includes spots for local stores and cinemas and a few products that are manufactured or assembled by state or local industries; the local commercials generally feature a slide of the product or a poster giving details of the product or service with a voice-over. Neither the video nor the audio quality of the commercials is very good and the contrast of their faultiness with the high technical quality of Sudanese television in general is stark—due in part to the fact that the audio for commercials is taped on home—rather than broadcast—quality audio tape equipment, in a small studio operated by the radio and television sales office. There is almost no communication between that office and the radio and television administration. While the broadcast administration recognizes that the commercials do produce revenue, it believes that the clustered commercials detract from its programs; and, unfortunately, it realizes no direct advantage from the advertising income, all of which goes directly to the Ministry of Finance. The government estimated that about $600,000 was realized from broadcast advertising in 1979. However, to reiterate what has been noted previously, the chaotic political and economic situation that has existed in the country since the mid-1980s has not helped foster the advertising industry in what amounts to a bankrupt country.

TELEVISION VIEWING PATTERNS

In 1968, Sudan Television commissioned a survey of viewers in the Khartoum-Omdurman area to determine viewing patterns, program preferences, and attitudes toward news and commercials. The study, "The First Survey of Television: 1968–1969," was done by university and secondary school students; the methodology, data collection, and interpretation must be read with that circumstance in mind. Following are several findings of the study.

1.   Of the 1,481 people interviewed only 30 were illiterate. [Author's note: This indicates that the sample was not a cross section of the Sudanese population.]

2.   In Khartoum, 94.9 percent of those questioned said that they owned television sets. [Author's note: This may be an accurate figure if the word "own" is taken as "have access to."]

3.   The most popular local program was *Taha't El Adwa* ("Under the Light"), a program of live Sudanese music.

4.   About one-third of the sample said that they liked television commercials while the remainder said that they did not.

5.   About three-quarters of the respondents said that they liked foreign films on television (Sudan Television, n.d., "First Survey").

As is the case in most other Islamic countries, conditions for television viewing in the Sudan are favorable: members of its family-centered culture have neither the general opportunity nor the funds to seek entertainment outside the home. Several families may contribute money to purchase a set, or working family members, including children, may all help finance the important purchase. The communal nature of television is perhaps best illustrated by an incident that occurred in Khartoum in February 1977. On a warm evening, an American friend and I were walking from the main downtown shopping area to a house in the suburbs and paused at the open gate of a home to see what was being televised on the set placed in the garden. Immediately there was an invitation to watch television with the family.

Since independence, problems have hindered the development of Sudanese radio and television. Lack of trained personnel and funds, a disruptive civil war, destruction of some equipment during an attempted coup, and poor transmitter design and installation have all affected media development. During the 1960s, various aid programs helped to establish radio facilities and to train personnel for what it was hoped would be the beginning of a well-organized national radio system—yet as outsiders were puzzled to note, when the federal government was trying to stop the fighting in the Southern Region, there was almost no media campaign to parallel the military one. After 1972, both radio and television transmitters were placed in Juba, but they have tended to be for the rebroadcast of the national programs, with little attempt to allow local radio programs or local television.

At one time the government was considering a proposal from broadcasting officials that would have created a semiautonomous public corporation for radio and television. This would have functioned under the Ministry of Information as a similar one does in Egypt. It would have considerable financial freedom, and it would at last give Radio Omdurman control over its own transmitters and engineering personnel—though television appears now to have been categorically successful in becoming the national electronic medium, its signal being so successfully distributed via satellite ground stations and local transmitters.

Whatever the Sudan's eventual solution to the problems of its electronic media, television will continue to be the most effective means of providing the citizens of Africa's largest country with information and entertainment. At least the visual medium gives those who have access to a television receiver a moment of escape from a difficult political and economic environment.

CHAPTER 4

LEBANON

THE BASIC GEOGRAPHICAL BOUNDARIES of present-day Lebanon were first defined by the Ottoman Empire, which ruled the area for 400 years prior to World War I. The present boundaries were established in 1920, when France administered both Syria and Lebanon under a League of Nations mandate. Lebanon achieved independence in 1943, but it was not completely free to manage its own affairs until the end of World War II.

The population of Lebanon can only be estimated, as no official census has been done since 1932. At that time, it was found that the population was almost evenly divided between Moslems and Christians. The various ethnic and religious communities have always vied for political power, and when Lebanon became a modern state, these factions tended to fractionalize the population. It is an oversimplification to assume that the basic division in the country is between Moslems and non-Moslems. Groups such as Armenians, Greek Orthodox, Palestinians, Nasserites, Communists, and Druz have helped make the political history since 1946 colorful and, in 1975, explosive. The Lebanese Civil War of 1975 suggested that the free-wheeling Lebanese economy that had attracted transnational business concerns in the 1950s and 1960s had neglected some of the basic needs of the population. The initial fighting did not end until an Arab League peacekeeping force dominated by the Syrian Army occupied parts of the country in 1976. Tens of thousands of people were killed during the long-lasting civil war and much of Beirut was destroyed.

The Syrian Army brought a measure of stability to Lebanon, and by 1979 a facade of normality had returned to sections of the country. But by the early 1980s chaos reigned again. One result was a multinational Western force, including American Marines. Terrorist attacks against Western forces—most notably the bombing of the U.S. Marine barracks—motivated the departure of the armies and once again plunged this state into violent civil war. It was not until 1990 that Syria once again regained the upper hand and that some of the most violent aspects of the long-term civil war began to disappear.

The country's 4,015 square miles and estimated population of 2.7 million make it one of the world's smallest nation states.

It is estimated that there are 2.2 million radio receivers, 850,000 television sets, and 350,000 videocassette recorders in Lebanon (British Broadcasting Corporation, 1991b).

RADIO

The first identifiable radio station in Lebanon was constructed in 1937 by the French government and was operated by France with the help of local employees (UNESCO, 1949, p. 225). One motivation for the construction of the early French station was to counter the Arabic-language radio propaganda of the Italians and Germans. In 1941 the transmission facilities of "Radio Levant" were destroyed by the Vichy French government to frustrate the Allies when they occupied the country (N. Dajani, 1979, p. 21). The facilities were rebuilt and for a period, until formal independence took place in 1946, both the French and British legations supplied programming for the one shortwave and one mediumwave transmitter.

The studio and transmitters were formally handed over to the Lebanese government in 1946. An agreement with the French allowing a specified period of use per day was signed and is still in effect. The radio system was renamed the Lebanese Broadcasting Station and put under the Directorate of Propaganda and Publishing, part of the Ministry of the Interior (N. Dajani, 1979, p. 21). After this formation of a broadcast operation under the complete control of the Lebanese government, several attempts were made to expand programming and facilities. The government was not convinced that radio was an important part of national development and the low-power service remained essentially unchanged until the 1958 Civil War, which was precipitated by a changing political mood in the Arab world, starting with the Egyptian Revolution in 1952 and continuing through the overthrow of the royal family in Iraq in 1958 and the instability in Jordan during the same year. The Lebanese government asked for and received help from the United States, and in 1958 the U.S. Marines landed in Lebanon.

Prior to 1958 the government had decided to allocate funds for the construction of the building to house the Ministries of Tourism and Information and for new and more powerful medium- and shortwave transmitters. Because of the appearance of several clandestine radio stations during the war, this project moved forward with some speed. It became obvious to the government that the coverage of the mountainous country by the low-powered transmitters was incomplete and that the population was not particularly loyal to the station, which was perceived to be a government-controlled outlet for those in power. By the late 1950s, Lebanese could tune to broadcasts from Israel, Jordan, Syria, and Egypt for news and entertainment. A new Ministry of Information building was completed in 1962 near the Hamra area of Beirut and new transmitters were installed. The Ministry of Information and the broadcasting section underwent several reorganizations, and the government reached agreement with the various clandestine stations to stop operating. The equipment of these illegal stations was stored rather than destroyed or sold as the owners believed that the day would come when the equipment would again be needed. The new building provided ample room for what were thought to be present and future needs of the Lebanese Radio Station, later called Radio Lebanon. Six production and on-air studios in the building utilized German equipment, most of which has been well maintained.

Perhaps the biggest problem between 1962 and 1972 was an increasing awareness among listeners that the radio service reflected the attitude and policies of the government. The station served not so much as a voice for the government's public relations office as a means of denying access by various political groups to the airwaves. There were few frank discussions about the myriad of problems that faced the country. The political leaders believed that discussions might only fan smoldering political beliefs. Access to the radio medium was further restricted by the policy of not allowing advertising on radio. The station has been financed by government funds in a manner consistent with many other radio stations in the Arab world, a policy thought by the Lebanese to be inconsistent with their traditional freewheeling economy. Some opposition leaders wanted political advertising so that they could purchase airtime for the dissemination of their views.

During the 1960s, Lebanon experienced an unprecedented period of economic growth. Egypt was not a hospitable environment for wealthy Arabs from the Gulf states. Beirut, on the other hand, offered numerous investment opportunities as well as an active nightlife and pleasant weather for vacations. These same factors attracted international businesses, which established Middle Eastern headquarters in Beirut. Particularly visible were American and European banks that came to do business in the "Switzerland of the Middle East."

Even up to the 1975 Civil War, when the system fell into chaos, the transmissions of Lebanese radio had not been as highly structured and defined as was the case, for example, in Egypt. Services centered around transmissions, which were predominantly in Arabic. A secondhand FM transmitter was acquired and used for the music program in the late 1960s and the facility was modified in the early 1970s for stereo transmission. Shortwave transmitters were added relatively early in the history of Lebanese broadcasting. It was believed that Lebanon should have a voice that reached other Arab countries as well as countries to which large numbers of Lebanese had emigrated, mainly in Africa, Europe, and North and South America.

Furthermore, there were omnidirectional shortwave broadcasts of programs during specified periods of the day. There is no evidence that these broadcasts were listened to with any degree of regularity or enthusiasm in other countries; the Ministry of Information has not commissioned research that would provide such information.

The criticism that the state radio denied access of political groups to the airwaves came to a head in 1972. Lebanon has always had an active press that has afforded an outlet for all manner of political thought. The printing of numerous daily, weekly, and occasional publications prior to the 1975 Civil War actually constituted a sizable portion of the Lebanese economy and helped the development of Lebanon's once-thriving book publishing industry. In fact there were too many disreputable outlets for political thought, and the few respected papers tended to express either the government point of view or the prevailing political philosophy of the major established political parties. The Lebanese political factions did not lack outlets for political expression; they did lack access, however, to the government-controlled radio.

The spring 1972 Lebanese elections brought the radio access problem to the forefront. Kamal Jumblatt, a Socialist Deputy, stated that he would start his own radio station to compete with the government operation. The government made it clear that such an act would be illegal despite the stipulation in the Lebanese Constitution that guaranteed freedom of expression. There is no specific law prohibiting the establishment of a private station, but there is a procedure that stipulates how one must go about it. During one of the Radio Lebanon reorganizations, a government decree (No. 3870) issued in 1960 stated that the licensing of radio stations was the province of the Ministry of Posts, Telegrams, and Telephones (Phipps, 1972, pp. 4–5). The elections did not force the establishment of private stations, but the entire atmosphere surrounding Lebanese radio changed after 1972 in that political groups knew that they would not gain access to the state radio.

The elections did create an interesting and short-lived alternative to the Ministry of Information radio outlet. Farid Salman, who owned a cinema newsreel, "Actualité Libanaise," purchased a block of time on the Cyprus Broadcasting Corporation's mediumwave service, which reaches Lebanon with a clear signal. Salman, who appears to have acted out of financial motives as well as a desire for freedom of expression, recorded political messages, including one from the Prime Minister, which were aired on the Cyprus "Radio Magazine." The project lasted only four days. The government jammed the station and caused the practice to be discontinued (Mirshak, 1972, p. 7).

By the time the 1975 Civil War started, domestic coverage had improved, although Lebanon had not become an important international broadcaster because shortwave transmitters remained few in number and low in power. The main domestic service was boosted by the construction of a new 100-kilowatt mediumwave transmitter outside of Beirut in Amsheet.

TELEVISION

Television was organized in a totally different manner from radio. In the mid-1950s, a group of Lebanese businessmen approached the government and proposed that they build a television station financed by the sale of advertising. They signed an agreement with the government in 1956 for the construction of a station that would operate two channels, one for Arabic-language and the other for mostly foreign programs. The 1958 Civil War interrupted the station's construction, but the services started in May 1959 (N. Dajani, 1971, p. 172). La Compagnie Libanaise de Télévision (CLT) thus became the first non-government-operated, advertising-supported television station in the Arab world. Article 21 of the agreement addresses some of the stipulations under which CLT would operate:

1. The government does not give the company monopoly rights.
2. Broadcasts should be under government scrutiny, and should not include programmes which threaten public security, morals, or religious groups, or enhance the image of any political personality or party.
3. Programmes should be restricted to education or entertainment, and advertising should not exceed 25 percent of broadcast time.
4. There should be at least 20 hours per week of programming, and the company undertakes to broadcast free of charge news programmes and official bulletins provided by the Ministry of Guidance and Information.
5. The first phase of the project will include the construction of a main transmitter with 400-watt power, to be increased later to 4 kilowatts, and the installation of relay stations to cover the whole of Lebanon.
6. Television is to respect all laws and regulations relating to the rights of the press and of authors, and shall be subject to all laws and internal or international regulations dealing with wireless communications and broadcast institutions. It shall also exchange sound programmes with the Lebanese radio in the sphere of overall cooperation.
7. If the television station stops broadcasting for 30 days on two occasions in one year without a compelling reason which the government considers to be valid, the government has the right to take over the station directly and to operate it on a commercial basis. The government can cancel the license without indemnification by giving advance notice which shall not exceed four years.
8. The agreement, once approved officially, shall be in force for 15

years, at the end of which the government has the full right to buy all facilities connected to the project, at prices specified by two experts, one representing the government and the other the company whose agreement has been ended. In the event of any dispute on the estimates the two parties shall seek an international arbitrator to decide the points at issue. (N. Dajani, 1979, pp. 26–27)

The original studios and transmitters and some of the original equipment are still operating in a building in a residential area in Beirut. The transmitters, operating on Channels 7 and 9, and a tower are located atop the building. At first the transmission hours were limited and employees few because the venture was almost totally concerned with making a profit rather than with providing a comprehensive national television service. As the above stipulations indicate, the government placed severe restrictions on the kinds of programs which could be telecast. Obviously, the government had in mind a television service that was not unlike radio where news was guided by the government in power and programming was almost entirely entertainment. The economic situation immediately after 1958 was not conducive to commercial advertising and revenue was small; profits went to investors rather than being returned to the station in the form of training of personnel or buying new equipment and studios for local production.

Shortly after transmissions started, CLT established a separate company to handle station administration and advertising sales. Advision, as the organization was known (Sobh interview, 1972), had the American Time-Life organization as a partner for a short period of time. In 1967, the French government corporation SOFIRAD purchased Advision in partnership with a group of Lebanese investors (N. Dajani, 1979, p. 28). CLT modified its transmitters in the late 1960s to transmit SECAM color, but it was not until the mid-1970s that cameras and associated studio equipment were installed for local color production.

CLT faced additional financial problems in mid-1962, when a second commercial station began telecasting. Compagnie de Télévision du Liban et du Proche-Orient (Télé-Orient) reached agreement with the government in 1959 for a second television station in Lebanon. The organization, which agreed to the same conditions as CLT, was partially financed by the American Broadcasting Company (ABC). Later ABC sold its interest in the station to the British Thomson Organization and the Rizk brothers, a wealthy Lebanese family (N. Dajani, 1979, p. 29). Télé-Orient built a studio in Hazmiyeh, about 15 kilometers from Beirut, and telecast one program on two channels, 5 and 11. The Télé-Orient facility was designed to house two medium-sized studios and additional space for administrative offices and equipment such as tele-cine. The 1962 design, which was still operational in 1980, would allow one person to operate lighting controls, switching, and audio. When no live studio news or interviews were to take place, only a transmitter, a master control, and a tele-cine operator would be needed to run the operation in addition to the "director," who would do the job of several other employees.

Until the late 1960s, little local production was done by either station. The Lebanese audience was not large enough to make such undertakings profitable. Some Egyptian films were shown but a substantial percentage of the relatively short telecasting day was devoted to American, British, and French programs that were broadcast with the original sound, but subtitled in Arabic. Neither the stations nor the Ministry of Education appears to have been interested in any kind of educational programming during those hours when commercial programs were transmitted. The Ministry of Information was not unhappy with the services since they did not telecast political or controversial programs and were essentially free of charge to the government. That advertising sales were allowed on television, it was reasoned, softened the criticism of noncommercial radio.

These two stations were motivated almost entirely by the desire to return a profit to both local and foreign shareholders, and they were not interested in such program development as local news. The Ministry of Information controlled both local and international news; television newsfilm from VISNEW5 and UPITN were sealed on arrival at the Beirut airport and delivered to each station. The seals were broken in a special viewing room by government censors.[1] The television organizations did not resent this state of affairs because the government-controlled news freed them of responsibility for what was broadcast.

Beginning about 1970, the stations and their employees benefitted from increased local musical and dramatic production efforts that were shown in Beirut and then sold to stations in the Gulf states. Some programs were produced under the auspices of the stations. Independent producers often rented the studios and videotape facilities from the stations. Télé-Orient was particularly active in the Gulf television market and served as a distributor of foreign programs in addition to acting as sales agent for Arabic-language material produced in Lebanon.

Despite efforts to increase revenue by producing programs for export, financial problems plagued both stations from the very beginning. Unable to compete successfully for limited viewers and financial resources in Beirut, the two organizations started to cooperate with advertising sales and even broadcasting the same program simultaneously. In 1968 Advision had become the sales agent for Télé-Orient as well as CLT, and in October 1972 TeleManagement was created to undertake complete marketing and advertising sales of all television channels. Advision continued to assume the responsibility for the operation of CLT.

Between 1972 and the outbreak of the civil war in 1975, the television business seemed to stabilize. Both stations were returning a profit, and local production had increased because of the export market for Lebanese taped television programs. Both stations maintained a limited broadcasting schedule of only 6 hours per day.

BROADCASTING DURING THE CIVIL WAR

As one might expect, the fighting in Lebanon greatly affected the Ministry of Information radio service and the two commercial television stations. The fighting did not start on one particular day. Rather, a series of shootings and kidnappings led to the acquisition of guns, ammunition, and explosives by the various Moslem and Christian factions. The large expatriate community in Beirut stayed throughout the initial 1975 skirmishes, but when fighting intensified they left and closed the company offices in Beirut. The city seemed to erupt into full-scale war after the destruction of many of the luxury hotels not far from the Ministry of Information building. Beirut became a fractionalized city with predominantly Moslem and Christian neighborhoods fighting each other. The Lebanese police and defense forces were ineffective in controlling the fighting. The various groups continued to support daily newspapers, many of which continued to publish.

The electronic media were clearly not responsive to the needs of the Lebanese population during the civil war. The radio service attempted to stay neutral: the official Ministry of Information Service broadcast some essential information, and people listened for reports about fighting, news about proposed cease fires, casualty figures, information on where essential services could be obtained, and even personal news about families. But there were times, even during the heaviest fighting in 1975 and 1976, when one would not know from radio programs that the country was in the midst of a devastating war. Television reflected the situation even less. Both stations continued to operate and some companies continued to advertise. The stations reran old programs and telecast censored news as if nothing of great importance were occurring. Both stations lost a great deal of money. The equipment that was not damaged during the fighting deteriorated because of lack of maintenance and spare parts. Normal communication between the two stations was impossible at times, since they were located in different parts of the city. Each station had installed relay transmitters around the mountainous country to fill in areas that did not regularly receive one of the three television programs. Almost all of these facilities were damaged and many were destroyed.

In March 1976, however, the broadcast media became heavily embroiled in the dispute. In the middle of the CLT evening Arabic newscast on March 11, 1976, a Moslem Lebanese Army officer, Brigadier Aziz Al-Ahdab, forced his way into the studios of Channel 7 and demanded airtime for "Communique No. 1." Owing to his status and his armed entourage, he was granted his wish. After televising the statement that proclaimed that he was the new ruler of Lebanon and stating that the President should resign, Al-Ahdab moved to the Ministry of Information radio studios and broadcast what had been said on CLT. Thereupon he returned to CLT to supervise the French-language version of the communique on Channel 9. Employees of Télé-Orient, which had been transmitting the CLT Arabic program, immediately stopped transmission after the statement was read. Al-Ahdab did not become an important force in the civil war, but he sparked a media war that had been avoided until that March evening.

Hearing that these broadcasting facilities had been "occupied" by a Moslem faction, supporters of the Christian president took control of Télé-Orient and the radio transmitters at Amsheet. Thus, each major warring group had a radio and television outlet that could enthusiastically broadcast programming in support of its own side. Although these major facilities became targets for gunners, damage was relatively light. One CLT employee observed that his station was an easy mark for artillery because the tower on the building seemed to provide an easily recognizable homing device. One week after the occupations took place Claude Khoury, a Lebanese journalist and television newscaster, made the following observation in *Monday Morning*, a weekly Beirut English-language magazine:

> The Al-Ahdab information forces are entrenched in the Lebanese Television Company (Channels 7 and 9) and the Lebanese Radio Station-Information Ministry (Sanayeh, Ras Beirut).
> The Franjieh information forces have dug in at Télé-Orient (Channels 5 and 11, the latter, however, being out of order) and the Amsheet radio relay station near Jbail (Byblos).
> For ammunition, they're using contradictory news flashes and endless rounds of threats, insults, "we shall overcome" speeches, patriotic songs and military marches.
> Caught in the middle are the listeners and the viewers—and, possibly, the troops themselves, the men and women who are reading the news and the various statements prepared for them by the two camps. (Khoury 1976, p. 41)

It was not until a new elected government took power and the Syrian-dominated peacekeeping force entered Lebanon in 1976 that the respective transmitters and studios were returned to their owners. The government radio service was reunified on December 12, 1976 (BBC, n.d., *Clandestine* Part 4, p. 1). The civil war had a more lasting effect on Lebanese radio listeners—particularly those who became regular listeners to the clandestine or rebel radio stations that were operated by political factions. Perhaps a more descriptive name for these stations is "unofficial," as their origins and locations were known but they broadcast on frequencies that the Lebanese government had not registered with the International Telecommunications Union, a United Nations agency.

UNOFFICIAL RADIO STATIONS

Several factions tried radio broadcasts in 1975 and 1976. The stations were of course intended to disseminate the views of the faction that operated the station. A partial explanation for the proliferation of stations was the need to provide vital communication to people in light of the inability of the national electronic media to do so. During the 1958 disturbances, three radio stations—"The Voice of Arabism," "The Voice of Lebanon," and "The Voice of the People's Resistance"—had not been very professionally run (N. Dajani, 1979, p. 48). When the stations ceased operation in September 1958, "The Voice of Arabism" ended its transmissions by announcing, "The national interest made it necessary to stop this broadcasting station. So we agree to stop it voluntarily as a move for cooperation with the new regime" (Brewer, 1958, pp. 1–2).

In 1975 and 1976 some of the former radio rebels reactivated stations that had been dormant for 17 years. Many factions attempted to broadcast, but only the more professional and well-financed operations lasted throughout the civil war and continue. Possibly, they have become permanent additions to Lebanese media. "The Voice of Lebanon," a pro-Phalangist (Christian) station, was first heard on September 24, 1975 (BBC, n.d., *Clandestine* WBI/5 and 7, p. 1). One day later, "The Voice of Arab Lebanon," a pro-left-wing station, started broadcasting programs that lasted until January 26, 1976 (BBC, n.d., *Clandestine* WBI/5 and 6, p. 1). These were not the only stations that operated during the war; but they are the only ones that were adequately financed and protected to become identifiable broadcast entities. The arrival of the Syrian peacekeeping force apparently renewed interest in rebel radio stations and on May 22, 1977, the pro-Phalangist "Free Radio of the Voice of South Lebanon" started transmissions (BBC, n.d., *Clandestine* ME/5520/A/2 and WBI/21, p. 2). "The Voice of One Lebanon," an anti-Syrian station, was first reported on May 11, 1977 (BBC, n.d., *Clandestine* ME/5515/A/1 and WBI/20). These stations tended to motivate various other political factions to begin stations, and "The Voice of the Arab Revolution," hostile to right-wing elements in Lebanon, emerged in May 1979. "Free Lebanon Radio," anti-Phalangist, and "Radio of Free and Unified Lebanon," pro-Franjiyah (a former Lebanese president), were first heard in 1978 (BBC, n.d., "Monitoring"

129/78, p. 2). On the more unusual side, "The Voice of Hope" started in 1979 in southern Lebanon in an area where some Christian Lebanese, under the leadership of Major Saad Haddad, had been cooperating with the Israelis. The operation is reportedly financed in part by an American religious group that includes Pat Boone, and the station features country and western music and inspirational messages in English.

"The Voice of Lebanon" deserves closer examination. Located in Ashrafieh, in the Christian sector of Beirut that resisted the presence of the Arab League peacekeeping force, what started as an informal operation became a viable business whose news is respected by listeners and is quoted in the international press. What makes the operation unusual is its size and the fact that it is a successful commercial radio station with over 100 employees in a former apartment complex that houses one mediumwave and one shortwave transmitter.[2] There are numerous brochures and a published quarterly program schedule in station media kits that provide programming information and station advertising rates. The modest, well-equipped studios contain some equipment from 1958 and are similar to what one would find in smaller medium-sized markets in the United States. Other stations survived the civil war, but they lack the organization of this station, which is located in an area largely outside government control: Ashrafieh is a city within a city. Another unique feature of the station is the fact that it claims to have a license to operate. Immediately prior to the 1976 elections that resulted in a change in leadership, the President signed a permit supposedly authorizing the station to broadcast. It is this action, claims the station management, that legalizes the operation (Khoury interview, 1979), although the telecommunications authority and Parliament did not act to legitimize the broadcasts.

The radio station is apparently quite popular and its news is respected by some listeners because they know that it is not provided by the government. The news operation is extensive and uses local and international correspondents who telex and phone stories that are used on the Arabic-, French-, and English-language broadcasts. The station subscribes to the Agence France Presse Arabic wire service. An indication of the station's popularity can be gleaned from a survey done in June 1978 in selected Lebanese cities by Associated Business Consultants of Beirut. Of those surveyed who claimed to have listened to radio the previous day, 20.5 percent said that they heard "The Voice of Lebanon" between 0800 and 0900. The heaviest time for listening was between 0700 and 1000 (Associated Business Consultants, 1978, *Extracts*, Part V, p. 1). The future of this and the other stations is uncertain. As long as supporters remain tenacious about their "voices" and have the means to protect them physically, they will probably continue to operate. Until Lebanon is able to muster a strong, respected national government, it is unlikely the stations will stop broadcasting. A strong national government, on the other hand, requires the support of the factions that operate the stations, and compromise, therefore, is possible—a compromise wherein a selected number of private commercially supported stations are allowed to broadcast legally in return for a pledge to support that government. The more popular operations have become an important part of the national electronic media offerings, and it is possible that listeners would resist closing the stations, because the stations provide an alternative to the Ministry of Information radio service for both entertainment and information. (For a detailed description of the unofficial broadcasting outlets in Lebanon until 1991 see Boyd, 1991.)

TELEVISION REORGANIZATION

Between late 1977 and 1980, Lebanon concentrated on reestablishing a somewhat normal situation with the return to a prewar status of the many necessities of life and basic government services. Some rebuilding has taken place in Beirut and other cities, but the peace that has come to this country is an imposed rather than a negotiated one. Because a comprehensive settlement has not been reached and the Arab League peacekeeping force will not stay indefinitely, the various factions still support private armies and stock weapons for the next round of fighting. The economy is recovering. The government, however, does not reap all of the benefits, as Lebanon's virtually open borders invite smuggling of easily marketable items such as liquor, cigarettes, and perfumes. An economy that seems to be recovering, as well as changes in the administration of Lebanese television, have produced an entirely new television organization. The Lebanese appear to be more enthusiastic about television since 1977 because it provides entertainment in the home and it enables them to avoid the streets during evening hours. Lebanon has joined virtually every other Arab country, where the legitimate electronic media are either heavily influenced or controlled by the government.

In 1974, CLT reached agreement with the government for a new license to operate its two television channels. The original contract stipulated that the agreement would last for 15 years. As the civil war temporarily deescalated in 1976, the 15-year Télé-Orient agreement was up for renewal. In 1977, both stations asked the government to consider an arrangement whereby the television system could be rebuilt. A devastated economy, damaged transmitters, and sections of the country without electricity for receivers had left both stations at a point where it was amazing that the stations were operating at all. In late 1977, the two television organizations and the subsidiaries, Advision and Télé-Management, agreed to form a partnership with the Lebanese government for the creation of a single new national television system known as Télé-Liban. The new organization is half government owned, with the remaining half equally divided between the Rizk Brothers and the French government SOFIRAD corporation (Rizk, 1979). Télé-Liban's president is appointed by the President of the Republic and reports to a board of directors. While this move is obviously a sound step toward the creation of a national television system, several years of operation have not dramatically changed the two formerly privately owned stations. There is more program coordination than there was and each station specializes in the kind of activity it has the personnel or equipment to do best—local production, taping of satellite feeds, etc. The employees at each station site tend to remain loyal to the former companies rather than to Télé-Liban. They recall vividly the time when the respective stations were occupied and the staffs were polarized. Because the economy stabilized and the television channels provided national coverage, advertising increased to the point where several rate increases in 1979 alone did not discourage advertisers. In fact, available slots for either spot commercials or sponsored programs were difficult to find (Yasmie interview, 1979). Advertising rules in effect in the 1980s lowered the total amount of advertising time per hour to 12 minutes and forced the clustering of commercials. These commercials promote products such as cosmetics, candy, disposable diapers, and jeans. Local advertising can be seen for clothing stores, soft drinks such as K-Cola and Miranda, computer schools, and restaurants.

The increased program planning and cooperation under Télé-Liban has resulted in three available television services. They are seen throughout Lebanon on various channels from newly installed relay transmitters, but they originate from Channels 5, 7, and 9 in Beirut, start at 1800, and end at midnight. Channels 5 and 7 occasionally show the same program that may be in Arabic or imported from the United States or Europe. One of these channels almost always features an Arabic program. Arabic news is telecast nightly at 2030 and a taped replay is shown toward the end of the evening's programs. Channel 9 is mostly a channel for Western programs in English or French which are subtitled in two languages, Arabic and either French or English, depending on the language of the original sound track. This channel features at least 1 hour daily of programs supplied free of charge from one of the three French television networks. There is no English-language television news, but the news in French is available each night. Imported American programs apparently are among the most popular.

Under a grant from the International Communication Agency, William E. Osterhaus of Varitel Communications of San Francisco, California, spent several weeks in Beirut studying the Télé-Liban operation. His October 1979 final report included 15 recommendations that, if accepted, could have provided a more solid basis for Télé-Liban. The recommendations included the suggestion that services such as Télé-Liban 1, 2, and 3 be emphasized rather than channels that are heavily identified with the previous ownership. He recommended a campaign to promote Télé-Liban more heavily among advertisers, so that sales would be more tied to the concept of Télé-Liban than Télé-Management, still the main sales organization for television. Another recommendation suggested making one station site a transmission headquarters, the other production. Still another involved the elimination of the politically expedient but inefficient and disruptive practice of switching weekly the origination of the main Arabic news program between the former CLT and Télé-Orient studios (Osterhaus, 1979). The Lebanese television situation became further complicated in July 1980. As the result of armed conflicts in east Beirut between two rival Christian factions—the Christian Phalangist party and the national Liberal party—Charles Rizk, Télé-Liban president, was kidnapped and held for several hours until he agreed to resign. He had refused to stop transmitting on one of the channels used by the Hazmiyeh (previously Télé-Orient) facility. The Phalange Party is interested in using any available channel to broadcast an "illegal" television service. If the government is unable to prevent the telecasts, it is likely that similar television services will start. The most likely sponsors of such undertakings are the same factions that have successfully started illegal radio stations.

UNOFFICIAL TELEVISION STATIONS

Bashir Gemayel, the young president-elect who was assassinated in 1982 before he could take office, was apparently the first to propose an unofficial television station. In 1980, studios were built and two transmitters installed in a Christian-held area of Beirut. In August 1985 the Lebanese Broadcasting Corporation (LBC), operated by the Lebanese Forces paramilitary group, went on the air with a modest telecast schedule. As of 1986, most air-time consisted of French and U.S. television programs that could be seen in Beirut and the western part of Mount Lebanon (Labaki, 1986). In September 1988 LBC added a separate channel operating in English and Arabic (British Broadcasting Corporation, 1988).

Television was an essential medium during the fierce fighting that started in late 1989 between rival Christian factions in east Beirut. Julie Flint of the *Observer* wrote that during conflicts, "Beirut's two Christian television stations, one controlled by General Michel Aoun's army and the other by Samir Geagea's militia, bombarded viewers with celebrations of war" (Flint, 1990). In fact, LBC, Geagea's station—part of the government network taken over by Aoun—continued commercial-oriented programming.

Another television station, Fihe TV Channel, reportedly operates occasionally from the village of Fihe in northern Lebanon. It is apparently under the control of the National Syrian Social Party and former Lebanese President Franjieh (Labaki, 1986). Hezbollah, the Iranian-backed Lebanese Shiite militia—widely believed to have held several Western hostages from the mid-1980s on—also wanted to have a television station in the Bekaa Valley. In December 1987 *U.S. News and World Report* stated that the French government agreed to supply Hezbollah with a complete television station as part of the release of two French citizens held in Lebanon ("French swap arms," 1987).

Clearly, the most unusual television station among the small number of unofficial operations is U.S.-based Christian Broadcasting Network's (CBN) Middle East Television (MET). The station was initially built in 1981 by High Adventure Ministries, the same organization that started the Voice of Hope radio station. Like the radio operation, the television station's creation was actively encouraged by the Israeli government, which permitted equipment to move through the port of Haifa (Tabori interview, 1982) and then be trucked over the Israeli border into southern Lebanon. After one year of operation, the station was given to CBN "in response to the direction of the Lord" (High Adventure Broadcasting Network, n.d., p. 2). By 1984, MET had become popular in Israel and Lebanon where viewers watched news in English, CBS's *60 Minutes,* American football, *I Love Lucy, Bonanza,* and *700 Club* ("Arab station vying," 1984), a talk show hosted by 1988 U.S. presidential candidate and CBN founder Pat Robertson. Most MET programming is still from the United States, although there is an Arabic film on Friday night and Sunday afternoon (Middle East television, 1990).

In July, 1983, a bomb destroyed most MET facilities, but the station returned to the air shortly after the incident with the help of television equipment from Israel ("Terrorists blow up," 1983; Cobbs, 1984).

It is impossible to predict the future of broadcasting in Lebanon because the country's future is still so uncertain. Although 1991 once again saw the return of Syrian army forces to stabilize the situation in some parts of Lebanon, and the release of the last long-held American hostages in late 1991 seemed to signal a change in attitude of the radical groups holding hostages such as Terry Anderson of the Associated Press, a return to the pre–civil war days of Lebanese prosperity seems unlikely—at least in the short term.

The devastating civil war has obviously forced the electronic media to change. Radio listeners have become accustomed to the return of the government's pre-war radio service and a multitude of unofficial radio stations that the government is powerless to stop. Television has been reorganized with the government as half-owner and with a board of directors that is more responsive to the needs of the population. Unofficial television stations have joined the unofficial radio stations. Since both government-sponsored and private television are financed by commercial advertising sales, any renewed fighting could once again force the television system into a situation where government may attempt to take control, at least financially.

CHAPTER 5

SYRIA

APPROXIMATELY 12 MILLION PEOPLE live within 71,498 square miles of what is known officially as the Syrian Arab Republic. Part of the Ottoman Empire prior to World War I, the area includes most of what was known as Greater Syria and included parts of present-day Turkey, Iraq, Jordan, Lebanon, and pre-1948 Palestine. France administered the country under a League of Nations mandate between 1920 and independence in 1945.

Syrian politics have been heavily influenced by the Ba'ath (resurrection) Party, which was founded in Syria in the early 1940s. The party, which is also strong in Iraq, believes that all Arab lands are essentially part of the Arab nation and should be united into one cultural and political entity. The political situation since independence has occasionally been volatile, with frequent military coups occurring between independence and 1970, when Hafez al-Assad became president. The country's economic plight has hampered development. With an essentially agricultural economy, Syrian leadership has encouraged the private sector at times, but has maintained the Ba'ath ideological commitment to socialism. The Soviet Union was Syria's main military supplier after the ill-fated union with Egypt between 1958 and 1961, when the two countries formed what was called the United Arab Republic (U.A.R.). Syria lost territory to Israel during the 1967 and 1973 Middle East Wars, and the Golan Heights area, which separates the two countries, is patrolled by a third party—a United Nations peacekeeping force.

There are an estimated 3 million radio sets, 2 million television receivers, and 500,000 videocassette recorders in Syria (British Broadcasting Corporation, 1990b).

SYRIA'S NEIGHBORS, with whom it has had variously hostile and good relations, are Turkey, Iraq, Jordan, Israel, and Lebanon. Recognized internationally during the 1980s as a nation supporting various terrorist groups, Syria joined the military effort organized by the United States against its Arab arch-rival, Iraq. In part because of Syrian support for the

American-inspired military action during the 1990–1991 Gulf conflict, Syria has had much better relations with some of its neighbors as well as with Western countries. Following successful pressure from the United States, Syria agreed to participate in the fall 1991 Middle East peace conference in Madrid.

RADIO

Radio broadcasting in Syria dates from 1946, when the Syrian Broadcasting Organization was founded. The radio system has expanded since its beginning but it has not achieved the status of systems in other Arab countries. This is due to a lack of funds and a lack of government commitment to radio until the early 1960s. Unlike Jordan and Egypt, Syria has not had the strong, stable leadership that would have enabled planning for orderly expansion of radio personnel, studio facilities, and transmitters.

By 1950, four mediumwave transmitters in the two main cities of Aleppo and Damascus broadcast about 9 hours of Arabic programming between the hours of 0600 and 0800, 1300 and 1500, and 1800 and 2300. Foreign-language broadcasts between 2300 and 2400 presented programs in English, French, and Turkish (UNESCO, 1951, p. 541). Also in the 1950s, Hebrew broadcasts to Israel started.

Syria's broadcasting was heavily influenced by the country's union with Egypt between 1958 and 1961. Particularly during the early enthusiastic period of the union, Egyptians came to Damascus, where all broadcasting was headquartered, and Syrians went to Egypt. During this time Egypt already had a firm commitment to a large broadcasting system with multiple services and numerous high-power transmitters. Syrians trained in Egypt and in Syria by Egyptian radio employees also learned the Egyptian philosophy of radio propaganda, later useful in defending the country against attack from Egypt after the 1961 disintegration of the UAR. Between 1950 and 1965 important changes took place, including the construction of the Damascus radio complex, which houses the radio studios. This complex is not on the grand scale of Egypt's or even Lebanon's and basically remains unchanged from its construction in the early 1960s. The most significant expansion was the construction of medium- and shortwave transmitters designed to serve domestic and neighboring audiences with Arabic programming and a wider international audience with Arabic and foreign-language programming. By 1965 the country claimed 16 radio transmitters that broadcast programs for the entire nation, plus other broadcasts in French, English, and Spanish (UNESCO, 1965, p. 106).

Shortwave transmitters were built near Damascus in the 1960s and were used to broadcast the domestic Arabic as well as the foreign-language programs. However, the country has not been enthusiastic about beamed shortwave programming and the transmitters were allowed to deteriorate, largely because of a lack of maintenance. In 1978, all shortwave transmitters were deactivated and a plan was finalized to install five new 250-kilowatt replacement transmitters with a sophisticated antenna system. Syria's one entry into the race to gain super-power transmitter status is a Czechoslovak-made 1500-kilowatt Tesla mediumwave facility with an intricate antenna system that allows switchable omnidirectional and directional transmission. In late 1979, the antenna was oriented to broadcast to Iraq and the Arabian Gulf states, but the transmitter is excessively expensive to operate according to the Ministry of Information, requiring 16 tons of oil per day to generate sufficient electricity (Karkoush interview, 1979).

RADIO SERVICES

Main Program

The Main Program operates from the studios in Damascus for 21 hours per day, generally not broadcasting between 0230 and 0530. Coverage within Syria is complete, with mediumwave transmitters in larger cities such as Damascus and Aleppo, as well as low-power stations in other cities. Although essentially designed for a Syrian audience, broadcasts are also intended to be heard in neighboring states. Newscasts, drama, interviews, and even music are supportive of the Ba'ath Party and specifically the policies of President Al-Assad. This service has been used by Syria to communicate with neighboring countries in order to defend its role in the Syrian-dominated peacekeeping force in neighboring Lebanon. A widely accepted practice in the Middle East, the main Program is continuously monitored by Jordan and Iraq for clues to possible shifts in government policies that may affect them. Syria's relations with those countries have occasionally been volatile and Syrian newscasts are therefore closely monitored by many listeners in neighboring countries.

Voice of the People

Having started in September 1978, the Voice of the People contains several programs that at one time were featured on the Main Program. This service is designed for a less sophisticated audience than the Main Program. In late 1979 the service operated in Arabic from 0600 to 1000 and from 1700 to 2100 on several mediumwave frequencies. The time between the two Arabic program periods was used to transmit foreign-language programs and some music on mediumwave.

National radio coverage is a reality. Syrian listeners have a main national program as their primary source of news, information, and entertainment. The successive government changes during the 1950s and 1960s, however, did not allow or encourage a planned expansion of the radio system. The situation with the shortwave transmitters is a case in point. It is unthinkable that Egypt or Saudi Arabia, for example, would allow the main transmission source for its international service to deteriorate to the point that facilities would have to be completely shut down, and only then have plans drawn for new transmitters. Syria does not import talent for its broadcasting productions or for its engineering staff. The country has a long tradition of drama, writing, and art that has not been tapped to any significant degree to help with the construction of a first-rate comprehensive radio system.

TELEVISION

Syria's construction of a television system in 1960 resulted from its brief unification with Egypt. The UAR contract with the Radio Corporation of America (RCA) for a comprehensive television system included a station in Damascus. It was obvious from the beginning, however, that the Syrian system was not to be developed on the same scale as Egypt's. When the station officially started on July 2, 1960 (Helwani interview, 1977), the same date as the beginning of Egypt's television service, a good deal of the programming was live or taped. Egyptian programming comprised a substantial portion of the limited nightly telecasts. Those Syrians who worked in Egypt as part of the exchange-of-personnel agreement and in Syria itself recall that Nasser dominated programming intended for the Syrian station in order to disseminate his point of view. More specifically, they accuse Nasser of having promoted the Syrian television system in order to have an eastern relay for Egyptian television programming. In addition to the main transmitter in Damascus, stations were built during the 1960s in Aleppo and Homs that broadcast "bicycled" tapes and films until these stations were connected in the 1970s to the main station by microwave.

Aside from the construction of these two stations, both distant from the Damascus television headquarters, there was little expansion of physical facilities between 1960 and 1975. The Syrian economy did not permit the luxury of additional television production or transmission equipment or, for that matter, the large-scale importation of television receivers. During this period, Syria was involved in the two Middle East wars of 1967 and 1973 and most of her foreign exchange went toward the war effort or other nonbroadcasting national priorities. As previously noted, frequent changes in government leadership during this 15-year period did not provide the broadcast media with strong direction. Because of the Arab League boycott of RCA in the late 1960s (the Boycott Office is located in Damascus), spare parts were always a problem, and eventually the original RCA cameras acquired in 1960 were replaced with Polish cameras. However, the majority of the equipment in Damascus remained RCA, except for the Ampex videotape recorders, until about 1975, when the decision was made to upgrade the equipment and convert to SECAM color (Haffar interview, 1979). During the mid-1970s, plans were finalized to replace the old monochrome television transmitters and to install new ones to increase coverage in Syria and to provide a signal to neighboring countries.

One motivation for the upgrading and expansion of the Syrian television system was the increasing availability of signals from other countries. Israel, Jordan, and Iraq had increased the number of relay stations, including some near the Syrian border, and Syrians were able to receive more foreign signals. Particularly attractive were the Jordanian channels that featured large amounts of American entertainment programming. New color transmitters and antenna systems have been installed in Hassaka, Aleppo, Slemfe, Damascus, Sheikh Saleh, and Homs. A transmitter has been built in Deirlellour to broadcast the Syrian television service to Iraq, and another in Tabqa to broadcast a directional signal to Turkey.

The Damascus studios were converted to color, and new monitors, switchers, and cameras installed. Syria does not import personnel for its television system, as there appears to be an abundance of technical and artistic talent. Lacking in the late 1970s was any enthusiasm for creative programming or innovative production techniques. At the time Syria's Ministry of Information did not seem to feel that videocassette recorders were a threat to its own captive television audience. Even when it was obvious that Syria had increased the quality of domestic television productions, the country did not attempt to become a television production center for the creation of programming to be sold to other countries. Still many of the television employees work in relative isolation from the rest of the Arab broadcasting world. Only a few have been attracted to high-paying jobs in the Arabian Gulf. When studio color transmissions started in 1979, technicians did not then understand how properly to light the news set or to light for a simple chroma-key picture. For a short time in 1979, the U.S. International Communication Agency supplied an American lighting expert who worked with problems primarily associated with the news set. The news on television, considered to be important by the government, was greatly improved.

TELEVISION PROGRAMMING

Programming done in Syria consists of the same television offerings—news, drama, music, and political programs—as found on other Arab world systems. A good deal of time is devoted to interviews and discussions of the Syrian economy and to politics and Islamic religious thought. These programs are relatively easy and inexpensive to videotape, and they provide the government with a means of giving national exposure to those people it believes best reflect the thinking of the Ba'ath political leaders. Some drama is taped and shown. A locally produced children's program is scheduled every day for early evening transmission. Taped music programs ranging in length from 5 to 30 minutes are interspersed with other kinds of programming. These music tapes, some quite old, are used as "fill" until a program such as news needs to be telecast as scheduled. Films and videotapes from non-Arab countries are shown. Many of these, such as documentaries from the East European countries, are provided without charge as part of cultural agreements. Relatively few programs from the United States and Europe have been shown on Syrian television. An occasional segment of *Kojak* appears, but Syria neither believes that it can afford to purchase large amounts of Western programming nor thinks that such offerings are appropriate for Syrian viewers. The Director General of television does believe that Western programs have some social value for Syrians because they show life, albeit in a dramatized form, in other cultures (Bellatt interview, 1979).

Possibly the most important program to both government and viewer on Syrian television is the news. Because so much time during the various newscasts is devoted to the activities of the President and other government officials, television personnel put a good deal of time and effort into television news. Viewer interest in these newscasts derives in part from the fact that government policies and directives are often featured. Actual news items and guidance regarding the basic ordering of stories are supplied to both radio and television by the Syrian News Agency. When the President travels outside of Syria on official visits, more news is generally available and the newscast is extended beyond its normal length. The main newscast includes local, Arab world, and international items from wire services and the European Broadcasting Union (EBU) daily satellite news feeds. Prior to sign-off the final newscast of the day is aired, consisting mostly of headlines. Some local stories are filmed with 16mm film equipment, but Syria uses Electronic News Gathering (ENG) and has acquired state-of-the-art video news gathering equipment. The interest in tape, versus film, for television news came about in the mid-1980s when the Ministry of Information realized that it had to convert from film to tape in order to get stories on the air faster and to pass them on tape or via satellite feeds to Western news organizations. A few readers may recall some of the 1990 and 1991 releases of the Western hostages held captive in Lebanon. Virtually all of the releases were done from Damascus and in at least one case featured an English-language tape of an interview with one of the hostages as he was driven from Beirut to Damascus.

Emphasized throughout this publication is the fact that the electronic media in the Arab world are especially important in governmental efforts to create a type of social, political, and economic reality in the minds of viewers. Although this is the case in virtually every Arab state, Syria is an especially relevant example. Television is, for example, used to remind Syrian viewers, as well as those in other states who can see Syrian television, just who "won" the 1973 Middle East War. Peter Waldman of *The Wall Street Journal* observed:

> Black-and-white images pop like gunfire on the television screen: Soldiers charge a hillside, tanks roll across a desert plain, MIG jets fly, howitzers sound, paratroopers drop from the sky.
>
> The action fades and a smiling fellow in a black tuxedo and a dark mop of blow-dried hair—a Syrian Tony Orlando—appears as narrator. In the gentle voice of a lullaby, be begins telling of the glorious October War of Liberation.
>
> "Arab soldiers made history" in that 1973 conflict with Israel, he explains. "They won because they were defending a just cause."
>
> They won?
>
> History of a sort. (Waldman, 1991, p. 1)

The Syrians do not have any idea of the number of viewers who actually believe that Syria won the war. Syria, like virtually all other Arab states, does not do social scientific research that could help understand the audience. However, as long as the electronic media are operated by governments, the images on Syrian and other Arab television systems will primarily reflect governmental hopes rather than reality.

Television in Syria is financed directly by the government and by advertising time sales. There is almost no contact between those who are responsible for programming television and those who are charged with selling commercial time. A small staff is employed to organize commercials on television—a reflection of the fact that, although commercials have always been allowed, the Ministry of Information is not particularly enthusiastic about them. This is apparently due to the financial arrangement within the government regarding advertising time sales. Thirty percent of the revenue from advertising is retained by Syrian Television; the remaining 70 percent goes to the Syrian Ministry of Finance, which supposedly returns that amount and more as part of the government's yearly financial allocation to all ministries (Al-Sharif interview, 1979). A good deal of paid advertising appears to be for state-run industries, which manufacture soap, shoes, clothing, etc. Increasingly, however, commercials that are also seen in other Arab countries are for products such as Japanese watches, imported candy and cosmetics, and processed cheese. The government may reap a kind of psychological benefit from television advertising: the commercials may serve to remind the nation that the Ba'ath Party has not proscribed the concept of free enterprise.

It seems unlikely that Syria will build an elaborate national multichannel television system on a par with that of some other Arab countries. Economic constraints and national priorities appear to be major limiting factors. Syria has not been and probably will not be an important Arab world radio broadcaster equal to Egypt, Iraq, or Saudi Arabia. The government has not supported research on set ownership or listening preferences. Color television did not start until the late 1970s; and apparently very few color sets are available, although some are featured in stores. Many families are content to acquire a monochrome set to enjoy national as well as neighboring channels.

CHAPTER 6

JORDAN

THE HASHEMITE KINGDOM OF JORDAN consists of 37,738 square miles (including the occupied West Bank) and is inhabited by a population of about 4 million people. The term Hashemite indicates that the royal family traces its history to the Prophet Mohammed. Neighboring countries are Syria, Iraq, Saudi Arabia, and Israel.

The original territory was ruled by the Ottoman Empire until after World War I. Great Britain had limited administrative control over what was then called Transjordan and administered a League of Nations mandate in what was then called Palestine. After the 1948 war that followed the departure of the British from Palestine, King Abdullah's territory was increased by an area negotiated by the Arabs and Israel that included part of the city of Jerusalem. Unlike vast portions of the country that are desert, the West Bank is agriculturally rich and has some light industry. That part of Jerusalem that was Jordanian is a popular tourist attraction. In 1951, King Abdullah was assassinated and his son Talal was named king. Talal served as ruler for only a short period of time, allegedly because of a nervous disorder, and was succeeded by his son, Hussein. The country was ruled by a regency council for one year, until the King reached the age of 18 and completed his schooling in Great Britain.

There are estimated to be 1.5 million radio sets, 900,000 television receivers, and 400,000 videocassette recorders in Jordan (British Broadcasting Corporation, 1991b).

IN 1967, during the Six-Day War, Israel gained control of the West Bank. The territory is occupied and administered by Israel and has been the focus of international news since the mid-1970s because of the Jewish settlements that have been built there. The West Bank is where the Palestinian uprising against Israel—the *Intifada*—started.

The loss of the West Bank was a serious financial blow for Jordan. In addition, the migration of Palestinians from the West Bank to Amman, the capital, increased the already sizable Palestinian population. In 1970, there was a brief but bitter civil war that pitted the Palestinian forces in Jordan against those loyal to the King. The basic result of the action was that Hussein remained in control of the country. The economy became healthier during the 1970s largely because of the expatriate salaries that Jordanians working in the Gulf states sent home, and because of foreign aid and loans from countries like the United States and Saudi Arabia. However, with the drop in worldwide oil prices in the early 1980s resulting in decreased employment in the Gulf, the Jordanian economy has suffered serious decline. After Jordan's implied support for Saddam Hussein after the August 1991 Iraqi invasion, the country lost a good deal of its international good will and suffered additional financial instability.

RADIO

Jordanian Radio, officially known as the Hashemite Broadcasting Service (HBS), traces its beginnings to the Palestine Broadcasting Service (PBS), which was established on March 30, 1936, by the British government under its mandate authority. The station was an early radio outlet in the Arab world and broadcast limited local programming in three languages—Arabic, English, and Hebrew. Studios were located in Jerusalem and a 20-kilowatt transmitter and tower were placed in nearby Ramallah (*Palestine Department of Posts . . . 1935*, 1935, p. 5; *Palestine Department . . . 1936*, 1936, p. 6). The station was established by the British to facilitate communication with the Arab and Jewish residents of Palestine, as well as to provide an alternative to the hostile Italian propaganda broadcasts from Radio Bari (see Chapter 20, Early Broadcasting to the Arab World). During and immediately after World War II, the station facilities and transmission time were expanded and the BBC's Empire Service was at times rebroadcast over the station.

When the British left Palestine in May 1948, Jewish forces captured the radio studio complex and the Arab forces took control of the transmission site in Ramallah. After the 1948 peace agreement with Israel, Jordan used the Ramallah transmitter site on the West Bank while Israel refurbished the damaged Jerusalem studio complex, which still serves as the headquarters for its domestic and international radio services. Through Jordanian military authority on the West Bank, Jordan operated an Arabic service from the Ramallah site, to which studios had been added. On April 24, 1950, the West and East banks of Jordan were unified officially, and the military (Hashemite Broadcasting Service, n.d., p. 2) gradually handed over broadcasting to the Ministry of Information, which, in a manner similar to other Arab states, administers the radio service. Financial constraints hampered the expansion of the radio service after 1948. At the time, the government did not realize the importance of providing citizens with a viable radio service. This situation changed markedly in the mid-1950s, when Radio Cairo started attacking King Hussein and other government leaders for taking orders from the British—particularly from Glubb Pasha, a British officer who headed the Arab Legion, Jordan's army. When the government realized that Cairo's Voice of the Arabs was in fact having an impact, plans were made to construct a new radio studio facility and transmitter in Amman. On September 1, 1956, King Hussein—himself an avid amateur radio operator—inaugurated the new Amman radio transmitter, which broadcast limited programming of about 4 hours per day on one shortwave and one mediumwave transmitter. This station assumed the greater part of the responsibility of counter-programming the Egyptian services while the Ramallah site featured the domestic main service.

In 1958, neighboring Iraq underwent a bloody revolution resulting in the deaths of the Iraqi prime minister and most members of the royal family, which was closely related to the Jordanian royal family. This situation, coupled with the general instability of the Middle East between 1956 and 1960, caused the Jordanian government to take more notice of the need for a reliable, comprehensive radio service that would also serve neighboring states. The basic importance attached to radio in Jordan dates from expansion plans that were drawn in 1955 and 1956 and became reality in 1959. On March 1, 1959, King Hussein dedicated the Amman broadcasting service and on August 23 of that year he opened the studios of the radio service in Jerusalem. During the March ceremonies Hussein said:

> As Jordan listens today to its vivid voice, energetically defending Arabism and Islam, with the portraits of glory embodied in its vibrations, and with the guiding light of holiness radiating from within its depth, Jordan finds itself empowered to propagate such lights as would illuminate the way for humanity. The way of Jordan is the path of the Almighty God; the mission of Jordan is unity, amity and fraternity. (Hashemite Broadcasting Service, n.d., p. 1)

After 1960, the Jordanian government's commitment to a radio system was firmly established and plans were drawn for the introduction of a television service. Financial priorities did not allow the government to allocate funds to construct a large radio complex with a large staff like Nasser's in Egypt. A lack of money to operate a system in the 1950s had motivated Jordan to allow commercial broadcasting on radio; an aggressive sales staff, oriented toward research, was organized for this purpose. In the late 1950s, the country had asked for American help with its then fledgling radio system and a contract was signed between the Hashemite Broadcasting System and Syracuse University. The contract stipulated that Americans employed by Syracuse University would work in Amman as advisors (Hamilton interview, 1972; Jarrar interview, 1979). However, there is evidence of an even closer relationship with the Syracuse team that is especially interesting in light of the anti-Western, anti-imperialist feeling that was pervasive in the Middle East at that time. William E. Minette (letter, 1961, p. 1), then the Commercial Manager of the Hashemite Broadcasting Service, wrote to an American government official stating:

> The important point here is that the Commercial Section of the Hashemite Broadcasting Service is being operated by a team of professional American broadcasters. The basic contract is held by the Radio Television Center at Syracuse University, under which the University supplies the management team.
> Probably the most pertinent point of that contract is the following:
> "The Management Team, under the supervision of the Director General of Broadcasting, shall have full authority for the operation of the Commercial Department. This authority shall be considered equivalent to that delegated to any other department within the Broadcasting Service. However, the ultimate responsibility for the operation of the Hashemite Broadcasting Service shall remain with the Director General of Broadcasting.
> The members of the team will not be considered advisors, but members of the staff of the Broadcasting Service with clearly recognized responsibility and authority to make command decisions in regard to commercial broadcasting."

The relationship with the Syracuse group probably fostered the early research interest of HBS in determining audience size in both Jordan and neighboring countries in order to establish commercial advertising rates. In the 1960s, when little if any media research was being undertaken in the other Arab countries, HBS undertook a radio preference survey in Riyadh, Saudi Arabia, during a period when the Saudi Arabian government was not receptive to this kind of activity. This survey was probably the first of its kind to be done in Saudi Arabia (Associated Business Consultants, "A seven-day").

The above-mentioned survey was undertaken by Associated Business Consultants (ABC) of Beirut, Lebanon, which formed an alliance with an American firm by the name of RTV International, with offices in New York City. The company was founded in 1963 by Richard Bertrandias, for over 6 years a former director of Radio Liberty, an American radio organization headquartered in Munich, Germany, that broadcasts to what used to be the Soviet Union in various vernacular languages. Originally named Radio Liberation, the station is known to have been started and then operated by the U.S. Central Intelligence Agency (CIA), until the source of funds became public knowledge in the early 1970s. Radio Liberty and a sister station, Radio Free Europe, which broadcasts to Eastern Europe but not the former Soviet Union, still operate; now they are funded openly by the U.S. government.

It has become popular to accuse American organizations that operate

in the Middle East of having some connection with the CIA. Mr. Bertrandias' background and RTV's interest with ABC in media research and
mass communication in Arab countries has led to suspicion that RTV had
CIA connections or that it was actually owned by the U.S. intelligence
agency. For a time, RTV held contracts with Arab and African countries;
in many cases funding was arranged by the Agency for International
Development (Associated Business Consultants/RTV International, n.d.).
But rumors and speculation about the company apparently hurt its chances
for success, and by the late 1970s it had ceased to exist. At one time, RTV
attempted to secure a transmitter location on Cyprus for a radio station that
would broadcast to the Arab world in a manner similar to Radio Monte
Carlo (see Chapter 20, Western Europe). In 1972, RTV successfully
negotiated a contract with Bahrain to start a commercial television station
that it operated until the Bahrain government took it over. Other RTV
activities in the Arab world included hotel management contracts in Riyadh,
Saudi Arabia, and Beirut, Lebanon, as well as the introduction of television
in Jordan. When the U.S. Army Corps of Engineers sought contract bids in
the late 1960s for the operation and maintenance of new Saudi Arabian
television stations in Qassim and Medina, RTV was financially disqualified
because it did not have a firm enough economic base. Speculation about
involvement with the U.S. intelligence community may, however, have
influenced the Corps of Engineers' decision (West interview, 1972).

The Hashemite Broadcasting System did not become a strong
commercial service in the region. HBS lacked the transmission power to
reach large audiences in Syria, Israel, Iraq, or Saudi Arabia. Nevertheless,
the commercial income did help pay the bills for a radio service that until
1967 had studios in Amman and Jerusalem. Its international shortwave
service provided programs in Hebrew, Spanish, and English. The basic
orientation of Jordanian radio has been to defend Jordan's political position
in the Arab world rather than to engage in the type of hostile propaganda
frequently favored by Syria, Iraq, and Egypt.

The June 1967 Middle East war affected Jordan profoundly. The West
Bank was occupied by Israeli forces, resulting in a stream of residents
leaving it for Amman, the economic loss of potential tourists to East
Jerusalem, and the loss of West Bank agriculture and light industry. Jordan
also lost the Jerusalem radio studios and the transmitters at the Ramallah
site. After the war, operation of HBS was centered in Amman. Plans were
drawn to expand the number of transmitters and the studios as soon as the
economic situation would permit. The government realized more than ever
the importance of a reliable radio system. With this, it could encourage the
indigenous population stunned by the loss of its land, and maintain contact
with Jordanians living under Israeli occupation, as well as with active
Palestinian elements determined to retake the West Bank.

One of the changes following the 1967 Six-Day War was the general cooling of radio propaganda in the Middle East. Egypt had been a leader in suggesting that the Hashemite and Saudi Arabian royal families should be overthrown. The occasional vindictive broadcasts from Iraq and Syria did continue; but many countries, including Jordan, took the position that they should concentrate on the organization of a domestic service as well as broadcasts to reach other countries to help explain Jordan's Arab world position. Although television took some attention from HBS, by the early 1970s plans were made for the transmitters that would have to be added to provide coverage to areas such as Aqaba on the Red Sea. Plans also were made to join the ranks of the Arab countries that had decided to build super-power mediumwave transmitters. HBS operates three basic radio services, which are broadcast on mediumwave, shortwave, and FM transmitters, all of which originate from the broadcasting complex in Amman.

RADIO SERVICES

Main Arabic Program

The Main Arabic Program is the primary provider of HBS's news, information, and entertainment. The basic format is similar to Radio Cairo's Main Program and many other services in other Arab countries where programming is presented in blocks that include special features for children, women, and laborers, interspersed with music and regularly scheduled newscasts. This service is also intended to be heard outside of Jordan, as it is broadcast from a 200-kilowatt mediumwave transmitter in Amman and a 1-kilowatt mediumwave facility in Aqaba. At selected times during the day and night, portions of this service are broadcast by one of several 100-kilowatt shortwave transmitters in Amman.

An innovation of Jordanian radio that is almost unique in the Arab world is a daily call-in program, *Direct Broadcasting*. Started in the early 1970s, this program is aired seven days per week for an hour in the morning. Although the broadcast is not live and there are some restrictions on topics that may be discussed, the program seems to have a popular following, especially among those who wish to comment on and hear about government-sponsored development projects (Ayish, 1990).

English Service

Jordan has always broadcast some English-language programming because of the Palestine Broadcasting Service heritage and the fact that English is widely spoken in an area where Great Britain once had considerable presence. After the 1967 war, HBS discontinued its Hebrew schedule and decided to concentrate on English as an alternative to its Arabic service and as a kind of program that might be popular among both Arabs and Jews in Israel. The service is broadcast from Amman using a 20-kilowatt mediumwave transmitter, an FM transmitter, and, at specified times during the day, a shortwave transmitter. Programming is blocked in a manner similar to the Arabic service, but the overall format is heavily weighted toward music and news. Some drama is broadcast and specific times are set on a published schedule for classical music, American country and western music, jazz, and various request programs ("Radio Jordan English Service," 1979, p. 2). In order to be more competitive with radio services such as Radio Monte Carlo, the very latest popular American and European music is played from a supply flown weekly from London by the Jordanian national airline (Zada interview, 1979a). The service identifies itself as Radio Jordan and does not accept advertising.

FM Stereo Service

The motivation for an FM stereo continuous music service appears to have been King Hussein's interest in such an undertaking. In addition, people with home stereo equipment imported mostly from Japan were tuning to such a station that broadcast from Jerusalem. In 1979 a studio in the broadcasting building was renovated for an FM stereo control room and in January 1980 test transmissions were started.

JORDANIAN SUPER-POWER TRANSMITTER

Throughout this study of Arab world broadcasting, the intense interest in high-power mediumwave transmitters has been noted. With neighboring countries either planning or constructing super-power transmitters, Jordan decided that it must also build a powerful facility if its radio voice was to be heard among the clash of broadcast signals that crowd the mediumwave spectrum at night.

The Ministry of Information contracted with Continental Electronics of Dallas, Texas, for the construction and installation of a 2000-kilowatt mediumwave transmitter in Ajlun, near Amman (King communication, 1979; Continental Electronics, 1979, p. 1). Such a powerful facility would provide a strong signal to all neighboring countries. As the transmitter was intended to broadcast the HBS Main Program, additional revenue might result from an increased coverage area.

About the same time that the government ordered the new facility from Continental, Saudi Arabia finalized with the same company its Northern Stations Project, which consists of one 1000-kilowatt and three 2000-kilowatt mediumwave transmitters, located at Qurayat and Duba in the northern

Saudi Arabian desert. Both countries applied to the International Telecommunication Union International Frequency Registration Board for 594 kHz and were registered as having made the request. The frequency was noted as belonging to both countries. Continental Electronics started building in its Dallas plant two of the world's most powerful mediumwave transmitters that would operate on the same frequency while located only a few hundred miles apart. In the fall of 1979, both transmitters were installed and started test transmissions, at which time both governments realized that serious interference problems existed. Jordanian and Saudi Arabian Ministry of Information officials and broadcast engineers held a meeting that resulted in an agreement that Jordan would not broadcast on 594 kHz (Ashfoura interview, 1979). In return, Jordan received undisclosed compensation, and agreed to a change of frequency at the expense of the Saudi government (Odeh interview, 1979). The Saudi Arabian Ministry of Information defended its acquisition of the frequency by noting that although Jordan apparently registered the frequency first, it did so with the understanding that considerably lower power would be utilized. Officials took the position that the problem was Jordan's, because Jordan changed the intended power of the transmitter after the frequency had been registered (S. Nasser interview, 1980).

PATTERNS OF RADIO LISTENING

In a February 1972 study of radio and television audiences in Jordan, Associated Business Consultants of Beirut, Lebanon, made the following major findings (1972, pp. 1–2):

1. In the six cities surveyed there were an estimated 135,000 radio sets.
2. 90 percent of those surveyed listened to radio daily.
3. 94 percent of those surveyed owned at least one radio set.
4. Adult listeners averaged 2 hours and 45 minutes per day.
5. The most popular hour for radio listening was between 0630 and 0730.
6. The most popular type of radio program was news, followed by music.

The Jordanian radio audience, like that in other Arab countries, listens to foreign radio stations. A survey done in Jordan for the International Communication Agency in May 1977 concluded that 71 percent of an estimated 426,000 Jordanians listened regularly to non-Jordanian stations. An overwhelming number of listeners said that they listened to foreign radio stations on mediumwave; and among those surveyed who listened "once a week or more often" in Arabic, 34.3 percent listened to the BBC, 33.6 percent heard the Israeli Broadcasting Service, and 23.4 percent listened to Radio Damascus (USICA, 1978b, pp. 11–12; Jarrar, 1970, p. 16).

What these data do not indicate is the effect of these broadcasts on listeners. What seems clear is that Jordanians are similar to other Arabs with respect to a curiosity about hearing what neighbors, whether friends or enemies, are saying. Listeners appear to realize that in most cases the governments are the broadcasters and that tuning to a government radio station provides the listener with the government view. The BBC's news is uniquely popular because it is acknowledged by many to be essentially objective since the British government itself is not the broadcaster.

TELEVISION

By 1964 it was obvious to government officials that Jordan must build a television system. Jordan's Arab neighbors had started television broadcasts in the early 1960s—in the case of Iraq, in the 1950s. When Saudi Arabia, the most conservative of the Arab countries, announced its plans in 1963 for a national television system, Jordan had no choice but to begin steps for the expensive undertaking. In 1965 and 1966, the government allocated funds for a feasibility study, which was undertaken by an international team of consultants. About the time that the report was made to the government, a group of local businessmen proposed that they construct a television system along the lines of Lebanon's. The proposed system was to be commercial, but the government was to be allowed a good deal of control, including supervision of programming. The Jordanian Cabinet at last agreed to the basic plan proposed by the businessmen; but when the programming proposal was received and it became obvious that it was to be mostly entertainment, the Cabinet ruled against a private/ government partnership and decided to operate a system itself (Jarrar, 1970, p. 20). International bids for the creation of a television system were advertised and, by May 1966, bids had been received for the construction of a television system by 16 firms from the United States, Europe, and Japan. A board reviewed the bids and decided to allow several firms to supply and install in Amman various parts of the system. The bulk of the studio and transmission equipment was supplied by Marconi of Great Britain. The government created the Jordan Television Corporation, which would gain income from both commercial advertising and license fees; King Hussein laid the cornerstone for the television building outside Amman on July 11, 1966 (Madanat, 1976, p. 1).

The June 1967 Middle East War delayed the official introduction of television. During the economic, political, and military readjustments immediately following the loss of the West Bank to Israel, television lost some government attention. The construction of the studio complex and the delivery of equipment were delayed. Also, many Western technicians left

Jordan during the war, further slowing plans for installation of equipment. In retrospect, the decision to locate the main studio complex in Amman rather than in Jerusalem was a sound one. The initial plan called for a transmitter in Jerusalem to broadcast the Amman signal to the West Bank and to Israel, which at the time had no television. Some television equipment, notably a transmission tower and antenna, had been delivered to Jerusalem and was captured by the Israelis, who later used the equipment for their own service. In the fall of 1967, equipment deliveries resumed and British engineers continued equipment installation. Jordan Television (JTV) contracted with RTV International to supply a team of people to act on behalf of the government in certifying the equipment installation and to provide some production and technical training for those Jordanians who would actually begin the service.

On the evening of April 28, 1968, television officially started from the Amman studio with a 3-hour daily transmission on Channel 3. The initial stages of program development included some local programming—news, interviews, and children's programs. After two years of limited transmissions, the daily schedule had been lengthened to 4.5 hours, and increased local programming had been made possible by the addition of a large production studio and lighting equipment, additional cameras, and more videotape recorders. The addition of another transmitter on Channel 6 expanded the service to reach approximately 65 percent of the combined population of Jordan and the West Bank.

The 1970 Jordanian Civil War, which pitted Palestinian forces in the country against King Hussein's army, temporarily halted the development of television. However, planning continued for more space and equipment. By 1972, the basic administrative structure of the television service and the programming philosophy were established. The first channel to become operational, Channel 3, became the main Arabic service, broadcasting from approximately 1730 to midnight. Channel 6 features mostly foreign-language programs that are imported primarily from the United States and Great Britain. News is presented nightly in French, Hebrew, and English. Both channels simultaneously televise the main nightly Arabic news program at 2000 both to increase coverage and to discourage alternative viewing. Transmissions are extended during religious holidays and on Fridays.

By the mid-1970s, both channels had acquired additional production equipment including outside broadcasting vehicles and videotape recorders. The country became a member of INTELSAT, thus allowing the broadcast of such events as the Munich Olympic games and American space shots. Through the Arab States Broadcasting Union, Jordan became the coordinating center for several Arab countries' participation in the European Broadcasting Union (EBU) satellite news feeds (Boyd, 1975a, p. 317). On the sixth anniversary of JTV in April 1974, Jordan began color television transmission using the PAL system. Color brought new television production equipment to Jordan, resulting in an increase in the quality of the signal of both channels. In the mid-1970s, a national telecommunications project was completed that allowed the Amman headquarters to supply repeater stations in Petra, Ma'an, and Aqaba. By 1980 JTV was using 15 transmitters (Jordan Television Engineering Department, 1979) that provided reliable color coverage to most of the country. Some of the transmitters have been positioned so that the programming can be seen in neighboring Syria, the West Bank, and Israel.

LINKS WITH OTHER ARAB COUNTRIES

The size of the administrative, production, and engineering staffs for television increased significantly during the 1970s as new studios and equipment were added and as local production increased. Jordan television, which has never been heavily subsidized by the government, found that there was a market in the Gulf states for some of its productions. The studios in Amman are kept busy with taping programs that are used for domestic consumption and then offered for sale to other countries. An interesting by-product of the television system is that Jordan is probably the major exporter of engineering and production talent to the Gulf states. Egyptian actors and directors still tend to dominate the Arabic serial and television play syndication market, but Jordanians are widely employed in the Gulf in all facets of development, and television is no exception. In 1979, the two large stations in Oman hired some 20 Jordanian engineers and production specialists to replace the Germans and British who were there on contract (Jarrar interview, 1979). The export of television personnel is good for the Jordanian economy because expatriate salaries contribute to the flow of hard currency into the country. However, the continuous departure of trained people means that there is almost always a shortage of competent people to operate the Jordanian television system. In 1978, JTV made the decision to build a television production center adjacent to the existing television complex. The venture, which included government as well as private money, undertook the production of commercials and series for other countries (Ashfoura interview, 1979).

To some extent, developments in the early 1990s changed the employment patterns of Jordanian television personnel in the Gulf. First, the Gulf states made progress in training their own technical and production personnel. Second, it soon became obvious to Gulf television administrators that Arabic-speaking engineers were not essential in a technical field where the language of choice was English. Thus, it was cheaper to hire technical help from Pakistan and India. Third, after Jordan supported Saddam

Hussein during the Gulf War, Jordanians—many of Palestinian origin—were no longer welcome in the Gulf.

TELEVISION PROGRAMMING

The main Arabic program on Channel 3 telecasts productions made in Jordan and Egypt. Foreign-language programs are shown with the original soundtrack but with subtitles that have been added electronically. This process, which is used heavily in Jordan and in a few other Arab countries, allows the soundtracks of films and videotapes to be translated into Arabic and typed on a white scroll by an electric typewriter. When the foreign program is aired, the subtitling is done by a machine that uses a monochrome camera with the polarity reversed, so that the black letters ultimately appear white when superimposed or keyed over the picture. An operator sits in a special booth during the broadcast, listens to the soundtrack, and advances the subtitles on the scroll according to the prepared script. This procedure, because of the human factor, produces erratic results, but it saves the enormous expense of dubbing programs onto videotape or of subtitling films. The procedure is also used on the programs that are telecast on the predominantly foreign Channel 6.

The nightly Arabic newscast at 2000 is a nightly 30-minute program that features news about the royal family, domestic government news, international news from wire services, and the twice-daily EBU news exchange satellite feed. The program from Channel 6 is telecast simultaneously on the Arabic channel for special events. The early evening French-language programming is the result of a cultural agreement between Jordan and France that stipulates that the French government will supply programming on film and videotape and two French citizens who write and deliver a daily newscast.

Although Jordan probably adheres more faithfully to its published television schedule than most other Arab television services, changes do occur almost daily. Occasionally special programs of local interest are substituted for scheduled programming on both channels. Times are only approximate because of the emphasis on foreign programs, which, lacking commercials, do not conform to standard program times. There is often a good deal of fill, slides, and music to help bring the program times in line with the published schedule. Although the times for the various news services are published, the news does not always fill the scheduled period and is occasionally extended.

On both channels, there are several reasons for the emphasis on foreign programming. First, the television administration believes that the programming is popular among Jordanians. It tries to provide those who have television sets with popular entertainment. From the start, Jordan Television has attempted to attract Arabs from the West Bank and the citizens of Israel to its television service; popular foreign programming was one way of realizing this goal. Whereas Israel, like Jordan, established a television service after the 1967 war, the one Israeli channel has not featured much foreign programming.

The Jordanian services, which are very concerned about expenses and income, apparently use foreign programs to attract advertisers. In 1977, the Minister of Information indicated that the effects of foreign programming were minimal, but that some viewers confessed a frustration about not being able to afford some of the products that are advertised on television. After watching an episode of *Hawaii Five-0*, the minister said, his son asked why they did not have a house as nice as those of the important people on the program; their present house, the son said, was not good enough for a person as important as a Jordanian minister (Odeh interview, 1977). The minister apparently had not realized the possible impact of television on his own family.

Because Jordan uses so much Western television programming, suppliers are interested in having Jordan show their television series, as a showing on Jordan television can help program sales in other Arab countries. Thus, Jordan is in the position to telecast programs first and at a relatively low price. The television administration also gets foreign programming relatively cheaply by allowing its electronic subtitling scrolls to be duplicated and used by other Arab countries, a feature attractive to suppliers.

It is impossible to discuss Jordanian Television without mentioning the important role played by its first director. Mohammed Kamal, Jordan Television's founding director, was the driving force behind the development of Jordan's visual medium. From its inception until the mid-1980s, Kamal built the technical and production sectors of Jordan Television because he understood that television was an essential part of national, social, and political development. In the early 1980s, there was a joke in Jordan that the country really had three kings: King Hussein, the head of the country's national airline, and Mohammed Kamal. Mr. Kamal left the directorship of television when King Hussein appointed him Ambassador to the United States in the mid-1980s.

THE ISRAELI AUDIENCE

Jordan discontinued its Hebrew radio service after the 1967 war and has not resumed it. The basic philosophy has been to reach Israeli citizens instead through English-language radio broadcasts, popular foreign programming on television, and a daily Hebrew news program on Channel 6. The newscast started in October 1972 and is intended to provide information about Jordan as well as to disseminate the Arab view of the Middle East problem (Odeh interview, 1979). In addition, the newscast seeks to provide Israelis with an alternative view of events in Israel. Occasionally, items in Israeli newspapers and the foreign press about Israeli society, politics, or the economic situation are included as news items. Many newscasts include a political cartoon drawn on a camera card by an artist at Jordan Television.

It is difficult to assess the impact on Israelis of the JTV Hebrew news. The newscast is probably watched by those Israelis who are curious or who have sets tuned to JTV for the entertainment programs from the West and do not change channels when the news is aired. Unlike the reaction of some Israelis to the Hebrew radio broadcasts of Egypt, Syria, and Iraq, which they see as propaganda, the JTV Hebrew news is generally given good reviews by many citizens and media professionals. The language is generally accurate; moreover, the basic approach includes an effort not to portray Israeli society in a derogatory light (Bar-Haim interview, 1980). Jordan's basic media policy has always differed from other countries that broadcast to Israel in that the Ministry of Information officials know that inflammatory anti-Israel rhetoric will not attract or keep broadcast media consumers. Not only do Israelis seem to recognize the attractiveness of the two Jordan television channels, but the JTV schedules continue to be published daily in the *Jerusalem Post*, a well-known Israeli English-language newspaper.

Although there are no known survey data to support this conclusion, almost surely the Jordanian channels are not as popular now among Israeli Jews as they were in the early 1980s. Two major technical developments have changed viewing options. First, the Israeli government started a second television channel. Second, the major urban areas have become cabled, thus permitting a greater variety of entertainment programming and news that was not previously possible. Some programming, such as CNN news, comes from Western satellite-delivered services.

THE TELEVISION AUDIENCE

Jordanians' ability to receive foreign television signals depends on the location of the viewer. Even within the hilly city of Amman, the quality of foreign and domestic signals varies greatly. Signals from Israel and Syria can be received during most parts of the year. During the summer months, the Egyptian, Lebanese, and Cypriot channels can be received in some parts of Amman by people who have installed antennas with rotors, an increasingly popular practice. The last available survey of television viewing patterns in

Jordan was done in 1972; since then important changes, such as an increase in the number of owned television receivers, have taken place in Jordanian society. Nevertheless, the main findings of the study are of interest (Associated Business Consultants, 1972, p. 1):

1. The estimated number of television sets was 105,000.
2. Average number of viewers per set was 6.5.
3. 73 percent of surveyed households had a set.
4. 81 percent of viewers surveyed watched television daily.
5. Most viewers (80 percent) watched in their own homes, while 17 percent watched outside the home, and 3 percent watched both at home and outside.
6. The most popular time slot for viewing was 2000 to 2030—the time of the Arabic newscast.
7. The most popular foreign series included wrestling and *Hawaii Five-0*.

The Jordanian television system differs in several respects from the services operated by other Arab countries. The system has always tried to operate with little or no expense to the Jordanian government. Financial support comes from license fees and advertising. About 1,000 people work with the two channels, a relatively lean staff compared with that of other countries such as Egypt that have built large systems with a vast number of employees. JTV programming philosophy includes the desire to reach a non-Arab country, Israel, with attractive programming and news. Programming that helps with the priorities for Jordanian development has not been totally neglected, but the percentage of Western entertainment programs is higher on JTV than on any other Arab television system. Finally, Jordanian television serves as the main training ground for television engineers and other technicians who work in the Gulf countries.

CHAPTER 7

YEMEN

NORTH AND SOUTH YEMEN are not the first Arab states to merge. But they may be the only ones that have apparently succeeded in doing so. As noted previously, Egypt and Syria tried to combine governments in the early 1960s. Libya offered to merge with several Arab states during the 1980s. Despite very different political and economic backgrounds—South Yemen was the only Marxist state in the Arab world—the two Yemens are economically and culturally similar. The attempted overthrow of the South Yemeni socialist government in January 1986 by forces within the country destabilized what was believed to be a well entrenched regime. The formal merger of the two states took place in May 1991. Since the country is still relatively new, it is essential to explore the background of the two formerly separate states of North and South Yemen.

According to the BBC, there are 1.4 million radio receivers, 400,000 television sets, and 90,000 videocassette recorders in Yemen (British Broadcasting Corporation, 1991b).

NORTH YEMEN

NORTH YEMEN, officially the Yemen Arab Republic, was located in the southwest corner of the Arabian peninsula, with Saudi Arabia to the north and the People's Democratic Republic of Yemen (South Yemen) to the south and east. The population estimates varied between 5 and 6 million people, about one-quarter of whom were employed in other countries. Many were in the Gulf states working as laborers and in service industries. The three main cities were San'a (the capital), Taiz, and the Red Sea port city of Hodeida. Agriculture was an important activity in North Yemen, a relatively poor country blessed with fertile land. Coffee was the main source of foreign exchange, along with cotton. Qat, a plant whose leaves when chewed produce a mild narcotic effect, was also a source of income for farmers.

Politically North Yemen witnessed some dramatic changes in this century. After the dissolution of the Ottoman Empire in 1918, Imam Yahya gained control of the country and remained in power until he was assassinated in 1948. Yahya's son Ahmed defeated the forces who had assassinated his father and proclaimed himself Imam. After Ahmed's death in 1962, his son Mohammed succeeded him, but Mohammed's rule lasted only a few days; the military deposed the new leader and proclaimed the Yemen Arab Republic. In 1967 the Yemen civil war ended. Royalist forces (those who supported the Imam), supported by Saudi Arabia, had been pitted against republican forces, supported by Egypt. North Yemen's political stability was threatened beginning in 1968 by South Yemen (People's Democratic Republic of Yemen), a proclaimed Marxist state. There was open warfare between the two Yemens in 1971, followed by a cease-fire and an agreement between the two countries to merge. This merger, however, did not occur. Occasional changes in the government continued to take place during the 1970s. Again fighting between the two Yemens erupted in February 1979, and again a cease-fire was signed, along with a pledge to unite the two countries. The United States supplied North Yemen with arms during this fighting, but the country moved closer to what was the Soviet Union, with which it concluded an arms deal in November 1979.

RADIO

Egyptian radio services, most notably the Voice of the Arabs and Radio Cairo, played an important part in the eventual development of radio in Yemen. During the 1950s, Egyptian services were well received in the southern part of the Arabian peninsula. There was, in fact, no real alternative to the Egyptian programming. Local broadcasts from the San'a station were limited in hours and, compared with those of Egypt, unprofessional.

In September 1956, both Radio Cairo and the radio station in San'a broadcast programming that was designed to provoke actions against the British government's presence in the Aden Protectorate (South Yemen). A kind of mini radio war between Aden and North Yemen reached its peak in 1957. The North Yemen government apparently believed that this broadcasting activity would distract attention from its own internal problems (Macro, 1968, p. 105).

During the civil war in the 1960s, broadcasting to North Yemen intensified as Egypt and Saudi Arabia openly used their radio services to support efforts of the opposing groups. After the 1962 military coup, the government moved to centralize the mass communication media under a Ministry of Information. The construction of a viable internal radio system that could be used for national development was not possible until the end of the civil war.

Since 1967, the government increasingly realized the importance of radio as a means of communicating with the largely illiterate population. Under the administration of the Ministry of Information in San'a, three radio services, all broadcasting only in Arabic, have been built. Each one took the name of the city from which it originated: Radio San'a, the main North Yemen station, which transmits for 15 hours per day; and Radio Taiz and Radio Hodeida, each of which daily transmits 4 hours of programming (Nyrop et al., 1977, p. 225; *The Middle East and North Africa*, 1980, p. 1,170). North Yemen does have shortwave transmitters that simulcast programs from the domestic service. The government announced that in late 1980 or early 1981 a new 600-kilowatt mediumwave transmitter would be completed and afford better national coverage. Of the three medium-wave transmitters for the three existing radio services, none exceeds 60 kilowatts (Frost, 1980, p. 197).

TELEVISION

The economic and political situation in North Yemen did not provide strong motivation for the government to start a television system until radio facilities were first completed. In the early 1970s, a group of international businessmen, headed by an American, attempted to gain a government concession to operate a commercial television service in San'a. The businessmen, with the backing of an international television equipment manufacturer, were to provide the station itself and to operate it on a commercial basis, with a percentage of income going to the government. However, government changes during the final stages of negotiations prevented the conclusion of the proposed agreement. Also, the North Yemen government realized that although the station would be built at no cost to the government, there would not be total government control over programming.

The government formally opened its PAL color San'a-based television service in September 1975 (*The Middle East and North Africa*, 1980, p. 1,170), making North Yemen the last Arab country to start a television service. Programming is still confined primarily to the evening hours, with most programs imported from other Arab countries, especially from Egypt. To serve the important population centers, since 1975 two more transmitters have been built and linked by microwave to the San'a studios (Frost, 1980, p. 398).

SOUTH YEMEN

SOUTH YEMEN, officially the People's Democratic Republic of Yemen before union with North Yemen, was a country with an estimated population of 1.5 million people within 111,000 square miles bordered by Saudi Arabia, Oman, and North Yemen.

Historically, the country's fortunes were tied to the British, from whom Aden and the surrounding Protectorate of South Arabia secured independence in 1967. In 1839 the British East Indian Company occupied Aden, a port that was an ideal location for coal storage facilities used by ships traveling to and from India. Because of its port, Aden became a thriving trade center between World War II and independence. The area once known as South Yemen is not as agriculturally fortunate as what was North Yemen, although some coffee, cotton, and fruit are grown.

The loss of British prestige in the Middle East after the 1956 Suez War encouraged attempts to force the British to leave the area. Making a choice between the two main rival political organizations, the British handed power to the National Liberation Front (NLF), which became the only recognized political organization in the country. After independence, the government reorganized the country in order to gain more complete control of most commercial activities. In the early 1970s, banks, insurance companies, and many other businesses were nationalized. The South Yemen government became politically close to the People's Republic of China, the Soviet Union, and the East European countries. The country's Marxist attitudes, combined with its geographical location, led to increased isolation. The relationship with the former North Yemen has varied, depending on the political climate of both countries. In 1972 the two countries agreed to unite, with the new country to be named the Yemen Republic. Following armed conflict along the North and South Yemen border in February 1979, the countries renewed their pledge to unite. Whether these two countries, which have had very different political orientations, have been able to create a lasting single political entity remains to be seen.

RADIO

Radio broadcasting in Aden started in May 1954 with the local relaying of the BBC Arabic Service and the Cyprus-based, British-operated Sharq al-Adna. Programming from these stations was broadcast locally via a transmitter rented by the colonial government from the British telecommunications company Cable and Wireless. In August 1954, the Aden Broad casting Service was officially formed as a subsection of the Public Relations and Information Department. With the creation of the new radio service, local Arabic programming of about 2 hours per day replaced the relays. By 1960, the daily program lasted for 10 hours, 3 of which were a relay of the BBC Arabic Service from London.

Studio and transmission facilities were expanded during the 1950s. The original rented Cable and Wireless transmitter was replaced by a 250-watt mediumwave transmitter. In 1957, under a British Colonial Development and Welfare grant, two additional transmitters were purchased and installed—a 5-kilowatt mediumwave transmitter to serve the Colony and a 7.5-kilowatt mediumwave transmitter to reach the Protectorate. All broadcasting was done by the British government, and several BBC personnel were seconded for transmitter maintenance and the training of program production personnel (British Colonial Office, 1960, p. 8).

The British government's interest in providing a local broadcasting service for Aden was the result of an awakening, fueled by Egyptian radio broadcasts, that took place between 1953 and 1956 among both the urban and rural populations of the Colony and Protectorate. The Voice of the Arabs and Radio Cairo programs encouraged the population to join Nasser's Pan-Arab movement, and programs were designed to provoke anti-British feeling. Great Britain's involvement in the 1956 Suez War further motivated those who were planning to force the British to grant independence and leave the area. The Egyptian broadcasts came at an opportune time for residents of South Yemen. The port of Aden allowed free trade, and transistor radios from Japan were abundant; people purchased them with the hope of finding news and entertainment. With no local Arabic broadcasting available, it was only natural to tune to the popular Egyptian services. The British were at a loss to compete with the Egyptian broadcasts that circumvented the British-influenced local media and went directly to the population. In 1956 the British authorities realized the seriousness of the situation and opened a local Arabic station, but it could not compete in coverage with the Voice of the Arabs (Gavin, 1975, p. 333). Another problem was the actual use to which the medium was put by the British.

> The administration could not effectively use the radio to propagate broad and general ideas of political integration. Instead, broadcasting became one of the principal means by which popular sentiment was galvanized against British rule. As radios poured into Aden in a mounting flood throughout the 1950s and 1960s, legitimacy of the British presence was steadily sapped away. (Gavin, 1975, p. 334)

After independence, the government added more radio transmission facilities with the help of the Soviet Union and East European countries. These countries have provided a good deal of the military and civilian aid to South Yemen. South Yemen's radio has not, however, improved technically because the country's economy has not prospered since independence. When the National Liberation Front assumed power upon British departure from Aden, it moved to centralize governmental activities. A 1974 decree established state control of all forms of mass communication, and the Minister of Information was given the power to appoint newspaper editors and broadcasting station managers (Nyrop, 1977, p. 107). The South Yemen government may have been reacting to increased broadcasting efforts from neighboring North Yemeni- and Saudi Arabian-financed clandestine radio. Clandestine broadcasting sought to undermine the government's position much as did Egypt's broadcasts in the 1950s and 1960s, but there is no indication that these neighboring broadcasts had any effect on the general population.

TELEVISION

The idea for the introduction of television in Aden dates from the period in the 1950s when the British authorities realized that Egyptian radio programs were popular and that no effective means of countering them existed. By 1963, the British government had made the preliminary decision that a local television service would be beneficial. The medium, it was apparently reasoned, could provide an attractive alternative to external radio broadcasts. This reasoning was not, of course, unique to Aden. As noted elsewhere in this study, governments have attempted to use television as an alternative to foreign-radio listening, particularly at night. Saudi Arabia is a case in point.

In 1963, the British obtained television channel assignments at the African VHF/UHF Broadcasting Conference held in Geneva (*VHF television assignments obtained for Aden*, n.d.). In 1965, programming started, but coverage was limited to the populated areas surrounding Aden that were served by four low-power transmitters. Programming during the period between initiation and independence consisted of films obtained from U.S. and British television services. Because of limited local production facilities—there were no videotape recorders—Aden-based programming consisted of news in Arabic and English and live interviews. The original equipment, obtained from Great Britain, consisted of Pye and Marconi components (Patel interview, 1980).

After independence, the television service deteriorated because of lack of spare parts and maintenance. The government emphasized radio broadcasting. However, the television service, which interestingly enough accepts commercial advertising, continued to operate a monochrome service. At least one additional low-power transmitter has been added since 1967 (Frost, 1980, p. 398), and the service, still confined to the Aden area, operates a limited early afternoon and evening service.

The differences in the use of mass communication in Yemen and neighboring Oman and Saudi Arabia are due mainly to philosophy and economic constraint. The government decided to emphasize radio and maintain the status quo on television, since the country has limited resources to devote to its broadcasting services. The country's strategic location provided a military advantage for the former Soviet Union and other countries that had negotiated treaties allowing access to Yemen ports and airfields.

The unification of the electronic media of what were North Yemen and South Yemen will continue to be a difficult undertaking, but no less difficult than the unification of the two states' economic and political systems.

Part 3
The
Gulf
States

THE ECONOMIC AND POLITICAL IMPORTANCE
of the Gulf states was generally unrecognized until the
mid-1970s. The term *Arabian Gulf,* or more commonly,
the *Gulf,* is relatively new, having been promoted by
Arab leaders who felt that *Persian Gulf* was primarily a
geographer's term that added credibility to Iran's claim
of influence. Countries that border on the Gulf and
whose people speak Arabic qualify for membership in
the Gulf states' seven-member fraternity: Bahrain, Iraq
(at least until August 1990), Kuwait, Oman, Qatar,
Saudi Arabia, and the United Arab Emirates (U.A.E.).
During the 1970s, these countries emerged as a major
international economic force because of their petroleum
exports. Only two states, Bahrain and Oman, are not
major oil exporters, but they play an important part
politically and economically in the area as a result of
either their strategic location or their involvement with
petroleum shipping and services. Common factors
identified by the states themselves include religion, land,
environment, culture, the Arabic language, history,
mutual interests, and common will (*TV in the Gulf
states*, 1979, p. 3). Of these similarities, Arabic and

Islam are the most important. The states vary greatly in their size, political environment, national priorities, and income.

We in the West have become accustomed to newspaper, magazine, and television pictures of the modern government offices, hotels, schools, airports, and banks in Jidda, Riyadh, Kuwait City, Bahrain, Dubai, and Doha. However, most who see the physical results of wealth do not realize that this is comparatively new. Until the late 1950s, modern capitals such as Riyadh consisted of little more than mud and brick buildings. Modernization in the form of a telecommunications infrastructure, schools, roads, airports, and hospitals either did not exist or was inadequate.

The one country that obviously does not fit politically into the group is Iraq. This is especially true after the August 1990 Iraqi invasion of Kuwait. Nevertheless, Iraq is included in this part because it had been active in efforts by ministers of information of all seven countries to cooperate in various information activities, particularly in the dissemination of information regarding Arab culture. Before the August 1990 invasion of Kuwait, Iraq was a member of what is probably the most visible result of information-cooperation efforts, Gulfvision. Iraq is the only Gulf country that is not governed by a powerful head of state whose family historically ruled or otherwise was recognized as having influence, in the bedouin tradition, over its geographical area.

Prior to the discussion of individual media systems, several factors that are important to broadcasting developments need to be mentioned. As is the case in the other Arab world countries in this study, the Gulf states' electronic media are either directly or indirectly government controlled. Residents of one country have reliable access to the radio and television programming of other countries. The powerful mediumwave radio signals from these countries are usually available in other countries. Because of a phenomenon known as over-the-horizon propagation or "tunneling," normally line-of-sight FM radio and television signals travel long distances over warm salt water during hot, humid summer months. Viewing of television channels and listening to radio stations of Gulf states other than the one in which one resides is apparently a standard practice.

With the possible exception of Iraq, the Gulf states have almost no artistic tradition. Painting, sculpture, and drama were discouraged because many states, most notably Saudi Arabia, were influenced by a traditional interpretation of Islam that forbids reproductions of human forms. Nor did the bedouin culture, which dominated these countries until modern times, encourage artistic development because of constant tribal wanderings.

Except for Iraq, the Gulf states' radio and television systems are operated and maintained mostly by Arabs from Jordan, Lebanon, the Sudan, and Egypt. Most states do not have qualified personnel to undertake sophisticated broadcast equipment maintenance, and local talent is very limited for radio and television program production. Each country has an expatriate community that works with oil, shipping, and other industries. Kuwait and the United Arab Emirates have a population that is only about one-half native-born. The governments directly employ large numbers of nonindigenous Arabs, Pakistanis, and Indians as civil servants. In the case of the ministries of information and subordinate broadcasting organizations, Jordanians, Egyptians, and Palestinians hold some senior government positions and have policy influence as well as day-to-day operational responsibility. Because of the general support for Saddam Hussein by the Gulf Palestinian community, even long-time Palestinian employees of Gulf ministries of information have become at least somewhat suspect. This is, of course, especially true in Kuwait where Palestinians with Jordanian passports have traditionally held high-ranking administrative posts.

Radio and television receivers are available at fairly low prices. Most countries in the Gulf do not feel that they need income from import taxes on consumer goods, including home entertainment systems. Home video recorders have become so common in residences in Kuwait, Saudi Arabia, Qatar, and the U.A.E. that these countries probably constitute the largest home videocassette market in the world. Most of the cassettes available for rent or sale are pirated films and television programs from the United States and Europe. Many tapes of American programs are crudely edited, leaving intact entire commercials and even station identification. Also, residents of the Gulf appear to be enthusiastic listeners to international shortwave and mediumwave radio broadcasts from non-Arab countries.

The ordering of countries in this part is geographical. Starting in the north with Iraq and working down the Gulf, the remaining six countries are Kuwait, Saudi Arabia, Bahrain, Qatar, the United Arab Emirates, and Oman.

CHAPTER 8

IRAQ

FOR SEVERAL HUNDRED YEARS prior to World War I, Iraq was part of the Ottoman Empire. After the war, sections of the country were occupied by Great Britain until it was given a League of Nations mandate to administer Iraq that lasted until 1932. Faisal, brother of Abdullah, the first king of Jordan, was proclaimed King in 1921. Descendants of this Hashemite family maintained a royal house until 1958. During the preceding 26 years, the country underwent various changes that included or were influenced by the death, under suspicious circumstances, of Faisal's son, King Ghazi; political rivalries between pro- and anti-British factions and between communists and supporters of the Ba'ath Party; rebellions by the Kurdish minority; military coups; and religious friction between Shiite and Sunni Moslems.

In July 1958, Abdul Karim Kassem, an army officer, staged a military coup that resulted in the deaths of King Faisal, a second cousin of King Hussein of Jordan, and many other members of the royal family. Killed too was the pro-British Prime Minister, Nuri as-Said. Kassem was but one of a series of leaders who came to power during various military coups after 1958. The political situation was unstable during the 1960s and 1970s, with the power largely vested in the military, which has been influenced by communists and Ba'ath Party philosophy that believes Arabism should pervade all political and economic thinking.

Especially during the 1970s, the country had close relations with the Soviet Union and the East European countries, important Iraqi arms suppliers. Iraq, a major oil-exporting country, started using income from increased oil prices in the 1970s to foster national economic development. After Egypt signed a peace treaty with Israel in 1979, Iraq emerged from relative isolation in the Arab world to take part in the call for the boycott of Egypt. One result, until Iraq invaded Kuwait in August 1990, was better relations with Saudi Arabia and Kuwait, neighbors with whom Iraq has not traditionally had close relations because of land and OPEC price and production quota disputes. Saudi Arabia and Kuwait helped Iraq finance its eight-year war with Iran. Even before the Gulf War, Iraqi president Saddam Hussein's desire to push Iraq into a commanding Arab world leadership role put a strain on Iraq's relations with most other Arab states.

Eighteen million people are estimated to inhabit the country's 167,925 square miles; Iraq shares borders with Syria, Jordan, Saudi Arabia, Kuwait, Iran, and Turkey.

BBC ownership estimates are 4 million radio sets, 1.5 million television receivers, and 500,000 videocassette recorders (British Broadcasting Corporation, 1991b).

ON THE MORNING OF AUGUST 2, 1990, Iraq invaded Kuwait, after claiming that Kuwait had stolen Iraqi oil, that it had not adhered to OPEC production quotas, and that the Kuwaiti royal family was too pro-Western and had squandered the country's wealth. One week after the invasion, Iraq annexed Kuwait as its 19th province. However, the action was formally rejected by the United Nations. On January 16, 1991, 28 nations participated in the U.S.-led invasion of Iraq and Kuwait. This move restored the Kuwaiti royal family, and resulted in the defeat of the Iraqi army. Saddam Hussein's ill-fated attempt to take over Kuwait guaranteed his place in history. In the minds of many in the Arab world as well as in the West, Hussein's name ranks with other tyrants of the 20th century.

RADIO

The first radio station in Iraq started as a government enterprise in either 1935 (UNESCO, 1951, p. 533) or 1936 (*Present-day Iraqi culture*, 1970, p. 12), depending on the source consulted. Radio programming began from a lower-power mediumwave transmitter connected with the Telegraph and Mail General Administration, but administered by a government committee including a representative of the Ministry of Education. However, the government allocated insufficient funds to operate a reliable service and eventually a tax of one-half Iraqi dinar was imposed on the sale of radio receivers to help pay the seven full-time employees (Adwan, n.d., pp. 2–3).

Shortly after the government station began, King Ghazi—who was interested in things technical, thought to be rather odd, and known to be anti-British—started a privately owned station in the royal palace. He apparently operated the station irregularly, depending on his mood. The King was the only announcer and was known for his pro-Nazi broadcasts, including news bulletins supplied by the Germans (McKenzie, 1940, pp. 200–201). The station ceased to exist when Ghazi died under mysterious circumstances in April 1939.

The original government radio service operated until about 1939 for approximately 5 hours per day in Arabic. In 1939, a daily 15-minute program in Kurdish was started for the Kurdish minority located mainly in the northern part of the country. During World War II, radio transmissions were lengthened with the help of British program advisors and technicians. In 1945 the Arabic program contained a limited offering of music, news, poems, and some drama, from 1625 to 2205 hours. The Kurdish program had been expanded from its original 15 minutes to 1 hour between 1525 and 1625 (Adwan, n.d., pp. 6–7).

Between the end of World War II and the 1958 revolution, no major developments occurred in Iraqi radio. The government made little effort to communicate with minorities within the country, except for the Kurds. The pro-Western civilian government and the royal family apparently believed that they had support from the Iraqi citizenry and from other Arab countries as well. The government did not become concerned about hostile broadcasts from other Arab countries until Egypt's Voice of the Arabs started a campaign against Nuri as-Said, then Prime Minister, who was encouraging Arab support for the pro-Western Baghdad Pact.

Baghdad was apparently taken by surprise by the viciousness of the Egyptian radio attacks and did not have the skilled radio personnel to mount an effective counterattack. More importantly, Iraq did not have sufficient transmitter power to cover its own country completely with an Arabic service, much less to reach neighboring Arab countries with a reliable signal. In the mid-1950s as-Said approached the American Ambassador to Iraq with an urgent request that the United States supply high-power medium- and shortwave transmitters. The Prime Minister wanted transmitters "in a matter of days, or a few weeks at the latest," because the country's transmitters were inadequate to match the Egyptian signals. In return for American help—which incidentally was not supplied because of United States State Department bureaucratic inefficiency—Iraq offered to grant the Voice of America use of any American-supplied facilities (Gallman, 1964, pp. 49–50). In addition to the Voice of the Arabs, Egypt also had at least one clandestine station beamed to Iraq that identified itself as Radio Free Iraq. Some observers believe that Egypt's radio propaganda helped inspire the 1958 revolution. This may be true, although the broadcasts alone did not bring about the military coup on July 14, 1958, that dramatically brought an end to the Iraqi royal family.

The Iraqi character, which tends to be unpredictable and occasionally violent, showed itself in connection with the coup. The King, many other members of the royal family, and the Prime Minister were killed. Abdul Karim Kassem, the coup leader, became the head of government until he, in turn, was killed in 1963 in another coup. It seems that Kassem realized the importance of the electronic media to gain popular support internally and to communicate with other Arab countries. He also knew that the Egyptian broadcasts had been well received in Iraq and that his government had to take steps to increase radio transmission power. He turned to the

Soviet Union for several powerful medium- and shortwave transmitters. The new $3.5 million facility was dedicated by Kassem as part of a celebration marking the third anniversary of the 1958 revolution (Schmidt, 1961, p. 7; Adwan, n.d., pp. 11–12). The new transmitters gave Iraq transmission power equal to Egypt's. The Kassem period marks the beginning of present-day Iraq's interest in broadcast dissemination of its political philosophy to the Arab world.

An example of how quickly loyalties can change in the Middle East is the turn of events under Kassem regarding Egypt. Radio broadcasts had been pro-Nasser after the revolution, but when Iraq declined Egypt's invitation to join Syria in the U.A.R., broadcasts turned nasty and violently anti-Nasser. Egypt and Iraq entered into a radio propaganda war more violent than Egypt's had been against the King and Nuri as-Said years before. While many Iraqis undoubtedly admired Kassem for having brought an end to the monarchy, the majority believed that his tenure as national leader brought disgrace and fostered internal corruption. One observer comments on Kassem's use of the media:

> After the 1958 revolution, more publications appeared and cultural activities increased. Radio broadcasts were expanded to 15 hours per day and the programs became revolutionary and anti-imperialist in nature. Yet, this freedom led to confusion and conflict developed between papers and political parties. Kassem closed most of the opposition papers and only left the papers which supported him. He turned radio and television into tools for his government and personality. He selected the announcers who supported him and imprisoned those who disagreed with his policy. Radio and television became devoted to Mr. Kassem. His speeches and other information occupied most of the transmission hours. Only songs which glorified him were telecast and broadcast on radio. During the five years Kassem was in power he used the media extensively for his own purposes. (Adwan, n.d., p. 10)

The political leaders who followed Kassem maintained an interest in radio. The broadcasting complex in Baghdad, which once housed both radio and television studios, was expanded and modernized over the years. The radio studios date from the late 1950s and in the early 1980s appeared to be well maintained. New American Ampex audio tape recorders had been installed, but the audio consoles and other equipment were quite old. There are some production facilities elsewhere in addition to the main radio studios in Baghdad. As the 1990–1991 Gulf crisis showed, Saddam Hussein, who appears to have been clever enough to provide secret bunkers for himself, his family, and his trusted military leaders, apparently anticipated that an attack on his country might start with an attempt to stop his ability to broadcast to both home and neighboring audiences. The majority of production, however, took place in Baghdad under the supervision of the

Ministry of Information, which is responsible for the electronic media.

The main expansion of radio in postrevolutionary Iraq has been in transmitters rather than studio equipment. The political leaders who followed Kassem in the 1960s and 1970s continued to install transmitters to provide better signals both inside the country and to the rest of the Arab world. The external shortwave service used as many as 15 transmitters, located in various parts of the country; of the 6 mediumwave transmitters, 5 were over 100 kilowatts. A 2,000-kilowatt facility located in Babylon was primarily used for the Voice of the Masses Program.

By 1970, Iraq had become more internationally minded and was broadcasting 189 hours per week in Arabic, 70 in Kurdish, 28 each in Turkmanian and Persian, and 7 hours each in Urdu, Turkish, English, German, French, Hebrew, and Russian (Ali interview, 1980).

The basic program schedule in 1980 consisted of the following programs and languages.

Main Program

Iraq's major effort was devoted to the Main Program, which operated for 22 hours per day, from 0200 to 2400. The general tone and approach of this radio service was similar to the main radio service transmitted by most other Arab countries. News times were fixed and there were music programs, drama, interviews, and discussions. A good deal of time was devoted to political discussion, a dominant program type on Iraqi electronic media. News, music, drama, and interviews tended to promote the stand that the government was taking in the Arab world. Changes that took place in the tenor of radio programming since 1978 have been reflected in this important service. Radio broadcasting employees told me that in 1978 the President of Iraq had issued a directive to media officials to dwell less on the "sad" and "negative" aspects of Iraq and to make radio and television programs more entertaining and happy. When asked, the Ministry of Information denied that this had been ordered by the President but did admit that some lightening of program style had occurred. One reason for this change may have been that Iraqi officials believed people were turning to more attractive foreign radio stations.

Voice of the Masses

The Voice of the Masses was broadcast on both shortwave and mediumwave and was intended for both domestic and Arab world consumption. The service, entirely in Arabic, paralleled the 22 hours per day of the Main Program. The schedule was occasionally interrupted to broadcast special programs intended to be heard in other countries such as Egypt. Between 1800 and 2000 hours each evening the Voice of the Masses carried the Palestine Program, which was produced under Iraqi supervision by Palestinians. It was over the Voice of the Masses frequencies that one of the more interesting radio programs in the Arab world, the Voice of Egypt of Arabism, was broadcast. Observers have compared this program with Ahmed Said's style from the Egyptian Voice of the Arabs.

Possibly because of the relative isolation of Iraq prior to the Egyptian-Israeli Peace Treaty in 1979, there had been some clandestine broadcasting from Iraq directed mostly against neighboring countries—Kuwait, Saudi Arabia, Jordan, Syria—with whom at times it did not have good relations. Historically, Iraqi radio services have tended to broadcast rather strong political rhetoric. Occasionally, they have been known to transmit inaccurate information to see what the effect would be. It was as though Iraq were returning to the mid-1960s when violent radio propaganda was used. However, increased sophistication and the availability of radio programs from other countries have enabled Arab radio listeners to check the accuracy of news reports; this has reduced the effect such broadcasts used to have.

On May 27, 1979, the Voice of Egypt of Arabism was first heard over three shortwave and two mediumwave frequencies (Foreign Broadcast Information Service, 1979). The use of two frequencies—1035 kHz 2000 kilowatts (Babylon) and 692 kHz 1200 kilowatts (Basrah)—ensured that the nightly 2-hour program could be heard by the majority of Arabs with a standard radio receiver. The Ministry of Information denied that the program originated from Iraq. The transmission was divided into blocks that featured mini-programs about such subjects as peasant life, Islam, and music. The entire theme of the service was anti-Sadat and listeners reported that the programs were appealing in part because the announcers were Egyptian. Egyptian officials stated that the Iraqi program posed no threat to the stability of Anwar Sadat's government. Taking no chances, however, Egypt jammed this program.

Kurdish and Other Minority Language Programs

The Ministry of Information expanded the amount of time devoted to Kurdish broadcasts during the 1970s. The Kurdish minority has been a serious problem for Iraqi governments, which have alternately fought and signed peace agreements with them. The number of broadcast hours in this language appears to be dependent on the interest that the government has in communicating with Kurdish speakers. In 1980, the daily number of hours was approximately 20 (Ali interview, 1980). Assyrian and Turkmanian languages in Iraq also receive some attention from the radio authority. Programming in each language is transmitted for about 2 hours per day.

Foreign and Beamed Programs

Most of the expansion in the number and duration of foreign languages occurred during the 1970s, although broadcasts in Russian, English, and French date from the 1960s. About 2 hours per day are devoted to programs in French, English, German, Russian, Turkish, Persian, Hebrew, and Swahili. After the Shah left Iran in 1979, more attention was given to the Persian broadcasts because of the increased tension between the two countries and the resultant skirmishes at the border.

Philosophically, increased expansion of radio is consistent with Ba'ath Party policy, which states that all Arabs are "part of one nation both in the cultural and spiritual sense. . . . The different [Arab] countries . . . make up a politically and economically united fatherland" (Shibli-L-A'Ysami, 1977, p. 9).

THE IRAN-IRAQ WAR AND THE GULF CRISIS

Hindsight suggests that Saddam Hussein increased radio studio and transmitter facilities to reach his own people as well as a wider audience in the Arab world to support his August 1990 invasion of Kuwait. While it is true that Iraq used its massive oil revenue for a variety of civilian and military projects, its impressive medium- and shortwave transmitter expansion program during the 1980s is an indication that under the leadership of the Iraqi president, Iraq wanted to become a leading Middle East nation, or at least to sound like one.

For a brief period of time after the August invasion of Kuwait, Iraq jammed incoming radio signals—primarily those from the BBC, VOA, and Saudi Arabia. However, Iraqi Ministry of Information officials soon learned what many East European states and the Soviet Union concluded in the late 1980s: in the electronic world of the information age, a country can never effectively stop incoming radio signals. Those who try do not succeed; the attempt is expensive in terms of both personnel and equipment. Realizing this, Iraq stopped jamming VOA Arabic broadcasts in late September and BBC transmissions in early October 1990. The much joked-about (in the West) Mother of All Battles Radio stopped broadcasting altogether on February 3, 1991, after air attacks silenced virtually all of Iraq's radio transmission capacity (Voice of America, 1991).

Before most of the high-powered radio transmitters were destroyed by the January 1991 air attack on Iraq, the amount of medium- and shortwave transmitter power available to radio programmers in Baghdad was impressive, even by Middle Eastern standards. During the 1980s the French Thomson-CSF firm had installed a 2-megawatt mediumwave facility at Masisan. In 1985, the same firm built the largest shortwave transmitter facility in the world—the Balad site, consisting of 16 shortwave transmitters of 500 kilowatts each (Wood, 1991).

TELEVISION

Iraq was the first Arab country to establish a government-operated television service in the Middle East. As part of a trade fair, the British Pye electronics firm brought television equipment to Baghdad in 1956. The government was impressed with the equipment and purchased the modest studio facilities and low-power transmitter. The service officially started on May 2, 1956. Programming at first was experimental and irregular. Only a few television sets existed in Baghdad at the time and a regular service did not seem feasible. Television assumed importance in Iraq immediately after the July 14, 1958, revolution. Kassem, sensing that television like radio could facilitate social change, ordered an increase in the power of the Baghdad station. In 1959, a new 2-kilowatt transmitter was put into service (Fakery interview, 1980). Between 1958 and 1963, while Kassem was president, some updating of studio equipment took place; but political and economic conditions prevented construction of a countrywide network. Iraq did not, at that time, have national telecommunications relay facilities to distribute the Baghdad signal. Kassem made his mark by developing Iraqi programming rather than by expanding facilities.

Following the revolution, the Kassem regime established a Special Supreme Military Court, or People's Court, presided over by Fadhil Abbas Al-Mahdawi, Kassem's cousin, who possessed no legal qualifications (Penrose and Penrose, 1978, p. 220). Because of the broadcasting of the trials on both radio and television, Mahdawi became well known for his showmanship rather than his juridical leadership. Generally referred to as the Mahdawi Trials, the trials were an outlet for people's feelings against the old regime and served as a substitute for mob action. Khadduri (1969, p. 80) made the following observation about the televised events:

> The proceedings of the court were fully reported in the press and broadcast on radio and television, so that Mahdawi's name was familiar in almost every home and coffee shop. The people watched the trials as if they were watching a theatrical performance. They noted how he arrogantly entered the court at the head of a band of officer-lawyers, taking his seat amid the loud applause of the spectators. He opened each session with a resounding "In the name of God and the People." Before the trial began he always made a speech giving his opinion on the question of the day. He would then make a speech and shower insults on the men at the dock, treating them all as guilty and making no distinction between plaintiffs and defendants. He was often interrupted by one of the spectators, who asked him to recite a poem specially prepared for the occasion, and the recitation was likely to excite some of the spectators who would rise and perform a dabka, a form of folk-dancing, in support of the cause to which the poet had addressed himself.

The Iraqis have not generally been very successful users of the broadcast media. They lack the talent and humor of the Egyptians and the attention to detail often possessed by the Jordanians. Richard Cawston (1963, p. 5) made the following observation after a trip to Iraq in the early 1960s:

> At seven o'clock every evening, there was what is called the Government Program. This consisted of two unshaven army officers arriving at the station at 5 minutes to seven—script in hand. They walked straight into the studio and addressed the camera about anything from politics to personal hygiene for 25 minutes nonstop. The television authorities never had any idea what the officers were going to talk about.

An era in Iraqi political and broadcasting history ended when Kassem was overthrown in 1963. He was killed near the television studios and his body was displayed on live television.

After 1965, the government constructed additional television stations capable of some local production. Stations were opened in two major cities north of Baghdad: one in Kirkuk in 1967 and one in Mosul in 1968. In 1968 a powerful station was opened in Basrah, a southern city located near the border with Kuwait. This station was built during a period when there were hostile Iraqi-Kuwaiti relations because Iraq had claimed Kuwaiti territory during the Kassem regime. The station is received clearly in Kuwait and during the warm summer months as far south as Bahrain. Additional transmitters have been constructed, including one in 1974 to transmit programming mainly in Kurdish.

In the early 1970s a second television channel was started and in 1976 limited color broadcasts using the SECAM system were begun (Fakery interview, 1980). Additional studios capable of color origination were built in the early 1970s in connection with the inauguration of the second channel.

Unlike most other Arab television systems, Iraq's uses relatively little western television programming. The general philosophy of the government since the 1958 revolution has been to downplay things Western and imperialist, despite the fact that Iraq's most notorious leader, Saddam Hussein, relied heavily on the West for food, technology, and military equipment. The country broke diplomatic relations with the United States during the June 1967 war and has not reestablished them. However, some imported programming is shown with subtitles, the need for such programming having increased when the second channel was added.

President Saddam Hussein has provided some thoughts on the role of the Iraqi media:

> Information is one of our revolutionary democratic means for enlightening the people and acting as a surveillant. To function properly, information media

needs great care, not only on the part of those directly responsible for it, but also on the part of all of us. We are required to attend to it but not to spoil it, to guide it and to cooperate with it, to criticize it in case it errs and to provide it with all possible means of power and development so that it can properly play its role in enlightening and acting as a surveillant. (Hussein, 1977, p. 8)

Iraqi television is heavily political—perhaps it would be more accurate to say that it is heavily Saddam Hussein—and devotes a great deal of time to documentaries about the progressive stance taken by the government. Discussions and interviews with party officials and government leaders are presented almost every evening. An example of political programming on television is "Behind the News," a weekly broadcast in the early 1980s that provided, according to television officials, an Iraqi perspective of international situations and news events. Building on the government's then anti–Anwar Sadat theme, the program on January 20, 1980, featured old film footage of Egypt—crowded Cairo, primitive conditions in the countryside, pollution. These conditions, the commentator said, were brought about by the Sadat government.

A new television complex adjacent to the existing television studios in Baghdad was completed in 1981. The main motivation for the modern facility was to provide coverage of the proposed 1982 Iraqi-hosted meeting of the nonaligned countries. However, the Iran-Iraq war necessitated that the meeting be moved from the Middle East. The new facilities did, however, provide the basis for an expanded service, largely used to promote the image of Saddam Hussein as President.

IRAQI ELECTRONIC MEDIA: GULF WAR MOBILIZATION AND PROPAGANDA

Since Saddam Hussein came to power in the late 1980s, Iraq has probably devoted more time and financial resources than any other country in the world to using the electronic media to promote the image of its leader. To say that this effort has been devoted primarily to perpetuating a Saddam Hussein personality cult is a defensible statement. While radio and television are only part of the country's information effort, they are a very important part in this society where illiteracy is high. Hardly a moment is spent on Iraqi electronic media programming on images and words that do not directly deal with some aspect of Hussein or his Ba'ath Socialist Party. As previously mentioned, these are state-run enterprises that do his bidding.

Of course the Iraqi electronic media were ready for the invasion. Once August 2, 1990, arrived, all Iraqi media devoted virtually all airtime to the conflict. The aim was essentially twofold. First, the government wanted to keep morale high at home. Second, Iraq was intent on using radio broadcasts from its powerful medium- and shortwave transmitters—as well as those it captured in Kuwait—to promote its claim to its 19th province, Kuwait. One month after the invasion a writer for the *Wall Street Journal* observed:

> Nightly newscasts have an Iraqi bias so profound that one is left thinking that the United States—not Iraq—is under siege. Newspaper cartoons show camels urinating on U.S. soldiers in the desert. Only a small elite listening to the BBC or Voice of America appears to have any grasp of the gravity of Iraq's situation. (Horwitz, 1990, p. 1)

Horwitz (1991b, December 26) asserts that VOA Arabic broadcasts from studios in Washington, D.C., were made stronger by the U.S. military using modified C-130 aircraft retransmitting the signal.

During the summer of 1991, Hussein continued to use the visual medium as a primary means of communicating with viewers as well as those reporters and diplomats who monitored broadcasting with the aim of gaining information about what Saddam was doing. A great deal of television time was devoted to videotape of the president meeting with various Kurdish and Shiite delegations that had been attracted to the Iraqi capital with the hope of gaining some degree of autonomy. Paul Lewis (1991, p. 1) of the *New York Times* notes that "almost nightly, the President has been shown on television holding meetings with delegations of prominent Shiites from the south of the country."

The utilization of the electronic media by President Hussein or, for that matter, any leader who might succeed him should not be surprising in light of the history of Iraq's infusion of radio and television in politics.

CHAPTER 9

KUWAIT

THE STATE OF KUWAIT is small, comprising 6,880 square miles in the northeastern corner of the Arabian peninsula. It is located between Saudi Arabia and Iraq. Only about one-half of the approximately 1 million inhabitants are native-born Kuwaiti nationals. The resident alien community consists of Britons, Americans, Pakistanis, Indians, and citizens of other Arab countries who work with the oil industry and in service jobs.

In 1899, the ruling Sabah family established a relationship with Great Britain for the purpose of protection and international representation. Kuwait became a British Protectorate in 1914, further strengthening the relationship with Great Britain. The country became independent in June 1961, and in 1963 the government adopted a constitution. By law, the head of state is a member of the Sabah family, which has been a political force since the 1700s.

Kuwait is a major petroleum-exporting country, ranking second in the Arab world to Saudi Arabia. The capital, Kuwait City, features modern buildings and wide, well-planned streets. The country is small and its relatively well-educated, organized Kuwaiti civil servants and businessmen appear able to manage projects that in many other Arab countries would become delayed due to bureaucratic inefficiency. An interesting feature of Kuwait's foreign policy is its financial involvement abroad. The government makes loans and gives financial aid for development projects to other Arab countries and to African nations. Before the August 1990 Iraqi invasion, Kuwait's per capita GNP was among the highest in the world.

The BBC's receiver estimate should be considered pre-invasion: 1.4 million radio sets, 900,000 television receivers, and 420,000 videocassette recorders (British Broadcasting Corporation, 1991b).

RADIO

During World War II, the British operated a low-power radio transmitter in Kuwait. One purpose of the station was to counter Nazi broadcasts in Arabic as well as occasional pro-Nazi transmissions from neighboring Iraq. An official, identifiable Kuwaiti radio station dates from 1961, when Kuwait became independent (Monsour, 1980). Because Kuwait is so small and flat the country has not had the radio coverage problems of larger Arab world nations. A service could be provided to all within the Kuwaiti borders with a single mediumwave radio transmitter of modest power. However, during the 1960s and 1970s, as the country became increasingly wealthy and assumed an important leadership role in the Gulf, the number and power of transmitters rapidly increased. The government wanted to reach a large, regional audience with a Kuwaiti message. The Ministry of Information, under which both broadcast media function, appears to have decided that a state can partially overcome the psychological disadvantage of smallness by having a powerful radio and television service.

Using a variety of FM, mediumwave and shortwave transmitters, Kuwait provided several radio services prior to Iraq's August 1990 invasion.

Main Program

The Main Program is intended for local as well as Arab world consumption. The service features a mixture of news, drama, music, discussions, and educational programming. On mediumwave, the program is transmitted continuously on two frequencies, using one 750-kilowatt and one 1500-kilowatt facility. The latter transmitter on the low end of the mediumwave band renders the program accessible in most parts of the Arab world at night. An even wider reach is made possible by the use of nine shortwave frequencies during the day. This ensures reliable reception in all parts of the Middle East for those with shortwave radios and the motivation to tune to Kuwait.

Second Program

Intended to be an Arabic alternative to the Main Program, the Second Program broadcasts daily. The 6-hour schedule is broadcast by a 200-kilowatt mediumwave and one shortwave transmitter. Programming on the service is similar in format to the Main Program, but it is intended for a local and regional audience rather than a larger Arab world audience.

English Program

The English Program operates on the same medium- and shortwave frequencies as the Second Program. Most of the program time is devoted to music, with occasional news and interview programs. Kuwait is one of many Arab countries that operate an English-language radio service for their own citizens. English is widely spoken in the Arab world, particularly in the Gulf, and many countries apparently believe that such a service lends them prestige.

FM Music

Kuwait's newest service is continuous FM stereo "beautiful" or "background" music, only occasionally interrupted by news. It is apparently quite popular among Kuwaitis. One reason for this is the availability of a variety of multi-wave receivers.

Koran Program

Special radio programs that feature religious discussions and readings from the Koran have become a means of providing religious programs to Moslems as well as a way of reminding citizens and neighbors that Islam is still important. Kuwait's population is mostly Sunni Moslem but a sizable Shiite Moslem population also exists. The Iranian revolution has helped bring an increase in conservative religious activity in the Middle East and this daily program on the same facilities as the English and Second Programs provides a reminder that the modern State of Kuwait is a dedicated Islamic nation.

Persian and Urdu Service

For approximately 2 hours per day, Kuwait broadcasts Persian- and Urdu-language services on medium- and shortwave transmitters. Programming is intended for speakers of these languages who reside in Kuwait and for listeners in Iran and Pakistan.

The radio and television facilities are housed in a modern Ministry of Information building, located in the downtown area of Kuwait City. The formidable structure has become a landmark, one easily located by the invading Iraqis. The radio studios were first used in June 1978, after having been completed by a French company. Fifteen studios, all of which are equipped for stereo recording, contain Schlumberger audio equipment. Because the Ministry of Information was attempting to build for the future, more studios were built than are used, ranging in size from compact booths for news reading to large drama studios with "dead" rooms. The French technicians who installed the equipment have trained engineers in operation and maintenance. Although some Kuwaiti radio operators work with the equipment, the majority of those who work in radio engineering are non-Kuwaitis.[1]

RADIO AUDIENCE

The percentage of foreign-radio listening in Kuwait is high mainly because of the large resident alien population interested in hearing transmissions from home. Data from an April–May 1974 survey commissioned by the United States Information Agency indicated that the BBC's

Arabic Service and Radio Baghdad (Main Program) were almost equally listened to. Of those surveyed, 22.4 percent reported listening to Radio Baghdad during the previous seven days while 22.3 percent said that they had listened to the BBC. The third and fourth most listened-to stations were Egyptian—Radio Cairo (Main Program) and Voice of the Arabs (USIA, 1975a, p. 10). Data provided by Radio Monte Carlo from a February–March 1979 McCann Erickson Middle East Media Study indicate that Radio Monte Carlo Middle East (RMCME) is the most listened-to foreign commercial radio station. Nineteen percent of those surveyed said that they had listened to RMCME during the past seven days. The second and third ranked commercial stations in terms of popularity in the study were Cairo's Middle East Program and Bahrain Radio ("Audience, penetration and listenership," 1979, p. 1).

RADIO AFTER THE IRAQI INVASION

It is not an exaggeration to say that the Iraqi invasion forces took virtually all radio production and control equipment to Iraq before they left Kuwait. An American broadcast engineer who spent several days in Kuwait in the late summer of 1991 reported that virtually all equipment was taken from the Ministry of Information studios in downtown Kuwait. Likewise, all of the medium- and shortwave transmitters and associated buildings from the transmission site near Kuwait City were destroyed by the Iraqis. Ironically, the transmission towers were left standing.

TELEVISION BEFORE THE IRAQI INVASION

The following section is intended to give readers an overview of Kuwaiti television prior to August 2, 1991, the date Iraq invaded Kuwait. It is important to understand how television in this Gulf state developed before describing some of the changes.

Television had an informal beginning when the local RCA television receiver dealer started a low-power American-standard transmitter in Kuwait City in order to promote set sales. At independence in 1961 the Ministry of Information became the television broadcaster and changed the system to the CCIR European standard. In about 1967, residents in the Eastern Province of Saudi Arabia and Bahrain started purchasing dual-standard receivers so that the Kuwaiti channel could be viewed. Until 1970, the only television station serving the Dhahran and Dammam, Saudi Arabia, area had been an Arabian American Oil Company (ARAMCO) station that operated on the American (525-line) standard. It was observed by many

Saudi viewers who were anxious to receive more than the one channel that the Kuwait station could be received in that part of Saudi Arabia during the warm summer months. The availability of Kuwaiti and other channels in the Gulf states has played an important part in television development in the area.

The transmission capability of the Kuwaiti Main Channel his been increased since the 1960s. A separate transmitter, Channel 6, rebroadcasts the Main Channel specifically toward Basrah, Iraq, in order to provide a television presence in a country that threatened in the early 1960s to invade Kuwait.

The expansion of television in Kuwait took place in 1973 as part of the completion of the radio broadcasting complex mentioned earlier. Kuwait started color television transmission in 1974 using the PAL system. When it moved to a new television studio building in 1979, Kuwait started a second color television channel. Prior to the Iraqi invasion, the television studios were impressive. The Kuwaiti facilities were the most modern and extensive in the Arab world until they were surpassed by the new television complex in Riyadh, Saudi Arabia. The equipment, with the exception of a few British Marconi cameras from the old studios, is French-supplied by Thomson-CSF. Some of the equipment, such as bilingual character generators that can produce subtitling in Arabic and English, is specifically designed for Kuwait Television. There are six studios, three for on-air programming such as news and interviews and three larger studios for videotape production. One studio, 800 square meters in size, is spacious enough to accommodate several sets at the same time; it was used for the production of *Iftah Ya Simsim*, the Arabic *Sesame Street* (Chapter 15).

There are no radio or television receiver license fees in Kuwait. The government is wealthy enough to provide radio and television programs for citizens. Commercial advertising is allowed only on the Main Channel for a maximum of 15 minutes per day between programs. The commercials are permitted because the government wishes to endorse the free enterprise system as well as to help viewers make choices about the kind of products they want to buy (Al-Fieli interview, 1980). Television officials do not know the amount of income that the commercials generate. Television advertising in Kuwait is similar to that seen in other Gulf countries where television advertising is allowed. Advertisements promote candy, Japanese watches, automobiles, processed cheese, disposable diapers, and products such as food processors and other small home appliances.

Kuwait Television operates two television channels. The first channel (KTV One), an updated version of the original service started in the 1960s, is considered to be the main program. The second channel started in 1978, preceded by research to determine listener needs and preferences (Ragheb and Haddad, 1979).

Kuwaiti television viewers apparently watch their own channels. The propagation phenomenon that sends television signals long distances does not bring the signal northward as easily as it does southward. While the main Kuwaiti television program is generally available in Bahrain, the Eastern Province of Saudi Arabia, and at times the United Arab Emirates, the signals from these countries do not tend to reach Kuwait. One channel from the Basrah, Iraq, station and another from Iran are easily received in Kuwait; but the political nature of Iraqi television and the rather bland educational and religious programming from Iran since the 1979 revolution do not seem to attract many viewers.

Main Channel (KTV One)

The Main Channel is predominantly in Arabic. Locally produced entertainment programs as well as those imported from other countries are shown. There are two newscasts nightly at 1700 and 2100. Regular daily hours of operation are from 1700 to 2330, but the broadcasting day is occasionally lengthened for special events, during religious holidays, and on Fridays.

Second Channel (KTV Two)

Generally referred to as the cultural service, the second channel might more appropriately be called the foreign cultural service. Although it does feature some Arabic programming, the majority of the offerings are imported from Australia, Great Britain, and the United States. The service daily shows Western cartoon series, some of which have been dubbed into Arabic. Later, programming suitable for children is shown, for example *Big Blue Marble*, *Wild, Wild World of Animals*, and *Bewitched*. From 2000 to 2030 the news in English is featured. From 2030 until about 2300, selected Arabic films and serials for television are scheduled. However, the majority of programs are U.S. and European programs and made-for-television films. Officials are not concerned about the cultural effect of imported programs because they believe that it is up to the viewer to make a choice between what is offered on the two services. They indicate that even if imported programs from the United States and Europe were not offered on Kuwait television, they are available in local cinemas or on videotape for home video systems.

The prevalence of home videotape systems is noted at several points in Part 3. Kuwait's concern about the pervasiveness of tapes is slightly different from that of other Gulf countries. Since independence, public cinemas have been widespread. The country's 11 major movie houses show both Arabic (mostly Egyptian) films and Western films with Arabic subtitles. Many of Kuwait's cinemas are in financial trouble, though, because, according to their owners, television and home videotapes have reduced attendance (*Gulf Mirror*, 1980a, p. 3).

Because Kuwait was well equipped for television production and transmission, relatively few changes took place in the late 1980s. There were, of course, program refinements on both channels, although the second channel continued to show English-language productions exclusively. Because the country could afford to do so, there was a renewed interest in local—or at least Gulf-oriented—productions. Yet, the Ministry of Information was fully aware that it faced stiff competition from the home video market.

TELEVISION AFTER THE INVASION

The status of television facilities in Kuwait after the American-led invasion in 1991 is easily summarized: the Iraqis took virtually all of the production equipment, but left the transmitters. The existing transmitters were important because they rebroadcast Iraqi television from microwave feeds.

While Iraq occupied Kuwait it moved most valuable equipment from banks, hospitals, offices, and schools to Iraq—television was no exception. As previously mentioned, Kuwait's television facilities were well equipped with technology that Iraq could use in Baghdad. The Iraqis also took television scenery, costumes, and props. A particularly significant loss was sets, costumes, and even the puppets from *Iftah Ya Simsim* (see Chapter 15). The Iraqis took Melsoun (a parrot) and Noaman, the popular life-sized Big Bird–like character (roughly a cross between a camel and bear) who was a favorite of children throughout the Arab world (King, 1991).

Via a temporary low-power transmitter installed after the multinational force ejected Iraq from Kuwait in early 1991, Kuwait has been operating a temporary service that features a very limited amount of local news and a great deal of Egyptian satellite-provided programming. In September 1991 a ranking Ministry of Information official told a visiting American broadcast engineer that the country's number one priority was getting television back on the air.

Of the countries in the Gulf, Kuwait had the most developed radio and television system until the Iraqi invasion. The country is small enough readily to achieve complete signal coverage; the broadcasting complex built in the late 1970s provided adequate facilities. The country is at an interesting point in the development of the electronic media. Since the system was completely destroyed as a result of the invasion, it can now reconsider what type of system it wants.

CHAPTER 10

SAUDI ARABIA

SAUDI ARABIA shares with what was known until May 1990 as North Yemen the rare distinction of never having been colonized or otherwise dominated by a foreign power. Even the Ottomans could not occupy the whole of Arabia on a continuous basis. The area's modern history began when Abdul Aziz ibn Saud captured the old walled city of Riyadh from the Rashid family in 1902; over the next 30 years, his sons and followers conquered various sections of the country, which occupies most of the Arabian Peninsula and borders on Jordan, Iraq, Kuwait, Qatar, the United Arab Emirates, Oman, and Yemen. In 1932 that land was proclaimed Saudi Arabia.

The two factors that have most influenced Saudi Arabian society are religion and oil. The kingdom is the most conservative of all Arab countries, adhering to the basic beliefs of a Sunni Islamic sect that follows the teachings of Mohammed Abd-al-Wahhab. The consumption of alcoholic drinks is illegal and public cinemas are not allowed; the country's legal system follows closely the teachings of the Koran. In the 1930s, oil was discovered in the Eastern Province, but almost no revenue was realized by the government until after World War II. Income then increased steadily, during the 1950s and 1960s, but not until the rapid increases in OPEC oil prices after the 1973 Middle East War did the country accumulate enormous wealth and put into effect its remarkably energetic development plan. An important supplier of oil to the United States, Europe, and Japan, Saudi Arabia is the largest oil exporter of the Arab countries. Estimates of its population, between 6 and 8 million, have remained approximately the same since the 1970s.

The British Broadcasting Corporation estimates that there are 4.5 million radio sets, 3.25 million television receivers, and 2 million videocassette recorders in the kingdom (British Broadcasting Corporation, 1991b).

IT WAS THE IRAQI INVASION of Kuwait on August 2, 1990, that placed the Saudi desert kingdom firmly in the minds of those in the West and much of the rest of the world. With the possibility of Iraq's invasion of the Saudi Eastern Province, the U.S. government proposed a multinational force composed primarily of American, British, French, and Egyptian troops. Subsequent Operations Desert Shield and Desert Storm gave the world a comprehensive view of the religion, culture, and character of Saudi citizens. Those paying attention also were witness to some of the activities of the government-run broadcasting services.

PRE-BROADCASTING DEVELOPMENTS

Before discussing the contemporary development of the electronic media in Saudi Arabia, some background information is necessary. By the mid-1920s, the followers of ibn Saud had captured the Hijaz, the Western Province, which contains the holy cities of Mecca and Medina: its former ruler, Sharif Hussein of Mecca, was expelled. (His sons Abdullah and Faisal were to become the kings of Jordan and Iraq respectively.) That part of the peninsula had been heavily influenced by Westerners, and the Turks, who had had nominal control over the area until World War I, had left behind Telefunken wireless stations and a telephone line between Jidda and Mecca (Philby, 1952, p. 173). The king realized that he would need the help of wire and wireless communication facilities in order to rule effectively over such a vast, sparsely populated country: he purchased and installed a network of transmitters in various cities in the kingdom and also ac-quired—from his friend the British Marconi agent H. St. John Philby, Arabist and historian—portable transmitters that would accompany him when he traveled (Williams, 1933, p. 248; Philby 1955, p. 316). But he realized at the same time that he and those who followed him would need to strike a delicate balance between modernization and Islam, for the Wahhabi religious supporters of his family—especially the *ulema,* the religious leaders—were grimly opposed to the Western gadgetry that would almost surely change the traditional bedouin ways of the area. Their objections to wireless communication were more absolute even than their objections to automobiles and telephones. Being unable to see the manner of its working, they had to suspect that it was literally the work of the devil (Philby, 1955, p. 316). Ibn Saud's way of proving that it was not was characteristic of him: he devised an "experiment" to satisfy them. He asked a group of *ulema* to travel to Mecca, where they were to await a wireless transmission from his headquarters in Riyadh. At the appointed time he had passages from the Koran read to them over the system and then had the men in Mecca read sections of the Holy Book to others of their sect with him back in Riyadh. He then reportedly observed in the presence of the religious leaders that, as the devil could not pronounce the word of the Koran, the "miracle" they had just witnessed had to be the work of man and nature rather than the devil (Eddy, 1963, p. 258; Benoist-Mechin, 1958, p. 205; Nadir, 1971; Walpole et al., 1971, p. 182). Although music and photography continued to be forbidden for the time being, opposition to wireless communication ceased. In 1927, its future was sanctioned by an official *fatwa,* or legal opinion, in which the religious leaders decided not to rule on the legality of radio technology: "We abstain from answering the question and without knowing about science we will not discuss it from the viewpoint of the teachings of God and His Prophet" (Nallino, 1939, p. 119). Television, however, was to be another matter.

RADIO BROADCASTING BEFORE 1960

It is said that very early ibn Saud occasionally listened to Arabic-language radio broadcasts from Europe and that he had transcripts made of them in the late 1930s and during World War II. But there had been no such early need for a radio broadcasting service in Saudi Arabia, as in Egypt, Lebanon, and Iraq. No foreign power was at the time influencing government decisions. The king ruled the country with an ongoing system of interpersonal communication, visiting the various tribes on a regular basis and often inviting tribal leaders to meet with him when he traveled to the kingdom's major cities. But by the end of World War II, when he was showing signs of age and had begun to give some administrative responsibilities to trusted advisors and to those of his sons who might potentially come to the throne, he may have reasoned that when he became older and found it difficult to travel extensively, radio could be a substitute for his visits. Also, Saudi citizens started acquiring radios after World War II, and they listened to Arabic programs on foreign stations in order to get news and other programming. The Minister of Finance arranged in May 1949 for International Telegraph and Telephone, Inc., to build a mediumwave transmitter and studio in Jidda, and ibn Saud put his son Faisal, later crown prince and king, in charge of the station ("Saudi Arabian broadcasting," 1980, p. 2). Service was at first restricted to 5 hours per day—2 hours in the morning, and two 90-minute periods in the afternoon and evening; neither women's voices nor music (military marches excepted) was allowed on the air. Most of the broadcasting time was devoted to religious programming, including some broadcasts that originated from Mecca ("Saudi Arabian broadcasting," 1980, p. 2).

The original 3-kilowatt transmitter in Jidda was soon replaced by a 50-kilowatt RCA facility and the hours of programming were expanded; Faisal was influential in 1953 in establishing the first identifiable office within the government to handle broadcasting and information activities—the Directorate General of Broadcasting, Press, and Publications—an organization later given the status of a Ministry of Information. But no other major broadcasting developments took place in Saudi Arabia in the 1950s, though the number of Saudi radio receivers increased because of growing affluence and the new availability of electricity. Smaller, more reliable battery-operated transistor sets also appeared on the market and, as was the case in many other Arab countries, coffeehouse owners acquired radios to attract customers. As the decade ended, the radio service was still restricted to the Western Province and operated for only a limited number of hours per day. Listeners interested in news events tuned to the BBC; those more interested in entertainment, especially popular Arab music, tuned to one of the Egyptian radio services. And when, in the late 1950s, the Egyptian services (most notably the "Voice of the Arabs") started attacking the Saudi royal family and suggesting revolution, the government was initially powerless to counter them. The popular Egyptian radio services, which were only to grow more hostile during the 1960s, were therefore probably the single factor most responsible for the expansion that took place in Saudi Arabian radio in that decade. The kingdom could not defend itself against radio attacks without adequate transmitting facilities.

RADIO BROADCASTING, 1960s

Primarily because of increased listening to foreign broadcasts, the government announced in 1957 that it would build a station in Riyadh ("Battling radios vie," 1957, p. 48). The first Saudi radio station outside the Western Province, the Riyadh Domestic Service, was on the air about 16 hours per day (Walpole, 1971, p. 183). Then in the early 1960s construction started on a new broadcasting studio complex in Jidda: its service was to be known as Radio Mecca even though it did not originate from there, and it operated for about 17 hours per day. In 1965, these two domestic radio services were operating quite separately, 500 miles apart, with no means existing—other than the low-quality radio-telephone link that was used for special announcements or speeches by the king—to connect them. They reached only their respective cities and the surrounding towns: national coverage was not yet a reality. Indeed, the only radio broadcasting in the large oil-rich Eastern Province was done by ARAMCO, the American company later acquired by the Saudi government. Not until the late 1960s did the Ministry of Information inaugurate a mediumwave transmitter, in Dammam, to serve the eastern portion of the country. But it had been announced in 1964 that a series of 1-kilowatt transmitters would be built in major Saudi Arabian cities to rebroadcast the Mecca service, and plans for a series of shortwave transmitters had been commissioned: construction had begun in Riyadh in the middle 1960s on a 1200-kilowatt mediumwave super-power station originally meant to broadcast a "Voice of Islam" program to compete with the anti-Saudi Egyptian radio services. The last plan was frustrated by failure of the French-built transmitter to operate as designed until it was refitted in the early 1970s—by which time, after Nasser and King Faisal had met in the wake of the 1967 war and reached agreement over the chief source of friction during the 1960s, the civil war in Yemen, the need to counter Egyptian broadcasts had diminished.

As the 1960s ended, the fact that the kingdom was no longer under constant radio attack by other countries gave planners an opportunity to review the future of radio broadcasting in Saudi Arabia. During this period, a plan was conceived to provide a strong signal to the sparsely populated northern portion of the country and to reach countries such as Egypt, Lebanon, Iraq, and Jordan (Kingdom of Saudi Arabia Central Planning Organization, 1970, p. 140). All major government offices except for the Ministry of Foreign Affairs, which has traditionally been located in Jidda, were moved to Riyadh: the Ministry of Information was relocated in 1967, and plans were consolidated to centralize radio administration and most production and transmission there as well. The U.S. Army Corps of Engineers, which had built the initial television facilities in the kingdom, was asked to supervise the design and construction of the new central radio studio and administration building: that project was completed in 1972 and became operational in 1974. The chief problem of the period was that the Ministry of Information had grown dramatically and it was hard to find enough qualified Saudis to fill the major management positions in expanding radio and television services. In Saudi Arabia those positions were reserved for natives of the country—as was not true in Gulf states such as the United Arab Emirates—though it had always been the practice to use non-Saudis to do equipment installation, maintenance, announcing, and program production. All too often, those who assumed administrative responsibilities had no previous media experience, although many had been university educated.

RADIO BROADCASTING, 1970s

The October 1973 Middle East War had a great effect on Saudi Arabia and consequently on its radio system. Though not directly involved in the armed conflict between Egypt, Syria, and Israel, the kingdom for a time joined other Arab countries in stopping shipments of oil to the West, quadrupling the price upon resumption of shipping. Saudi Arabia found itself with more oil income than it could absorb—and a new international role. The increased income was earmarked for an energetic development plan that included additional high-powered radio transmitters able to reach other countries: Ministry of Information planners reasoned that Saudi Arabia's pro-West orientation and moderate stands on increases in OPEC oil prices would necessitate a particularly strong external radio service, one able to defend the kingdom's political, religious, and economic policies to its neighbors.

In the mid-1970s, the completion of a Saudi national telecommunications system made reliable networking possible. Originally planned in the late 1960s, the project was delayed because of its expense and the Ministry of Communication's indecision as to what kind of technology should be used. After an International Telecommunication Union study, the decision was made to utilize a combination of underground cable and microwave links. The desire to distribute radio and television signals was only a small part of the motivation behind the construction of the system, which was designed also to be used for military and commercial telephone communication within the country; but with the networking capability it supplied, the Jidda and Riyadh radio studios would be able to feed to any combination of medium- and shortwave transmitters and thus at last provide a national service. Moreover, the country had lacked sufficient high-power mediumwave transmitters capable of reaching neighboring countries during the day as well as at night: with the increased oil income following the 1973 Middle East War, Saudi Arabia could afford to purchase, at a price of $4–$5 million each, super-power mediumwave transmitters to do that job. As part of what had first been conceived as the Northern Stations Project, the Ministry of Information purchased from Continental Electronics one 1000-kilowatt and three 2000-kilowatt mediumwave transmitters, to be located at two sites (Continental Electronics, 1979) and linked to the Riyadh and Jidda studios to transmit the General Program. In addition, Continental installed one 2000-kilowatt and one 1000-kilowatt transmitter in Jidda and another 2000-kilowatt transmitter in Dammam. In 1980 a super-power facility was planned for Jizan in the southern part of the country. With all this transmitter construction completed, Saudi Arabia may have the most powerful mediumwave transmitter system in the Arab world. Between 1979 and 1981, 12,000 kilowatts of mediumwave transmission power were added to a country that at one point not very long before had not had the ability to reach its own population with a radio signal: it can now be heard reliably throughout the Arab world, except in the North African countries. For a time, radio services expanded ahead of studio space, but a new addition in Riyadh built by the Corps of Engineers added studios and thus helped solve this problem.

RADIO SERVICES

Dependent on announcers and producers from other Arab countries, Saudi Arabia can claim relatively little that is uniquely Saudi about its programming: Egyptian, Jordanian, and Lebanese personnel particularly have had a major influence on programming style and format, and some of the recorded music and drama broadcast in Saudi Arabia was taped in other Arab countries prior to the time when the kingdom built adequate studios for its own productions. By the early 1960s, the initial restrictions on music were gradually changed, one reason being that popular songs could easily be heard on the Egyptian radio services. Religious leaders did object to the introduction of female announcers on the Jidda-based radio service in 1963—but King Faisal reportedly told the protesting *ulema,* "You'd better get used to women's voices on the radio, because you'll be seeing their faces on television soon" (Holden, 1966, p. 117). The first part of this prediction was fulfilled by the late 1960s when women's voices became a daily part of Saudi radio programming.

The following discussion covers the Saudi Arabian radio services as they operated in 1990.

General Program

The General Program is transmitted for 20 hours per day on the powerful mediumwave transmitters, and at various times during the scheduled broadcasting period over 12 shortwave transmitters. It originates from the studios in Riyadh and Jidda with a certain number of hours going out from each location each day. Intended to be the country's main domestic and international Arabic radio voice, the General Program is structured so that special programs appropriate for military personnel, children, women, students, and housewives are aired at appropriate times.

Much of the religious programming offered on the General Program is supplied by another radio service that, originating from the holy city of Mecca, is heard on the frequencies of the interrupted General Program, at the times of the daily prayers. Besides the calls for prayer from the Mecca Mosque, this service—called "The Voice of Islam" like the anti-Egyptian Riyadh service of the previous decade—broadcasts news and features about Islam. In 1980, plans called for it to become independent from the General Program and to assume, with its Islamic religious character, a separate existence.

Holy Koran Broadcast

The Holy Koran service traces its origins to 1972 and is actually two separate services, one from Riyadh, the other from Mecca, transmitting on both mediumwave and shortwave. Designed for listeners in Arab, Asian, and African Islamic countries, the Riyadh service lasts for 18 hours per day, 0600 to 2400. The Mecca service broadcasts from 0600 to 1200, and then from 1600 to 2400; it does most of the shortwave broadcasting, on six frequencies. The Holy Koran Broadcast appears to differ from the Voice of Islam in that the latter is more oriented toward news and information about the Islamic world while the former is designed rather to broadcast serious religious discussion and lectures, as well as readings from the Koran.

International Foreign-Language Programs

Saudi Arabia's external language services are beamed primarily to Islamic countries. Two of the services, the Indonesian and Urdu, were started as early as 1949 and were transmitted for a short time each day on the facilities constructed for international telegraph traffic. The original enthusiasm for this kind of broadcasting did not continue because of limited facilities and the higher priority given to the establishment of a domestic service in the 1950s and 1960s. Essentially a product of the 1970s, then, the language services feature religious subjects and some information about Saudi Arabia as an international economic entity.

European Service

In January 1965 the Ministry of Information began an English service in Jidda in the hope both of reaching the large foreign community there and of communicating Saudi news, views, and other information to diplomatic missions that might not (it thought) have personnel to translate the daily Saudi newspapers from the Arabic. For the first two years of the service, the staff consisted of two full-time British ex-BBC announcers and one full-time American announcer[1]; special programs were taped on a weekly basis by native English-speakers who were employed part time. The hours of the service have fluctuated, depending on availability of transmission time and programming personnel. During the first five years, there were two 1-hour transmissions, one in early morning and one in early afternoon; the evening program lasted for 3.5 hours. On Friday, the afternoon transmission was lengthened to include a program of popular Western music for people at the Red Sea beach, introduced with patter by a popular Saudi Arabian disc jockey. Between 1966 and 1968 the Jidda service was broadcast simultaneously from Riyadh, using the radio link supplied by the telephone authority: the link was of poor quality, a fact that discouraged listening in Riyadh, and the rebroadcast was discontinued when a separate Riyadh-based English service was started. In 1980, that Riyadh service broadcast from 1400 to 1600 and 2100 to 0100 daily; the Jidda English service included an afternoon and evening transmission for a total of 4 hours per day.

The Jidda French service, which began in 1965, has not received much attention because French is not an important language in Saudi Arabia. The kingdom has good relations with France, however, and appears interested in continuing the service locally for public relations purposes.

Although intended mainly for listeners within the kingdom, at specific times the English and French services are broadcast on shortwave for listeners in the rest of the Middle East and in Europe.

After construction of the basic studio and transmitter infrastructure for Saudi Arabian radio was completed, few changes, mostly related to programming, have been made. Those that have taken place are part of the normal programming adjustments that are made to meet the needs of the audiences or governmental information goals. However, there has been one development that seems to have had an impact on Saudi radio listeners, especially the young.

As part of the infusion of military personnel into Saudi Arabia after the Iraqi invasion of Kuwait in August 1990, the British and U.S. military secured permission to operate FM radio stations to entertain and inform troops in central and eastern Saudi Arabia. Both the British and Americans have had a policy since World War II of providing troops with entertainment and news from "back home." For U.S. troops, the Armed Forces Radio and Television Service (AFRTS) operated several stations under the generic title: "Desert Shield Radio." Beginning in late October 1990 one station came on the air in Riyadh and several in the Eastern Province. I monitored several of these stations for a week in late December 1990 and early January 1991.

In Dhahran, for example, a station operated on 99.9 MHz with the on-air call: "This is your oasis station, FM 99.9 on the Desert Shield Network." In Riyadh the FM station could be heard on 107 MHz. Much of the programming came via satellite from the Los Angeles studios of AFRTS. Music oriented, with public service announcements for military personnel in Saudi Arabia, "AP Radio News on the Hour," sports, and some local DJ-type programs, the stations seem to have been popular with some Saudis. Although no audience figures are available, from discussions with a number of Saudis and from listening to the Western music coming from car radios and shops, it seems that the popular music stereo service was a change from either the conservative-oriented government radio or the numerous medium- and shortwave radio services available from neighboring or Western states.

In the Eastern Province, the British operated an FM station on 103.5. Known as British Forces Broadcasting Service (BFBS)—and similar to the service provided to British troops stationed in Germany—this was a satellite relay of BBC World Service news and information from BFBS London.

TELEVISION BEFORE 1970

Although relatively late in establishing a government-operated television service, Saudi Arabia is the location of the second television station in the Arab world.[2] On June 17, 1955, station AJL-TV went on the air in Dhahran on the Arabian Gulf (*USAFE television story,* 1955, p. 3). It was operated by the U.S. Air Force and was intended to provide entertainment for the American personnel stationed at Dhahran Air Force Base, then a Strategic Air Command facility: some local production was done by base personnel, but programming came mostly from American networks. Another station, operating on the same American 525-line system as the Air Force station, opened in September 1957 on the Dhahran ARAMCO compound ("Aramco tv on," 1963, p. 6). Station HZ-22-TV, which still broadcasts (see Censorship), telecast American programs and some locally produced Arabic-language productions. Until the station became an entirely English-language operation after the government opened its own television station in the Eastern Province, all English programs were dubbed into Arabic: the Arabic sound was transmitted with the picture, and the English sound was provided by FM radio. ARAMCO's American employees, for whom the service was originally started, used a standard American television set with an FM radio tuned to an ARAMCO FM radio frequency—but in those early days few Saudis had sets.

The Saudi government had several reasons for announcing in late 1963 that it would build a national television system. First, it needed to provide the population with an innovation that was at least symbolically modern. Despite the fact that the Wahhabis had interpreted sections of the Koran to mean that any kind of cinematic art was a form of idolatry, wealthier Saudis had by that time traveled to Lebanon and Egypt and had become enamored of television. National television, it was reasoned, would at least give the government some control over the kind of news, developmental, and entertainment programming that was provided to Saudis at home. The second reason for the introduction of television was the preoccupation of the Ministry of Information with hostile broadcasts from Egypt's radio stations: a television service operating during evening hours would provide an attractive alternative to Radio Cairo and the Voice of the Arabs, which were thought to be widely heard in Saudi Arabia at night. Third, the government counted on using television for educational purposes—to help with basic health and literacy training as well as to support classroom teaching. Finally, television would help provide a sense of national unity not before possible, a unity also being promoted at the time by increasing numbers of inter-province domestic airline flights and new telephone and telex systems. No longer would the Eastern Province be isolated from the capital and the cities near the Red Sea.

Television was and is still organized in a manner almost identical to radio. It is operated by the Ministry of Information, and funding is provided by the government and commercial advertising on both channels: there is no license fee. For the first eight years, the United States was deeply involved in television planning and operation in the kingdom. The American connection started when then Crown Prince Faisal, who later became king, made a visit to American Ambassador Parker T. Hart: he asked for American help in "solving the problem of contracting for a reliable television system" (Hart communication, 1970), believing that the United States could build stations for him quickly, bypassing the Saudi Arabian commercial firms that could be expected to slow the introduction of television and increase the cost of the project. Ambassador Hart passed the request for help to the State Department, which in turn contacted the Federal Communications Commission (FCC). Edward W. Allen, then the FCC's chief engineer, came to Saudi Arabia, and after visiting various locations wrote a report (Allen, 1963) that served as a blueprint for television facilities construction throughout the 1960s. The implementation of the Allen Report became the responsibility of the U.S. Army Corps of Engineers (COE), whose efficiency in constructing the Dhahran airport facility and several small projects involving the Saudi Arabian military had impressed the Saudi government. Their responsibility was formally defined in an agreement signed in January 1964 by Ambassador Hart and Omar Sakkaf, Saudi Deputy Minister of Foreign Affairs (U.S. Department of State, 1964, pp. 1,864–75).

The Corps of Engineers hired an American firm to construct two buildings, one in Riyadh and one in Jidda, to house the studios and equipment. Contracts were awarded to RCA to supply the equipment; another contract went to the National Broadcasting Company International (NBCI) for the operation and maintenance of the stations. American television engineers and production specialists were stationed in each. Test transmissions started at both stations early in the summer of 1965: on July 17, 1965, the date generally accepted as the formal beginning of Saudi Arabian television, both stations officially went on the air (Watson, 1965, p. 1).

OPPOSITION TO TELEVISION

It is unlikely that the full story of the opposition to television from conservative religious elements in Riyadh will ever be known. What is certain is the profound and far-reaching effect that one incident had on the country many years later.

Interestingly, the Saudi religious establishment had not objected to the early American Air Force and ARAMCO broadcasts in the Eastern Province, just as it had given only minor opposition to early programming on the first radio station in Jidda in the Western Province. Those two areas had been more exposed to the outside world, specifically to the West—the American oil companies having been present there since the 1930s—than had the central area of the country, the more religiously conservative Nejd. But essentially the same religious leaders who had opposed radio broadcasting opposed television, and television was a more serious problem because of its visual element. Even still photography had been unacceptable to the *ulema* until the early 1960s, when ibn Saud had exercised his own masterful brand of rationalization on the point:

> He summoned his detractors and convened the *'ulema* . . . and put forth questions: Painting and sculpture are idolatry, but is light good or bad? The judges pondered and replied that light is good; Allah put the sun in the heavens to light man's path. Then asked the King, is a shadow good or bad? There was nothing in the Qur'an about this, but the judges deduced and ruled that shadows are good, because they are inherent in light, and even a holy man casts a shadow. Very well then, said the King, then photography is good because it is nothing but a combination of light and shade, depicting Allah's creatures but leaving them unchanged. The battle was won in the King's characteristic way, by persuasion and not by force. (Eddy, 1963, p. 258)

Saudi Arabia was changing only slowly, however, and television continued to be seen both by theologians and by radical religious zealots as blasphemous: moreover, it was potentially corrupting in their eyes as yet another Western influence. In the summer of 1965 during the test transmission period in Riyadh, a conservative royal family member named Khalid ibn Musad gathered supporters for a march on the television station, intending to destroy its tower and transmitting equipment. What happened next is still a matter of speculation. Several sources reported that the transmitter had been destroyed: this was not true. When police dispersed the crowd, Khalid returned to his house—where he was shot and killed during a struggle with an official of the Ministry of the Interior.[3] Though Khalid's immediate family appealed to King Faisal to punish the person who shot him, Faisal ruled that the policeman had acted appropriately, and his identity was never officially disclosed.

But the incident was not really over. Almost ten years later, Faisal ibn Musad, Khalid's younger brother, shot and killed King Faisal while he was receiving guests in Riyadh: *Newsweek* ("The murder of," 1975) reported that after the shooting Faisal ibn Musad shouted, "Now my brother is avenged" (pp. 21–23). King Faisal's death came when his leadership was badly needed in the kingdom. He was a moderate who had attempted to balance social progress with the constraints imposed by conservative Islamic beliefs, and it is one of history's ironies that he was thus killed over an incident involving television—a medium he had supported and helped to develop.

TELEVISION EXPANSION

In 1967, two years after the opening of the Jidda and Riyadh stations, a second television project was completed by the COE: a series of microwave relays was built to send the Jidda station signal to transmitters in Mecca and the adjacent city of Taif, the government's official summer residence. (No additional programming facilities were needed in Mecca and Taif, as all transmissions were still to originate at the Jidda station.) In that same year an operation called the "Training Transmitter Project" was also completed—one that the COE and RCA undertook only reluctantly. The innocuous name of the project notwithstanding, its four transmitters in a building near the Jidda television station were, in fact, intended by the Ministry of Information to jam Egyptian television signals, broadcasting on the same channels as the Egyptian channels most likely to "tunnel" across the Red Sea. The importance of this project to the government can only be understood within the context of the anti-Saudi Egyptian radio propaganda that was so virulent prior to the 1967 Middle East War; and indeed by the time the transmitters were operational, improved relations between Saudi Arabia and Egypt had made them—like the Riyadh "Voice of Islam" radio transmitter—unnecessary. As television signals from Egypt did not reach Jidda until the mid-1980s, there was no opportunity even to test the system. Eventually the transmitters were used either for genuine training purposes or for standby facilities.

In early 1968, two more television stations came on the air. Designed for limited local production only, these stations in Medina, north of Jidda, the second most holy city in the kingdom, and Qassim, a conservative Islamic area northwest of Riyadh, were smaller than the Jidda and Riyadh facilities—though they contained living quarters for the foreign engineers who were needed to operate them. The Jidda and Riyadh stations supplied more of the programming on videotape and film until they were connected to the national television network for direct rebroadcast in the 1970s: RCA and National Broadcasting Company International (NBCI) built and operated the new stations.

The final Saudi television project involving the U.S. Corps of Engineers was the construction of a powerful television station in Dammam in the Eastern Province: the good working relationship that the COE had with the Ministry of Information soured when the station became operational. The Saudi government had placed a high priority on the completion of the Dammam station: neighboring countries were building stations that might reach the Eastern Province. A Kuwait station was already available there during the warm months; and Saudi Arabia, which had traditionally had a friendly rivalry with Kuwait, wanted especially to make a similar showing in that neighboring oil-rich state. ARAMCO, moreover, was tired of providing the sole television service in the area and of trying to find programming that both its own employees and its Arab hosts would find enjoyable and appropriate. With uncharacteristic speed, then, a letter of credit for the $3.25 million needed for the construction of the station moved through the kingdom's financial bureaucracy to the Chase Manhattan Bank in New York and to the U.S. Treasury Department. The Minister of Information also approved the use of RCA as the prime supplier of equipment, despite the fact that the company was on the Arab League boycott list: the Ministry assumed that no violation of the boycott agreement had occurred inasmuch as the RCA Dammam contract was not a new one but rather was written as an amendment to an older, pre-boycott contract. RCA supplied two 12.5-kilowatt transmitters, designed to operate in parallel and to feed an antenna mounted atop a 1,200-foot guyed tower. The effective radiated power of the station at that time was possibly the highest in the world (Radio Corporation of America, 1969, p. 1). But apparently RCA had misinformed the Corps, or the Corps of Engineers had misunderstood some of the technical advice provided by RCA—and its transmissions did not reach Kuwait. The government was furious, and with the cooling of relations between the COE and the Ministry of Information, the Corps stopped contract work on broadcasting in the kingdom. Furthermore, by 1971, the COE had numerous contracts with the Ministry of Defense and Aviation, its original Saudi employer, and had lost interest in the other (and always secondary) type of work that it had found in Saudi Arabia. Ultimately, the Corps of Engineers' involvement in the kingdom had far-reaching consequences and brought the United States and Saudi Arabia closer together. It was the COE that designed and supervised the construction of the large military installations in the kingdom that later accommodated the multinational force assembled in the kingdom following the Iraqi invasion of Kuwait in August 1990.

TELEVISION, 1970s

Considerable changes had taken place in Saudi Arabian television by the mid-1970s. After a decade of experience with television, the Ministry of Information felt more comfortable with the medium. Under the supervision of the Corps of Engineers, a small number of Saudi television employees had been sent to the United States for training in all facets of television: production courses, English-language training, graduate work in broadcasting, and electrical engineering.

In 1969, NBCI had lost a competitive bid to AVCO, an American corporation then owning broadcasting stations, for the operation and maintenance of the kingdom's television stations: AVCO, which had underbid NBCI in order to get a start in Saudi Arabia, was to contract directly with the government after the Corps of Engineers withdrew from television there. But most notably, by 1974 the entire television system was Saudi managed: a local Saudi company, BETA, had taken over the AVCO contract. In 1980 BETA still had the operations and maintenance contract with the Ministry of Information—though the technicians and engineers who worked for the company were virtually all non-Saudi Arabs. European personnel generally supervised the work done by Jordanian, Egyptian, and Lebanese engineers.

Before any additional stations could be built or existing stations upgraded, the government had to make a decision about the type of color system it would adopt. The feeling in Saudi Arabia and many other Gulf states was that the German PAL system ought to be the common Gulf states color standard. In 1971 the Ministry of Information hired Hammett and Edison, a San Francisco, California, broadcast engineering consulting firm, to study the SECAM and PAL systems to determine which would be better for the kingdom: they too concluded in their 1972 report that PAL should be the choice. Despite this, the country decided on the SECAM system, invented and promoted by the French, who have been successful in some countries in tying SECAM-standard acceptance to various economic, military, or cultural agreements.[4] The SECAM decision was thus political rather than technical (Edison communication, 1979), and was made by the Saudi Arabian cabinet, possibly at the request of King Faisal. In any case, whatever length the French went to in order to secure the acceptance of the SECAM color system in the kingdom, it was worth it to them: the majority of the color equipment bought by the Saudis since, whether for new stations or for upgrading older ones, has been purchased from French manufacturers. In 1983, for example, a new broadcasting complex, the largest and most technically advanced in the Arab world, was due to be completed in Riyadh—using French equipment exclusively. The main consulting group for the project was a French state-owned organization. Inconveniently for the Saudis, of course, the remaining Gulf states (with the exception of Iraq) use PAL—and PAL is incompatible with SECAM for color transmission. In order to compete in international television in the Gulf states region, Saudi Arabia had to convert its powerful twin RCA transmitters in Dammam to PAL so that those outside the kingdom could see the Saudi signal in color. Another transmitter (UHF) was constructed in 1976 to broadcast the Dammam signal locally in SECAM (Al-Warthan interview, 1979).

In August 1977 a new television facility was opened in Abha in the southwestern part of Saudi Arabia ("Saudi Arabian television," n.d., p. 3). The station is used to broadcast the national television service and has the capability of producing local programming. But it is the only station with production facilities that has been built since the Dammam station was completed: the growth in Saudi Arabian television has been in the increase in coverage provided by transmitters that broadcast the Riyadh signal by a leased INTELSAT system satellite transponder to 20 ground stations scattered throughout the kingdom. The same system is planned to link the new industrial towns that are under construction. Thus, although behind other Gulf states such as Kuwait on the construction of production facilities, Saudi Arabia has expanded its television coverage to include the entire country; and, moreover, two ground stations linked to the INTELSAT system—Taif and Riyadh—are used to receive and transmit television signals internationally. (Radio also uses the INTELSAT satellite for standby purposes for linking the Jidda and Riyadh stations and the powerful mediumwave stations that form the Northern Stations Project.) In December 1979, when the national telecommunications network malfunctioned, the satellite circuit was activated so that the distribution of radio signals would not be interrupted (S. Nasser interview, 1980). Saudi Arabia is an active participant in the ARABSAT project headquartered in Riyadh—in which members of the Arab League participated in the launching of two satellites in order to improve all forms of communication, including the distribution of broadcast signals among Arab countries. At one time Saudi Arabia had plans to design, build, and launch a satellite for its own exclusive use. The government apparently believed that having such a satellite would lessen its dependence on INTELSAT for circuits, and the $500 million voted for the project by the Council of Ministers in December 1979 (S. Nasser interview, 1980) was thought to be a good investment of excess funds gained from oil exports. However, ARABSAT was more expensive than anticipated and as the mid-1980s approached, it was clear that the kingdom would not have the funds for its own satellite because of declining oil prices.

TELEVISION, 1980s

Three developments most affected the visual medium during the 1980s: (1) the decrease in worldwide oil prices that dramatically slowed the booming Saudi economy; (2) the addition of a second channel; and (3) the decision to permit advertising on television.

Between early 1974, when King Faisal dramatically raised the price of oil sold on the international market, and 1980, the high price of OPEC oil fueled a financially healthy Saudi economy, resulting in an immense transfer of wealth from the West to Gulf states. Large sums of money were spent by the government on development projects; the electronic media received large sums of development money. Old television equipment in the stations built by the U.S. Corps of Engineers in the 1960s was replaced, and some new buildings were built. However, the most impressive project was the new state-of-the-art studio and administrative complex for Saudi television in Riyadh. The additional studio space and associated equipment made possible the addition of a second national channel. From its beginnings in August 1983 (al-Najai communication, 1983) the second channel has evolved into a genuine alternative source of broadcast television for viewers who know English. The entire channel consists of locally produced or imported programs that are in, dubbed into, or subtitled in English.

TELEVISION PROGRAMMING

It is easier, given sufficient funds, to acquire hardware than to produce software, and generally speaking the Saudi Arabian television administration has been more successful in managing the equipment-related aspects of television than the programming side. The Corps of Engineers and NBCI were ready to provide production advice when asked by the government, but programming decisions have been the responsibility of the Ministry of Information—and, when television was first introduced, very little thought had been given to the kind of daily schedule that the ministry would provide. It was after the incident in Riyadh, which showed how militant the opposition to the medium could be, that officials became concerned about the possible consequences of the start of actual programming.

In July and August 1965, the test pattern was telecast in the morning; in the early evening about an hour's worth of programming was provided, including Koran readings, background music, and scenic slides of various sections of the kingdom. Mighty Mouse cartoons were shown, and off-camera announcers read the news while still news pictures appeared on the screen. By almost any measure, these first television signals were received with tremendous excitement by the citizens of Riyadh and Jidda, the majority of whom had not seen a motion picture before films were shown on television. I remember the scene in downtown Jidda during the brief evening transmissions in August 1965: people stood five and six deep on the sidewalks to catch a glimpse of the television sets in shop windows. Every morning when the test pattern transmission stopped, the station's switchboard was flooded with calls wanting to know where the "programs" were (Watson, 1965, p. 2). The Minister of Information would drop by the station at night to see how the programming was progressing. On one occasion he came to the station with a press delegation and decided on the spot that the visit should be televised: on that evening, the programming was extended to 70 minutes (Watson, 1965, p. 1).

Early planning by the Ministry of Information and NBCI projected that nightly programming was to be limited to about 2 hours; and the programming, maintenance schedules, and number of personnel to be hired were arranged accordingly. But receiver sales soared. Those who could not afford to buy, such as males from lower-income families and expatriate workers, watched television in the coffeehouses and restaurants at night. By the end of the first year of operation, the stations were each operating between five and 6 hours daily.

The Jidda and Riyadh stations had only one studio each; and although the studios were large, only limited amounts of local programming could be produced in a single studio that could be used only when the station was off the air. Programs were moreover limited by the lack of production, engineering, and artistic personnel. Some dramas were taped, then, but most locally produced programs consisted of interviews with officials and religious leaders. Children's programs and dramas were (and still are) written and produced by Arabs from other countries, most of them from Syria: because of the Yemen Civil War, Saudi Arabia did not have close relations with Egypt, and Jordan had no television system at all at the time. The only live programming consisted of the news and press reviews, reviews of the evening's schedule (which was not yet published in Saudi newspapers), and station identification.

Religious programming, important in all Arab countries, has special importance in the country in which the two most holy cities of Islam are located. Each telecasting day begins with a Koran reading. Evening prayer calls are heard over a slide or short film of the famous mosque in Mecca. King Faisal reportedly promised religious leaders, when he was trying to secure approval for the construction of the system, that television would be used as an important means of disseminating religious doctrine (Eilts, 1971, p. 27); and one of the first programs to be videotaped at the Jidda station, a popular religious series that continued into the 1970s, therefore deserves special mention. Former U.S. ambassador Hermann Eilts (1971, p. 28) described it and its creator thus:

> At least one distinguished *alim*, Shaykh Ali Tantawi, is demonstrating the value of television in the cause of religion. Possessed of an engaging television personality, this savant conducts a regular question and answer program on religious subjects. He invites written questions, reads them before the television camera, and with homely anecdotes about and relevant allusion to contemporary everyday life instructs his viewers. Lacking his imagination, some of his colleagues shortsightedly criticize him. He deserves more credit.

When the Jidda station acquired a mobile broadcasting unit, it began originating both live and taped broadcasts from Mecca during the important religious days of Ramadan and Hajj: before the completion of the national telecommunications system, the programs were taped and distributed to other stations. By 1980, about 25 percent of unified programming was devoted to religious subjects ("Saudi Arabian television," n.d., p. 5) while the Qassim and Medina stations, in traditionally conservative areas, had formerly programmed as much as 50 percent. There is some evidence to suggest that the kingdom's commitment to religious television will increase. The revolution in Iran and the attempted mosque takeover in Mecca in 1979 were reminders that the country should move cautiously toward modernization, which might be perceived by conservatives as rejecting (or even as encroaching on) traditional Islam.

The increase in programming hours during the first year of operation required buying material from other countries. Egypt, as previously noted, was not considered to be an acceptable supplier: not only were relations between the two countries at an all-time low between 1965 and 1970, but the material that Egyptian television made available to other countries often contained objectionable references to Nasser's various Pan-Arab policies. Some programming, generally of low quality, was purchased from the two privately owned Lebanese stations. At that time, Arabic programming was not being taped in Europe, and the Arab production centers in Jordan, Bahrain, and Dubai had not been constructed. The only answer to the immediate need of even more additional programming, then, was to purchase packages of old movies from the United States and Great Britain. Some of these films were shown, but many proved to be unacceptable because of unsuitable themes. During the first five years of television in the kingdom, imported made-for-television programs were limited to those that had been sold to other Arab countries and therefore were already dubbed or subtitled in Arabic. These programs proved to be so popular that the Ministry of Information was willing to purchase additional such programs to help fill the expanded television schedule. Until about 1972 the percentage of imported Western programming on the Saudi Arabian television system ranged from 25 percent to 33 percent. After 1972, the kingdom started purchasing large amounts of Egyptian programming while continuing to buy from Lebanon; and by the late 1970s, it was also buying programs from Jordan, Bahrain, and Dubai, in addition to special productions done by Egyptian producers working in Europe. While the percentage of imported, mostly entertainment programming has not decreased, the percentage of imported programming has decreased. This is due not only to increased program production in the Middle East but to the new permissiveness in television programming in the West: the earlier programs had been more acceptable and had required little editing.

The infusion of oil money into the Ministry of Information coffers in the late 1970s, the completion of the new Riyadh television headquarters, and the addition of the second channel had a great impact on programming.

TELEVISION ADVERTISING

Advertising was not considered necessary to help finance the system until the kingdom started experiencing financial difficulties in the early 1980s because of the drop in OPEC oil prices. The Ministry of Information had had trouble finding trained Saudis to operate and repair equipment and otherwise manage the system; the government did not have sufficient personnel to deal with the complex issue of advertising sales, production, and billing. However, financial considerations—and lobbying by some of the influential businessmen in the kingdom—quickly changed government attitudes.

At first advertising was permitted only on the English-language Second Channel. But, after its January 1, 1986, start, wide acceptance on the part of the public allowed the Ministry of Information to permit advertising on the Arabic-language First Channel.

The Saudi government has really never objected to advertising per se. In a consumption-oriented, market-driven economy, advertising appears in Saudi newspapers and magazines, on billboards, and in stores. However, at least during the period when the government could afford it, the Ministry of Information felt that it did not have sufficient numbers of trained personnel to operate the stations, and that the organization of advertising would only make matters worse. All of this changed when the second channel began and the Ministry of Information was forced to find an alternative source of funding to that provided by the government. In January 1986 advertising started first on the second channel and soon spread to the main (Arabic) channel.

Not only did Saudi television wish to gain income from television advertising, but also the government had grown resentful of Western and Asian manufacturers of consumer goods who were selling millions of dollars worth of products in the kingdom by advertising on the commercial radio and television stations in other Gulf states and via international radio operations such as Egypt's Middle East Radio and France's Radio Monte Carlo Middle East (al-Yusuf, 1989). The economic impact of Saudi Arabian television advertising on outside media is obvious from what happened to advertising revenue on the most popular Western radio station heard in the Arab world: after the introduction of advertising on both Saudi television channels, gross advertising revenue on Radio Monte Carlo Middle East fell 50 percent (Taquet interview, 1989).

As is occasionally the situation on commercial television systems, some of the commercials on Saudi television are more interesting than the regular programming. Many of the commercials, featuring automobiles, cooking oil, watches, processed food, soap, bug sprays, and cosmetics, are produced in the West or in Egypt. Some commercial producers have gone to great lengths in an attempt to attract viewers. For example, in early January 1991, just prior to the Gulf War, some influential conservative religious elements in the kingdom are said to have officially protested to the Ministry of Information about females being used on some commercials.

As noted previously, from the very beginning of Saudi television in 1965, the topic of females—especially Arab females—on television has been a very sensitive matter. There has been a general understanding that females will not appear in commercials, especially those that do not directly advertise female-oriented products. But the television administration became rather lax about this, particularly when commercial producers became very clever. For example, males and females are never seen dancing on Saudi television. However, in a very clever bath soap ad shown in 1990, bars of a brand of soap—rather obviously sex typed as male and female—did dance! This was reportedly one of the commercials to which the religious authorities objected. The Ministry of Information decreed that females would only appear in commercials where their presence was appropriate, e.g., in commercials for disposable diapers (al-Najai interview, 1991).

Generally speaking, however, female roles in commercials are very carefully presented. For example, in a 1991 commercial for a brand of cooking oil, viewers see only the hands of the woman using the product. Another commercial shows an obviously satisfied husband and children eating food prepared by the wife and mother. The woman is not shown; she assumes the position of the camera viewing the happy family.

Television authorities did not give reasons for suspending all television commercials during the Desert Storm Gulf War, but it is widely believed that this was done in an attempt to focus attention on coverage of the fighting, without commercial distraction. Also, this action helped avoid conservative criticism of Western product advertising during a time when some believed that foreign armed forces, for whatever reason, should not be in the kingdom.

To reiterate, the role of conservative religious elements in Saudi society cannot be overemphasized, particularly after the Gulf War when religious conservatives, especially underemployed or unemployed younger men, became more aggressive in calling for prayer-time shop closing and protesting against women who did not veil in public. Television almost always reflects what the Ministry of Information believes to be the mood of the country. Commercials, as well as other aspects of Saudi television programming, took a more conservative turn as the *mutawain*—officially the

Committee for the Promotion of Virtue and the Prevention of Vice—became more forceful in protesting virtually anything they believed to be anti-Islamic, i.e., Western.

CENSORSHIP

One of the advantages of television over public cinemas was that television could more easily be controlled by the government. This was especially true before Egyptian television could be seen in Jidda, before U.A.E., Kuwaiti, Bahrani, and Qatari television could be seen in eastern Saudi Arabia, and prior to the proliferation of videocassette recorders in the kingdom. News and other information about the royal family and the country itself could be—and was, and is—placed first on the news: the royal family and ranking government dignitaries have thus always been assured a great deal of exposure on the medium. The government believes moreover that it must regulate cultural trends toward modernization, and controlled television is one means of expressing and affecting, often indirectly, the prevailing mood. The use of the medium itself, of course, reflects a government orientation on the question of how quickly society should move away from traditional Islamic practices. The alternations of cultural liberalism and conservatism in Saudi Arabian society since the introduction of television have been clearly seen on it: for example, women were only gradually allowed to be seen on television, and there remains a kind of double standard on the two national channels. Western women are considered to be properly attired when their arms are covered and their skirts are not above the knees. On the other hand, Arab women are usually more conservatively dressed, with at least a scarf covering the hair. Following the 1979 Mecca Mosque incident, Saudi women were banned from television altogether for a short time.

Every program purchased for Saudi television, whether bought from an Arab or a Western country, is reviewed by a special department within the Ministry of Information that must screen both its visual and its audio portions. For example, some words on the English sound track of an American-made program may be deleted even in a subtitled program because the original sound track can be heard. The basic guidelines established in the late 1960s for censoring imported programs still apply and prohibit:

1. Scenes which arouse sexual excitement
2. Women who appear indecently dressed, in dance scenes, or in scenes which show overt acts of love
3. Women who appear in athletic games or sports

4. Alcoholic drinks or anything connected with drinking
5. Derogatory references to any of the "Heavenly Religions"
6. Treatment of other countries with praise, satire, or contempt
7. References to Zionism
8. Material meant to expose monarchy
9. All immoral scenes
10. References to betting or gambling
11. Excessive violence (Shobaili, 1971, pp. 272–73)

Of course, Saudi Arabia is not the only Arab country to screen programs before showing them on television, and these criteria are generally used by all the Gulf states; but they are more strictly applied in Saudi Arabia. An example of what can happen to a program when the guidelines are applied to an ordinary American Western film was related to me by an employee of the film department in 1966:

> The town sheriff walks into a bar—censored because alcohol is forbidden. Sheriff talks to woman who is unveiled—censored because woman's face is shown. Sheriff pets dog as he walks down the street—censored because the dog is considered an unclean animal. Finally all scenes involving the sheriff are omitted because it is discovered that the sheriff's badge closely resembles the Star of David and is unacceptable because of the association with Israel. (Boyd, 1971, pp. 76–77)

Except for some residents of the Eastern Province and those in the Jidda area with equipment to see Egyptian television, viewers have little opportunity to compare the Saudi television service with that of other Arab countries and are therefore unaware of the extent of program censorship. But in the early 1990s, fewer programs are imported from the West—and those that are, such as *The Rockford Files* and *Columbo,* are considered to be easily edited for Saudi television. Because the kingdom is such an important market for Arab television programs, particularly dramatic programs dealing with Islamic history and bedouin culture, many are conceived and made with the requirements of the Saudi system in mind.

The censorship requirements of Saudi Arabian television depend on the prevailing political, economic, and social climate in the kingdom. *Index on Censorship* (1992) published a list of what is not permitted in Egyptian-made programs shown on Saudi television:

1. Unmarried couples acting the part of a married couple are not allowed to sit on the same bed together.
2. Unmarried actors are not allowed to be shown sitting in the same room together with the door closed.
3. A father cannot be shown kissing his daughter, nor a mother her son, unless the actors themselves are so related.

4. Certain names cannot be used as they are theologically suspect, such as Abdel Nabi or Abdel Rasul.

5. Women are not allowed to be shown singing or dancing.

6. No women may appear on Saudi television during the month of Ramadan.

7. It is forbidden for any character to use the expressions "by my life" or "by your life."

8. The name of the Lord may not be taken in vain.

9. No statues of figures may be shown that represent the human or animal form as these are graven images and hence forbidden by Islam. ("Saudi Arabia: No," p. 22)

TELEVISION PROGRAMMING, 1980s

Riyadh is the center of program transmission, providing the bulk of programs for all stations and relay transmitters in the kingdom. The cities with studios large enough to tape programs—Jidda, Riyadh, Dammam, and (to a limited extent) Abha—are each assigned the task of specializing in the production of certain kinds of programs that are then placed on the national network. Both Riyadh and Jidda tape some programming for children; quiz programs are taped in Dammam, as is a program about Saudi Arabia that is made as part of a Gulf states cooperative programming arrangement. Riyadh is the originating center for almost all news.

The government has commissioned several studies on how the television medium can be used for educational purposes, but relatively little educational programming is shown, except for a few programs on health, safety, and literacy as the Ministries of Information and of Education have never been able to agree on which has primary responsibility over such programming. At one time the television service considered employing a company to produce a series on basic adult literacy, but that plan did not come to fruition. The Ministry of Education, which closely controls the national school curriculum, has expressed an interest in a comprehensive television instruction program to be shown in schools with the goals of improving the quality of teaching and of furthering unity in the curriculum. This plan too has been shelved, apparently because the Ministry of Education wants its own production studios and transmitters. Some form of televised supplement to classroom instruction is likely to be given national priority in a country that is very concerned about education and that must import the majority of its teachers from other Arab countries.

Some of the government's programming choices have unquestionably helped unify the country. The visual medium has been able to do what radio was unable to do, for lack of transmitters, even into the late 1960s—to provide a sense of national direction and to explore various ramifications of the kingdom's culture and history. National leaders, most of whom are members of the royal family, have been given the kind of national visibility not possible before the introduction of television. The medium has been used with some degree of effectiveness during periods of crisis, the first instance being in 1967, when a series of bombings occurred in Riyadh. Yemenis, allegedly supporting Egypt's role in the Yemen Civil War, were arrested and executed; but first they were shown on television in an interview during which they admitted their role in the bombings. These telecasts were apparently well received by citizens. Seeing the people responsible for the acts somehow added credibility to the government's statements about the nationality of the bombers and their motive and stopped rumors and speculation about the causes of the explosions. During the November 1979 Mecca Mosque incident, television helped again in a national crisis—though it began the exercise less than smoothly. The takeover of the large mosque on the day corresponding to the end of the Islamic fourteenth century caught Saudi Arabian authorities by surprise: for several days, Ministry of Information officials withheld information about the "incident," and Saudi citizens listening to foreign radio reports began to suspect that the government was minimizing the seriousness of the situation in the mosque. When the government decided to release specific information about the extent of the fighting, television was unable to react promptly: pictures of what was actually happening were difficult to obtain because no trained Saudi national was available to take the necessary news footage, and Arab expatriate employees of the film department hesitated to undertake the assignment until their security in Mecca could be guaranteed. But as soon as film of the fighting became available, it was included in newscasts and some was released to the television services of other countries. Following his capture, the leader of the takeover was interviewed on television. The Ministry used this and other footage to produce a 90-minute documentary that was shown on what was then the national channel and was offered to the services of interested Arab countries:[5] it showed Mecca and provided some history about the mosque itself; then the fighting was shown, followed by footage of the final group of holdouts, including the leader, being given medical attention in prison. As the interviews with the Yemeni bombers had 13 years earlier, this program defused rumors—and it apparently helped satisfy Saudi concern about the extent of damage to a holy Islamic structure.

ARAMCO RADIO AND TELEVISION BROADCASTING

A discussion of the broadcast media in Saudi Arabia would not be complete without further examination of the broadcasting activities of the Arabian American Oil Company (ARAMCO). This organization was originally owned by major American oil companies that first participated in Middle East petroleum exploration in the 1930s. Company headquarters are in Dhahran, in the Eastern Province, where almost all oil activity is centered. During the 1970s the kingdom purchased the company, but it continues to contract with a consortium of American oil firms to manage and market the country's entire output—and, of course, the country is the Arab world's largest oil producer. Americans have always played an important part in Saudi Arabia's oil industry, and acquisition of control by the kingdom has not decreased the number of its American personnel. Indeed, the country's booming oil business during the 1970s increased the American presence in the Dhahran area: by January 1980, 3,000 Americans were directly employed there by ARAMCO and 3,600 more were employed by various company subcontractors. Also resident were many employee dependents (Nawwab interview, 1979). The ARAMCO Compound in Dhahran, then, could function as a model American community, complete with cinemas, a bowling alley, supermarkets, beauty shops, and a school system with an American curriculum; women, not allowed to drive in the rest of Saudi Arabia, were there permitted to do so. Naturally, in such a setting, an American-type broadcasting system would operate.

It was noted earlier that ARAMCO started television transmissions from HZ-22-TV in September 1957 and soon was providing entertainment not only for its American employees but for Saudis in the surrounding area who could receive the signal—broadcasting its soundtracks in two languages, both English and Arabic. In 1963 the station's coverage was extended by a transmitter built in the Hofuf area, about 60 miles from the main ARAMCO compound; and in 1964 the company moved its studios from their previous location above a snack bar to a larger building, specifically to accommodate an increased local production schedule including religious programs, drama, a children's series, and a bedouin show (Al-Warthan interview, 1979)—mostly in Arabic. ARAMCO television has employed several American production specialists to advise on local production and to work on the instructional and various public relations films that the oil company has produced. (Programming is under the direction of the ARAMCO Public Relations Department.)

When the government's Dammam station went on the air in 1970, HZ-22-TV ceased all Arabic-language transmissions. ARAMCO actually welcomed relief from the responsibility of being a major television broadcaster in Arabic, never really having sought that role, but its station still continued to provide English-language—mostly American—programming from its 525-line monochrome transmitter. Local Saudi nationals continued to receive this predominantly entertainment-oriented programming by purchasing dual-standard sets that were able to receive not only both the ARAMCO and the government stations but, in the summer months, the services of other Gulf states as well. In November 1976, ARAMCO modified its transmitter to broadcast NTSC color. In March 1979, a new Harris 625-line PAL color transmitter became operational, thus making ARAMCO TV's signal compatible with the neighboring Gulf states and the Dammam high-power PAL transmitter. The station operates daily from mid-afternoon to approximately 2200, featuring those American and British programs that the company believes conform to local Saudi cultural standards. Indeed, all programs are censored by the ARAMCO Public Relations Department in spite of the fact that most offerings purchased for the station are intended primarily for a Western audience. Minimal editing is usually required. The station features mostly entertainment programs that come on 3/4 inch U-Matic cassettes. Public service announcements and some safety and training films are televised daily between programs such as *Sesame Street, The Muppet Show, Lou Grant, Strange Report, Different Strokes, Anna Karenina, Electric Company, Grizzly Adams,* and *Secret War.* Station HZ-22-TV—presented by ARAMCO as Channel 3 and never identified as operated by ARAMCO—is bigger than ever, then—but all programming is in English and Arabic subtitles are no longer provided.

When American and other "Coalition" partners arrived in the Eastern Province of the kingdom to participate in Operation Desert Shield, and later Operation Desert Storm, Channel 3 was important because it was an immediate source of American television programming for U.S. and other English-speaking troops. In fact, the Saudi Arabian military asked ARAMCO television to increase transmission hours slightly to meet what was believed to be a need for "home-style" entertainment for the mostly American military contingent (al-Muhaiteeb, 1990).

As of early 1991, Channel 3 programming consisted of mostly American-produced television shows and made-for-television films: *L.A. Law, 60 Minutes, Wonderful World of Disney, Hunter, Growing Pains, The Jim Henson Show, 227, The Cosby Show, Beauty and the Beast, Mission Impossible, Jake and the Fat Man, Wiseguy, Murphy Brown,* and *Alien Nation.* Additionally, the channel provides sporting events and educational programs acquired from British television and the U.S. Public Broadcasting Service (al-Muhaiteeb interview, 1990; *Channel 3 program schedule: January 9–15, 1991*).

Like its television services, ARAMCO's radio broadcasting dates from the 1950s: not until the mid- to late-1960s did records and tapes become generally available for sale in the kingdom, and ARAMCO reasoned that FM radio music would fill a real void. So too would a 15-minute newscast of international news from United Press International (UPI)—read by an employee of the ARAMCO PR department at 1145, with taped repeats at 1245 and 1745—incorporating items about American sports activity and the weather forecast for the Eastern Province. But the original small radio operation of the 1950s has, like the company itself, greatly expanded. By 1963, popular and easy-listening music services were available on both FM and mediumwave. After 1970, the company decided that more variety was important and designed a new system to broadcast four separate 24-hour FM stereo music services: the operation, assembled wholly from components, resembles an American automated radio station down to its automatic system of voiced time signals.

As was the case with Channel 3 television, the two ARAMCO FM stereo radio services provided the military troops in the Eastern Province during the Gulf crisis with a variety of 24-hour music services. These were especially important until British and U.S. military stations came on the air. There are two ARAMCO radio stations: Studio One (91.4 FM in Dhahran and on two other frequencies in other areas) provides contemporary American popular music. Arranged in blocks, there are several hours each day of country, adult contemporary, and the latest U.S. popular song hits. Music is supplied on tape from various American radio programming services. Studio Two (101.4 FM in Dhahran and on other frequencies in neighboring areas) features what is commonly knows as a "beautiful" or "easy-listening" format (al-Muhaiteeb interview, 1990; *Studio One and Studio Two program guide,* 1990).

VIDEOCASSETTES

In the early 1980s, the business of providing equipment for home video recorders and cassette programming in the Gulf states, particularly in Saudi Arabia, was a major industry. By the mid-1980s, Gulf state businesses became more active in videocassette software—both the production, mostly from Egypt, and distribution of tapes for rent. The Gulf area is probably the largest home videocassette market in the world; it is surely one of the world's largest outlets for pirated tapes of first-run American and British films and television programming, as well as Egyptian video and film material. Part of the explanation for this situation can be found in the cultural and economic conditions that exist in the kingdom. Only a few private cinema enterprises have been allowed to operate—small businesses that rent 16-mm projectors and older Egyptian and Western films for home showing—and no public cinemas exist, though companies such as ARAMCO and some large defense contractors such as Raytheon and Lockheed and U.S. government agencies have been permitted by the government to import films for showing before their own employees. In most areas of the country, excluding the Eastern Province, the only television programming available is on the two national Saudi Arabian television channels. Yet, from their travels in Europe, the United States, and other Arab countries, upper- and middle-income Saudis have become accustomed to a diverse film and television diet. That Saudi Arabia's is a culture that is fascinated by modern gadgetry also boosts business, as does the fact that import duties on home entertainment equipment are low to non-existent. Saudi Arabians in such large cities as Jidda, Riyadh, and Dammam had also been accustomed, since the 1960s, to buying audio cassettes of U.S. and European music recorded from the BBC or the Voice of America and Arab music illegally recorded from Radio Cairo or the Voice of the Arabs.

The videocassette business, more technically advanced and profitable than the audio, started in Saudi Arabia in about 1972, with the sale of Sony U-Matic "industrial format" machines. At that time Sony was making these recorders available mostly to the U.S. market, and consequently the first machines sold were 525-line NTSC American color standard: they were used with the Sony dual- and later triple-standard (NTSC, PAL, SECAM) 525/625-line sets that were becoming popular. The American-standard U-Matic sets were purchased both by individuals for home entertainment and by foreign firms with local contracts that wanted to provide employees with entertainment in construction camps located in isolated areas. When the VHS and Sony (Beta) home video recorders became available in the kingdom, however, interest in these larger and more expensive U-Matic units declined.

Once cassette machines became popular, the immediate problem was to provide enough programs on cassettes to meet the demand. At first, cassettes were openly imported into the kingdom: before the arrival of high-speed duplicating equipment, a company would acquire the rights to programs and then have the duplicates shipped to Saudi Arabia. The customs inspectors and the Ministry of Information, which is responsible for censoring such material, were initially accommodating: they did not understand what the cassettes were and had no means of previewing the programming. When they awoke to the realities and required that all material be censored, the importers simply circumvented the system by smuggling. Several businesses operate in Saudi Arabia selling selected television programming taped in various American and British cities: so little attention is paid to the editing of their tapes that in many instances identifications from stations in New Orleans, Louisiana, and San Francisco, California, may be seen and heard. Even the commercials are often left in the programs. And after the advent of copying machines, pirated American and British first-run films were regularly shipped to Saudi Arabia for duplication and local sale or short-term rental. Eventually, the pirating importers almost wholly prevailed over those who were purchasing the rights to programming. Foreign business firms in the kingdom became their willing customers because their wares cost so much less than legal equivalents. That the tapes for VHS and Beta units are considerably smaller than those for U-Matic recorders had much to do with the supplantation of the latter machines by the former: not only was their programming less expensive; it was more easily smuggled past customs.

The videocassette business has, then, circumvented the government's policy of controlling the kind of visual material shown in the kingdom. One need no longer rely wholly on Saudi Arabian television for entertainment. Indeed, in some instances the censored Western programming shown on the national television channel is locally available in full on videocassettes. The efficiency of the cassette pirates is evident from the speed with which the controversial British program of April 1980, *Death of a Princess,* reached the kingdom. Purporting to detail the death of a Saudi Arabian princess and her lover for adultery, the film was flown to the Eastern Province the morning after its showing on British TV; copies were duplicated and made available in Dammam for sale the same day. Though luggage is thoroughly searched by Saudi customs authorities, a compact VHS or Beta tape may—as before noted—be carried through customs in a coat pocket. So, doubtless, came the "Princess" to Arabia. The videocassette business is still growing rapidly throughout the Middle East. Though Saudi Arabia is the liveliest market, because of its prevailing cultural conditions and the economic position of its citizens who want video programming, the kind of activity described above occurs in many other Gulf states. The duplication and sale of cassettes has increased even in the less affluent countries such as Yemen, the Sudan, and Egypt.

THE BROADCASTING AUDIENCE

Relatively little audience research has been done by commercial firms in Saudi Arabia. First, the government has been hesitant to allow foreign companies to come to the kingdom and ask questions that might, by local standards, be sensitive. Second, when permission has been granted for survey work, it has been given with the stipulation that women not be interviewed, even by trained female interviewers. Whatever reliable data are available, then, regarding radio and television audiences in Saudi Arabia apply only to the male half of the population. The Hashemite broadcasting Service of Jordan may have done the first radio research in the kingdom—apparently without official permission—in 1965. In December 1972, Associated Business Consultants (ABC) of Beirut, Lebanon, did a survey of the radio, television, and print media habits of priority audience groups in the kingdom: this study was sponsored by the U.S. Information Agency and the BBC. Extensive surveys were also done in Saudi Arabia by Cyprus-based Middle East Marketing Research Bureau as part of the 1977 and 1979

McCann Middle East Media Study: McCann refused to grant permission to quote from its studies but Radio Monte Carlo, one of the McCann participants, released some material to me.

Although in 1990 the British Broadcasting Corporation (1990) estimated there to be 4.5 million radio receivers and 3 million television sets in Saudi Arabia, it is impossible to know the exact number of receivers there. Customs figures on the importation of sets are not helpful because many of the imported receivers are purchased by Arab expatriate workers, mostly Egyptians and Jordanians, and taken home to their families or to sell to friends. Even a low-paid laborer from another Arab country can afford to buy an imported radio in Saudi Arabia; and the same statement may apply to television sets, as many workers come to the kingdom without their families and several men, often renting a small apartment or room, pool their financial resources to purchase a stove, refrigerator, television set, and VCR.

Since Saudi Arabian television did not permit commercial advertising ("Ads go on," 1986) until 1986, one common reason for undertaking research to determine audience size and makeup did not exist. The 1972 USIA survey did ask respondents some questions about television viewing habits: 87 percent said they owned a television set and 52 percent said that they watched television daily (USIA, Office of Research, 1973, pp. 8–11). But the only known comprehensive study of television use in Saudi Arabia was done in 1972 by Boyd. This project involved 120 interviews conducted in Riyadh among middle-class and upper-class Saudis. Below are some of its major findings.

1. 90.8 percent of respondents owned a television set; 29 percent owned two television sets.
2. 60 percent of respondents said that they watched television daily.
3. The average number of viewing hours per week among those sampled was 14.8.
4. The average number of people who watched television with the respondent was 5.9.
5. The most popular programs among respondents included the Egyptian films and programs shown on Thursday and Friday, over the Arab weekend.
6. 98 percent of respondents believed that television had an impact on Saudi Arabian society, most people noting that it provided information of an overall educational nature to viewers. Secondly, respondents said that television served to keep the family together: they reported fewer instances where the adult male family members had to leave home to seek entertainment with male friends. Television appeared to be a family-centered form of entertainment

which could be enjoyed by all. (Boyd, 1972, pp. 269–302)

In January 1982 Boyd and Najai (1984) collected television viewing information from 600 male and female students between the ages of 15 and 20 in the capital, Riyadh. Contrary to what was hypothesized, male and female viewing time did not differ significantly. As expected, males listed sports as important programs; females did not. Respondents did not believe Saudi television to be an important source of news, despite the fact that it is featured during prime evening time. Consistent with a finding in the above-noted (Boyd, 1972) study, 90 percent of respondents said that television had had an impact on society; 86.4 percent said the impact was positive.

Data from a 1992 BBC survey show that 88 percent of Saudi Arabian adults watch television daily. The most surprising finding of this survey was the audience for London-based Middle East Broadcasting Centre (MBC)—a daily audience of 10 percent that was made possible by MBC's retransmission to the eastern part of Saudi Arabia on a Bahrain TV channel (Eggerman, 1982).

The 1972 USIA survey of radio listeners indicated that 88 percent of those sampled tuned to the Saudi service at least once per week. It is apparently, then, as common a practice in Saudi Arabia as in other Arab countries for people to tune to the government stations to hear what the government is saying—but the survey also indicates how very usual it is to tune to foreign radio stations. Seventy percent of respondents said that they tuned at least once a week to Radio Cairo and 53 percent to the Voice of the Arabs; at least once a week 73 percent listened to the BBC, 62 percent to Radio Kuwait, and 37 percent to the Voice of America. Radio Monte Carlo (RMCME) is apparently the most popular among the commercial radio stations that can be received in Saudi Arabia, but Jordan's HBS, Egypt's Middle East Program, and the Bahrain Commercial service are also well liked (Pan Arab Computer Center, 1978, pp. 1–6; "Audience, Penetration and Listenership," 1979, pp. 1–10). The government seems to be aware of the popularity of Radio Monte Carlo: during the fighting that followed the November 1979 Mecca Mosque incident the government jammed RMCME, which was reporting the incident more thoroughly than were the Saudi Arabian radio services. It took several weeks and a considerable amount of work by RMCME officials in Saudi Arabia to get the government to cease jamming (Regnier interview, 1980).

In 1987 Boyd and Asi (1991) undertook a kingdom-wide study of the international radio-listening habits of 2,000 Saudi university students. Students were most likely to listen to Radio Monte Carlo Middle East and the BBC, preferring the BBC for news and public affairs programming and RMCME primarily for entertainment as well as news. This finding is generally consistent with results of studies done by the leading foreign international radio broadcasters. The BBC's long tradition of credible service to the Arab world as well as its signal strength advantage make it an important information source, particularly during times of crisis. There was no more appropriate crisis during which to examine radio listening than during the time that Iraq occupied Kuwait.

A U.S. Information Agency (USIA) study in Saudi Arabian urban areas between December 5 and 25, 1990, highlights Gulf crisis radio-listening levels in the kingdom. All respondents in the USIA national Saudi survey used radio as a daily information source. To illustrate the impact of radio listening before and after the invasion, Saudi nationals were asked about regular listening before the August 2 invasion, during August and September, and finally in December. Results indicated that before the invasion 1 percent listened regularly to the BBC; in August and September, 35 percent were regular listeners; in December the percentage had increased to 40 percent. All radio services, but especially those from the West, had increased listenership. The percentages of radio listeners in the kingdom were higher for non-Saudi residents (U.S. Information Agency, 1991).

The kingdom faces in the 1990s the difficult problem of coping with an escalating demand for appropriate programming. But the future of radio and television broadcasting in Saudi Arabia depends on many factors, including the stability of the present government, the future level of oil incomes, and the kingdom's position internationally and within the Arab world. The kingdom has completed the installation of the most extensive system of radio and television transmitters in the Arab world; added studio space allows the production of as much locally produced radio and television programming as the government deems appropriate. The second television channel that started in August 1983 (al-Najai communication, 1983) provides a choice of programming for those viewers who do not have access to alternatives from other countries: that additional service, when the English channel is not operating, could also be the opportunity for the Ministries of Information and Education to cooperate on educational/instructional broadcasting, particularly instructional programming designed to help alleviate the kingdom's lack of qualified native teachers.

But, the country's development has been so rapid since 1965 that the government has still not been able to install within the Ministry of Information a cadre of skilled administrators able to establish, and then effect, a consistent broadcasting policy. Most particularly, the government has not agreed on the manner in which it will present itself to its own citizens, to the Arab world, or to the rest of the world. The government's practice has customarily been to react to events, usually after a period of silence during which rumors abound: the information apparatus of the kingdom must then act to attenuate the rumors and minimize the incident or situation that started them. This procedure may be culturally Arab in nature, but the government appears to be interested in making changes in it, especially in light of its position in the international political and economic community.

The event that caused leaders to re-think their way of reacting to events was the November 1979 Mecca Mosque incident: though Saudi reporting on it was ultimately extensive, the limited amount of information available from the government media during its course—not to mention the jamming of Radio Monte Carlo—gave rise to speculation among Western and Arab countries that it was actually part of a larger plot to change the form of government in the kingdom. Saudi leaders admit that some of the speculation could have been avoided or negated if the government had itself provided more information about the situation from the beginning, not waiting to react to external comment on the state of affairs. In an interview published in a London-based Arabic-language magazine, *al-Hawadith,* then Crown Prince and Deputy Prime Minister (later King) Fahd was to admit that Saudi Arabia had not then had an information philosophy, adding that clearly the country should "facilitate the task of the [foreign] press instead of neglecting to put the facts to it" (Al-Lawzi, 1980).

The Council of Ministers created a commission to study and deal with such information problems. Known as the Higher Media Council, the organization is headed by the Minister of the Interior, rather than the Minister of Information, in part because of the widespread belief that it was the information ministry that was the gatekeeper causing the information flow problems. The government realized, then, that it must be more aggressive and prompt in providing information about internal matters. An example of such a possible change in the previous policy is the manner in which the media handled the Saudi Arabian Airlines jumbo jet disaster at Riyadh airport in August 1980. Immediately after the catastrophe, the state radio and news service released information about its extent and speculated about the cause of the fire, which killed over 300 people. Film of the returning plane taken by Saudi Arabian television was fed by satellite to all interested television organizations and quickly appeared on American network television news. Subsequently, problems during the annual Hajj ceremony in Mecca, such as the summer 1990 death of 1,400 pilgrims in a tunnel accident, have been dealt with in a relatively straightforward manner.

The acquisition of the broadcasting infrastructure has been the easy, albeit expensive, part of the establishment of a comprehensive Saudi Arabian radio and television system. More difficult to achieve is a lasting, practical consensus on the way in which that nation's broadcasting facilities are used. The videotape revolution in the kingdom presented the television programmers with a considerable challenge. With VCRs in almost all Saudi television homes, the two national channels are no longer a monopoly outside the eastern part of the country where signals from neighboring states are available. Owners of videotape recorders are, in fact, their own television station program directors. However, the ultimate test of the system will be when direct satellite broadcasts become more financially practical to viewers and satellite receivers are officially permitted by the Saudi government.

Direct satellite television programming is already available in the Gulf. Egyptian television offers programming via SpaceNet, although for the most part this is a satellite-to-television station service whereby the Egyptian Ministry of Information distributes material to stations in the Arab world. The satellite service with the most potential to have a major impact is, in fact, Saudi backed. London-based Middle East Broadcasting Centre (MBC) is owned by a group of wealthy investors headed by Walid al-Ibrahim, Saudi King Fahd's brother-in-law. MBC started operating in September 1991; in late June 1992 MBC purchased, with the agreement of a New York Bankruptcy Court, the American wire service United Press International (UPI) that had been in financial trouble for a number of years (Ibrahim, 1992b; Goldman, 1992). The kingdom is not only moving to take advantage of new communication technology, but it is expanding its decade-long policy of starting Arabic-language media outlets in and outside the Arab world with the apparent goal of favorably influencing public opinion both inside and outside the kingdom.

When satellite services become possible, those in the affluent state can do with television what they do with shortwave and mediumwave radio broadcasts—tune to the outside world.

CHAPTER 11

BAHRAIN

BAHRAIN, eight islands situated about 15 miles off the coast of Saudi
Arabia in the Arabian Gulf, is the smallest Arab country. Approximately
0.25 million people live within its 231 square miles. Bahrain Island is the
largest island, and it is here that the capital, Manama, is located. In the
1500s, the Portuguese established a presence on the islands, but the British
and the Khalifa family have influenced the country in more recent times.
Great Britain became responsible for Bahrain's protection in 1861, having
established a relationship that lasted over 100 years. Following the 1968
British decision to leave the Gulf area, Bahrain declared its independence
in 1971. For a period of time Bahrain discussed with Qatar and the United
Arab Emirates the possibility of forming a federation, but this did not
come about. In 1973 a constitution was promulgated that established the
country as a constitutional monarchy, with Emir Al-Khalifa as the head of
state. The nation is ruled by an administrative body comprised of the
heads of various departments and ministries.

Oil was discovered in Bahrain in 1932, but production has steadily
declined and the economy increasingly depends on the service industries
that support the petroleum exports of neighboring countries. During the
1970s the country became an important tourist center in the Gulf area
where Western and Arab residents of the more conservative countries,
most notably Saudi Arabia, could come to relax, to enjoy live entertainment imported from Europe and Asia, and to enjoy alcoholic beverages.
In the mid-1980s, Bahrain was connected to the Arabian coast by a
causeway financed largely by Saudi Arabia. This has made the country
more accessible and has increased the tourist business from Saudi Arabia.

BBC receiver estimates for Bahrain are 260,000 radio sets, 170,000
television sets, and 80,000 videocassette recorders (British Broadcasting
Corporation, 1991b).

LACKING THE FUNDS to do otherwise, Bahrain started broadcasting on
a small scale in 1955. The island group has not felt the need to use the
broadcast media to make its presence felt outside its boundaries. With a
small, concentrated population, the country had no internal communication

problems that might have motivated a large investment in broadcasting.

RADIO

In 1955, the Bahrain government started on Bahrain Island an Arabic-language radio station that provided limited news, music, and dramatic entertainment. The station gradually increased the hours of transmission, up to 14 hours per day by 1980. The studios are still at the original site near the capital, Manama, although they were refurbished and new equipment was added in 1972 (Suliman interview, 1980). The 20-kilowatt mediumwave station can be heard in neighboring Gulf states, but its power does not compare with that of stations in the area that have joined the race to acquire super-power transmitters. This situation apparently reflects the government's lack of interest in competing with regional Arabic-language stations and its contentment with providing an essentially local service. The one national Arabic service provides various kinds of programming similar to those that most other Arab countries provide on a Main Program.

In 1977 the Ministry of Information, which operated all broadcast media, started an English-language radio service. Because English is widely spoken in Bahrain and in the eastern region of neighboring Saudi Arabia, it was believed that a commercial English-language service would be popular on the islands and in other Gulf states that could receive the signal. Furthermore, income derived from such a station would help finance activities of the Ministry of Information. Radio Bahrain's basic format is similar to that of a popular U.S. music station. Disc jockeys (DJs) host blocks of time, featuring popular music almost exclusively. News is regularly scheduled and throughout the day there are short features about sports, books, cinemas, etc. Most of the personnel consists of housewives who have been trained at the station—native English speakers who are married to expatriate Britons or Bahrain nationals. The other employees are the DJs, most of them male, who came to the country from Great Britain to work as disco DJs and who were trained locally to work at the more lucrative job of announcing for Radio Bahrain (Suliman interview, 1980). The most expensive air time is during the popular "Radio Bahrain Top 20" program (Radio Bahrain Commercial Rate Card No. 5). The service broadcasts commercials for local businesses, including hotels, restaurants, and clubs, and in this respect serves as a type of promotional voice for the tourist activities that many people from other countries find attractive.

International companies are attracted to this service primarily because of the potentially large audience in Saudi Arabia's Eastern Province, only a few miles away via a causeway completed in the mid-1980s. Because of the neighboring Saudi market and the fact that Saudi Arabian radio does not permit commercial advertising, products such as small home appliances, cold drinks, food products, and automobiles are advertised on Radio Bahrain. Of course, the main audience of the station consists of those who speak English, and in this respect the audience is quite different from and smaller than that of commercial Arabic services in the area: in the McCann and PACC surveys, Radio Bahrain ranked consistently behind Radio Monte Carlo and Egypt's Middle East Radio (Pan Arab Computer Center, 1978, pp. 1–6; "Audience, penetration and listenership," 1979, pp. 1–10). Probably the main competitor of Radio Bahrain is ARAMCO's two 24-hour popular music services that provide similar music without commercials.

TELEVISION

In several respects the introduction of television in Bahrain is more interesting than radio, although the service operates in a manner similar to the English-language service, i.e., it programs largely for viewers who live in neighboring countries.

The activities of the American company RTV International have been mentioned previously in this study with regard to the introduction of television in Jordan. (See Chapter 6, Radio.) RTV International also attempted to start a commercial radio station to broadcast to the Arab world from Cyprus, and tried to bid on a television operations and maintenance contract in Saudi Arabia. In 1972, RTV International signed a contract with the Bahrain government giving the company a concession to operate a color commercial television service (Hamilton interview, 1972). A small studio was completed in 1973 and telecasts, using the 625-line PAL color system, started the same year. Viewers in Bahrain and Saudi Arabia were apparently enthusiastic about the station at first because it provided an interesting alternative to the then monochrome ARAMCO 525-line service and the Saudi Arabian national channel. The color signal was clearly an advantage. Initially, advertisers were attracted to the service because of the audience in the Saudi Arabian Eastern Province. During the initial two years of operation, most programming was imported from the United States, Great Britain, and Egypt. Little local production outside of news and interviews was done because of the limited studio space and equipment. RTV had started the station with as little money as possible and much of the equipment first used was not of broadcast quality—U-Matic videotape machines used without timebase correctors, inexpensive studio cameras, and 8mm film chains. Apparently acceptable by local standards the signal was not of broadcast quality at first. Moreover, construction of a new building and purchase of associated equipment to increase local programming and improve the quality of the broadcast signal led RTV into financial difficulties. This situation, coupled with Bahrain's clear desire to operate its own television service rather than one operated by an American company with rumored CIA connections, motivated the Ministry of Information to assume operation of the station in 1976.

Bahrain television has continued the commercial orientation started by RTV International. With the exception of some advertising by hotels wishing to attract tourists from Saudi Arabia, relatively little local advertising is done and most commercials feature the kinds of products promoted on other television stations in the area. Before Saudi Arabia permitted advertising on television in 1986, Bahrain was in an especially advantageous position because of its proximity to the Saudi Arabian market: advertisements are often for the kinds of luxury items and consumer goods purchased in Saudi Arabia more frequently than in Bahrain itself. The importance of Saudi Arabia to the commercial success of the station is evident from advertisements that Bahrain television placed in newspapers in the early 1980s that serve the Gulf states. Usually appearing on the same page as the radio and television program listings, they remind readers to view the station—"Bahrain Television: Best in News and Entertainment"— and seek to attract advertisers:

> Click! TV. It's an appeal to the senses. Showing, telling, selling. Presenting your product story to over 400,000 households in Bahrain, Eastern Province of Saudi Arabia, Qatar and U.A.E. Click! Advantage Two: TV has your audience captive. Talking to them in their homes, in a relaxed mood. Switch to Bahrain TV. It's quite clearly the most powerful medium of today. And tomorrow. (*Gulf Daily News*, 1979, p. 6)

As of late 1991, Bahrain's two television channels operate for about 85 hours per week with extended transmissions on Thursday and Friday. Programming consists of limited local production; imported Arabic serials from Egypt, Dubai, and Jordan; and American and British series subtitled in Arabic. There are two daily newscasts, in Arabic on Channel 4 at 2000 and in English at 1900 on Channel 55 ("TV," 1991; "TV today," 1991). Bahrain and regional news is furnished for the most part by the state news agency; international news comes from the major wire services, commercial television news from Britain, and CNN.

The 1990–1991 Gulf crisis—and the resulting influx of Western service personnel into eastern Saudi Arabia and Bahrain—presented Bahrain with several opportunities, especially in radio and television broadcasting. Drawing on its traditional Western orientation because of the long-standing relationship with the United Kingdom, the island's radio and television exports became even more aggressive. First, as mentioned in Chapter 20, the island nation permitted the Voice of America to install a mediumwave transmitter for its own use. Second, some satellite-delivered Egyptian programming was used on the Arabic channel. Third, on the mostly English-language television channel, Cable News Network (CNN) was broadcast for an hour each evening on a tape-delayed basis. Finally, in November 1991 the British Broadcasting Corporation's new World Television Service signed a contract with the Ministry of Information, stipulating that Bahrain would broadcast the satellite-delivered service 18 hours per day until January 1992 when the service would become 24 hours ("Persian Gulf to," 1991).

To a large extent, the broadcast media in Bahrain have been organized by the government to reflect the basic economic orientation of the country: to attract people to the tourist-associated industries on the islands and to gain income from the petroleum-rich neighbors. The commercial radio and television services are economically sound largely because of the Saudi Arabian market that attracts advertisers to Bahrain media.

The country probably will not become a major broadcasting force in the Arabian Gulf because it lacks the funds for the extensive facilities it would take to gain this status. The greatest potential for expansion lies in the production of television series that can be sold to other Arab countries. The Bahrain television organization already is active in program taping, but it has not been as active as Dubai or Jordan. In order to be competitive, a considerable investment in studios and equipment will be necessary, in addition to more aggressive and creative management and promotion.

CHAPTER 12

QATAR

THE STATE OF QATAR contains some 100,000 inhabitants within its 4,250 square miles. Qatar is actually a peninsula that protrudes about 100 miles into the Arabian Gulf; it is bounded to the southwest by Saudi Arabia and by Abu Dhabi, part of the United Arab Emirates.

The Ottomans occupied the area for four decades until World War I. In 1915, Great Britain recognized as rulers the Al-Thani family, with whom it signed a treaty that stipulated that Great Britain would handle external political affairs for the country. Petroleum was discovered in small amounts in the 1940s. Since then, oil production has increased steadily with the discovery of new oil fields, many offshore. The economy of the country is heavily dependent on oil income, and the traditional pearling and fishing industries have all but disappeared. There is some agricultural development; however, the basically desert country is not self-sufficient in the production of food. The oil industry has created the need for skilled labor and large numbers of people from Jordan, Lebanon, Iran, and Pakistan have settled in Doha, the capital.

The British Broadcasting Corporation estimates that there are 160,000 radio sets, 130,000 television receivers, and 90,000 videocassette recorders in Qatar (British Broadcasting Corporation, 1990b).

AFTER THE BRITISH DECISION in the late 1960s to leave the Gulf area by 1971, Qatar and Bahrain discussed the possibility of forming a federation with the Trucial States—now the United Arab Emirates. However, this was not to be, and Qatar, like Bahrain, declared its independence in September 1971 and joined the United Nations. The country, now an important oil exporter, is an independent sheikhdom with a constitution that provides for a consultative assembly. The ruler is a member of the Al-Thani family. Culturally, Qatar is almost as conservative as Saudi Arabia because it has been influenced by Wahhabi religious doctrine.

RADIO

Two major developments motivated Qatar to begin a radio broadcasting service: the announcement that the British were leaving the area and increased income from oil. The service was inaugurated on June 25, 1968, with 5 hours of Arabic programming per day from a 10-kilowatt medium-wave transmitter. Since then there has been a steady increase in the number of transmitters, radio services, and studio facilities. Six months after the initial Arabic service began, the mediumwave transmission power had increased to 50 kilowatts and in 1969 to 100 kilowatts (Said, n.d., p. 1). Qatari nationals hold responsible positions in the Ministry of Information under which the broadcast media function; however, much of the program planning and production and virtually all of the technical operation and maintenance is done by nationals of other countries.

After the introduction of radio in the late 1960s, and more earnestly after independence in 1972, the government decided to use the electronic media in order to make its presence felt in the Gulf area. Unlike its less affluent island neighbor, Bahrain, Qatar had the funds to provide its small population with a major broadcast facility.

The following describes the radio service in 1980.

Arabic Programs

The main Arabic service was broadcast for 18.25 hours per day, from 0545 to 2400. Similar to the various main radio programs of other Arab world countries, the daily schedule included blocks of news, music, drama, government announcements, and educational features. This program was broadcast by two 750-kilowatt mediumwave transmitters on 954 kHz. The super-power station could be heard clearly throughout the Gulf area, particularly at night. This service was also broadcast by means of a 100-kilowatt shortwave transmitter operating in the 31 meter band. There was a second Arabic program that was broadcast by two low-power mediumwave transmitters, primarily for residents within the country. Known as the Colloquial Service, the 2-hour, 1600 to 1800, daily program featured programming in a local dialect, including some of the local folklore music that has been recorded.

Urdu Program

A 1-hour daily program in Urdu was broadcast locally on mediumwave for Pakistani expatriate workers.

English Services

Aside from the main Arabic program, the Qatari English Services were the most extensive. There were two separate transmissions, FM and mediumwave. The FM program was continuous automated easy listening music; the mediumwave service operated from 0600 to 2400 hours. Two transmitters were used to broadcast the program, one for the morning and one for the afternoon/evening transmission. This program featured a great deal of popular music from Europe and the United States within a DJ format. There were regularly scheduled segments for classical, country and western, and music requested by listeners (*Gulf Mirror,* 1980b, p. 17). Newscasts and some drama and short features about beauty, health, and education were broadcast. Some of the informational programs were produced locally by Ministry of Information employees and some were imported, mostly from Great Britain. Between 2000 and 2400 hours, music from the automated FM music service is simulcast. In 1980, the evening automated segment of the English Service on FM was expanded into a separate program that provided continuous and essentially uninterrupted easy listening music.

To a large extent, relatively little has happened since the above developments occurred in 1980. With the assistance of the French government, 3 hours of French language programming started in January 1985. Also, the number of employees working has increased to over 400; half are Qataris. When radio started in 1968, only one-fifth of the staff were natives of Qatar (*Radio Qatar from Doha,* 1986).

Qatar is in the unusual position of having some excess transmitter capacity in that many of the low-power but still functional facilities have been replaced with new, high-power transmitters. This situation exists despite the fact that Qatar has not involved itself in the super-power transmitter race characterized by other Gulf countries. A new Doha radio studio complex was completed in 1983. The additional studio space was to be utilized, according to the plan, to add separate religious and educational radio services (Said, n.d., pp. 3–4). These were to be broadcast on existing, but currently unused, facilities.

TELEVISION

Qatar started television on August 15, 1970, with a daily monochrome 3- to 4-hour transmission (*TV in the Gulf states,* 1979, p. 84; Ibrahim communication, 1980). This first television effort was intended to be temporary, as it provided a period of time to train local staff and to hire nationals of other Arab countries, upon whom the system heavily depended, especially during the 1970s. During this initial introductory stage of television, new color facilities were being readied. A new three-studio complex housing American and European equipment was completed in late 1973, and on July 1, 1974, Emir Sheikh Al-Thani officially opened the PAL color service ("State of Qatar," p. 8). Between this opening date for color television in Qatar and the beginning of the 1980 program schedule, many changes took place. Those in charge of scheduling appear to have finalized a sequence of programs that balances imported Western and Arab productions with some local production of entertainment and information programs.

The Arabic program is telecast on two channels, 9 and 11, and provides complete national coverage. The program can also be seen year-round in Abu Dhabi, Bahrain, and the Dammam-Dhahran area of Saudi Arabia. During the summer months, the signal occasionally reaches Kuwait and areas of the United Arab Emirates. The television service is on the air for a few hours in the morning, featuring religious and other programs. That transmission time is increased during the summer months to include a 4-hour 0900 to 1300 series of programs, presumably for the entertainment of school children who are at home during this time. On Friday, as is the practice in virtually all Arab world television systems, the transmission is extended. Qatar concentrates on programming for children on Friday mornings, featuring cartoons and *The Wonderful World of Disney*.

The normal telecast day started in late afternoon with the Koran reading, a religious discussion, news, and the daily television program review. From approximately 1630 to 1730, cartoons and other programs for children were featured. The 1980 schedule featured *Iftah ya Simsim*, the Arabic *Sesame Street;* a mixture of educational and informational programming; a short religious dramatic series; and the nightly Arabic newscast. The news closely duplicated the established format for other Gulf state countries: news about the activities of the Emir and about Qatar itself was then followed by other Arab world news and international stories that relied heavily on EBU satellite feeds. Before another channel was started primarily for Western-oriented programming, musical features and imported Western and Arabic productions followed the main evening news. In the early 1980s, Arabic and Western entertainment programs were shown between 2015 and the final newscast (usually headlines) at midnight. As of 1990, this main national service is entirely in Arabic.

New studios, control rooms, and transmission facilities permitted Qatar Television to start another channel in the mid-1980s. Operating on UHF Channel 37, Qatar's second television service follows the lead taken by neighboring states such as Saudi Arabia, Bahrain, and Dubai in featuring a television service operating entirely in English. Operating from 1300 to midnight, seven days per week, Channel 37 programs sports and some feature-length films. However, the mainstay of this service is imported Western television programs, mostly from the United States. In 1989 and 1990, for example, this service showed *Rags to Riches, Falcon Crest, Simon and Simon, 227, Dallas, L.A. Law, Miami Vice,* and *The Judge.* There is a 30-

minute English newscast daily from 2200 to 2230 (TV, 1990; *Cycle of programs*, 1989).

Qatar television accepts commercials, most of which are for locally available products from Europe and Japan. They do so despite the fact that the majority of funds needed to operate the television system are provided by the government. There is no receiver license fee. Perhaps an obvious question is why a relatively wealthy country like Qatar permits advertising when that small amount of income is not needed. One answer is that the Ministry of Information, which controls television advertising, wants the television system to help communicate to its citizens that the country still embraces an essentially free-market economy—reasoning similar to that used in Kuwait. In addition, advertising helps the local merchant families, who are most likely to benefit from television commercials. Advertisements meet established standards before being accepted. No alcoholic beverages may be advertised, and there are prohibitions against comparative advertising, gambling, and products of a personal nature that may be offensive to a family audience. Commercials are clustered between programs and may not be shown adjacent to religious programs or political commentaries ("Advertising rates and," 1980, pp. 3–4). Fifteen-, thirty-, forty-five-, and sixty-second commercials are accepted, with a premium price charged for commercials adjacent to popular international sporting events.

As a relative latecomer to both radio and television broadcasting in the Gulf area, Qatar has progressed fairly rapidly—particularly with the construction of radio and television transmitters and studios. Both broadcast media schedules are extensive for a small Arab country with a correspondingly small population. Despite some progress in training Qataris to work with the electronic media, this situation necessitates the use of large numbers of nationals from other Arab countries in order to maintain and operate equipment and to provide some local programming. The country must also rely heavily on importing both English and Arabic programming from other states.

CHAPTER 13

UNITED ARAB EMIRATES

THE 1968 DECISION by the British government to leave the Gulf area affected the collection of sheikhdoms known as the United Arab Emirates (U.A.E.) much the same as it did Bahrain and Qatar. On December 1, 1972, these entities—previously known as the Trucial States—ended their relationship with Great Britain; the U.A.E. was officially formed on December 2, when six of the emirates, Abu Dhabi, Dubai, Sharjah, Ajman, Umm Al Quwain, and Fujeirah, declared themselves a federation. In 1972, another emirate, Ras Al Khaimah, joined the U.A.E. as the seventh member. Bahrain and Qatar, as has been noted, considered joining the federation but decided against it.

The British came to the area in the 1800s to stop the pirates who operated from the coastal areas; hence the original term *Pirate Coast*. British presence is still strong in the area and English is widely spoken.

About 0.25 million people live within the federation's 32,280 square miles. Saudi Arabia, Qatar, and Oman border on the U.A.E. The oil industry, centered in Abu Dhabi and Dubai, has necessitated the importation of skilled labor for petroleum operations. There are Arabs from other countries as well as Iranians, Pakistanis, and Indians who work with the oil, oil service, and local businesses. The expatriate population exceeds the indigenous inhabitants.

The British Broadcasting Corporation estimates that there are 900,000 radio sets, 600,000 television receivers, and 300,000 videocassette recorders in the U.A.E. (British Broadcasting Corporation, 1991b).

THE FACT that the U.A.E. is a federation greatly complicates government administration, including control of the electronic media. Abu Dhabi is the official capital and is the largest emirate with the most oil. Dubai, the traditional capital of commerce, is the second largest emirate and has some oil. The remaining five emirates are not oil-rich, but they vie for a share of

the national wealth. The country embraces a monarchical form of government. The rulers of the seven emirates comprise the Supreme Council of
the U.A.E., of which the ruler of Abu Dhabi is the president and the ruler
of Dubai vice-president. Oil was not commercially available until the early
1960s; since then money from this industry has permitted rapid development
and some drastic cultural changes. Even in the early 1990s, in Abu Dhabi
it is not unusual to see camels tethered near new Mercedes automobiles; in
Dubai there is an ice rink where bedouin in traditional dress may be seen
skating.

The result of the federation system is that broadcasting in the U.A.E.
is unique in the Gulf states. A radio and television system is operated by
the federal government. In addition, broadcasting is done by individual
emirates.

RADIO

British forces first brought radio broadcasting to the area by establishing a station for their own use in Sharjah. Abu Dhabi was the first emirate
to introduce Arabic radio broadcasting when limited programming started
in 1969. After the creation of the U.A.E., this facility became the headquarters for the official federal Arabic radio service. Upon independence, the
service changed its identification from "Abu Dhabi Radio" to "United Arab
Emirates Radio from Abu Dhabi" (Mubarak interview, 1980). After 1971,
new modern studios were added to the complex. The transmission power
of this station was increased with the addition of a super-power (1500-
kilowatt) transmitter. Other lower-power facilities rebroadcast the main
(and only) national service throughout the federation. One shortwave
transmitter is used to reach the Arab world. The linking of these additional
transmitters was made possible when the national telecommunications
network was completed. The service, which is the usual mixture of blocks
of news, drama, music, and informational programs, operates for 19.5 hours
per day.

The second radio service operated by the federal government is a
foreign-language program, originating from Abu Dhabi and heard widely,
but not as extensively throughout the federation as the Arabic program.
English, one of the three foreign languages broadcast, is featured over a
single mediumwave transmitter. Music is an important part of the daily
offering on mediumwave, but a good deal of informational programming is
also provided. Besides news and commentary, daily programs inform
residents and visitors about activities, receptions, and other social events.
Originally, several full-time British contract employees were brought to Abu
Dhabi specifically to work with the English service. However, as of January

1980, only part-time employees were working with the English section. There is French, Urdu, and English programming. The 3-hour nightly program consists of music played by a disc jockey who solicits requests by mail and by phone. This service is staffed by many of the same part-time people as the mediumwave service. The setting of the FM studio and transmitter is unique in the Arab world. The Ministry of Information radio and television compound, like the others in the Arab world, is heavily guarded by the national armed forces and one needs to have permission to enter this complex. By contrast, the FM facilities are housed in the same building as the television transmitter and are completely unguarded.

TELEVISION

The first transmissions were started under the auspices of the Abu Dhabi sheikhdom as a monochrome service on August 6, 1969, prior to the formation of the federation. When Abu Dhabi became the U.A.E. capital, the system became the national television channel, owned and operated by the federal government in a manner almost identical to that of radio. The Abu Dhabi broadcasting complex was expanded after 1971 and new PAL color equipment was installed, enabling color television to start on January 4, 1974 (*TV in the Gulf states*, 1979, p. 18).

Because of a serious shortage of educated, skilled citizens in the U.A.E., television had to rely heavily on outsiders to start and continue to operate the system. Nationals are in charge of various departments of the Ministry of Information that supervise television, but even in the late 1980s over half of the planning and production staff and virtually all technical staff were from Jordan, the Sudan, Egypt, and Lebanon. The first two successive directors of television were from Jordan and the Sudan. The result—not at all unique to the U.A.E.—is that the television service is not entirely programmed with the local culture in mind. There is also little local production aside from news and other informational programming, the majority coming from other countries in the Arab world—primarily Egypt—and the West—mostly from the United States.

In the early 1980s, the daily television schedule started at 1700 and continued until midnight. After the traditional opening and Koran reading there was a period of programming for children—cartoons and *Iftah ya Simsim*, the Arabic *Sesame Street*. Then came an Arabic feature, often a program in a 13-part series, and a locally produced informational program. At 2100, the main Arabic daily news was telecast. It included stories about the activities of the U.A.E. president and vice-president and items about the emirates. Arab world news and international items from the EBU satellite feed followed. After the news, a locally produced film or videotape feature about some aspect of the U.A.E. was shown. At 2230, the news was presented in English. This was almost always identical to what was shown 1.5 hours earlier on the Arabic news and was read by two native English speakers, one of whom was usually a part-time employee of the radio service. The closing program was an entertainment feature, either in Arabic or in English.

By the late 1980s, several developments changed the federal television system. First, following the practice of virtually every Gulf country, the U.A.E. added a second national television channel. The main channel, Abu Dhabi 5, became an Arabic all-day service, operating from 0900 to midnight. In many respects, this channel resembles the type of programming found on a Western station. That is, in the morning, programming concentrates on the female audience, followed by news, educational programming, and entertainment programs—Arabic soap operas—until midnight. The second channel, Abu Dhabi 35, is primarily but not entirely in English. Programming starts at 1630 and operates until approximately midnight. With mostly imported Western programs such as *Remington Steele*, this is where the English news is telecast daily at 2130 (TV, 1990).

Using a series of repeater television transmitters, the federal television service reaches about 90 percent of the population. The national microwave telecommunications system provides network interconnection.

There is competition for viewers in the U.A.E. from other television services within the federation, in addition to signals that can be received from Oman, Saudi Arabia, and Qatar. The federal Ministry of Information is aware that its service has a responsibility to uphold and promote the national interests of the entire federation. Thus, entertainment programming is not emphasized; informational and cultural programming, within personnel and budgetary limitations, must take priority on the main Arabic service. The broadcast media have problems similar to those faced by other branches of the Ministry of Information. The federal government, in an attempt to include personnel from all seven emirates, has been forced to appoint people who are not educationally or administratively qualified. In addition, these employees from other emirates, though working in Abu Dhabi, continue to maintain their residences in the other emirates. Therefore travel time between home and job often means loss of two days per week. The four-day work week for commuters adds to the responsibilities of the nationals of other countries who, in reality, do most of the planning and actual work. All federation members realize that a national radio and television service plays a necessary role in the unification of the country. However, individual emirates have the right to broadcast; and in one emirate, Dubai, commercial radio and television programming is a major business.

DUBAI AND THE FEDERATION

The creation of the federation of emirates in 1971 did not remove the right of members to undertake certain activities that they believe important to their own development. Indeed, there is competition among the seven for the more visible aspects of development such as airports, hotels, schools, etc. Dubai, though not oil-rich, has been a thriving commercial and banking capital since the 1950s. The city itself is a blend of old and new buildings and modern Western-owned hotels that cater to the international business traveler. Dubai probably has more international bank branches per capita than any other city in the world. The economic health of this city is due in large measure to the U.A.E. vice-president and local ruler, Sheikh Rashid, who is an aggressive businessman. Although not well known outside the Middle East, Rashid's name became a daily press item in mid-1990 during the Bank of Credit and Commerce International (BCCI) scandal. One of his advisors, Riad Shuabi, a Palestinian, was the main force behind the initial introduction of radio and television as well as its later expansion into what at one time was the most aggressive production and marketing organization for Arabic television programming outside of Egypt. Shuabi increased his financial holdings in both print and electronic media to include an interest in advertising and in *Eight Days*, a London-based English-language magazine specializing in the Arab world.

DUBAI TELEVISION AND RADIO

Dubai television started broadcasting a commercial monochrome service from Dubai in 1972 (Robertson interview, 1980). Essentially operated during the evening hours, the station showed imported Arabic and Western entertainment programs that would attract a large audience for those who were interested in advertising on the station. Relatively little local production was done at first, except for limited news broadcasts. This Channel 2 service was popular among the large expatriate population in Dubai and Abu Dhabi as well as with the local population. Advertisers were attracted to the service, which seemed to be a natural part of the thriving commercial activity in Dubai. With the success of Channel 2, plans were made for a more extensive service, which by the late 1970s had produced two separate commercial channels (one Arabic and one English), a commercial FM radio service, and a major television production and marketing company. The contrast between the radio and television services in Dubai and Abu Dhabi is striking, primarily because of the completely different orientations of the two services. While the Abu Dhabi-based national service programs respond to the needs of all seven emirates, Dubai concentrates on commercially oriented broadcasting. The Dubai radio and television services rely exclusively on expatriates. Even some management positions have been held by British citizens. The television facilities are superbly maintained and among the most elaborate and modern in the Arab world.

Program One

Program One, known as Dubai 10, is a PAL color station intended mostly for Arabic speakers. The signal does not reach all of the country because it is essentially a regional service that is operated by a company controlled by Sheikh Rashid—in effect representing the Dubai government. The signal is received reliably in Abu Dhabi, Sharjah, and Umm Al Quwain on three channels. There is some limited local programming in the form of news, interviews, and religious programs. Yet the majority of the schedule is a mixture of older imported subtitled programs and relatively new Arabic features. Occasionally, the facilities of the two services are linked to transmit the same program, such as a popular Western film ("Dubai radio and," 1980, p. 2). Program One, however, caters almost exclusively to speakers of Arabic, and some of the Arabic programming that is telecast is produced in the adjoining Dubai production center.

Program Two

In June 1978 a second television service started. The audience for this English-language color channel is primarily the expatriate population and Western-oriented local residents. The station is also called by its channel number, 33.

These two television services operate from separate control rooms and use one of two studios available for news and other limited local informational programming. The Dubai radio and television complex also contains studio "C," which is used exclusively for the taping of Arabic productions. Completed in December 1978, this facility constitutes the main production facility of the Arabian Gulf Production Company. The organization was created by Riad Shuabi to produce programming for Arab world television stations and to market productions from Dubai as well as those done in other Arab world studios. Only the main 1,100-square-meter studio in the Egyptian television complex is larger than studio "C." This Dubai studio was designed to allow 1,050 square meters of studio floor space—intentionally 50 square meters more than the main BBC television studio in London. It is equipped with the latest television production, lighting, and videotape editing equipment. The studio is usually in continuous operation, with as many as four separate sets in the studio at one time. Often as one scene from a series is being taped, a different part of the studio is being readied for another scene from the series or for another series.

The economic conditions that motivated the creation of this business have been noted in the chapter on Egypt (see Chapter 2, Television, 1974 to 1981). However, toward the end of the 1980s, Egypt's peace treaty with Israel became more accepted; thus, Egyptians and Egyptian programming became once again a staple of Gulf, and U.A.E., Arabic television programming.

There is a basic need for more Arab world productions among Middle Eastern television stations—particularly those in the Gulf states that can afford to pay the prices such productions demand. Until the mid-1980s, the marketing efforts of the official Egyptian television sales organization were hampered by that country's peace agreement with Israel and the resultant attempts by Arab countries to boycott Egyptian products and services. The Dubai production center was frequently rented by Egyptian directors and producers who brought Egyptian actors to the facility to make programs. Egyptian material is still the most popular in the Arab world; moreover, Egyptians who produce and appear in productions that are not taped in Egypt are not subject to the boycott. The Arabian Gulf Production Company has helped the Egyptian Television Organization sell programs taped in Egypt by editing that makes them appear to have been shot elsewhere. This highly professional facility includes an adjoining hotel and restaurant that caters exclusively to artists who come to Dubai to undertake television productions.

Dubai Radio—Arabic Service

The Dubai Radio—Arabic Service started in 1971. Using a staff that is comprised of over 50 percent Arab expatriates, the service is essentially music-oriented with some news and brief features (Ahmed interview, 1980). The mediumwave signal can be heard throughout the United Arab Emirates and the commercial rates are slightly higher than those on the sister English radio service.

Dubai Radio—English Service

This service is broadcast exclusively on FM. Western popular music is played throughout the day by DJs who are native English speakers, and record requests are taken.

The commercial success of the two television and the Arabic and English radio services in Dubai has made the U.A.E. an important broadcasting center. Even more significant is the impressive Dubai-based Arabian Gulf Production Company, which supplies facilities for the majority of taped syndicated Arabic productions sold in the Middle East. The success of the Dubai operations has given rise to imitators in at least one other emirate. There is a station in Ras Al Khaimah that operates like the first

Dubai television station, with nightly transmission of imported programs and no local production. It is, however, unlikely that Dubai's fellow federation members will become competitive threats. The smaller emirates to the south of Dubai do not have the economic base or the capability to organize production activities on the scale of what has been built in Dubai.

The unique political and economic nature of the U.A.E. has produced two distinct systems of radio and television broadcasting. One, operated by the national government headquartered in Abu Dhabi, features a noncommercial radio system and a commercial television system. The programming philosophy of both media is oriented toward the tastes and interests of the population of all seven emirates. The Dubai system, the second major one in the country, is run as a profit-making venture. Its programming is designed to attract a large audience for potential advertisers. The Arabian Gulf Production Company is a major production facility for the Arab countries and provides an example of how quickly the media have developed in the Arabian Gulf area.

CHAPTER 14

OMAN

APPROXIMATELY 1.4 million people live in Oman, an independent sultanate of 82,000 square miles in the southeastern part of the Arabian Peninsula. Oman's neighbors are Yemen, Saudi Arabia, and the United Arab Emirates (U.A.E.). The small Musadam Peninsula, separated from the main portion of Oman by the U.A.E., is strategically located on the Strait of Hormuz, through which 40 percent of the world's oil passes.

Known until 1970 as Muscat and Oman, the country was one of the less developed in the Middle East until a 1970 coup organized by Qaboos bin Said resulted in the exile of his father to London. The country's development since 1970 has been impressive, particularly when one considers that progress has been accomplished largely without the oil income that most other Gulf states have. Oman does have some petroleum, but the amount only meets domestic needs, with little left over for export.

The BBC estimates that there are 700,000 radio receivers, 300,000 television sets, and 200,000 videocassette recorders in Oman (British Broadcasting Corporation, 1991b).

IN THE 19TH CENTURY, Oman and Great Britain established a special relationship that, to some extent, still exists. British civil servants and military officers hold positions as advisors at the request of the ruler, himself educated at Sandhurst. Qaboos believes that these and other Western advisors are necessary to help organize the country in light of its location. South Yemen was through the years a particularly hostile neighbor: the Marxist government there supported a separatist movement that was militarily active for about 10 years in the Dhofar area until successful Omani military efforts brought the fighting to a halt in 1975. Oman faces no significant internal threats: the military concentrates on security along the 1,000-mile coastline.

The two major cities that constitute the capital area, Muscat and Matrah, are probably the most picturesque on the Arabian coastline. Old Portuguese ruins, a reminder of a former European influence, and modern buildings combine to create an unspoiled effect not found in neighboring countries.

RADIO

The attitude of the government toward the broadcast media changed immediately after Qaboos bin Said took power. Prior to 1970, the country lacked many—some say any—elements of modern development. The first mediumwave transmitter, built near Muscat, had a power of 1 kilowatt. Programming was limited to a few hours per day. In 1973 the power was increased to 100 kilowatts, and on November 17, 1974, a new Muscat mediumwave transmitter was inaugurated. In Salala, a 100-kilowatt mediumwave facility was built to serve the section of Oman near what was then South Yemen. The national Arabic program is also transmitted from a shortwave transmitter, providing coverage to all parts of the country not already served by the mediumwave signals. Until an English-language program started in the late 1980s, English, the only other language then used on Radio Oman, replaced Arabic daily from 1300 to 1500 hours (Siyabi interview, 1980). Programming emphasizes news and information concerning government development policies and accomplishments. Most of the program and production personnel of the station are Omani, but Arabs from other countries help with equipment, transmitter operation, and maintenance. Until the mid-1980s, British advisors helped with some of the program and technical planning.

At first, the ruler was especially concerned about the lack of radio coverage. As a result, plans were made to increase the number of medium-wave transmitters (Ashworth interview, 1980). Not only did the government want to reach all citizens with its development, cultural, and political messages, but it wanted to provide a viable alternative to the then frequent hostile broadcasts from what was then South Yemen on behalf of the Popular Front for the Liberation of Oman. South Yemeni transmitters had broadcast anti-Oman propaganda for years; activity increased in 1979, when Oman was reported to be considering providing military facilities to the United States, which was seeking a stronger military presence in the Middle East. These broadcasts decreased considerably by the mid-1980s and essentially stopped after the South Yemen coup in January 1986 and the eventual reunion with North Yemen.

The English Service, available on mediumwave, operates from 0700 to 2200 and features a mixture of imported packaged music of various types, locally produced news, and some musical programs ("Radio," 1991).

Masirah, an island off the Omani coast in the Arabian Sea, is the location of the British Broadcasting Corporation's Eastern Relay medium-

and shortwave transmitters that rebroadcast the Arabic, Hindi, Persian, Urdu, and English services originating in London. The Omani government does not use any of these transmitters.

TELEVISION

Television is considered by the government to be an important part of development. The medium's development has gone according to a plan whereby first a station would become operational in the capital area, then a second station would be built in the Dhofar region, and finally the signal would be provided to major population areas by microwave and satellite. On November 17, 1974, the Muscat station went on the air with limited programming. For five years this station was operated and maintained by a German company that had a contract with the Ministry of Information. In 1975, a second and almost identical station became operational in Salala. This facility was operated under contract by a British company. In 1979, when both contracts expired, the government determined that it was capable of operating the stations itself with the help of Arabs from other countries and a few of the Western contract employees. In late 1979 Oman hired about 20 Jordanian television engineers and technicians who became responsible for both stations under the supervision of a few Europeans employed under the original contract. The distribution of the Omani television channel is at least as widespread as Omani radio. This is accomplished by a leased satellite circuit that distributes the signal to ground stations and transmitters in addition to the main transmitter sites located at the two major stations ("Oman colour television," n.d.). The same distribution network makes it possible for the two stations, Muscat and Salala, to feed local news items and productions to each other.

The organization of television is relatively streamlined. A director general of radio and television reports to the Minister of Information. The Director General, in turn, appoints and is responsible for various engineering, administration, and programming heads. There is no license fee for broadcast receivers in Oman and advertising is not permitted. The entire budget for these operations is supplied by the government.

TELEVISION PROGRAMMING

The one Omani national PAL color program operates from approximately 1500 to midnight daily, except on Friday, when programming starts earlier. Imported programs from the Arab world and the West constitute the bulk of the daily schedule. Egypt is Oman's main television program supplier. Imported Western programming is deemphasized and limited to older serious documentaries and entertainment programs such as *Star Trek*, *Project U.F.O.*, *Kung Fu*, *Chopper Squad*, and *The Odd Couple* ("Oman television schedule: January 1 to March 31, 1980"). There are two daily 30-minute newscasts—English at 2000 and Arabic at 2200 hours ("Television schedule," 1991). Video for the international news is taken almost exclusively from daily satellite news feeds such as the one provided by the European Broadcasting Union.

Several programs are scheduled for production each week, mostly from the Muscat studios. These include a family program, a quiz show, a musical variety program, a children's program, and various programs of an educational nature on, for example, health, traffic, or the country's history. Religious programs are also taped and telecast each week. When television was first started, there was concern among government officials that there would be opposition to the medium from some conservative elements, in a manner similar to fears of Saudi Arabian officials in the mid-1960s. However, the concerns of religious leaders were allayed by the government when they were told that television would be used to extend the religious message (Siyabi interview, 1980).

There is almost no interest in making Oman a production center to compete with Dubai or some of the other countries that rent studio space for Arabic program production. The Ministry does not believe that it is a sound financial investment. In addition, for security reasons the government has been very hesitant to grant visas to Arabs from other countries. In the late 1970s there was one exception. People were brought from other Arab countries to direct and act in a series of locally taped programs that dealt with Oman's history as a maritime country. Some of the programs were shown in other Arab countries, but this is the only effort of this kind that Omani television has undertaken.

Among ranking Omani cabinet ministers, there is a great deal of interest in improving Omani television. They, along with most of the Omani television staff, understand that because of the location of the major cities they do not compete with neighboring signals; television does, however, compete with home video recorders. After a month-long study in January 1986 under a U.S. Agency for International Development contract, I proposed a specific training plan to improve staff quality, but the proposal was not funded.

THE AUDIENCE

Set ownership is pervasive, especially among those in the upper-middle and above income brackets. In an effort to make television available to those who could not afford a set during the early television years, the government placed large-screen color receivers in public places. Oman is the only Gulf state to have undertaken a program of placing sets in populated areas. The other countries apparently felt that citizens had the financial means to acquire receivers. In 1980 one of the public sets in Muscat was located at a major intersection on the harbor road. The large crowds attracted caused some traffic congestion at night. By 1986 all public sets had disappeared.

Oman does not intend, in the short run, to become an important international radio broadcaster to the Arab world. The country's radio goal is to provide most citizens with the national service on mediumwave. This goal, when accomplished, will spread the Omani message of development and will offer a viable alternative to the hostile broadcasts from South Yemen, directed primarily toward the Dhofar area. Probably no television service in the Gulf states is more aware of the necessity of linking programming to the government's goals. Imported programs from the West are shown, but not as extensively as in some other countries in the area. Local production of a nondramatic nature is accomplished with a small staff that achieves relatively high-quality results.

CHAPTER 15

Conclusions

EACH GULF STATE has developed a broadcasting system that it believes best suits its needs and that is different from the systems of other states. However, there are many similarities among these countries in the way they program their electronic media. These similarities may also apply to the systems in other countries in the Arab world, but, for reasons noted at the beginning of Part 3, the Gulf countries have banded together to cooperate in areas where they feel common interests exist.

The following observations are offered after extensive on-site examination of the Gulf states' systems.

Gulf television is heavily entertainment oriented. Programs that are imported from the West or from other Arab countries or those that are taped locally are essentially for entertainment. Some programming of an educational/developmental nature is done for each country's television system; but music, drama, and other forms of entertainment dominate television. Probably the major reason for this situation is a lack of understanding on the part of programmers about how television might be used for purposes other than entertainment. Officials are often too busy keeping the stations running and coping with technical expansion to plan programming that will meet educational/developmental goals. This also applies to radio.

Arab expatriate workers are used extensively in the Gulf states. Jordanian engineers and technicians are employed in large numbers in all area countries except Iraq. Egyptian, Lebanese, and Sudanese radio and television personnel have been used in the technical operations of broadcasting. Attracted by the high salaries in the Gulf states, Arab expatriates are found in programming, commercial sales, news, and local production and administration.

Also, the Gulf area has become a major production center. Due primarily to the Dubai television production studios, the Gulf states have attracted top Egyptian writers, directors, and actors who have produced programs that rival those made in Egypt. Factors that have allowed this development include the move among Arab countries to boycott Egyptian-made television productions, the increased desire among Gulf countries for Arabic productions that they do not believe they can produce themselves, and the willingness of Egyptian and other artists to come to the Gulf, where high salaries and professional facilities permit a short production schedule. Abu Dhabi and Bahrain rent studios to those who wish to undertake productions, but these locations have neither the facilities nor the atmosphere to rival the Dubai operation.

International radio and television broadcasting is pervasive. The climate and proximity of the Gulf states mean that citizens of one country can and apparently do receive broadcasts from neighboring countries. Depending on the time of year, as many as seven different television channels can be seen in Saudi Arabia's Eastern Province, Bahrain, Qatar, and the U.A.E. Radio signals from these countries are receivable on mediumwave as well as on FM. Some countries such as Saudi Arabia have intentionally built stations that will reach other countries in order to extend influence, while other stations, such as the one in Bahrain, attempt to reach neighboring markets in order to make their service attractive to advertisers.

English-language programming and news are used extensively. Each Gulf state system broadcasts a daily television newscast in English. All countries in this region have radio services that broadcast domestically in English. Some states—Bahrain, Dubai, Qatar—operate full-time English services. Most of the program time on these services is devoted to music, specifically British and American popular music, including country and western. There are also imported television programs from the United States and Great Britain. Programmers believe that these programs are popular among viewers and are relatively inexpensive to show. Television programming in English tends to be used more heavily on systems that have two channels, such as in Kuwait and Dubai, and on systems that permit advertising, as are found in Qatar and Bahrain.

Still another similarity is that news items from outside the Arab world are alike. All systems in the Gulf area feature nightly television newscasts. There is usually one major newscast in addition to scheduled times when headlines are read. For international news, each country receives, tapes, and uses items supplied by the EBU daily satellite feeds. The second of the two daily feeds occurs about 2000 hours, depending on the local time in summer and winter. With little time before the Arabic news, news personnel view the feed as it is taped and note the stories that seem appropriate for use. The stories are used in order of taping as the tape is put on fast forward during the on-air transition provided by the newsreader. The effect is to create international newscasts that are similar and, in some cases, identical.

The videocassette markets in Kuwait, Bahrain, Saudi Arabia, Qatar, and the U.A.E. are thriving. There are sufficient numbers of people with both the financial means and the motivation to purchase equipment and to purchase or rent mostly pirated tapes of first-run films and television programs. Saudi Arabia sees the most activity of this kind in the Gulf area, and possibly in the world, because of the few entertainment choices available to people who do not live in the Eastern Province.

Beginning in the 1960s, some of the Gulf states began coordinating telecommunication, defense, banking, petroleum, and civil air transportation policies. One part of their overall attempt to promote communication and cooperation is their cooperative effort in the broadcasting field. In the early 1970s, cooperation was encouraged within the framework of the Arab States Broadcasting Union for news and program exchanges (Boyd, 1975a, pp. 311–20). Because of similar interests in the information field, the Gulf Ministers of Information started meeting to discuss ways in which cooperation in radio and television broadcasting could be increased. By the second ministers' conference in 1977, Gulfvision had been formed to promote news and programming among member states. Gulfvision is an organization to which all seven Gulf states belong. The wealthier states believe that cooperation is in their best interests, and countries such as Saudi Arabia, where Gulfvision is headquartered, subsidize membership of the less wealthy countries. These excerpts from the Gulf States Television Charter reflect some of the basic concerns of the member countries with respect to television programming standards:

> One of the targets which the Gulf States Television endeavour to achieve is to maintain the local cultural characteristics as these are considered among the major tributaries of the Arab culture.
>
> In all its programs the television service should maintain the moral and social values of conduct originating from the Islamic Faith, which are the corner stone of the spiritual, educational, and cultural basis of this region.
>
> Obscene or vulgar expressions injurious to any public taste should under no circumstances be used. Any scene or term inviting degradation, nudity or provocating sexual instincts or vice should be deleted.
>
> When selecting foreign programs it should be taken into consideration that these do not include any offense to the religious, social or cultural values of the viewers or any insult to their national or human feelings, or any embarrassment to the political authorities of the states.
>
> Foreign programs based on provocation of sexual desires or violence, or causing fear or displaying violence in contradiction with common human values shall be excluded.
>
> Care should be taken that the program shall not include anything which may lead in words or picture to teach the public new criminal methods which can be imitated even if the criminal and the crime are condemned at the end of the program.
>
> Care should be taken when presenting foreign programs to the children

or youth so that no specimens conflicting with their upbringing according to the society's objectives are presented. (*TV in the Gulf states*, 1979, pp. 119–25)

Once per month, on a rotating basis, each Gulfvision member country tapes a program about its country. Copies are distributed to member states, which, in turn, attempt to telecast the program at a specified time and day. Other plans for cooperation have been discussed; however, the most tangible effort made by the Gulf states has been in the area of children's programming.

In 1976, the Kuwait-based Arabian Gulf States Joint Program Production Institution was formed. This organization is an outgrowth of the cooperative efforts among the Gulf states, with the exception of Oman ("Facts about Iftah," n.d., p. 1; Al Yusuf interview, 1980). The organization produces documentaries about the region, and dubs Western cartoons into Arabic for the use of members and for sale to other Arab countries. This most ambitious effort has established a new standard for children's programming in the Arab world.

The idea for an Arabic *Sesame Street* appears to have originated with Abdulrahman Shobaili, a former director general of television in Saudi Arabia. Shobaili was impressed with the American program while he was completing his graduate work in the United States. Consequently, he purchased the program to be shown without subtitles or dubbing in Saudi Arabia in 1972. The possibility of producing an Arabic version of the program was discussed in Riyadh, Saudi Arabia, with representatives of the Ford Foundation and Children's Television Workshop, which owns the rights to the program. Initial financial support was supplied by the Ford Foundation and the Kuwaiti Arab Fund for various linguistic studies. The result is a visually impressive and extremely popular 130-program series, which was taped in the modern Kuwait television production center. *Iftah Ya Simsim* was first telecast in all seven Gulf states in the fall of 1979 and is available for sale to other countries.

Before the series was taped, and after pilot programs had been made, extensive research was done in several Arab countries. Even before the pilots were planned a team of linguists attempted to devise a form of modern standard Arabic that would be acceptable in all Arab countries. The various educational goals of each program were finalized with a group of Arab educators and psychologists representing several regions of the Middle East. The final product has some obvious similarities to the American counterpart: the setting is Street No. 26, where various adults live and interact with children; there are some Muppet characters; there is Malsoun (a parrot), and Noaman, a cross between a camel and a bear, serves as the Arab Big Bird. All Gulf countries telecast the program between 1530 and 1830 hours, with somewhat predictable results. The production is so superior to the various children's programs done by individual stations that it has set a new standard for children's programming. As with the initial reaction to *Sesame Street* in the United States, some of the most ardent fans of the program are parents who watch it with their children. The reaction to the program in Saudi Arabia was so enthusiastic that the government suspended the production of locally produced programs for young children.

The program is not without its critics, however. Dr. Nawaf Adwan, who heads the Arab State Broadcasting Union Research Center in Baghdad, Iraq, agrees that the program is visually exciting but also observes that it tends to reinforce one of the main features of the traditional Arab systems of education—rote learning (Adwan interview, 1980). The Arab countries outside the Gulf region have been hesitant to purchase the program for a variety of reasons. Egypt, a country that could possibly benefit most from televising the program, resisted purchasing it even though the Gulf Production Center arranged a special low price for the package. The Egyptians say, among other things, that they do not like the language. However, they are also concerned that *Iftah Ya Simsim* would reflect unfavorably on their children's programs. In addition they are not purchasing programs from countries that support the Egyptian boycott. Whatever the criticisms, the productions are the largest cooperative television effort in the Arab world. The fact that the shows were taped and are being shown in the Gulf states is an important achievement for states concerned about maintaining their unique cultures.

Part 4
North Africa

CHAPTER 16

ALGERIA

Yahia Mahamdi

ALGERIA is located between Morocco and Tunisia on the coast of North Africa. Its 900,000 square miles of land area consists mostly of mountains and desert; only 12 percent of its land, a fertile coastal strip 750 miles long where the majority of the population lives, is cultivated. As of 1989, the population of Algeria was estimated at 24.6 million, with an annual increase of 2.8 percent. Around 60 percent of the population is under 20 years old.

The Atlas mountain range divides the country into northern and southern regions and acts as a natural barrier to radio and television signals, a barrier that prompted Algeria to use mediumwave frequencies for national radio and satellite for television. The official language of the country is Arabic, but French continues to be used as a working language, especially in business, higher education, and international communication. About one-fifth of the population speak a variety of Berber dialects: Kabyle (in the central coastal area), Chaouia (in the Aures mountains), Mozabite (in the South), and Targui/Zenati (in the extreme South).

In addition to its oil, Algeria has huge reserves of natural gas, estimated at 12 percent of the world's reserves. About 97 percent of Algeria's export revenues are from oil and gas and related products. The declining price of oil in the early 1980s, combined with a considerable drop

Following Yahia Mahamdi's four years as a cinematographer for Algerian television, he studied cinema and communication at the University of Paris, where he earned BA and MA degrees. His Ph.D. is from the Department of Radio-TV-Film at the University of Texas at Austin. He has taught film and video production and media studies at several universities in the United States and Norway. He is Senior Lecturer and Director of the Television Production Section at the Department of Mass Communication, University of Bergen, Norway. Professor Mahamdi is currently working on a book about the international television program trade.

in export revenues and the $20 million debt load (as of 1987), resulted in a sharp economic downturn in the mid-1980s and led the government to adopt unpopular austerity measures. Algeria's GNP was $2,550 in 1986 but has been declining steadily since. Its official unemployment rate is 17 percent, but the actual figure is much higher.

Until very recently, Algeria was a one-party Islamic socialist state under the FLN party, the Front de Libération Nationale. The Constitution of 1989, whose content and urgency were prompted in part by the October 1988 uprising[1] staged by unemployed youth and high school students, has ended the one-party system and opened the door to economic liberalization.

Modern Algeria was shaped by two historical processes: French colonization, which lasted 132 years, and a 7-year war of national liberation, which led to the creation of the Algerian nation.

During the 132 years of French colonial administration, Algerian society underwent drastic social, political, and cultural transformations. Under colonization, the traditional social and political system, which was based on family and tribal organizations, was disrupted as the French established a new administrative infrastructure to rule the new colony and imposed a capitalist model of agricultural and industrial production to replace the traditional (feudal) economic organization.

As French settlement increased and as Algeria was proclaimed an integral part of France, French language, administration, and culture were imposed on the indigenous populations of the urban centers through the replacement of Arabic by French in the schools, the entrenchment of the French model of government, and colonial control over the country's key cultural institutions. However, the rural areas where most of the indigenous population lived were not developed as intensively as the urban centers and prime agricultural areas. The absence of schools in these areas resulted in increased rural illiteracy and reduced the average Algerian's access to French culture. This, combined with the oppression of colonial rule and the marginalization of traditional Algerian culture, resulted in generalized cultural alienation.

The Algerian nationalist movement addressed this cultural alienation by focusing on the problems of language and religion in rallying Algerians against colonial rule. While the French language provided access to the dominant culture for a restricted urban elite, its imposition on the rest of Algerian society resulted in the suppression of traditional Arabic language and culture and a bifurcated cultural landscape. Thus, the Algerian nationalist movement promoted Arabic as the language of resistance, social unification, and, with Islam, the vehicle for national identity. As the Algerian cultural historian, Lacheraf (1965, p. 324) points out, "The [Algerian] people declared the French language a worthless and passing language, by opposition to Arabic, which became the language of spiritual merit in the afterlife."

After independence, and once the Algerian state was established, the task was to define a new Algerian identity and work toward its consolidation and development. This task was further complicated as Algeria took the challenge to modernize at the same time as it reclaimed its Arabic-Islamic heritage, suppressed during the years of colonization. This dualism between tradition and modernity, or "essentialism and epochalism" (Geertz, 1975), has been a fundamental characteristic of Algerian society since independence and has complicated the task of defining national culture because, while modernization in Algeria appears to lead inevitably to westernization and increased reliance on the French language, tradition calls for a return to Arabic language and Islamic civilization.

Although since independence Algeria has staunchly pursued a policy of *Arabisation* (an emphasis on Arabic and Algerian culture and the progressive abandonment of French language and culture) and has made Arabic mandatory in elementary education, the adaptation of Arabic to science, technology, and higher education has been slow. French is still used as the working language in international communication, business, trade, education, publishing, and in the mass media in general, where the reliance on French technical know-how, personnel training, and programming, in the case of television broadcasting, persists.

Arabisation has been a source of conflict and ideological struggle between factions of the governing elite. The pro-French faction argues that a modern, universal, and scientific European language is better suited to Algeria's modernization program. Algeria, according to this argument, although belonging to the Arab world, should maintain its ties with the West both because of its economic and technological dependency and because of the Mediterranean cultural heritage it shares with France and other European countries. The pro-Arabic faction argues that Arabic can be adapted to the modern world and that if the emphasis on the Arabic language is lost, the Arab-Islamic renaissance in Algeria would be incomplete. This faction argues that other countries (notably Japan and Israel) have developed their economies without sacrificing their languages, and that Algeria can do the same. This conflict over language, itself a part of the larger debate concerning modernity and tradition, is nowhere more predominant and visible than in the domain of broadcasting, particularly in television, which has emerged as a major cultural force.

The BBC estimates that there are 5.5 million radio sets, 33.8 million television receivers, and 670,000 videocassette recorders in Algeria (British Broadcasting Corporation, 1991b).

BROADCASTING DURING THE COLONIAL PERIOD: SERVING THE INTERESTS OF THE COLONISTS

Radio broadcasting began in Algeria in 1937 as a service to the 1 million French colonists and was called France Cinq (the fifth French channel). Most of the programs were relayed from Paris as production facilities were very limited. As new production facilities were created during and after World War II, radio broadcasting was expanded to include an Arabic channel in 1940 and a Berber (Kabyle) channel in 1948. Studios were expanded in Algiers and built in Oran and Constantine. The Arabic and Kabyle channels were conceived as part of a local service called Emissions des Langues Arabe et Kabyle (ELAK) whose purpose was to provide publicity and support for the French "civilizing" presence in Algeria. Broadcasting was limited during these early years of radio in Algeria (3 hours weekly for the Kabyle station).

Transmission facilities in Algiers in the 1950s consisted of 100-kilowatt transmitters for the French and Arabic channels and 20-kilowatt transmitters for the Kabyle channel as well as for the stations transmitting from Oran and Constantine. With the beginning of the war of liberation in 1954, the French government increased the number of small transmitters and broadcast hours to cover the populated areas of the North. By this time, the three radio stations were broadcasting 84 hours per week in French, 60 hours per week in Arabic, and 26 hours per week in Kabyle to an estimated 255,000 radio sets (*L'Algérie Contemporaine*, 1954, p. 190).

The armed rebellion against French colonialism also spurred the creation of television broadcasting in 1956, just two years after the outbreak of hostilities. The French broadcasting organization Radiodiffusion Télévision Française (RTF) installed transmitters in the key northern cities of Algiers (50 watts), Blida (100 watts), Constantine (50 watts), and Oran (100 watts). Programming was first imported from France in the form of films and telerecorded programs which were then sent over the air using the tele-cine. In 1958, however, RTF engineers introduced a tropospheric transmission system that enabled programs to be transmitted directly from France. In these early days of television, receivers were the near-exclusive property of the colonists, programming was predominantly in French, except for a few news programs in Arabic and Kabyle, and local production remained very limited.

When the Evian accords between the French government and the Algerian leaders were signed in 1962 to end the war, the terrorist organization Organisation de l'Armée Secrète (OAS), a third force opposed to any settlement between France and the FLN, started a wave of violent attacks and sabotage, concentrating on telephone exchanges, radio and television transmitters, power plants, libraries, bridges, factories, and stores in the hope of undermining the Evian agreements. The communications infrastructure was badly damaged and the situation was exacerbated by the sudden departure of nearly all the French technicians and engineers, who were needed for the repair and operation of the installations. By October 1962, approximately 90 percent of the French had left, leaving behind an Algeria in desperate need of doctors, engineers, technicians, and other vital professionals (Ottaway and Ottaway, p. 10).

At the end of October, the RTF in Paris ordered all of its French staff in Algeria to return immediately. Broadcasting came to a virtual halt, but there was enough enthusiasm and dedication on the part of the Algerians who took over to keep the system running, with a practically nonexistent stock of local programs and insufficient staff.

BROADCASTING AFTER INDEPENDENCE: THE FRENCH LEGACY AND THE CREATION OF THE RADIODIFFUSION TÉLÉVISION ALGÉRIENNE (RTA)

In January 1963, the RTF became the RTA and a governmental decree (*Journal Officiel,* 1963) defined it as a "financially autonomous public authority of commercial and industrial character under the authority of the Ministry of Information." This status was copied almost word-for-word from the RTF model, perpetuating the French model of government control of broadcasting with little attempt to explore new alternatives. The continuation of the French system of broadcasting by the Algerian government after independence was explained not only by reasons of expediency and the automatic inheritance of French institutions following independence, but also by the absence of a clearly defined role for television in the platform of the FLN party. Nonetheless, because the overall plans of the FLN called for the construction of a modern state that would take charge of the nation's vital resources, the French system of government control of broadcasting fit the Algerian government's desire to establish its control not only over radio and television, but also over all the means of information.

Thus, from its inception, the RTA was subject to close ministerial control: the Ministry of Information and Culture appointed the RTA's general director, the directors of the main services (radio, television, technical services, and general administration), and the Conseil Supérieure de la Radio Télévision, whose task was the coordination of informational programs, artistic production, and matters of policy. Finance was controlled, as in France, by the Ministry of Finance, which provided the budget for broadcasting established by the government.

Another indication of French influence on Algerian broadcast legislation was the creation of the administrative council (conseil d'administration) during the 1967 organizational reform. The administrative council of the RTA was a body that was supposed to act as an intermediary between the government and the television staff and also as a buffer against excessive governmental interference. It was composed of representatives from five ministries, a representative from the presidency, three members of the Ministry of Information, a representative of the Algerian Press Service, a representative of the RTA, and one other person selected on the basis of his interest in broadcasting.

An almost identical reform had been implemented in France three years earlier, in 1964, when the RTF was renamed the ORTF (Office de Radiodiffusion Télévision Française) and the same "conseil d'administration" was created for the same purposes. In both the French and Algerian systems, governmental control was exercised over the appointment of council members. In spite of the similarities between the French ORTF and the RTA, the Algerian system remained more overtly connected to the government than did the French system. In addition, if the new structures of the ORTF allowed some relaxing of state control and paved the way for the forthcoming introduction of advertising in 1968, the RTA, despite some gains of independence in terms of the management of its operations, remained under the close supervision of the government.

Thus, the 1967 administrative reform gave the RTA more independence at the managerial level, but government control over editorial policy remained as powerful as before. The real reason for the reform was the deficient performance of RTA in the production of local television programming. Apart from news and studio discussions of current affairs, little local programming had been produced, partly because of bureaucratic inertia and partly because of the lack of financial resources available for production (most of the RTA's resources are used to pay the salaries of administrative personnel).

After the reorganization, the RTA attempted to reduce its heavy dependence on French television programs that the ORTF had provided for nominal cost and began to initiate its own purchase operations in the international market. Despite this effort, however, the growth of local programming remained very slow. In 1969, only a quarter of the RTA's output was locally produced, most of it consisting of information and news programs. A substantial increase in local production would not occur until broadcasting was called upon to play an enhanced role in the country's drive for development and economic and cultural independence during the Boumedienne regime.

BROADCASTING UNDER STATE MONOPOLY: THE BOUMEDIENNE ERA

Houari Boumedienne came to power through the military coup of 1965 that toppled Ahmed Ben Bella, the first Algerian president. Under Boumedienne's presidency (1965–1978), the processes of modernization and of establishing state socialism[2] that had begun with Ben Bella's short-lived government were accelerated as Boumedienne gave the government the instruments needed to implement its economic strategy of industrialization and development—nationalization of enterprises and banks and the creation of a planning institution that set the priorities of development. Among the first industries to be nationalized were the film and broadcast industries. This policy of nationalization of the media (which included the print media) was motivated by Algeria's desire to build its own press and broadcast news institutions, as well as a national cinema and television, in order to achieve cultural independence from the West, particularly France.

Between 1967 and 1990, five plans were implemented by the Algerian government. As a rule, the evolution of Algerian broadcasting from the mid-1960s onwards depended greatly on the state's appropriation of funds under various economic plans. During the first plan, called the three-year plan (1967–1969), the Algerian government concentrated on the repair and rebuilding of damaged systems, the electrification of the country, the extension of broadcasting coverage to unserved areas, and the expansion of broadcast facilities.

With the help of a French company, Télécommunications Radio-électriques et Téléphoniques (TRT), a microwave system was designed to connect all the major towns in northern Algeria and also to link Algeria to Tunisia and Morocco through what came to be called "Maghrebvision." Under the same plan, television transmission between France and Algeria was improved and the one-way television link was replaced by a two-way television system. Production equipment was also improved. The planners used foresight in purchasing color-capable television equipment during this first plan period to facilitate the conversion to color, which was carried out during the second plan.

The second plan, called the first four-year plan (1970–1973), accorded a major cultural role to broadcasting in promoting the Arabic language and supporting the government's development efforts. The plan set out three objectives: the extension of the transmission network, the increase of domestic program production, and the multiplication of links to facilitate inter-regional and international program exchanges. On the transmission side, the plan provided for the investment of $50 million for the installation of a high-power mediumwave radio transmitter near Annaba (in the eastern part of the country) and the upgrading of existing transmitters to improve their overseas coverage. More television transmitters were installed at Médéa and Tindouf to extend coverage further south into the interior of the country and new television production equipment was added in Algiers, Oran, and Constantine to increase local production.

In 1970, while industrialization was fully under way, the Algerian government launched a cultural revolution which stressed Arabisation and the return to an Arab-Islamic heritage. At the level of the Algerian Radio and Television (the RTA), the policy of Arabisation coincided with a major administrative reorganization that was characterized by an important influx of managerial staff from the Ministry of Education, most of whom were educated in Arabic. This reorganization brought to the surface the ideological conflicts between different factions of the elite in power concerning modernity and tradition, the use of French or Arabic, and the strengthening of Algeria's ties to the West or to the Arab world. At the level of the RTA, these conflicts were apparent in the clashes that occurred between the management, composed mostly of bureaucrats educated in Arabic who had no broadcasting or production experience, and a technical staff mostly educated in French who either had worked with French radio and television or had been trained in France.

The new management personnel from the Ministry of Education had the task of making sure that local production in Arabic was given priority and that the amount of imported programs was reduced. This reorganization dramatically increased the proportion of locally produced programs as well as the proportion of programs in Arabic. From 1970 to 1973, the RTA's domestic television production rose to 49 percent of the output. During this time, several Algerians who spoke little French and whose cultural orientation was distinctly Arab were appointed to key positions, a move that resulted in an increase in Arabic-language programming.

However, this policy of forced Arabisation was met with some resistance from the producers and the staff of the RTA as well as from the viewing audience, which did not understand the classical Arabic used in broadcasting (Algerians speak a different dialect from the Arabic spoken in most of the Middle East) and preferred imported programming to the poorer quality productions of the RTA. Because technical professionals were badly needed for the development of the country, the use of Arabic as a working language was not forced on the RTA's technicians or for that matter on any scientific workers. The intense drive for Arabisation at the RTA lasted only until 1975 after which time productions in French and the colloquial Algerian dialect were resumed. From that time to the present, Algerian television has maintained a balance of 35–40 percent locally produced programming to 60–65 percent imports.

The schism between "Francisants" and "Arabisants," as the two main orientations of the Algerian elite came to be known, reflects deeper tensions concerning the major economic, political, and cultural challenges Algeria has faced since independence. The Francisants, who regard the French-speaking world and the West in general as their partners in building a modern economy, seek to establish Algeria in the international community and favor a technocratic and state-socialist approach to government. Francisants comprise the majority of the technocratic class and have been in positions of control in state enterprises and institutions.

The Arabisants, in addition to pushing for the increased role of Arabic language and culture, are committed to nonalignment and Pan-Arabism. Perhaps in response to the key technological and economic roles played by Francisants in the economy and government, the Arabisants have identified the domain of culture as their primary arena. They also oppose the overall approach to development pursued by the Francisants and object to their close ties with the West, seeing in this relationship a continuation of the economic and cultural dependency that characterized Algeria under French colonial rule.

A total expenditure of $15 billion was allocated under the third plan, called the second four-year plan (1974–1977), which occurred during the oil and gas boom, a period of general prosperity. Two major television developments resulted from this plan: the installation of a satellite distribution system to ensure full national coverage and the full colorization of the television system.

Satellite technology offered itself as a way of bringing the country together and of facilitating the much-needed communication between the different regions of the country by extending telecommunications to the most remote areas of the Sahara that were previously reachable only through high frequency radio. In 1974, GTE was awarded a $9.6 million contract to install with SONELEC (the Algerian electronics and telecommunications state enterprise) a domestic satellite system consisting of 14 earth stations scattered across the country. The system uses a single transponder leased on a preemptable basis from spare capacity by INTELSAT. The main station, constructed by Mitsubishi, is located at Lakhdaria and is equipped with 12 telephone-telex channels and one video transmit/receive channel. The other remote stations are equipped with television-receive-only (TVRO) channels. The system was designed for expansion through the increase of the number of earth stations. The number of earth stations grew to 18 in 1982 and to 33 in 1984.

Color television transmissions began on an experimental basis in 1973 when both the French system SECAM and the German system PAL were evaluated. As Franco-Algerian relations were very strained in the early 1970s and as a closer relationship developed between West Germany and Algeria, the RTA chose the PAL system. Under the second four-year plan, the process of colorization of the television system proceeded rapidly.

Until the late 1970s, the budgetary priorities in broadcasting had favored investment in production and transmission equipment and technical training as opposed to program production. However, with the change of the RTA's directorship in 1978 that brought a Francisant to the position, emphasis was again placed on local production, and the RTA's output of entertainment programming increased from 20 hours in 1977 to 60 hours in 1979. However, this output remained negligible when compared to the RTA's programming needs, which continued to be met by cost-effective imports.

Both 1978 and 1979 were transitional years during which previous plans were evaluated. Boumedienne died in 1978 and was succeeded by Chadli

Benjedid, another military officer who, unlike Boumedienne, is less committed to the ideals of socialism. As Algeria entered the decade of the 1980s, world oil prices plummeted and so did Algeria's export revenues. The sharp decline in oil revenues, combined with the mismanagement of the country's highly centralized economy, have pushed Benjedid's government to rethink the Algerian strategy of development, a strategy characterized by centralization and planning that prioritizes industrialization over agriculture.

The abundance of hydrocarbon resources, mainly oil and gas (95 percent of Algerian exports) generated the cash needed to create a base for heavy industry. This is how the Algerian model of development came to rely on "industrializing" industries with emphasis on chemicals, steel, and construction. These industries were expected to generate financial as well as technical capital and to have a "trickle down" effect on agriculture by modernizing it through the delivery of mechanical (tractors and other machinery) and chemical (fertilizers) support. However, by emphasizing industrialization over agriculture, Algeria aggravated its food dependency on the international market and increased rural to urban migration, as people from the countryside moved to the urban centers in search of employment.

Even the agrarian revolution launched in 1971 did not succeed in alleviating the problem of urban migration or in increasing agricultural output. By 1986, 65 percent of the Algerian population were urban dwellers. During the same year, Algeria, which used to be France's granary and wine cellar, imported 65 percent of its cereals, 85 percent of its green vegetables, and 75 percent of its eggs (*Africa Research Bulletin,* 1985). Under the government of Benjedid, most of the cooperative farms created during the agrarian revolution were rented to private farmers and the marketing for fruit and vegetables that used to be controlled by the state was liberalized, an indication of the failure of the agrarian revolution to improve the agricultural sector.

As long as oil prices remained high and the revenues were sufficient to support heavy industry and to allow the government to subsidize food prices, the Algerian model of development seemed to work. However, the drastic decline in oil prices (from $41 a barrel in the early 1980s to below $10 a barrel in 1988) reduced Algeria's revenues from $13.7 billion in 1980 to $7.3 billion in 1988 and aggravated a $24 billion (as of 1990) debt load (*Jeune Afrique,* 1990) to produce a period of bitter austerity in the second half of the 1980s. 1986 was the first year in which the economy grew more slowly than the population, which translated into falling per-capita income and soaring food prices that stagnating salaries ($250 was the average monthly salary of a worker in 1988) could not offset.

Due to the economic collapse and growing popular discontent, Algeria under Benjedid has been moving toward economic liberalization and political reforms in an attempt to resolve the economic and political crises that have plagued the country. The movement toward decentralization and the dismantling of the big state enterprises that characterized the 1980s included the breakup of the RTA into smaller enterprises, a move that has lessened state monopoly and opened the door for the first time to private initiatives in the business of film and television production.

ALGERIAN BROADCASTING IN THE 1980s: GLOBALIZATION AND THE BREAKUP OF THE RTA

During the fourth plan, called the first five-year plan (1980–1984), the Algerian government decided to create a second channel to be used for educational and cultural purposes and a radio broadcasting facility using satellite for national broadcasting that would include short-, medium-, and long-wave broadcasting, a project estimated at $10 million. While a budget was allocated for the second channel and some of these funds have been absorbed by the RTA, the second channel itself has not materialized. The reason given is the continued lack of local production and the reluctance of the government to start up a new channel that would wind up relying on imported programming. During this plan, investments were made in satellite news-gathering trucks provided by RCA, the expansion of the satellite distribution system to the South, and the provision of some of the new southern stations with production equipment for news gathering.

During the fifth plan, called the second five-year plan (1985–1989), the second channel remained in limbo as the government decided to concentrate on restructuring the RTA and formulated the plans for an $80 million television production center to be called La Maison de la Télévision. In addition, the government continued designing the new nationwide radio broadcasting facility begun during the previous plan. However, due to the worsening economic situation of the country, these projects were postponed to a later date. In the new age of austerity, broadcasting, which had received considerable investments in the past, was no longer an urgent priority.

However, the audiovisual landscape of Algeria underwent major changes in the 1980s. As part of the process of dismantling the enormous state enterprises and banks that had functioned as monopolies until the mid-1980s and transforming them into smaller, more efficient, and autonomous state enterprises, the RTA was split into four entities in 1987: the ENTV (National Enterprise of Television), in charge of news and programming; the ENPA (the National Enterprise for Audiovisual Production), which oversees the production of telefilms and other entertainment and cultural programs; the ENRA, in charge of radio broadcasting;

and the TDA, in control of television equipment. The purpose of the RTA's decentralization was to end its dependency on state funds and establish production policies and sources of financing that would enable the newly independent entities to function as profit-making enterprises.

Perhaps the most important of these changes was the creation of the ENPA (a cheaper alternative to the planned $80 million production center), which is allowed to coproduce both nationally and internationally, to produce for private companies outside the state structure, and to keep and reinvest the profits earned from these productions. The ENPA is the production arm of the national television network and has inherited production equipment from the ex-RTA as well as laboratories, post-production facilities, and 35mm film production equipment from the information service of the national army. The financing for the ENPA's productions for the national network comes from the ENTV when this last entity orders programming. Domestic and international coproductions as well as foreign sales (France, Belgium, and Switzerland are the major markets for ENPA's products), which constitute a new effort for the network, provide additional sources of financing.

The ENPA also provides services (equipment and crews) to foreign productions shot in Algeria. Between 1988 and 1990, the ENPA produced or coproduced 12 feature films, several mini-dramas, telefilms, and documentaries. The ENPA's relatively strong start is due in part to its General Director, Lamine Merbah, a film and television director who worked for many years with the RTA and who is familiar with the difficulties filmmakers and television producers face with regard to government agencies and bureaucratic procedures.

Three years earlier, in 1984, the national film enterprise ONCIC (Office National de Commercialisation et de l'Industrie du Cinema) underwent a similar restructuring and was divided into two national enterprises, one in charge of production (ENAPROC) and the other responsible for distribution (ENADEC). However, three years later (in 1987), as a result of the poor performance of the two enterprises, the Algerian government decided to go back to the one-enterprise formula, and the CAAIC (Centre Algérien pour l'Art et l'Industrie Cinématographique) was created as a profit-making enterprise in charge of production (including for television) and distribution.

Other manifestations of decentralization and liberalization in the media industries in Algeria[3] include the appearance of private capital and commercial enterprises in this domain. Private investments (both national and foreign) in film and television production are now welcomed by Algerian film and television production companies and there are now at least ten private audiovisual enterprises (Mostefaoui, 1988, p. 68). The creation in 1983 of OREF, L'Office Riadh El Fath, is one outcome of the policy of the Algerian government to encourage mixed corporations (incorporating private and public capital) in the domain of the media. OREF is a media enterprise that provides closed-circuit video distribution to supermarkets and stores and owns four movie theaters that are supplied by films imported by OREF, a practice that breaches the monopoly of the CAAIC over imports and distribution.

More significant to the process of liberalization is the creation in 1987 of Tipaza Audiovisuel, a joint venture between OREF and a private Kuwaiti company. Tipaza Audiovisuel is involved in the production, coproduction, sale and purchase, and import/export of theatrical films, television programming, and audiovisual products. The wide range of this company's operations indicates the Algerian government's desire to find alternative ways to generate funding in film and television to offset the pressures exerted by the economic downturn and restricted budgets.

Thus, the emerging transformation of the broadcasting landscape in Algeria that began in the 1980s is due in part to internal factors such as a ponderous and inefficient bureaucracy and shrinking government funds, which have coincided with pressures to expand the broadcasting system. However, external factors, such as the pressures exerted on Algeria's broadcast system by the new distribution technologies of satellite broadcasting and home video, were also instrumental in bringing about the current changes.

Due to satellite's ability to bypass geographical boundaries, Algeria's television institution, like those of many countries, was forced to acknowledge the competition constituted by the incoming flows of images and radio signals via satellite from neighboring countries. Algerian audiences receive programming from radio and television stations in Morocco, Tunisia, Spain, France, and Italy. With the proliferation of satellite dishes (approximately 40,000 in 1989), the reception of broadcast signals from these countries has been made even easier. As a result, the French Antenne 2 and the Italian RAI networks (which have been broadcasting in Tunisia since 1983 and 1985, respectively), as well as the French television services Canal Plus and TF1, have become part of the menu of many Algerian viewers with satellite dishes. As for radio, Algerian audiences were already exposed to international radio channels like Médi-1, a Franco-Moroccan station broadcasting from Tangiers, and Radio Monte Carlo from France.

In Algeria, the private ownership of television has not yet come about, but the few changes in Algeria's media industries described above could indicate that commercialism lies ahead. The second channel, if it is realized in the 1990s, for example, might be allowed to combine advertising revenues and public funds to face the ever-increasing costs of broadcasting. Already, the battle to end the monopoly over advertising by the state enterprise ANEP (Agence Nationale d'Edition et de Publicité) has begun as private companies are lobbying to change the law regulating advertising in Algeria.

ALGERIAN RADIO AND TELEVISION TODAY
AND THE EMERGENCE OF TELEVISION AS
THE MOST POPULAR MASS MEDIUM

As a result of the tremendous investments made in broadcasting technology during the two decades between 1965 and 1985, Algerian radio and television today cover virtually the entire country. There are three radio channels: two domestic (Channels 1 and 2), using mainly mediumwave transmitters, and one international service (Channel 3). Channel 1 is national as it broadcasts 24 hours in Arabic to the entire country through a network of relays. Channel 2 broadcasts in Kabyle 12 hours per day: 3 hours in the morning (from 0600 to 0900), 3 hours in the afternoon (from noon to 1500), and 6 hours at night (from 1700 to 2300). The international service, which uses a 1500-kilowatt long-wave transmitter, broadcasts 7 hours a day (from 1800 to 0100) mainly in French but also in Spanish and English.

Television broadcasting is provided by one channel (ENTV) whose 9 hours daily average broadcast time (approximately 64 hours per week) are distributed by microwave in the northern region and by satellite in the South. Some 170 transmitters constitute the terrestrial microwave distribution system in the North. Although the coverage in this region is comprehensive, there are still reception problems in some areas due to the mountainous geography of the North. The South is covered by the satellite network installed in 1974 that includes over 30 terrestrial stations scattered throughout the Sahara. There were between 30 and 40 thousand private satellite dishes as of 1989 for an audience of between 2.5 and 5 million satellite viewers.

For a population of more than 24.5 million, there were 3,100,000 television sets in 1989 ("The Maghreb at," 1990, p. 53), most of which (2,235,000) were black and white because of the high price of color television sets ($800) and the relatively low income of most Algerians. As of 1984, there were 4.5 million radio sets. Both television and radio receivers are manufactured by the state enterprise ENIE (Entreprise Nationale des Industries Electroniques). Since 1985, ENIE has produced 50,000 television sets per year (Mostefaoui, 1988, p. 60) and (as of 1987) has manufactured 200,000 radio sets annually (*El Moudjahid,* 1987, p. 11). Both radio and TV receivers are subject to license fees that are collected directly by the RTA, although fee collection appears to be somewhat lax in spite of the fact that license revenues traditionally have represented a considerable portion (30 percent in 1979) of the national network's budget.

Today, Algeria's television network, the ENTA, is a member of the Arab States Broadcasting Union (ASBU) and the European Broadcasting Union (EBU), and is linked to both Eurovision, the Western European television exchange network, and Maghrebvision, as well as to the other Arab states via the Arab satellite system ARABSAT. In addition, Algiers houses the headquarters of the coordinating center of the URTNA (Union des Radio-Télévisions Nationales Africaines), the African organization that was created to facilitate and encourage program exchange between African broadcasting institutions.

Broadcasting has always received most of the budget allocated to the Ministry of Information. In 1987, for example, broadcasting was allocated $42 million whereas the print media received $14 million (Mostefaoui, 1988, p. 57). Television has always been perceived as a cultural priority and receives on average between 50 and 60 percent of the Ministry of Information's budget.

These investments are a reflection of the government's perception of television and other media as key cultural institutions of Algerian society. The National Charter, for example, states that "cultural and educational dissemination, which gives an important place to ideology, aesthetics, and arts, must be the major task of all the means of education, notably the press, radio, and television" (*Révolution Africaine*, 1979, p. 61). In other words, the priorities of the media are to disseminate state ideology and policies and in this context they are seen as a tool for the education and mobilization of the Algerian population around government policies and programs. Radio and television, in particular, offer themselves as the best way to convey state ideology since the illiteracy rate is high (50 percent). However, beyond the state's interest in broadcasting, there are social and cultural factors that have fostered Algeria's television revolution.

Television provides an immediate source of information and entertainment for a large portion of the population as half the population is illiterate and thus has no access to libraries or newspapers (which also suffer from a lack of credibility due to their ownership by the state). Secondly, as women are primarily confined to the home and are practically excluded from the cinemas (which have become the turf of young male adults), television has emerged as a popular entertainment alternative. According to Chevaldonné's study (1981), the introduction of television into middle-class homes in the interior of Algeria coincided with the elimination of the special cinema screenings reserved for female audiences (which had begun following independence and had lasted several years). These screenings were canceled because they attracted male adolescents who harassed women as they entered the theater.

The third factor behind the popularity of television is the cultural vacuum that exists in the country. One source of this vacuum is the dilemma of a dual culture inherited from colonialism. On the one hand, French culture is accessible and visible (through the media as well as via the million Algerians living in France), but it is perceived as the culture of the colonizer and is thus criticized by the state, which promotes Arabic language and culture. On the other hand, Algerian culture, still in the process of self-definition, is often restrictive because state control over national culture has tended to exclude cultural and artistic expression outside the mainstream.

An additional source of this cultural vacuum is the considerable gap between the material temptations of Western culture as seen on television and in movies—fast cars, the latest fashion and music, general affluence, and a lot of sex—and the actual limitations of Algerian reality, which confine young urbanites to run-down cinemas, crowded cafés and stadiums, and more recently to mosques, a result of the Islamic revival.

Finally, the failure of the Algerian government to provide an adequately wide range of cultural outlets by supporting local music, theatre, and dance festivals that would appeal to Algeria's young population, and the relative monopoly the government exercises over "national" culture (Mahamdi, 1989), have resulted in a very limited and unsatisfying cultural landscape. In these circumstances, television becomes a viable alternative for entertainment. As the editor-in-chief of the cinema and television review magazine, *Les Deux Ecrans,* rightly points out, "Social life revolves around it, it has no competitor! There are no nightclubs, no nice restaurants, no concerts. What remains is 'our' RTA" (Stoltz, 1983, p. 234).

While television is popular in Algeria because of the absence of alternative forms of entertainment, its programming remains problematic. The content of imported programming, constituting the bulk (65 percent) of ENTV's air time,[4] appears out of place next to locally produced news, educational and current affairs programs, documentaries, and religious programs that follow an anti-imperialist and Islamic revivalist line. The ideological and cultural content of Western programming is perceived as being in conflict with the cultural policy of Algeria and has been described by Algerian newspaper critics as promoting "capitalist alienation" and "Western consumerism."

In 1985, for example, out of 2,300 hours of broadcast air time, 2,000 hours were imported and only 300 hours were locally produced (*Algérie Actualité,* 1986). On average, 90 percent of all imports come from the United States, Britain, Canada, France, and the Middle East. The primary supplier of television programming to Algerian television is the United States, and as a consequence, most of the prime-time schedule is filled with French-dubbed American series such as *Kojak, Ironside, Starsky and Hutch, Dallas, Beauty and the Beast, Kate and Allie,* and other American serials.

Several attempts have been made to improve programming and inter-Arab program exchange, but so far the results have been unsatisfactory. As early as 1970, Maghrebvision was created to stimulate television exchange between Algeria, Tunisia, and Morocco, but political difficulties among them, particularly between Morocco and Algeria over the question of the Western Sahara, have overshadowed the initiative and very little exchange has been generated through this network. Similarly, in 1985, ARABSAT, the Arab satellite system, was launched in the hope of increasing the exchange between Arab television systems. However, due to mismanagement and the lack of programs available for distribution, satellite use for inter-Arab television exchange has been negligible, reaching only 32 percent in 1987, comprised mainly of news items and variety shows.

Sixteen percent of the ENTV's programming is devoted to educational material provided by the Centre Nationale d'Enseignement Généralisé (CNEG) and aimed primarily at older students and adults. However, the primary function of television in Algeria (as elsewhere) is entertainment. The dilemma of reconciling television's informational and educational role (which services cultural integration and development) with its function as an entertainment medium is an old problem. Katz (1977, 1979), for example, has addressed this issue, noting that while broadcasting in the Third World was initially directed toward geographic, ethnic, and cultural integration and was perceived as a tool for development, the entertainment function of the medium, which was initially overlooked, gradually emerged as its primary function. This function was more immediately recognized by the audience, which was predominantly urban and middle class. Thus, the initial developmental role of television was eclipsed by its use among the urban middle classes as an entertainment and increasingly commercial medium.

In conclusion, the breakup of the RTA into four smaller, more manageable enterprises, the process of decentralization, and the probable multiplication of production entities with the evolution of the private sector indicate a first step toward liberating the creative energy that has been stifled by the bureaucratic presence of the state in Algeria's media industries since their inception. If the ENPA is provided with the necessary resources to produce domestic television programs, and if the writers, directors, and producers are allowed enough freedom and given the incentive to be innovative, Algeria might be able to create an indigenous form of television that both reflects and responds to Algerian cultural diversity and effectively competes with imported programming.

The Algerian government is planning to create a cinema department at the Art and Drama School of Bordj-el-Kiffan and a film and television production center in Algiers. In addition, it has planned, with the help of the Italian RAI, the creation of a dubbing center to be built in Algiers, a move that will allow Algeria to dub its own imports and break its dependency on France for dubbed programming. These plans, if they come to fruition, will allow Algerian television to play an active role, not only in the Arab Maghreb Union (UMA) which was born in 1989, but on the African continent as well, as it has the most developed audiovisual infrastructure in Africa.

The task that lies ahead for Algerian television is to redefine its role in the cultural landscape of the country. This can be achieved through continued decentralization and liberalization as well as through a recognition of the importance of pluralistic cultural expression that would include the voices of women, ethnic minorities, and youth. By voicing the social and cultural concerns of all regions and segments of the population, Algerian television might be able to formulate an effective and appealing alternative to the state-controlled news and imported entertainment fare it has offered over the last 30 years.

CHAPTER 17

LIBYA

Drew O. McDaniel

LIBYA is situated at the center of North Africa, bordered on the west by Algeria and Tunisia and on the east by Egypt. Libya's Mediterranean shore stretches across the north, and Chad and Niger lie to the south. Although it was known as the prosperous breadbasket of the Roman Empire, its lush farmlands have disappeared. Due to the Sahara's encroachment, almost 95 percent of Libya's territory is considered desert now, and only a narrow strip of land along the northern coast and scattered oases support agriculture.

Like much of the rest of the Arab world, Libya fell under control of successive invaders. Once part of Phoenicia and later ancient Greece and Rome, Libya was incorporated into the Ottoman Empire from the 16th century until 1912. For three decades afterwards, it was an Italian colony. Following World War II, it passed to Allied administration before finally winning independence in 1951. By this time, Libya had been reduced to one of the world's poorest nations, having an annual per capita income of about $35. The feeble economy was dependent on exports of esparto grass and scrap metal from abandoned war armaments.

After commercial oil discoveries in 1959, petroleum earnings erased a balance-of-payment deficit in excess of $100 million within a year (Farley, 1971). By the end of the 1960s, per capita Gross National Product (GNP) had grown to $640. Libya became the largest petroleum producer on the African continent. Today, oil exports constitute the single biggest sector, officially about 45 percent, of the national economy, but McLachlan (1987) indicates that in real terms at least 80 percent of the Gross Domestic Product (GDP) is derived from oil. Even though petroleum

Drew McDaniel is Professor of Telecommunications and Director of Southeast Asia Studies at Ohio University. His primary research interest is mass media and national development.

revenues have improved the quality of life, the global oil market's volatility has caused wide fluctuations in national income. Recent estimates place per capita GNP at about $5,400 annually, roughly half the figures reported in the late 1970s.

Libya's urbanization is high, around 75 percent, and the population is concentrated in its main cities. The capital, Tripoli, is situated on the western Mediterranean shore, at the eastern extremity of the Maghreb. Benghazi, also on the coast, is in the eastern region formerly called Cyrenaica. Sebha is deep in the southern desert district known as the Fezzan. Current population estimates total more than 3.9 million residents, including a large expatriate work force.

The BBC estimates that there are 1 million radio sets and 450,000 television receivers in Libya (British Broadcasting Corporation, 1991b).

POST-INDEPENDENCE DEVELOPMENT AND THE MEDIA

On December 24, 1951, Libya gained independence through an arrangement worked out in the United Nations. A constitutional monarchy was established, and Mohamed Idris al Sanusi was named as leader. He was chosen as king because of his position as patriarch of the Sanusi Islamic order—a religious clan similar to Saudi Arabia's *Wahhabis*.

At independence, the country found itself in shambles. Decades of Turkish and Italian rule left it socially fragmented. This, plus deep regional divisions, undermined its sense of nationhood. Libya's economic situation seemed hopeless, with no apparent natural resources and a pressing need for land reform. A formidable handicap to development was the lack of trained human resources. According to Farley (1971, p. 83), despite efforts between the end of World War II and 1951, the country began independence with only 33,000 students enrolled in primary or secondary schools. Worse still, only 14 Libyans held college degrees and only 32 persons were enrolled in university-level education (Keith, 1965, p. 11).

Idris' government directed much of the earnings from oil exports into social development, most notably education. In 1954, illiteracy among Libyans was about 81 percent (Farley, 1971, p. 129). But gains came slowly; a decade later, the official estimate was 78 percent illiteracy, despite a four-fold increase in the number of students in primary and secondary instruction (*UNESCO statistical yearbook 1977*, 1978, p. 43). Even with this remarkable growth, only 59 percent of eligible children were believed to be enrolled in school (Farley, 1971, p. 90). Additional development objectives were improved agriculture, electrification, transportation, industrialization, and, above all, housing. Approximately one in four families had no housing in 1963 and many others were living in substandard dwellings.

Although the rapid increase in wealth afforded better living conditions, it brought about economic and social dislocations too. Petroleum riches fueled a rush from villages to the main urban centers. Soon thousands—later hundreds of thousands—of foreign nationals came to fill jobs that were vacant because there were no qualified Libyan workers.

These circumstances help to explain delays in the expansion of Libyan media. Because the country started its economic program from such a low level, it was forced to focus its resources on basic needs such as education, housing, food, and transportation. The 1963–1968 development plan set aside about $10 million for "news and guidance," only 1.5 percent of the total budget (Bearman, 1986, p. 46). Furthermore, the government seems to have had little interest in the media: the monarchy was an inward-looking regime and its intellectual grounding was in 19th-century religious perspectives. Estimates shortly after independence placed the number of radio receivers at a mere 5,000 sets distributed among about 1 million inhabitants (Johansen, 1955). Finally, the development model familiar in Egypt, one in which mass media were key agents, did not seem to *motivate* Libyan planners. At the time, newly independent nations frequently used media as channels of mobilization for needs such as capital formation and national unification. In Libya this "bootstrap" approach was unnecessary due to an abundance of capital and to a lack of ethnic and linguistic divisions. As a result, media played only a minor role in early development activities.

PRE-REVOLUTIONARY BROADCASTING

Broadcasting arrived in Libya about two decades after its appearance in neighboring North African countries. Under Italian colonial authority, radio loudspeakers were installed in public locations of the main cities to relay shortwave broadcasts from Rome during the late 1930s (Grandin, 1971). The first indigenous radio service started shortly after independence. In 1955, a single mediumwave 1-kilowatt transmitter was on the air from Tripoli, providing just 2 hours of Arabic programming each day (Johansen, 1955, p. 75), and a year later a similar station came on the air in Benghazi. The official opening of a national service was announced on July 28, 1957, when the two stations were joined in an organization called Radio Libya. American personnel were reportedly involved in programming the new broadcasting service. A UNESCO project in the late 1950s was mounted to develop the fledgling service, but the scale of the operation continued to be very small (Codding, 1959). Daily programming was increased to 4 hours, consisting mostly of recorded music and short talk features. Sweiden reported that short newscasts prepared under supervision of the Prime Minister's office were also scheduled (cited in Gartley, 1980).

By the 1969 revolution, five mediumwave and three shortwave

transmitters were on the air from Tripoli, Benghazi, Tobruk, and El-Beida. Four of these were high-power 100-kilowatt installations. Aid from the United States was used to construct the Benghazi station. Programming consisted of a 3.5-hour morning broadcast ending at 0800, and a 10-hour transmission that started at noon. In addition, two mediumwave radio transmitters were in operation at Wheelus Air Base, a large U.S. military installation a few kilometers east of Tripoli (*Guide to broadcasting stations*, 1970, pp. 58–59). These stations allowed programming from the American Forces Radio and Television Service to be picked up throughout the capital city. In the east, a station operated by British Forces Broadcasting Service in Tobruk could be received (Frost, 1970, p. 131).

Like radio, Libyan television was established at a comparatively late date. Through the late 1950s and early 1960s, a small number of sets were used in coastal cities. In locations close to the shore, reception of signals from Southern Europe and Tunisia was possible. Residents near the capital could receive daily AFRTS telecasts from Wheelus. This military television station was one of North Africa's earliest, beginning transmissions in 1956. In the absence of local broadcasts, programming from Wheelus became a significant source of entertainment for wealthy Libyan elites during the first two decades of independence. Wheelus' telecasts included the usual fare of local news and a mixture of shows from the American networks. Broadcasts in English were not a great deterrent to Libyan viewing: those who could afford a set were likely to speak English. After 1964, U.S. Air Force officials allowed a 1-hour program prepared by Libyan Radio to be televised each week (El-Zilitni, 1981).

No domestic TV service was available until 1966 when construction of a station in Tripoli was started. Regular broadcasting was officially begun on the anniversary of national independence, December 24, 1968 ("Libya, now 17," 1968). The Tripoli television facilities were installed by French technicians, and most operational workers were expatriates. Other personnel were seconded from Libyan radio. A few of these individuals were trained at the Wheelus TV station. The daily schedule was merely 3 hours, consisting mainly of imported programs (Souriau, 1975). Foreign shows were obtained from the United States, Egypt, and other Arab countries. Local programs included Quranic readings, news, occasional dramas, and musical shows.

THE REVOLUTION AND THE MEDIA

On September 1, 1969, a loosely organized group of junior officers known as the Free Officers Movement seized control of the Libyan government. In the early hours of the morning, arrests were made and police offices and radio stations were occupied. By 0630 that day, the Tripoli and Benghazi radio studios were linked and a broadcast by Mu'ammar Al Qadhafi, key organizer of the junta, was transmitted. His emotional speech announced the Idris overthrow and pledged to "build glory, revive our heritage, and revenge an honor wounded and a right usurped" (Cooley, 1982, p. 5).

The Free Officers Movement modeled its actions along the lines of Nasser's military takeover in Egypt 17 years earlier. At least three motives inspired this "revolution." First, the infusion of oil money into the economy under the king's management did not benefit all sectors of society; instead, his policies tended to increase the disparity between the haves and have-nots. Moreover, the Idris regime was seen as aligned with colonizing Europeans and other foreigners, about whom much bitterness was still felt. Finally, in addition to a more egalitarian society, the Free Officers Movement favored application of Islamic principles throughout national life. Affairs of government were taken over by a 12-person group called the Revolutionary Command Council (RCC) with members selected from the coup planners. First as head of the RCC, and later in a *de facto* capacity, Qadhafi has led Libya, his personality a constant presence in the country.

The military takeover halted all foreign broadcasting within the country and U.S. forces were required to evacuate Wheelus Air Base by June 1970. One of the junta's immediate goals was to reduce the social and economic involvement of Western interests and to encourage closer relations with Arab countries. Actions of the RCC government supported this aim in every ministry. In broadcasting, programs immediately cut Western content and began to promote pan-Arabist themes. Several scholars have noted the influence of radio broadcasts on Libyan leaders' political thinking. Harris (1986, p. 45) claims that Qadhafi in his youth "listened avidly" to programs from Nasser's Voice of the Arabs on Radio Cairo. It was therefore natural that Libyan radio began to echo its themes of Arab nationalism.

In due course, the Free Officers ideology behind the coup was revealed in the "Third Universal Theory," authored by Qadhafi a few years after he assumed power. His political philosophy rejected both capitalism and communism but sought a neutral socialist position based upon Islamic principles. Eventually, these concepts were drawn together in a publication called the *Green Book* (Qadhafi, 1976). The political dogma contained in this publication outlined a governance structure in which national authority is held by a body known as the General People's Congress (GPC). Its membership would be drawn from participants in local "popular con-gresses" as well as "people's committees, syndicates and unions" (Qadhafi, 1976, p. 63). The Revolutionary Command Council was replaced by the GPC in 1977.

While the RCC, like the Idris regime, did not seem to regard broadcasting as a primary vehicle for economic development, its value as a political instrument was not missed. Immediately following the revolution, media content became heavily weighted toward political issues and objectives. Sometimes this was shown dramatically, as in the televised trials in absentia of King Idris and his court (he was condemned to death, though he had taken asylum in Egypt) (First, 1974). It was reported that the TV stations were besieged with requests for rebroadcasts of these prime-time court proceedings. Many types of broadcasts were filled with heavy political overtones, especially programs built around speeches and discussions. An example was the "Revolutionary Intellectuals' Seminar," the broadcast of a series of public discussions just months after the RCC assumed power. These televised meetings focused on "a definition of the working forces of the people who have an interest in the revolution" (First, 1974, p. 125).

The objectives of the broadcast organization, as stated by the Ministry of Information, emphasized projection of Arab socialism and Arab unity to a national audience (Elgabri, 1974). Concern about the political conscious-ness of Libyan citizens was legitimate, for the nation had no tradition of popular participation in government. In one survey of political activity among rural Libyans conducted a few years after the revolution, 74.8 percent of those persons sampled were rated low or very low in predisposi-tion toward participation in political affairs (El Fathaly et al., 1977).

ORGANIZATION OF THE BROADCASTING SYSTEM

A term was coined to describe the Libyan political system, *Jamahiriya*, usually translated as "state of the masses," or as Qadhafi described it, "a state run by the people without a government" (Deeb, 1990, p. 149). This refers to an intricate structure of appointed or elected bodies that manage affairs within government bureaucracies. These "people's committees" are intended to represent interests of the public within government agencies and organizations. The concept is central to Qadhafi's political philosophy, and his *Green Book* instructed that "popular congresses choose administra-tive people's committees to replace governmental administration" (Qadhafi, 1976, p. 61).

Broadcasting was restructured on June 2, 1973, when people's committees assumed responsibility for radio operations in Tripoli and Benghazi ("Libya extends," 1973). By this time, hundreds of such commit-tees had taken charge of the operation of universities, hospitals, and other public agencies. Much of the committees' power rests with their chairper-sons, each of whom acts as the organization's highest-ranking staff member. Despite their professional responsibilities, the roles of committee chairper-sons are generally political in nature and therefore subject to partisan pressures.

Today, broadcasting is handled by a state enterprise called Libyan Jamahiriya Broadcasting (LJB), also known as the People's Revolutionary Broadcasting Company. Support for broadcasting comes exclusively through government appropriations. No receiver license fees are assessed, and advertising is not allowed. Even though radio and TV are guided by people's committees, these services are under the authority of the Department of Information and Culture. The department's Secretary provides supervision and liaison with government, along with fiscal and policy oversight. This post is equivalent to a cabinet-level appointment and is filled by a member of the General People's Committee. The department's objectives offer a glimpse of the atmosphere in which broadcasting operates. It aims to

> provide . . . the facts that refute falsehoods, as well as audiovisual and written material on both national and international achievements, . . . provide world public opinion with facts on the L.A.R., [and] to stand against defamation campaigns and refute all fabrications against the L.A.R. (Department of Information and Cultural Affairs, 1976, p. 239)

Reporting to the Information Secretary is the Director General and Chairman of the Broadcasting Committee. Radio and television are vertically integrated so that, for example, programming for both TV and radio are administered by the same department. Operational officers are dispersed among the main broadcasting locations around the country. Department heads are stationed at the national broadcasting headquarters in Tripoli, while deputy department heads are located in Benghazi. If a department head is out of the country, or is otherwise unable to report for work, the deputy will be temporarily moved to the broadcasting center in Tripoli. Staff of the broadcasting system number less than 2,000 in total. Of these, more than half are based in Tripoli and around 40 percent are stationed in Benghazi. A small work force is also stationed at the third production center, Sebha. Transmitter facilities elsewhere, such as Sabratha, employ a few additional technicians (Oun interviews, 1975, 1976).

Libyan Jamahiriya Broadcasting intends that all managers, from the highest level (the director-general) downward, will be professionally trained and will have previous experience in an operational position in the organization (that is, programming, production, or engineering). Since the revolution, broadcasting's growth has made filling positions with qualified personnel difficult. Indeed, overcoming staffing difficulties is one of the main responsibilities of the planning and training department. In spite of vigorous recruitment, it has been necessary to hire expatriates to fill certain vacancies, especially ones in engineering and technical areas. Personnel from Pakistan and from other Arab countries have been employed in the past. Assorted types of training programs have been arranged for senior employees. Courses of study in communication and engineering are offered by Garyounis University in Benghazi. Technicians have received instruction at European centers operated by equipment manufacturers and at private training organizations. More than 30 persons nominated by the Department of Information and Culture studied at universities in the United States during the late 1970s and early 1980s. This is no longer common, however, and until American-Libyan relations improve, there is little prospect that more Libyan students will enter the United States.

RADIO PROGRAMMING

National coverage by radio has been achieved in an interesting way, one that considers Libya's peculiar geography. The small population is spread thinly across a large expanse of territory. The country's area is approximately 680,000 square miles, roughly one-sixth the U.S. size, but its population is only about one-sixtieth that of the United States. Thus, Libya's population density is among the world's lowest at about 6 persons per square mile. Most residents live in the vicinity of one of the three urban centers of Tripoli, Benghazi, and Sebha. However, there are many tiny settlements throughout the country, along the coastal rim and in oases in the south. A system of local stations in the many widely separated settlements has proven impractical. Instead, a single service is provided through two high-power transmission facilities on opposite sides of the country. At Sabratha and Tripoli in the west and El-Beida in the east are 500-kilowatt transmitters that broadcast the national program service in Arabic. These two facilities alone can blanket virtually the entire country. Significantly, foreign audiences can receive these transmissions also; broadcasts cover large parts of Egypt, Tunisia, and Algeria from antennas located near their borders. The powerful mediumwave transmitters are supplemented by FM in Tripoli, El-Beida, and Tobruk (Sennitt, 1991, p. 169).

The national service is broadcast 19 hours each day beginning at 0600. There are nine major daily newscasts, as well as a variety of what might be called public affairs programs. Block programming is still the norm, based on shows of 5-minute to 30-minute lengths. Contemporary and traditional Arabic music is broadcast in specific programs. Dramatic shows are common, and ones based upon historical themes and personalities are believed to be popular (Megri interview, 1975). El-Zilitni (1981) found the most popular programs included *The People's Art*, a half-hour potpourri of music, poetry, and storytelling produced each day in a different region of the country, and *What the Listeners Want*, a long-running 60-minute request show.

Each day the European Program is presented in Tripoli and Benghazi beginning at 1500. Two hours of French shows are broadcast, followed by about 2 hours in English, with programs consisting of news and recorded (mainly European) music. Other informational programs on the European service include a series explaining religious beliefs and practices of Islam and programs devoted to political themes.

A few programs of a regional nature are broadcast from production centers in Benghazi, Tripoli, and Sebha. These are relayed by transmitters in Tobruk (from Benghazi) and Misurata (from Tripoli). Libyan Jamahiriya Broadcasting provides another specialized program service from Tripoli. Known as the Holy Quran Program, it transmits Quranic readings and religious services 14 hours daily starting at 0600.

INTERNATIONAL RADIO PROGRAMMING

Throughout the Arab world, distinctions between domestic and foreign broadcasts tend to be blurred. Because of radio-wave propagation conditions around the Mediterranean, and due to the small size of many countries, local broadcasts easily spill over into neighboring territories. Broadcast authorities are conscious of this and often shape programs with foreign listeners and viewers in mind. This is the case in Libya, and transmissions to other Arab countries are treated as though they were beamed to domestic listeners. The approach is justified on grounds of the "unity of Arab peoples."

One program service deliberately targeted to both internal and external listeners is Libyan Jamahiriya Broadcasting's Voice of the Great Homeland. Great Homeland offers a midday transmission of 2 hours and a 10-hour transmission beginning about 1900. Programs, exclusively in Arabic, are delivered on numerous mediumwave and shortwave frequencies. This is Libya's principal international broadcast voice, and the timing of its transmissions makes it possible to reach listeners in South and Southeast Asia and in North America at peak shortwave listening hours. The Great Homeland is modeled along the lines of Radio Cairo's Voice of the Arabs. It presents a Libyan—which is to say, sometimes radical—perspective on global political events.

Malta and Libya have a close but complicated and unstable relationship. Even though Maltese share many cultural values with Arabs, and the country's economy depends heavily on Libyan oil and tourism, there is tension on matters of religion and a range of political issues. Malta is a favorite vacation spot for middle- and upper-income Libyans, and it receives Libyan foreign aid of several tens of millions of dollars yearly. For nearly two decades, Libya has used facilities on Malta as part of a curious bilateral broadcasting activity.

In the 1970s, a program service called The Voice of Friendship and Solidarity was originated from Malta by the overseas department of Libyan broadcasting. At the time, facilities and offices of this department were housed in a rural villa on the island. Until mid-1980, shortwave transmissions by The Voice of Friendship and Solidarity were handled by the relay station of Deutsche Welle, also located on Malta. Programs were produced locally or were received from Tripoli by tropospheric scatter on microwave. The material was compiled at local studios, then delivered to the German transmitting station.

In addition to overseas transmissions, Libyan radio operated local AM and FM stations in Malta starting in 1975, broadcasting a full 12-hour schedule in Maltese. Programming consisted mainly of news and recorded European music. Several well-known local personalities, former staff members of the Maltese national service (Xandir Malta), were employed at this station. A treaty between Libya and Malta provided for this unusual arrangement as part of a package of special trade and diplomatic concessions.

Intergovernmental frictions continually disrupted operations of the Voice of Friendship and Solidarity. For instance, in 1979, broadcasts from the Libyan station were halted by pressure from Malta's opposition Nationalist Party. The party filed an application for a license to operate a station, complaining that the two existing radio services on the island were either pro-government or pro-Libyan. Nationalists professed a desire to "balance" radio programming. Furthermore, the party argued that Libyans were utilizing a frequency assigned to the Maltese people by international agreements. The interruption was short and Libyan AM and FM services resumed a few months later after the dispute had cooled, but the issue of the foreign stations continued to strain relations between the countries (Sweiden communication, 1979). Again in June 1980, all Libyan broadcasts, including transmissions by the Deutsche Welle, were halted following disagreements between Libya and Malta over offshore Mediterranean oil-drilling rights. For a time after local transmissions stopped, studios on the island were employed to produce Maltese programming and to prepare recordings which were shipped to Tripoli for broadcasts to Maltese listeners (Sweiden communication, 1980). This disagreement hastened a reorganization of Libya's shortwave services, which were transmitting in English, Italian, Arabic, and French by the time broadcasts were suspended.

After 1980, Libya's radio programs on Malta moved to Radio Mediterranean, a radio station carrying programs from several sources including local Malta radio, Adventist World Radio, and other religious organizations. In 1988, the stations were renamed the Voice of the Mediterranean and inaugurated under shared administration by the governments of Libya and

Malta. Maltese Prime Minister Dr. Fenech Adami underscored the cooperative nature of the project by stressing that "it is not a Libyan radio that will be transmitted from Malta. It is a joint venture" (McEwen, 1988). At present, 2-hour broadcasts in Arabic and English are aired on high-power shortwave and mediumwave transmissions. Steps are being taken to implement a French program soon.

TELEVISION PROGRAMMING

From an extremely rudimentary program service at the time of the revolution, Libyan television has grown into a full national system. Much of television's development occurred in the 1970s and early 1980s. Since then, the pace of expansion has slowed due to completion of projects such as construction of the national broadcasting center and due to stagnation of the economy and the consequent lack of government funds. Most programs originate in Tripoli, but other centers contribute a small number of locally produced shows to the national schedule. An occasional program, often international sports coverage, is relayed live through satellite.

The programming pattern has continued unchanged for more than a decade. Telecasts begin daily at 1600, with an hour of instructional programs when schools are in session. These presentations support subjects in the national primary or secondary curriculum. General programming commences at 1700. The majority of locally produced programs fall into three broad categories: music, documentary, and news. Early evening programs include children's shows, perhaps cartoons, followed by a religious program that includes a call to prayer. The television schedule revolves around the main evening newscast seen nightly at 2200. Content of the national channel tends to be serious rather than entertaining. Discussions, commentaries, documentaries, and programs focusing on history and folklife are staples of its schedule. After the nightly news, for instance, a current affairs magazine is usually broadcast. Regular transmissions end each day with a feature film or imported serial, usually an Arabic production, around 2330. Weekend programming on Thursday and Friday is expanded. On Fridays, sign-on occurs at about noon for religious programs leading up to broadcast of the main prayer service and continues with regular programming afterward.

The national telecast of news is typical of Libyan domestic productions. Its visual style is spare, and the news set is simple. The presentations of male and female anchors is formal in tone. Many domestic stories are read by the newscasters because costs and logistics prevent extensive field reportage. Stock slides, maps, wirephotos, and other visual materials are employed liberally to make the newscasts livelier.

Until recently, imported programs made up a significant part of daily TV schedules. Prior to the Lebanese Civil War, Libya depended heavily on Beirut television syndicators for programs in Arabic and for subtitling of foreign-language shows. After 1976, Libya began importing from syndicators in Greece. Programs subtitled in Arabic are still seen, including feature films and children's cartoons. Gradually, the portion of the schedule produced domestically has increased. Early television broadcasts relied extensively on shows from the United States and Britain. Among those aired were *Hawaii Five-O*, *The Brady Bunch*, and *The Untouchables*. Documentary shows were included and one of the most popular series was *The World at War*. Of course, all imported shows are stringently censored. El Jerary (1981, p. 159) mentions nine criteria that imported films must meet. He indicates that, among other things, imports should have a "moral," be free of racism, and not violate the "embargo on Zionist products." Libyan television has occasionally participated in coproductions with other Arab TV organizations. Examples include the Arab States Broadcasting Union's programs *The Arab Encounter* and *The Great Homeland* ("Recommendations," 1975; "News," 1979).

TECHNICAL FACILITIES

Libyan broadcasting relies entirely on three combined radio and television production centers. The largest facility is located at the organization's headquarters in Tripoli. Construction of the national broadcast center was started in the mid-1970s but it could not be completed until the early 1980s. The project was delayed by complications such as charges of bidding irregularities by European contractors. Despite this, the building was finished and the first stage of equipment installation begun by 1980. Benghazi's studios are somewhat smaller than those in Tripoli, and a very small facility is operated in Sebha.

Initially, television studios in Tripoli and Benghazi were converted from radio studios. Some equipment has been in use for many years, its lifetime stretched by careful maintenance. Technical upgrading has been gradual, in part as a result of the limited number of qualified technicians, and partly due to a lack of funds. For instance, color broadcasting in SECAM did not begin until the late 1970s.

High-quality videotape equipment is a must. In Libya, as in most developing countries, the majority of programs are supplied on videotape. Film is frequently used as well, but non-Arabic films require subtitling, which must be accomplished during a transfer to videotape. As a result, Libyan TV is forced to maintain a large tape library.

A national microwave network completed in 1975 linked all three production centers. This was a significant step not only because for the first time it united all of the country's regions, but because it permitted Libya to connect with Maghrebvision and Eurovision relayed through Tunisia.

Another step toward reducing the nation's isolation was taken with the opening of a satellite earth station in 1980 to connect with the INTELSAT global system. This facility is located near Tripoli and ties into the terrestrial microwave network. Currently there are three earth stations in this complex, two for Atlantic satellites and one for the Indian Ocean satellite. Libya is an active member and heavy user of the INTELSAT system. The country also is a participant in ARABSAT and initially held 18.2 percent of the organization's shares, second only to Saudi Arabia (Abu-Argoub, 1988).

THE LIBYAN AUDIENCE

Dependable statistics on the distribution of radio and TV sets in Libya are unavailable. Because receivers are not licensed, officials have no reason to monitor their ownership closely. Estimates of total radio receivers range from 135,000 to 1 million. The higher figure, equivalent to 25 sets per 100 population, is probably more accurate, but even this may be too low. A reasonable estimate of the total television sets in use is 600,000, amounting to roughly 15 sets per 100 population. This is a substantial increase over figures commonly cited a decade ago and probably results from growing interest in the medium and the spread of VCRs. The cost of receivers has been a barrier for many Libyan families whose income is lower than in other oil-producing countries of the region.

Radio continues to be a popular medium in Libya. Receivers are freely available in shops and traditional *souks* [open markets], where pocket radios typically sell for $6 and shortwave receivers can be had for as little as $30. Devoted listeners use sets in the workplace, coffeehouses, homes, and automobiles. El-Zilitni (1981) found that every one of the 400 persons he interviewed in a national survey listened to radio at least occasionally. It was also the favored source of news; 97.5 percent of those studied claimed it supplied most of their information on news events. Television was an important news source for 67.2 percent of those surveyed, and newspapers were preferred by 11.5 percent. Listeners expect radio to have news first, as it did in the 1969 revolution and in the confused weeks afterwards.

Foreign radio services still draw a significant audience, as they do in many other Arab nations. Shortwave and mediumwave signals from abroad can be heard throughout the country, even in the deep south. El-Zilitni (1981) discovered that programs from either Tunisia or Egypt were cited by 74.2 percent as important information sources. He also found that the most popular foreign broadcaster was the ever-present BBC Arabic Service. It was identified by 75.3 percent of his sample as a major source of news. This degree of exposure to a potential adversary naturally concerns the government. According to the BBC, Libya experimented with jamming its broadcasts during 1987, but discontinued the practice after three months ("Jamming ends," 1987).

Davis's (1988, p. 154) description of rural oasis communities in southern Libya includes an extensive analysis of media use. In particular, he found residents were "passionate virtuosi of the shortwave band selector." He noted that many listeners had memorized the times of newscasts from foreign stations. Audio cassettes were valued adjuncts to radio receivers and blank tapes were sold in many shops. Davis estimated that distribution of TV sets was no more than one in 25 households. The custom in oasis settlements was to watch TV outdoors on cool evenings, and anyone passing by was welcome to join the assembled group.

While imported television shows are well liked, quality local productions are more popular. El-Zilitni (1981) found that a domestically produced show about wholesome living, *Our Health*, had the highest popularity rating. It was mentioned as a favorite by 83.8 percent of those interviewed. Another local offering, a police show titled *Society and Security*, was rated second, with 79.7 percent of respondents preferring it. In contrast, a category of shows, "Imported Programs," was favored by 76.7 percent.

There is evidence that radio and television, which arrived late in Libya, are introducing significant social changes. Studies have indicated media's impact may be greater in villages, where few other entertainment options are available. El-Hammali's (1980) investigation of modernization in communities near Benghazi found that high levels of radio and television usage were more common in rural villages than in the city. He discovered that an acceptance of greater social freedom for women was associated with high levels of radio usage in rural areas and with high levels of TV viewing in all areas. The extent of radio and television usage was directly correlated with aspirations for higher educational goals. Finally, use of television was positively associated with acceptance of family planning in one village, but not in other localities.

In the current scheme of Libyan broadcasting, audience research is not a priority. This is due partly to the absence of an established research program, but it also fits current ideology. Officials of the broadcasting system can rely on the People's Revolutionary Broadcasting Committee for feedback on radio and television programs, as it represents the interests of audiences and presumably can act as a conduit for public opinion. Moreover, as Rugh (1979, p. 114) notes about Arab broadcasting generally, research enjoys a low priority because program decisions are not necessarily made "to fit precise needs and desires of audiences."

The conservatism of the Libyan social setting and the preference for watching TV as a family activity sometimes produce awkward moments. Groups of viewers, particularly ones of mixed age or sex, can be embarrassed by programs that offend family elders. Foreign programs and rapid changes in taste increase the possibility of value conflicts in Libyan households. To avoid these situations, younger members of the family increasingly watch TV shows and videos alone.

Video has been a fashionable alternative to television since the 1970s, and Libya has been among the world's leaders in its adoption. In 1980 one estimate (The Middle East connection, 1980) placed the proportion of Libyan TV homes with a VCR at 47 percent, a figure approaching that found in the Arab Gulf states. El-Zilitni (1981) reported that many homes had more than a single VCR, but few reported using the apparatus for recording TV shows. Playback of rented (or traded) videos seems to be the main use and, even in the countryside, shops renting videocassettes can be found everywhere. There is evidence that rural villagers are slower to adopt video than their city counterparts, possibly as a result of economic factors.

LIBYAN BROADCAST POLICY

Libya's GNP showed zero growth during the late 1980s due to slack demand for petroleum and a constant rate of exports. Thus, price inflation made the country's imports more expensive year by year. Since most of its food products and manufactured goods must be imported, Libya's economy has suffered. This, coupled with the high level of military spending (about 18 percent of GNP, proportionately one of the world's biggest outlays), has forced government to shrink its budget. This reduction, in turn, has produced cuts in development investment in all public sectors, including broadcasting. Often mentioned additional TV channels and radio services have remained on the drawing boards. Their construction in the near future seems unlikely.

Authorities' enthusiasm for mass communication as a vehicle of mass mobilization seems to have faded. In the 1970s, ambitious plans for expansion of radio and TV were developed, yet few initiatives have been realized. According to El-Fathaly et al. (1977, p. 183), Qadhafi has expressed disinterest in the media, stating that "we have little need for broadcasting." In his view, radio and television serve mainly to support the government in power, and in Libya "we do not have a regime, [therefore] we do not see any need to disseminate its voice." Criticisms are not confined to radio and television. In 1989, the national news agency JANA came under fire for inefficiency. In announcing drastic cutbacks in the press service as part of reform and liberalization of the national economy,

Qadhafi described JANA as a "huge octopus with hundred of officials—and it is still useless" ("Gadaffi to purge," 1989, p. 7).

The same attitude can be seen in the ungenerous financial support given media since the revolution. In the development budget for 1969–1974, the Information and Culture Secretariat was responsible for an allocation of $46.8 million, or about 1.3 percent of the development budget (First, 1974, p. 154). In the five-year development plan for 1976–1980, only 1.3 percent was set aside for information and communication ("Five year plan," 1976). Funding has been reduced even further in recent years. In 1984, for instance, information and culture's annual allocation was $51.6 million, or only 0.7 percent of Libya's development budget (Khader, 1987, p. 205).

At the time of the 1969 military takeover, Qadhafi was merely 28 years old. He and his colleagues represented an educated elite, something totally new in Libya. They were among the first generation of postwar school children, and were influenced by poverty and the country's history of domination by foreign powers. Such experiences have colored Libya's view of the world, and produced a foreign policy marked by conflict. As is well known, Libya's actions have led to confrontations with the United States and other nations. Western critics have characterized the government in Tripoli as "adventuristic." Qadhafi himself is frequently blamed for transgressions, and his political beliefs have been termed "eccentric." Setting aside the special situation in its relations with Chad, Libya's foreign policy has maintained two consistent goals: (1) the establishment of a literally unified Arab state; and (2) support of Palestinians against Israel, and by extrapolation, "oppressed peoples" everywhere. Libya has not used media as important instruments to reach objectives in its foreign policies. Its small-scale effort to develop an international radio presence has not been very successful. The "Friendship and Solidarity" service in Malta produced little of either friendship or solidarity.

Political considerations remain foremost in broadcasting. A special genre of Libyan TV is the political spectacle, through which political "lessons" are compellingly presented to some of the largest audiences achieved for any television program. In 1980, the corruption trial of Badri Ali Hassan, the head of Libyan Arab Airlines, was broadcast nationally. Videotaped excerpts of the proceedings were transmitted in hour-long segments over several nights ("Libyans televise," 1980). Many similar programs were broadcast at about the same time. Often, the featured personality is Qadhafi. An example was his lengthy speech on the occasion of the 1986 anniversary celebration of the U.S. expulsion from Wheelus. It came in the midst of tension over U.S. bombings of Libya and allowed him to respond to political questions in a manner that captured public attention ("Qadaffi fails," 1986). Qadhafi was also once seen operating a bulldozer, knocking down a prison wall, then announcing that Libya no longer had political prisoners (Deeb, 1990, p. 151). Some programs present shocking images, as in the 1987 prime-time televising of the execution of nine political dissidents, allegedly members of the Islamic Jihad Organization ("In Libya, wary middle class," 1987).

Finally, the need to strike a balance between television programs imported from the West and local Arab productions has been pointed out frequently. Abu Bakr, Labib, and Kandil (1983, p. 16) acknowledged that foreign programs project alien values but observed that "the same criticism extends to local production of entertainment and dramas." Libyan policymakers' goal of enlarging the domestic programming share of TV schedules appears to have been met. Only a fraction of shows on the air today are imported from the West. However, increases in popularity of imported videos makes the net effect of gains in television questionable. In any case, access to foreign media is easy for the majority of Libyans, and with the arrival of satellite-delivered television, the possibilities increase even further.

CHAPTER 18

MOROCCO

Claude-Jean Bertrand

NO ARAB COUNTRY lies farther west than Morocco, and none is closer to Western Europe. Morocco experienced Roman rule and Vandal invasion in ancient times; it occupied Spain between 711 and 1492; from the 18th century it had many contacts with European nations; from 1911 to 1956 it was a colony of France and Spain. Morocco thus looks upon itself as having a special calling to act as a bridge between two cultures. On the other hand, Morocco suffers from an internal split between the partly Europeanized middle class in the coastal cities and the more tradition-bound rural population of the interior. Moreover, about 40 percent of the population, mainly in the northern and eastern mountains, consists of descendants of Berbers who lived in Morocco long before the Arabs arrived in the 8th century and who normally speak one of their own dialects.

Unlike most other African states, Morocco has been a nation for many centuries. All Moroccans share the same religion, Islam, and nearly all share a language, Arabic. With the exception of Libyans, all Maghrebians share the legacy of long years of colonization by France, French as a second language, and the memory of the struggle for independence. Yet Morocco is different. It has retained freedom of enterprise within a planned economy. Its old-fashioned authoritarian monarchy has tolerated some degree of political pluralism; and, though Morocco does support Arab and Moslem causes, it has kept close to Western Europe and to the

Professor Claude-Jean Bertrand was born in Algeria, where he spent over 20 years of his life. He studied at the University of Algiers and then at the Sorbonne. He now teaches at the Institut français de presse (IFP) of the University of Paris-2. His fields of study are media in developed nations, especially the United States, and media ethics. He has maintained an interest in the Maghreb, which he has visited several times since independence. He is the author of numerous articles and books in French, English, and Spanish.

United States.

Morocco is more developed than most Third World nations and is growing at a more rapid rate; nevertheless it still faces problems. Its demographic growth rate is one of the highest in the world (3.2 percent): its population has grown from 4 million in 1900 and 6 million before World War II to an estimated 25 million in 1990. Since agricultural productivity and industrialization do not keep up with this, the result is continuing poverty: its per capita GNP is about $900. Additional problems are rapid urbanization and proletarianization. Though over 55 percent of the population are still rural, the 14 cities with over 100,000 inhabitants are plagued with shanty towns and unemployment. Casablanca has over 3 million inhabitants; Rabat, Fez, and Marrakech more than 500,000.

Another problem is social inequality. The lower 20 percent of the population has 7 percent of the national wealth, while the upper 20 percent has over 65 percent. To some extent that corresponds to the economic split between a traditional and a modern sector: on the one hand, quasi-feudal large landowners who grow commercial crops on irrigated land in constrast with small farmers, 90 percent of whom own fewer than 10 acres; on the other hand, a large quantity of craftsmen and an overabundance of tradespeople in contrast with a relatively small number of industrial concerns often controlled by foreign corporations.

After France granted Morocco independence in 1956, a series of conflicts began between the monarchy and the Istiqlal Party, which had been fighting against colonialism since the 1930s. The political crisis that erupted in 1971 coincided with two attempts on the king's life; King Hassan II sought and received diverse support. In the mid-1970s, the Saharan conflict broke out when Spain left that area. The Green March to the South in 1975 generated a "sacred union" of all Moroccans around the king. Political stability was the only remarkable feature of the next 15 years.

The BBC estimates that there are 7.5 million radio sets, 3.2 million television receivers, and 800,000 videocassette recorders in Morocco (British Broadcasting Corporation, 1991b).

RADIO

In 1907, the Sultan decreed a state monopoly on telegraphy, wired or wireless. A state Office chérifien des PTT had been set up by Franco-Moroccan agreement in 1913 and had been granted a monopoly over the post, the telephone, and the telegraph. A November 25, 1924, executive order enlarged its monopoly to include all electric communications. It was in February 1928 that the first radio broadcast was made from Rabat with a 2-kilowatt mediumwave transmitter, the power later being increased to 5 kilowatts (1932), then 20 kilowatts (1935). A 2.5-kilowatt shortwave transmitter started relaying the mediumwave signal in 1942. After World

War II, Morocco began building its communications infrastructure in earnest. In 1947, separate production and transmission facilities were given to the French and the Arabic programs—though at that point still only the major cities of Rabat, Casablanca, Fez, and Meknes were covered. Also, in 1947, Radio Maroc was granted by executive order a degree of legal and financial responsibility within the Post Office.

A 1948 conference in Copenhagen authorized Morocco to use eight transmitters. The next year, two new 20-kilowatt transmitters were inaugurated, one for the French program, one for the Arabic program. Then, in April 1953, the large Sebaa Aïoun transmitting station began operating with two 120-kilowatt mediumwave transmitters that, at night, covered almost the whole territory. FM was started in Casablanca in 1954. In 1955, an administrative and production center, La Maison de la radio (Radio House), was opened in Rabat. In 1956, Sebaa Aïoun was equipped with four shortwave transmitters. By the next year, Moroccan radio could use an aggregate 559 kilowatts of transmitting power for its three programs, the "A" Program in French (75 hours per week), the "B" Program in Arabic (60 hours) and Berber (20 hours), and the "C" Program in Spanish (10.5 hours) and English (5.5 hours).

Under the French Protectorate, the mission of radio was to serve French interests—those of the settlers and those of the Empire. There were programs in Arabic only for 3 hours a week from 1934 to 1936, then for 90 minutes daily from 1936. News and other programs were tightly supervised by the résident général. He appointed the director of Radio Maroc, who, in the absence of a board of governors or a board of management, had direct authority over all seven departments. If radio played a part in the fight for independence, it was through Cairo's Voice of the Arabs.

After 1956, the Moroccan government wished to unite a country long divided between a large French zone and a small Spanish zone in the north, and it wished to be heard on the international airwaves. Above all, it wanted to ensure its central control. French capital and experts were flowing out of the country, so little change could be brought in immediately. In 1959, the "A" Program was in Arabic (100 hours per week), the "B" Program in French (75 hours), and the "C" Program in Berber, Spanish, and English. As part of successive three- or five-year national development plans, technical facilities were expanded. By 1965, there were 24 transmitters, including 3 in Oujda in the east, 2 in Safi, and 1 in Agadir in the south. Expansion slowed down from the mid-1960s, except for two 400-kilowatt long-wave transmitters set up at Azilal (altitude 5,500 feet), and accelerated again as part of the 1973–1977 Plan.

Radio Maroc was not the only broadcasting institution in the country. In Spanish Morocco, the Sultan's deputy had granted the right to broadcast to a firm controlled by Torres Queveda, who already enjoyed a monopoly on the colony's telephone and telegraph. Its station, Radio Dersa Tetuan, used 2 mediumwave transmitters (25 and 5 kilowatts).

In Tangier, as early as 1937, in spite of French opposition, private entrepreneurs and hostile nations (e.g., Italy) had moved in. A first local station was soon taken over by French interests, then by the state. In 1939, Spaniards built a station that was protected so long as Spain ruled over the city (1940 to 1945), but in 1947 it was taken over by Radio Africa, whose principal owner was a Frenchman linked to Radio Andorre.[1] A year earlier, an American had launched Radio Tanger, of which 49 percent was owned by Spaniards and 33 percent by Americans.

When independence came in 1956, there were three private concerns in Tangier. Radio Africa owned five transmitters, two mediumwave for Radio Africa Maghreb (125 kilowatts) and Radio Africa Tanger (12 kilowatts), and three shortwave for Radio Inter Africa. The Spanish-speaking Radio Pan American operated a 2-kilowatt transmitter, and Radio Tanger International used two (50 and 10 kilowatts) mediumwave and two (10 kilowatts) shortwave transmitters.

In 1948–1949, the French government had yielded to U.S. pressure and given the Voice of America (VOA) a 10-year lease. VOA set up 12 shortwave transmitters with a combined power of 820 kilowatts to relay its broadcasts to Eastern Europe 24 hours a day. A condition was that it also relay programs of Radio Maroc and of the French radio.

An international conference gave Tangier back to Morocco in 1956. A ministerial decree then abolished all stations outside the state monopoly. It was only three years later, however, that the government decided that all those stations should go off the air by December 31, 1959, and, until then, would be strictly supervised. Radio Dersa and Pan American readily sold out. The Radio Africa people secretly shipped out all of their equipment. Radio Tanger was bought by the Moroccan government in 1960 and integrated into the state system. The Moroccans extended the VOA lease until 1963, provided it stopped relaying third-party (i.e., French) radio and that it loaned them two transmitters. In 1964, the United States transferred all the equipment to Morocco, which in return let VOA use it for a two-year renewable period.

EARLY TELEVISION

Television started earlier in Morocco than anywhere else in Africa. In 1950, two French firms obtained from the Office chérifien des PTT a 50-year monopoly on Moroccan television, as well as the right to take advertising *ad libitum* and to retain 85 percent of the annual fee on receivers. A year later another firm took over, TELMA. In March 1954, two years late, it started broadcasting 30 hours a week in Arabic and French, using a 4-kilowatt transmitter in Casablanca and another in Rabat: it reached 3,000 to 4,000 viewers. In May 1955 it stopped and went bankrupt in 1957, being 10 million (new) francs in debt. Circumstances could hardly have been worse for the TELMA project. With the Sultan exiled, agitation for independence was peaking. The French were getting ready to leave; few Moroccans could afford the sets; the Istiqlal had ordered a boycott of all French products. And, of course, newspapers fought the threat to their advertising revenues.

In late 1960, the government bought the equipment, much of it outdated, for 1 million francs. For two years, the Moroccans studied a relaunching with French experts—then suddenly initiated it in 1962 in order to cover the International Fair in Casablanca. For some years television was to be an improvised operation of Moroccan radio. As late as 1970, Moroccan television was on the air only 4 hours a day (1.25 hours in French) over a restricted area, the large cities in the north.

BROADCASTING REORGANIZATION—RTM

For a few years after independence, the status and structures of broadcasting changed only marginally. Several drafts of a constitution were proposed but to no effect. In the absence of a clear statute or rules and regulations, a tacit understanding enabled broadcasting both to function as a branch of the Postal Ministry and, politically, to be directly controlled by the Prime Minister. As late as 1978, the Minister of Information defined Moroccan broadcasting as "an instrument to publicize government policies."

A January 19, 1962, executive order resolved the ambiguity by creating the Radiodiffusion-Télévision Marocaine (RTM) and shifting it to the Ministry of Information, Fine Arts and Tourism. In the 1960s, various modifications were introduced, yet by 1980 RTM's legal standing and missions were still unclear. It was described as a separate government agency, legally responsible and financially autonomous, placed under the authority of the Minister of Information. There had been ministerial declarations (e.g., one in 1978 stating that the object of RTM-TV was both to preserve Moroccan and Islamic culture and to present a balanced picture of the world), but no specific Broadcasting Act had yet filled the "juridical vacuum" in which Moroccan radio and television are often said to be operating.

Originally, the budget of RTM was a *budget autonome* voted upon by the Board of Directors, not by Parliament, the expectation being that it would balance its accounts. Now it is a *budget annexe*, discussed in Parliament like the national *budget général*, because RTM both needs extensive financing by the state and has extensive revenues of its own. In 1987, for instance, its budget (250 million DH = approx. US$30 million) came from a state grant (52.4 percent), the fee (26.5 percent), and advertising on TV (20.8 percent).

The annual fee on radio receivers was eliminated in 1971. A television fee (a little over $1.00) is now automatically added every two months onto the electricity bill, whether one owns a TV set or not.

Advertising on radio had been allowed by a 1928 governmental order, and it was decided in 1961 that not only Radio Tanger could take commercials but also television when it came. Morocco was thus the first country in Africa to authorize radio advertising as a source of financing—and commercials appeared on the tube in March 1970. The part of advertising in the RTM budget has doubled since 1975.

Advertising is not plentiful in Morocco: the latest UNESCO figures (1986) put it at only 0.10 percent of GNP, $14 million in all, $0.61 per capita per annum. But in 1989, television got about 60 percent of it, as opposed to 15 percent for print media. On TVM (RTM-TV), the number of commercials grew from 1,000 per year at the start to 15,000 in the late 1980s. Naturally, most commercials are shown in the 1930 to 2300 period—in heavy blocks of 10 to 12 minutes, but they do not interrupt programs. Much of the advertising comes from foreign firms, many of them French as France is the country's major economic partner, but Moroccan firms are also present: the rates have been kept artificially low to make it easier for Moroccan companies to get commercials on the screen. The result is, even after the advent of pay TV, a long waiting list for those companies.

Except for Oujda on the Algerian border, the more important cities sit within an amphitheater of mountains, with Rabat and Casablanca in the center, on the Atlantic coast. They can easily be covered. The problem is with towns and villages in the mountainous Rif area (maximum altitude 8,000 feet) to the north and beyond it on the Mediterranean coast, and in the long Atlas chain (maximum altitude 13,660 feet) to the southeast and beyond it on the margins of the desert. Since 1975, moreover, Morocco (446,000 square kilometers) has been fast extending to the southwest over the vast sparsely inhabited former Spanish Sahara (226,000 square kilometers).

RTM RADIO

Since cooperation on a Maghrebian satellite has not materialized, RTM has gradually had to add transmitters to try to reach the whole population. By 1976 (just after the Green March), however, only the long-wave transmitter at Azilal (about 150 kilometers northeast of Marrakech) covered the whole country (not including Western Sahara). Only 18 percent was reached on mediumwave in the daytime by the first network, 12.3 percent by the second, and 5.5 percent by the third. Even in the early 1990s Moroccan broadcasting was still not accessible to the whole population.

In 1990, the RTM radio system, consisting of the three networks based in Rabat plus nine regional stations, could use

- 6 studios and 6 mobile units in Rabat,
- 3 studios in Tangier,
- 2 studios and 1 mobile unit in Casablanca,
- 3 studios and 1 mobile unit in Laâyoune,
- 1 studio and 1 mobile unit in Marrakech,
- 1 studio and 1 mobile unit in Agadir,
- 1 studio and 1 mobile unit in Fez,
- 1 studio and 1 mobile unit in Oujda, and
- 1 studio in Dakhla.

In all, there were far fewer technical means than 10 years before.

The A, or "national," network broadcasts 24 hours a day in Arabic on long, medium-, and shortwave. The B, or "international," network broadcasts 19 hours a day on mediumwave and FM: over 16 of those hours in French, the rest in Spanish and in English. The C, or "Berber," network also broadcasts 19 hours a day in various Berber dialects, but it also relays the A network. The regional stations air 3 hours of their own programs a day, in the afternoon, and they relay the A and C networks; on the other hand, most of them feed programs to the national nets once a week.

The three-network pattern reflects the inherited linguistic pluralism.[2] An excellent study done a few years ago (Chakroun, 1979, pp. 12–20) very precisely analyzed RTM radio programs.[3] It appeared that out of about 40,000 hours of programming a year, 62.6 percent was in Arabic; 18.5 percent was in French; 12.5 percent was in Berber; 3.7 percent was in Spanish; and 2.8 percent was in English. Each of the major networks corresponds to one of the cultural polarities, the traditional-rural on the one hand and the modern-urban on the other. As one Tiznit high school boy put it, "Arabic radio reminds me that I am Moroccan while French radio entertains me with programs all young people want." As far as subject matter is concerned, Chakroun found that overall air time was allocated as follows: entertainment, 67.44 percent; news and public affairs, 15.88 percent; education, 5.89 percent; culture, 6.39 percent; religion, 4.14 percent.

The National Network is the most important medium for that mass of the people who cannot read, cannot afford a television set, or know little or no French. It is more slow paced and rambling but more diversified and

Table 18.1. Regional radio stations

Station	Founded in	Broadcast Nationally	
Agadir	1971	Monday	9–12 A.M.
Casablanca	1936	Tuesday	9–12 A.M.
Dakhla	1980	Saturday	9–12 A.M.
Fez	1960	Friday	9–12 A.M.
Laâyoune	1976	Monday	0–5 A.M.
Marrakech	1958	Wednesday	9–12 A.M.
Oujda	1962	Thursday	9–12 A.M.
Tangier	1947	Six days/week	0–5 A.M.
Tetuan	1984	Only during Ramadan	

Source: Fattah-Allah, 1991.

popular than the others. Its format has not changed much over the years. Music fills over two-thirds of the air time. RTM has several orchestras, for "classical" (i.e., Andalusian) music, modern (Arab) music, and popular "malhoune" music; regional stations have some orchestras too. RTM also has several companies of actors to produce serials and plays. Among the more appreciated programs are the morning programs for women (sometimes lively discussions on problems of family life) and the phone-in programs introduced in the late 1970s. Most programs are taped, yet none is precisely scheduled except the news and press review, whose length may vary unpredictably. Nearly two-thirds of the non-news, non-music programming (14 percent of the total) is imported or obtained from United Nations agencies. Generally speaking, though, the National Network cultivates traditional values. On political and social subjects, it tends to sound rigidly Islamic and rather parochial.

The International Network caters to the younger, more educated, Western-oriented audience. Almost three-quarters of its air time is devoted to music, much of it Western pop, interspersed with world news. The format is more strict: the day is sliced into periods entrusted to one of several disc jockeys, who model themselves on their colleagues of the French peripheral stations. Quite a few of the programs are borrowed in their entirety from Radio France. Less than 5 percent of the non-news material is locally produced.

With Spanish on the decline and English never having been the tongue of either natives or invaders, even when the C network had to carry programs in those languages, the International Network was meant first and foremost for 40 to 45 percent of the population who speak Berber and do not know classical Arabic. Programs are aired several hours a day in each of the three dialects, tachelhit (in the southwest), tamazight (in the central mountains, to the east), and tarifit (in the north). What is most appreciated, especially by those Berbers who have migrated to the big cities, is the rich traditional music.[4]

RTM TELEVISION (TVM)

RTM television was launched in March 1962 with a speech by the king on the occasion of the annual Celebration of the Crown (la fête du trône), an apt symbol of RTM's political and economic subordination. It broadcast on 625 lines, using studios in Rabat, the modernized TELMA installations in Casablanca, and seven relay stations in Tangier and major cities in the interior. Only in the mid-1960s did expansion really start. Until then, the government seemed voluntarily to underfinance the new medium.

In 1990, RTM's 27 transmitters and 35 low-power repeaters, linked by microwave, covered all major urban areas. As early as 1972, it was claimed that 80 percent of the population were within reach of the RTM-TV signals—a claim that, even if accurate, ignored the fact that many town dwellings and many villages did not have electricity.[5] As late as 1980, a large part of the population remained untouched by television, especially in the mountains. On the other hand, as early as January 1970, Morocco became the first African nation to own an earth station. It was set up at Souk El Arba by the PTT in cooperation with INTELSAT; but the station was normally used for telecommunications and occasionally to receive Eurovision programs.

Whereas radio was somewhat decentralized, TVM programming in 1990 came from the Ain Chok center near Casablanca and predominantly from Rabat. Rabat had 2 studios, 4 large mobile units, 15 small video mobile units, and 15 mobile film units. Casablanca had 2 studios, 1 large and 1 small mobile unit. Laâyoune had 1 studio and 1 mobile film unit. Color had been introduced in 1972 using the French SECAM-B system.

In 1990, TVM was on the air an average of 46 hours a week, more in a festive period like Ramadan. Moroccan production capacities were still not equal to the transmission facilities. Since as little as 10 percent of the very small RTM budget went to creation, TVM could not originate even 1 hour of non-news programming a day. There was no policy to encourage production. Basically the only true Moroccan programs were the newscasts, the Saturday evening variety show, and reports on special events, like official ceremonies—plus a few plays and many taped songs. Most of the entertainment was imported. Originally, much came from France on a subsidized basis: those programs either were French or were U.S. shows dubbed in France. Since oil capital greatly increased Middle Eastern (mainly Egyptian) production of films and serials, arabization had progressed (75 percent of programs in Arabic), but not so morocconization.

After 20 monotonous years of French B-movies, Egyptian films, football games, and royal speeches, in 1985 TVM seemed about to change. The slogan was "La télévision bouge" (TV is on the move); young people were recruited, some trained by Médi 1, the commercial radio; the people looked

Table 18.2. Moroccan radio transmitters, 1991

Wavelength	Location	Power (kw)	Network/Station
Long wave	Azizal	2 × 400	RTM. Ch. A[a]
	Nador	2 × 1000	RMI Relay
Mediumwave	Agadir	600	RTM Ch. A + B +regional program
	Agadir	50	RTM Ch. C
	Agadir	20	RTM Ch. B
	Casablanca	1	RTM Ch. B
	Casablanca	1	RTM Ch. C
	Errachidia	15	RTM Ch. A
	Laáyoune	600	RTM Ch. A
	Laáyoune	50	RTM Ch. A + B +regional program
	Marrakech	1	RTM Ch. A
	Marrakech	1	RTM Ch. B
	Marrakech	1	RTM Ch. C
	Ouarzazate	15	RTM Ch. A
	Oujda	100	RTM Ch. B
	Oujda	100	RTM Ch. A
	Rabat	25	RTM Ch. A
	Rabat	10	RTM Ch. B
	Rabat	1	RTM Ch. B
	Safi	5	RTM Ch. B
	Safi	5	RTM Ch. C
	Sebaa Aïoun	300	RTM Ch. A +regional program
	Sebaa Aïoun	300	RTM Ch. B RMI relay
	Sebaa Aïoun	140	RTM Ch. C
	Sidi Benmour	600	RTM Ch. A +regional program
	Tanger	600	RTM Ch. A + B +regional program
	Tanger	1	RTM Ch. A
	Tanger	1	RTM Ch. B
	Tarfaya	10	RTM Ch. A
	Tetouan	10	RTM Ch. A
	Tetouan		RTM Ch. B
	Tanger	200	RTM Ch. B. RMI relay
	Dakhia	10	RTM Ch. A + B +regional program
	Ceuta	5	Radio Ceuta
	Mellila	2	Radio Mellila
		5	RNE (Spanish)

Table 18.2. (continued)

Wavelength	Location	Power (kw)	Network/Station
Shortwave	Sebaa Aïoun	50	RTM Ch. A + B towards Africa
	Tanger	100	RTM Ch. A towards Africa
	Tanger	50	RTM Ch. A + B towards the Middle East
	Tanger	50	RTM Ch. B
	Nador	2 x 500	RMI Relay
	Tanger	4 × 100	VOA
	Tanger	2 × 50	VOA
	Tanger	4 × 35	VOA
	Tanger	10 × 500	VOA - operational in 1992
	Oujda		RTM Ch. B
	Meknes		RTM Ch. B
	Fez		RTM Ch. B
	Marrakech		RTM Ch. B
FM	Casablanca	39	RTM Ch. A
	Casablanca	39	RTM Ch. B
	Oukaimeden	31	RTM Ch. A
	Oukaimeden	31	RTM Ch. B
	Rabat	39	RTM Ch. A
	Rabat	39	RTM Ch. B
	Sebaa Aïoun	1	RTM Ch. A
	Sebaa Aïoun	1	RTM Ch. B
	Tetouan		RTM Ch. A
	Tetouan		RTM Ch. B
	Marrakech	2.5	RMI relay
	Rabat	1	RMI relay
	Casablanca	1	RMI relay
	Fez	2.5	RMI relay
	Ceuta	1	Radio Ceuta
	Mellila	0.25	Radio Mellila
		1	Antena 3

Source: Radio France International, 1991.
[a]A = National Network, in Arabic
B = International Network, in French
C = Berber Network
RMI = Radio Méditerranée Internationale

more lively, the studios more colorful; the news sounded less shackled; more national products were announced.

But nothing much happened; in 1978, Chakroun (1979, p. 19) had found the following distribution of program types: advertising 4.35 percent; religion 5.56 percent; education 8.41 percent; culture 11.22 percent; news

Table 18.3. Moroccan television transmitters

Location	Channel	Power (kw) (PRE)	Network
Zerhoun (Meknés)	M 4	120	RTM
Laäyoune	BC 4	316	RTM
Boukhouali (Oujda)M	5	267	RTM
Azougar (Ifrane)	M 6	9	RTM
Rabat	M 7	180	RTM
Izeft (Errachidia)	M 7	14	RTM
Tazerkount (Beni-Mellal)	M 8	20	RTM
Touzarine (Al-Hoceima)	M 9		RTM
Ouarzazate	M 10	267	RTM
Essaouira	7	20	RTM
J. Kissane	M 5		RTM
Tiguelmamine	M 9	9	RTM
Bouigra (Agadir)	M 9	4	RTM
Tazekka (TAZA)	M 8	4	RTM
Tan-Tan	M 8	11	RTM
Sidi Bounouara	5 + 9	11	RTM
Safi	8	20	RTM
Jbel Lahdid	7		RTM
Fogo	5		RTM
Bouarfa	10	267	RTM
Figuig	6	9	RTM
Dakla	6	11	RTM
Zaïo (Nador)	M 4	10	RTM
Cap Spartol (Tanger)	M 5	20	RTM
Oukaïmeden (Marrakech)	M 6	18	RTM
Hafa Safa (Tetouan)	M 10	9	RTM
Casablanca	10	180	RTM

2M International has 6 transmitters (on Channel 33) in Rabat, Casablanca, Fez, Meknes, Marrakech, and Agadir.

Source: Radio France International, 1991.

Table 18.4. RTM television distribution of programs by genres, 1987

Type of Program	Number of Hours	Percent of Total
Fiction (movies, series, etc.)	619.41	21.39
News and information	475.26	16.40
Songs	375.55	12.95
Sports	353.37	12.19
Children's programs	328.56	11.33
Advertising	285.46	9.86
Culture	180.54	6.24
Religion	174.38	6.04
Documentaries	104.15	3.60
Total	2,897.00	100

Source: Rapport sur les statistiques des programmes télévisés, Service des études et de la planification de la RTM, 1987.

and public affairs 22.34 percent; entertainment 48.12 percent. Almost 10 years later, the RTM published the analysis shown in Table 18.4.

A glance at the listings for a normal day shown in Table 18.4 will give an idea of TVM programming at the beginning of the last decade of the 20th century.

THE DEMONOPOLIZATION OF THE 1980s

Sensitive probably to the fierce criticism of RTM, especially by the print media, by intellectuals, and by the young, the king took the initiative of opening new broadcast channels. Thus in the early 1980s Morocco became the first nation in the Maghreb with a privately owned commercial radio station, then in the late 1980s the first nation in Africa to have pay television.

COMMERCIAL RADIO: RADIO MÉDITERRANÉE 1 (MÉDI 1)

Between 1978 and 1980, an agreement was worked out between the Moroccan Information Ministry and the French SOFIRAD[6] on an undertaking similar to a Dutch-Swiss project dating back to 1969–1970. The Moroccan State would own 51 percent of the station and French firms (SOFIRAD, RMC, Hachette, and Thomson) the rest. The aim for the SOFIRAD was to exploit a market left aside by RMC: North Africa and West Africa. Morocco looked upon it as a means to build up its international image.

In September 1980, Médi 1 started broadcasting on mediumwave, using the transmitter of Radio Tanger (which then started withering into a small local station). By 1982, RMI was also broadcasting on long wave, covering the whole of Morocco, and on shortwave, reaching from Senegal to Egypt.

Over 10 years, using the easy and energetic style that made Europe 1 successful in France in the 1950s and made the Gabon-based Africa No. 1 a success from the late 1970s, Médi 1 has won about 8 million listeners, especially the young, a majority in the population. According to a SECODIP survey in 1987, 36 percent of Moroccans listened to it every day, 60 percent at least once a week: thus Médi 1, at 68 percent, ranked just behind RTM's National Network, which boasted 91 percent.

The format is music (a patchwork of Moroccan, French, English, and Berber music) with little talk, plenty of jingles—and news on the hour. A slogan of the station is "Dire bonjour en arabe et au revoir en français" (Say hello in Arabic and so long in French). A large part of its popularity comes from the fact that it uses *dialectal* Arabic, together with Berber and

French. By 1988 it alone drew 12 percent of advertising expenses in Morocco (but was expected to suffer from the advent of commercial TV).

Médi 1 is so different from traditional Third World stations that its impact has been felt throughout the Maghreb. Its penetration, on long wave, is estimated to be 50 percent from Tanger to Tripoli, in Libya. Every month about 3,500 letters are received from listeners.

In October 1990, RFM was launched: it was the first commercial *local* station in the country. With a 500-watt transmitter it has a range of about 40 kilometers around Casablanca.

COMMERCIAL TELEVISION: 2M INTERNATIONAL

The same month (July 1980) when the launching of Médi 1 was announced, another decision seemed to have been finalized: to open, within a year, a second television channel as a joint venture between the Moroccan state and private interests. But for 2M International to go on the air, Moroccans had to wait until 1989.

Two-thirds of the capital in the new company was held by Moroccans. The Omnium Nord-Africain[7] owned 31.5 percent and Moroccan banks 35 percent. The participations of SOREAD, the foreign consortium, were 8 percent for TF 1 (First French TV network, commercial), 5 percent for Bouygues (owner of TF 1), 5 percent for Maxwell, 15 percent for Videotron (Canada), and 0.5 percent for SOFIRAD. The king gave 2M the premises and equipment that had been prepared for a second public network, planned in the late 1970s.

The Second Moroccan (2M) network is scrambled 10 hours a day and clear 5 hours. It is non-scrambled from 1200 to 1400 (cartoons and series) and from 1800 to 1900 (diverse programming, including the news): those two are periods of heavy viewing, which advertisers appreciate. The clear programs are normally in Arabic (4 hours), while most scrambled ones are in French.

As regards programming, 2M had no obligations except to respect morality and religion. What it specializes in is movies in the morning, early afternoon, and after 2100 daily—Egyptian, French, and U.S. films. 2M also does music videos, quite a lot of sports, and, during clear periods, much appreciated live interviews of ordinary people. Its news tends to be more international, if only to play it safe. About 20 hours a week are of its own making: this limited (though growing) production caused some disappointment, but then it first had to invest in the training of staff and a technical infrastructure.

Considering the cost (180 dirhams = approx. $21 a month), of course only the middle classes can subscribe—about 100,000 to 150,000 households (no precise figure available) along the Atlantic coast and in the big cities inland, mainly people in the 30 to 45 age group. Cafés started getting decoders but the Centre du cinéma marocain got that forbidden in order to protect movie theaters. After operating three years, 2M expected to break even with 180,000 subscribers.

Since 1989, 2M programs have been sent by satellite to the north of France, where large numbers of Moroccans live, and later to some Paris suburbs. There were plans to distribute its programs to Benelux countries via cable systems—and later to make them available in the whole Maghreb and West Africa. 2M publishes *Télé-Plus* with its own listings and those of TV 5.

TV 5 (EUROPE)

TV 5 is certainly the most original of the newcomers. This multinational network gets its programs from public broadcasters in France, Belgium, Switzerland, and Québec. Then, riding an INTELSAT bird, it delivers them to 16 million potential viewers from Russia to Morocco. Since 1985 its signal has been received by a dish in the royal palace of Skhirat (near Rabat) and rebroadcast to other palaces in Casablanca, Marrakech, Rabat, and Salé. Of course, people living in those cities can benefit from this extra source of pictures except when the king interrupts the process, as he did in October 1990 when a French Antenne 2 talk show dealt with a book violently critical of Hassan II. By May 1991, even governmental dailies were requesting that the service be resumed. Up to 1988, RAI Uno (Italian) and RTL Plus (German) were also available; since then Sky Channel (British), Worldnet (American), Galavision (Mexican), for example.

Apart from the fact that the French net TF 1 was supposed to provide 2M with 1,000 hours of programming a year, Morocco had in 1989 signed an agreement with a new French concern, Canal France International: CFI offered 4 hours of TV material a day (fiction, entertainment, and information). This did not help Moroccan production but did provide diversity.

That was not all. At the turn of the 1990s, no plans for cable existed but, even when living away from the border with Algeria or from Spain, ingenious Moroccans set up antennas that enabled them to receive foreign programs (from the Iberian peninsula and the Canaries). The number of satellite dishes was estimated to be 200,000 to 300,000, increasing apparently since the interruption of TV 5. Though there were Moroccan manufacturers of the dishes, a permit had been instituted to protect 2M International. Besides, there were 300,000 to 500,000 owners of VCRs and they were served by about 1,000 video clubs renting (mainly francophone) cassettes for a little over $1.00. The choice, however, was rather mediocre and the arrival of 2M hurt the business.

It did not seem at the beginning of the new decade that competition had taught RTM much of a lesson: it did show a little more professionalism—but it was unable to create popular shows, was felt to be tightly controlled by the Crown, and still went on the air only at 5 P.M. A regional television project had been announced in 1988 but the regions were still only served by a news bulletin twice a week. The great majority of Moroccans who did not have access to the new television felt somewhat frustrated.

BROADCAST JOURNALISM

Information has always been looked upon as the primary mission of Moroccan broadcasting. It seems all the more important for RTM as so little is produced in other fields. One explanation given is that "interest in broadcast news, a characteristic of Maghrebian audiences generally, seems intensified here" (Elgabri, 1974, p. 34). Actually it has long been official policy that national attention must be focused on the king and his ministers,[8] and that no criticism whatever must be uttered of the king or his family—or of official stands towards Israel or the former Spanish Sahara.

The centrally important National Radio Network gives six 10- to 30-minute newscasts a day (the most important at 0700, 1300, 1800, and 2300) and 3- to 5-minute summaries every hour on the hour. The other radio services take their cues, and usually their texts, from the A Network, as does TVM. The early evening 45-minute TV news, read in classical Arabic with few pictures, can expand to 2 hours. Most of the news is domestic, the hierarchy of subjects being the king's activities, national news, news of the Arab world, news of Africa, news of the rest of the world, then sports and weather. The sources are the Royal Cabinet, the Ministry of Information, correspondents in the major cities, and the national news agency, Maghreb Arab Press (MAP).

RTM has links with the outside world other than MAP. It is connected to Spain by microwave and to France by cable. It has been receiving Eurovision programs since the mid-1960s. It is a member of the European Broadcasting Union (EBU), the African URTNA, and the Arab States Broadcasting Union (ASBU) and has at various times cooperated with nations in Western and Eastern Europe and in North America. Pooling resources with Algeria and Tunisia seemed an obvious move. A Maghreb-vision network was discussed from 1966 and started operating by microwave in 1970 but was promptly stalled by political conflicts.

Actually the closest cooperation has always been with France, in spite of friction between the governments. Following such agreements as the conventions signed in 1963 and 1972, France has supplied equipment, technicians and consultants, training, and programs. However, the 1975 fragmentation of the monolithic French ORTF (Office de Radiodiffusion-Télévision Française) into seven distinct and specialized units made for much confusion.

THE MOROCCAN PUBLIC

At the end of the 1980s, it was estimated that on average 65 percent of the population was illiterate, including 78 percent of women, 95 percent of rural women; these figures were much higher than those of Algeria and Tunisia. And while about half the population understand French in the cities, fewer than 10 percent do in rural parts.

This accounts in part for the popularity of broadcasting (as in all the Third World) and the low global circulation of dailies (less than 300,000 copies, almost two-thirds of them in French). Other causes are the geographical isolation of many villages, the social segregation of women, and the general paucity of entertainment. Further factors are the ancient Moslem and local tradition of oral communication and, of course, transistorized receivers, which appeared on the market just when radio stopped serving exclusively the French, the wealthy, and the intellectuals.

There are no longer any official figures on the ownership of receivers: one estimate is 1 radio set per 8 persons but another is of 6 to 7 million sets (to be compared with 133,000 licensed sets in 1950). As regards television, RTM reported 747,190 sets to the European Broadcasting Union in 1980; 10 years later, one estimate is of 1 TV set per 21 persons (1 to 1.5 million sets)—but according to a 1987 survey over 85 percent of Moroccans had a TV set at home (25 percent a color set), 69 percent among the poorer classes.

As for radio, the 15 to 30 year olds much prefer RMI (64 percent as opposed to 33 percent for the older people): the figure is 100 percent for Moroccans with only a primary education, but only 35 percent for the unschooled. RTM's "A" channel is preferred by the older people (50 percent as opposed to 8 percent for the young). RTM's two other channels are not accessible to all, by far: "B" (international) to 42 percent of the population and "C" (Berber) to 50 percent.

As for television, *Le Matin (du Sahara)*, the major daily, stated in November 1990 that 72 percent of the population could receive TVM, 30 percent 2MI, 17 percent TV 5, 7 percent Algerian, and 13 percent Spanish television. Most could not watch anything but RTM television, TV 5 being accessible only in the big cities and 2M only to subscribers.

A 1988 SECODIP survey showed that TV was even more popular in the cities than radio: it reached a rating of 60 percent between 2100 and 2200, whereas radio peaked at 25 percent between 1200 and 1330. In 1987 a survey showed that 67 percent of the women and 52 percent of the men watched TV every day. The proportion of those who watched TV regularly reached 90 percent on the west coast and went down to 72 percent in the mountainous east-central region.

How do they like what they see? On TVM they appreciate movies in Arabic and the news and they resent the commercials. On 2MI, they like the movies, serials, and series which they had long yearned for—but they would prefer more Moroccan shows and some find programs a little audacious. TV 5 is appreciated for news and culture. Overall, 39 percent are satisfied, 31 percent rather satisfied, and only 25 percent dissatisfied: the more pleased are women, rural people, and aged persons.

In the upper classes, a set will be acquired for the children and the domestics. For the middle classes, purchasing a set (on credit) is a priority; it provides prestige and tightens the traditional family bonds. Poorer men, the younger ones particularly, will view television in cafés. Television has so much become part of the café scene that prices go up when people come in for the shows after the news[9] and rise even more when sports are on. Though less than 60 percent of the territory (not including Western Sahara) was covered by television in the late 1970s, it was estimated even then that about 60 percent of the population, i.e., over 10 million Moroccans, had access to a set at least occasionally. Homebound women tend to watch more than men. Though moving pictures and stereotyped story lines make television relatively easy for all to follow, the young in particular find it more attractive, partly because, being better educated, they can understand classical Arabic and French.

PROBLEMS OF BROADCASTING

"Moroccan television is an institution that breeds obscurantism. . . . It serves as a garbage-can for the worst foreign programs. . . . It presents an abominable image of our country. . . . Not even our fiercest enemies could have invented such a mill of anti-national propaganda" (Lamrhili, 1980, pp. 6–7).

Though not all criticism of RTM is as shrill as that of this radical monthly, much of it does carry a similar message. Negative judgments come not just from French, American, or German consultants. Research work by Moroccan academics, assessments in the press, and speeches in Parliament have been remarkably openly critical. Strictures are clearly inspired by a patriotic desire for improvement. In a nutshell, RTM is accused of being politically shackled, professionally mediocre, and culturally alienating: this led to the creation of 2MI.

As there is no regulatory text, at RTM "self-censorship becomes an obsession . . . to avoid any risk of even vaguely alluding to any taboo topic" (*Lamalif*, 1977, p. 30). Not a word was said on RTM about the 1989 unrest in Jordan and Algeria. Whatever discontent there is with governmental policies (or lack of them), with bureaucratic abuse, with speculation and corruption, it never is heard on the air, not even under the guise of police blotter news items. RTM will not even accept free high-quality documentaries on remarkable achievements in other Arab countries for fear of generating disaffection toward the Moroccan regime. When in 1978–1979, TVM did produce a very successful weekly program called *Samar* in which VIPs from every section of the political spectrum (including the socialists and communists) were in turn invited, with guests of their choice, to talk about their experience of pre-independence history, even that topical a show came as a refreshing shock (*Lamalif*, 1979, p. 15).

It has always been taken for granted that all news is scrutinized beforehand, if not dictated, by the Palace and that the main task of broadcast journalism is to support king and government. 2MI is just as careful as TVM. The effect, everyone agrees, is that the "news" is uninformative and unexciting. In cafés, customers will only interrupt their games and conversation when at last the evening entertainment starts.

What the left-wing daily newspaper *Al-Bayane* had to say about RTM on October 28, 1990, was that public broadcasting "does nothing but carry sterilized, monochrome, one-way, unilateral official speech." It "stays locked and incapable of any change," a condition all the more regrettable as the printed press, though it must be careful and is often chastised, does express a modicum of political pluralism.

Ostensibly, state control is motivated by the need to keep the whole nation gathered around the throne and active in the effort to develop the economy; but mobilization for development necessitates feedback. "The total absence of relationship between the RTM and its listeners and viewers," Abderahim (1978, p. 49) notes, "represents a major obstacle to its action."

Given the close governmental attention, it is the more surprising that clear policies for RTM were never articulated or vigorously enforced. The resulting lack of quality is such that in July 1980 RTM was denounced in the semiofficial *Le Matin (du Sahara)* (1980, p. 2). "We too often forget," wrote the Grumbler in his column, "that our enemies too are listening and making great fun of our lack of discipline and our slovenliness as broadcasters." He added, "We would like every evening to watch an international movie. . . . Certainly we appreciate that so much air time is devoted to movies in Arabic—provided they be not lemons, which they usually are." Probably, 2M International has answered the wishes of this critic.

"The organization of the RTM is archaic, unadapted, and it should be reformed to face the new needs of television," a (confidential) official report affirmed. Apart from the absence of a precise legal framework, broadcasting has long suffered from a lack of leadership and expertise. Top executives have too often been political appointees, ignorant of radio and television, who did not stay on long enough to learn, but who, critics say, brought in untrained or hastily trained protégés who *have* stayed on. Hence, they claim, a "mafia" developed within the RTM monolith that has institutionalized muddling through and that resists any change. RTM management, according to French consultants, is definitely inferior to that of the huge RTA (Algeria) and even of the RTT (Tunisia). It was only in December 1979 that for the first time an engineer risen from RTM ranks was appointed its director general. This, however, was not considered totally satisfactory, for one problem with RTM is that investments have too often gone to transmitters (with little long-range planning) rather than to production facilities or to the training of administrative, technical, and artistic staff.

Low salaries and ill-defined functions do not breed professional fervor. Programs and schedules do not seem to be anybody's prime concern. "No one can tell you who exactly is responsible and on what criteria programming is determined," wrote Jibril (1977, p. 29). Nor does anyone know precisely, or really care about, what the public needs and wants. Too frequently some cheap foreign material is acquired and scheduled, and then the time is preempted by officialdom.

Political control of broadcasting is far more common in the world than broadcasting freedom, and Morocco is in no way exceptional. Failure to respect professional standards set by the more developed countries is unavoidable in developing nations. What then of the cultural complaints Moroccans make against television?

To many illiterates, much of TV entertainment, though fascinating, is irrelevant, especially as they cannot understand the dialogues. Even the sentimental Egyptian serials, which they are accustomed to by now, seem a little silly and alien to them. What they would most enjoy is local productions set in an environment familiar to them and dealing with their joys and concerns. The most traditional people object to TV programs for puritanical, even religious, reasons. Fathers, if uneducated, find them a threat to their authority, if only because children are prompted to ask questions that they are unable to answer. While only a few parents may object to the Syrian or Egyptian words, accents, and attitudes that some young people adopt, many adults hold TV responsible for youth's rejection of their values and ideals. Television is commonly accused of leading the younger generation to abandon the fields and forsake manual labor to seek conspicuous consumption as pictured on the screen.

Certainly broadcasting deepens the cultural gap between Arabic-traditional and French-modern. The Istiqlal Party has vigorously pressed for arabization, particularly since 1973. But here Morocco faces two problems. One is that neoclassical Arabic, though it has developed into an international idiom for media, still sounds foreign to many and, in its purer forms, can even be incomprehensible, especially to the children. The more colloquialized classical Arabic, used in variety shows, for example, is welcome, but popular experiments with news in dialectal Arabic have not been followed through. The second problem is set by the Berberophones. Since 1977, they have become more vocal in their opposition to the absence of their language on the major radio network and on television. Difficult as it is for a foreign observer to appreciate, many Moroccans simply do not clearly understand much of what is said on Moroccan radio and television.

In more sophisticated circles, it is vehemently regretted that broadcasting, TV above all, has done so little to conserve and enrich the national culture (Jibril, 1977, p. 32). It could, for instance, have stimulated the growth of a Moroccan cinema. Local investors find films too risky as compared to real estate, while the government-controlled Centre Cinématographique Marocain (CCM) is too propaganda oriented to promote creativity.

FOREIGN MEDIA IN MOROCCO

Just as many of the 0.5 million Moroccans in France will listen to RTM's National Network at night, Moroccans in their homeland consume foreign media, including TV.[10] Inhabitants of Oujda and the eastern border view Algerian television. Spanish TV is normally received in the north. A special antenna makes it possible to watch it, together with Portuguese TV, as far south as Rabat.

As for radio, older people who formerly turned for Arab music to Cairo on shortwave or to Algiers had probably, by 1980, switched to the Arabic program of the British Broadcasting Corporation (BBC). Radio France

Table 18.5. Foreign television services

Network	Audience		
	Total	Urban	Rural
TVM (RTM)	73.4%	88.5%	56.3%
2MI	25.6%	42.9%	5.9%
TV 5	9.0%	16.8%	0.2%

Source: La télévision étrangère, July 4, 1990.

Internationale (RFI) broadcasts in French but, unlike the BBC, RFI is more interested in Africa than in the Middle East. VOA seems to have a small following. Far less than 10 percent of the population regularly listen to anything apart from RTM and Médi 1, but those are people interested in news, and they are opinion leaders, whether they are intellectuals or small tradesmen and craftsmen.

Four stations broadcast from the Spanish coastal enclaves of Ceuta (in the north) and Melilla (in the northeast). Radio Ceuta (MW and FM) relays the SER network for 9 of its 24 hours. Radio Melilla (MW and FM) uses SER 24 hours a day. The RNE 1 station in Melilla is a station of the public Radio Nacional de España network. The third station in the enclave is an FM relay of the commercial Antena 3 network.

CONCLUSION

For years Moroccan broadcasting was considered inferior to that of Algeria or Tunisia. State control was tight and negative. A first turning point may have come with the 1975 Green March, for which RTM mobilized a mass movement and unified the nation as the media had never done before. This apparently came as a shock to both the authorities and the public. Plans were made to extend TV coverage, renovate the transmitters, expand production facilities, and better train personnel. Then economic considerations slowed down the movement.

But in 1980 came the launching of Médi 1, the first commercial radio station in the Maghreb, and its great success. And at the end of the decade 2M International went on the air, the first commercial TV network in the Maghreb. These were major undertakings that fit in the general Western trend towards demonopolization and media pluralism.

Certainly those major business undertakings have not cured all the ills that plague Moroccan broadcasting. The 1973–1977 economic plan had called for better, more diversified programming, adapted to the needs of society by use of audience research. It called for more educational broadcasting and for lively news shows based not on speeches but on field reports. That was wise, but it has not been done almost 20 years later. By the beginning of the 1990s, RTM has not changed much and most Moroccans cannot enjoy the new television nets either for economic (2MI) or for technical (TV 5) reasons.

Nevertheless, broadcasting did act as a powerful agent of modernization. As in the rest of the Maghreb, it also compensated for the disastrous effects of the now ended post-independence campaign for total arabization of the educational system.

With its bulging population and authoritarian regime, Morocco did not have the economic and political means to follow the broadcasting example of European democracies—but media-wise it seemed to do better than other Arab nations and other nations in Africa.

CHAPTER 19

TUNISIA

Donald R. Browne

TUNISIA has generally suffered by comparison with its North African neighbors. Smaller by far, and possessing none of the oil wealth of Libya or Algeria, it has gone largely unnoticed in the turmoil of world or even regional politics. Yet this modest-sized nation has won a considerable reputation for its resourceful approach to national development—an approach in which broadcasting plays an important, if not necessarily constant, role.

The history of modern Tunisia is quickly told. It became independent of French rule in 1956, after a struggle that saw a number of Tunisian intelligentsia jailed but very few killed. Its head of state was the Bey of Tunis—an office carried over from Tunisia's years as part of the Ottoman Empire. In the following year it became a republic. Thereafter, it has been governed by one political party, the Democratic Constitutionalist Rally (before 1988, it was called the Destourian Socialist Party), and up until 1987, was led by one chief of state, Habib Bourguiba. There have been various antigovernment protests and riots, some over religious and some over political issues, but little changed over the three decades of Bourguiba's rule, including the men who surrounded him and rotated from one ministry to another. Even in the four years (1987–1991) following the fall of Bourguiba, the degree of change has been modest, although the political climate has become decidedly more unstable. The Tunisia of today, however, is a considerable contrast with the newly independent Tunisia of 35 years ago, especially when one takes into account the limited resources

Donald R. Browne is Professor and Chair, Department of Speech-Communication at the University of Minnesota. He has written numerous books, monographs, book chapters, and articles about foreign and international broadcasting, including articles on Lebanese and Palestinian broadcasting. He lived in Tunisia from 1960 to 1963 and visited the country again in 1977.

with which it has had to fashion this transformation.

Not only is Tunisia not abundantly blessed with oil (although explorations continue), but other natural resources are also in short supply. Phosphate is the country's only major exportable natural resource. Other mineral deposits are hardly worth mentioning. Agricultural produce, chiefly olive oil, citrus fruits, and dates, finds its way to foreign markets, but the uncertain climate, with its long droughts and sudden torrential downpours, hampers maximum exploitation of this resource. Tourism has become a major source of foreign currency. As a result, hotel and resort construction has boomed; however, the country's frequently rocky coast and general scarcity of water, combined with limited capital and hotel expertise, restrict development of this sort.

The two resources that appear to have been most crucial for the country's progress are its people and its governmental policies. President Bourguiba often called Tunisians "the nation's greatest resource"; and even if one makes allowances for a certain degree of political hyperbole, the description seems apt. Tunisians are, on the whole, hard working, even tempered, and resourceful. Tunisia's governmental policies have aided the development process, too, in that the country has been able to seek the assistance of other nations, France and the United States in particular, without necessarily accepting priorities or philosophies that might accompany this assistance.

This does not mean that the country is without serious problems. The fickleness of the weather, combined with the aridity of much of the land in even the most favorable years, means that Tunisia lacks a stable agricultural base for the feeding of its own people, much less production for export. Two elements of progress—increased health care and educational opportunities—have led to further major problems: rapid growth of population and of a specific segment of that population that is overeducated and/or underemployed. They have been joined in recent years by a third major problem: religious fundamentalism. As President Bourguiba's health grew worse each year, predictions concerning the country's uncertain future circulated more and more freely—although not in the Tunisian mass media, which have remained under direct government control or strongly subject to its influence throughout the history of the republic. Indeed the mass media themselves, with broadcasting in the vanguard, appear to have conditioned the people to expect and desire stability and to see progress in evolutionary, rather than revolutionary, terms, although that stability has eroded somewhat in the face of rising religious fundamentalism over the past few years.[1]

The BBC estimates that there are 1.25 million radio sets, 3.2 million television receivers, and 200,000 videocassette recorders in Tunisia (British Broadcasting Corporation, 1991b).

RADIO BEFORE TELEVISION

On the whole, the French were slower to develop broadcasting in their colonies and protectorates than were the British. Development of the media came earlier and progressed more rapidly in those colonies where comparatively large numbers of French citizens settled; and Tunisia was certainly one of those. Its proximity to France, the relative arability of land on or near the Mediterranean coast, and the comparative docility of the Tunisians themselves, led tens of thousands of French nationals to settle there. A group of French amateurs came on the air from the Tunis *kasbah* in 1924 with an unlicensed radio service (Houidi and Najar, 1983, p. 106). It was intended primarily for the French colonists in and around Tunis, and consisted largely of material imported from France. Few efforts were made to extend radio beyond the areas where French colonists lived (primarily the northern third of the country), although private stations (French-run) were authorized in Bizerte and Sfax in 1935, and Sousse in 1937. The original private station in Tunis received official authorization in 1937. In 1938, the Tunisian and French governments signed an agreement establishing a government-run, license-fee-supported station, Tunis-PTT (Houidi and Najar, p. 106). The four private stations went off the air early in the Second World War and never came back (Houidi and Najar, p. 107). At the time of independence, there were an estimated 100,000 radio sets in the country, most of them in French households, the majority in and around Tunis. The beylical government and the French did sign a new convention on broadcasting in 1953. It contained a clause specifying that at least one-fourth of all broadcast staff in Tunis should be Tunisian (Houidi and Najar, p. 108), but the French nature and leadership of the service remained paramount, and it was operated as an adjunct of French Radio and Television (RTF).

Following independence, the Tunisian government lost little time in developing broadcasting facilities. A number of French advisors stayed on to help operate Radio Tunis, and these included administrative, technical, and artistic personnel. This would have been necessary in any event, since there were few higher-level Tunisians trained to step in and take over, but it also stemmed from the fact that the Franco-Tunisian independence agreement contained numerous provisions guaranteeing the rights of French citizens living in Tunisia, including certain cultural rights:

> The French shall continue to enjoy in Tunisia the cultural advantages from which they have benefitted up to now in the fields of thought and art, especially as concerns the entry, circulation and dissemination of all their means of expression. The Tunisian Government may nevertheless forbid publications which might jeopardize law and order or morals, with due respect for freedom of opinion and information. (*Le Monde Économique*, 1956, p. 196)

Thus, for the next several years, the French-language service of Radio Tunis maintained its pre-independence nature and scope: 8.5 hours per weekday, 12.5 hours on Saturday, 16 on Sunday as of 1960 (Voss, 1962, p. 223), and with a program schedule featuring such educational fare as Mallarmé's poetry, "Athens Before Democracy," and the Stoic philosophers (Celarie, 1962, p. 127). However, broadcasting in Arabic, which had taken second place to broadcasting in French in the pre-independence period—6 hours per weekday as compared with 7.5 hours in 1952—surged ahead during the late 1950s, and by 1960 the average weekday included 12 hours of Arabic broadcasting. Transmitters were also strengthened and services expanded. The southern city of Sfax received a 5-kilowatt transmitter in 1961, and a shortwave transmitter, intended to relay the Arabic service to southern Tunisia and to other parts of the Arab world, was installed in 1959. In 1960, the government initiated a plan to modernize and improve broadcasting facilities, at a cost of nearly $4 million (*Republic of Tunisia,* 1964, p. 23).

Programming in the initial years of independence was something of a struggle with respect to the Arabic service. Whereas the French service was able to draw upon the resources of ORTF in Paris (an October 1962 schedule lists such imported fare as a serialization of Dostoevski's *The Idiot,* jazz from the Champs Elysées, and "The Adventures of Tintin," a popular French comic book hero), the Arabic service had to fashion a schedule out of locally available resources. Some program material might have been available from Egyptian radio, but Egyptian President Nasser and Bourguiba were on poor to indifferent terms during much of this period. Certainly Egyptian popular music, widely available on disc, was played, as was a good deal of music by popular artists from Europe and the United States. Interviews with Tunisians from the world of arts were also prominent, and not surprisingly, since Tunisians pride themselves on their achievements in poetry, illustration, ceramics, and numerous other manifestations of cultural life. Visiting artists from the Arab world, Europe, and elsewhere were also interviewed, and their visits were frequent enough so that few weeks went by without a guest appearance.

News broadcasting posed relatively few problems. Tunisia's governmentally controlled news agency, Tunis Afrique Presse (TAP), drew upon the major American, European, and Arab news agencies, plus its own domestic reporters, to furnish a reasonably comprehensive service; and, with the aid of that service and its own reporting staff, the Arabic service of Radio Tunis was broadcasting news reports some 12 times a day by 1961. President Bourguiba's voice was frequently heard in those early days as well. His declarations and explanations of policy, his exhortations to the people to apply their collective efforts to the cause of national development, and his reviews of progress made since independence were weekly features in the broadcast schedule (Elgabri, 1974, p. 31).

But broadcasting as an arm of national development was another matter. Radio Tunis staff members were aware of the role that radio could play in this respect—UNESCO studies and other official and unofficial reports provided plenty of examples—but they had no tradition of their own on which to draw, since the French administration had rarely employed radio to that end. Gradually, and with the sometime collaboration of various ministries (e.g., Agriculture, Public Health) and organizations (e.g., the General Unions of Tunisian Students and of Tunisian Workers), the staff developed a number of weekly broadcasts designed to answer listeners' questions concerning national development and to induce listeners to think more deeply about those issues. There also were special daily broadcasts for women, dealing with subjects ranging from education to fashion (Celarie, 1962, pp. 126–27).

THE INTRODUCTION OF TELEVISION

Although broadcasting in the early years of independence was synonymous with radio, television was under active consideration by the late 1950s. Its imminent appearance was rumored yearly in the early 1960s, and a Franco-Tunisian accord of December 7, 1959, noted its eventual introduction (Houidi and Najar, p. 112). It was seen as "contributing to the creation of a national soul, to the political and civic education of the public" (*La Presse*, October 16, 1962, p. 2). The government recognized that the venture would be expensive, but probably worth the investment in terms of national development and national pride. However, the government was overtaken by events. Italy had erected a television relay transmitter on Pantelleria, an island just east of Tunis, in order to reach Italians on the island as well as the Italian community then in Tunisia. Wealthy Tunisians were beginning to purchase sets, both to receive the Italian signal and in hopes of soon being able to do the same with the Tunisian service. As many of those individuals were well placed in Tunisian society (several were high government officials), their hopes had the effect of further stimulating the government to take action.[2] However, several years passed before the Tunisian government committed the funds necessary for the introduction of television. The service was finally inaugurated on May 31, 1966, Tunisia's National Day.[3]

From the beginning, Tunisian television offered both information and entertainment: programs were both local and imported, some in French and some in Arabic. Broadcasts generally were limited to the early to mid-evening hours. National development received considerable attention, and some of the new programs bore resemblance to certain of the radio programs already mentioned: *Women and Society* and *New Home* stressed the rights and duties of women in national development, while *Young People's Club* attempted to prepare younger viewers for "future participation in the national effort."[4] Those in charge of the new medium also began immediately to lay plans for television programs on agricultural and industrial development, despite the fact that there were as yet few sets available in the villages, and coverage was limited to a relatively small segment of the country. According to official Tunisian estimates, there were only some 5,500 television sets in Tunisia as of the end of 1966.[5]

FROM THE TENTH ANNIVERSARY
TO THE FALL OF BOURGUIBA: 1966–1987

Ten years after Tunisian independence, then, radio broadcasting was firmly in place as an instrument of national development, while television was in its infancy but displayed every sign of enjoying a healthy future. Plans were in place for the development of a television relay system that would carry the new medium to all but the southernmost parts of the country, where, in any case, few people lived. The growth of both media over the next 20 years, in physical terms at least, was impressive, and television's was almost phenomenal, rising from 5,500 receivers in 1966 to 230,000 by 1976 and to 500,000 by 1986. That growth was certainly stimulated by the concomitant growth of both number and power of transmitters. Where in 1966 there were six radio transmitters—medium-wave, shortwave, and FM—most of them located just outside Tunis, and with a total power of a little over 200 kilowatts, by 1986 there were seven AM, one shortwave, and eight FM transmitters, distributed around the country and with a collective power of nearly 3000 kilowatts. Television, for its part, went from one 100-kilowatt transmitter just outside Tunis to a 1987 total of 9 VHF and 10 UHF transmitters all across the country, with a combined total of just over 1700 kilowatts on VHF and 4400 kilowatts on UHF.

Along with those increases in transmitter power, Tunisian Radio and Television (RTT) displayed increased dedication to the production of Tunisian programs, as opposed to imported fare. Agreements with France ensured the provision of radio (*Tribune of History, Crossroads of Knowledge*) and television (*History in Judgement, Dossier on the Screen*) series, but these were few in number, as were British (*Anna Karenina*) and American (*Grizzly Adams*) shows. Egyptian films and series were more numerous, and Lebanon had furnished many programs before its civil war began in 1975; but well over 50 percent of the television schedule and over 90 percent of the radio schedule for the Arabic services was Tunisian, making allowance for the fact that much of the popular music on various programs came from abroad, as did news clips, and that few of the domestic programs were in the more expensive formats (drama, comedy).

The range of Tunisian-produced programs was considerable: individual shows and series dealing with Tunisian history; economics; letters and music; original Tunisian drama for radio and television, in French and in Arabic; youth talent shows; serial dramas for preschool children; broadcasts from the Carthage Festival; medical and legal advice; quiz shows; Arabic poetry; tips on road safety; etc. News played a prominent role in both media: radio carried it 13 times a day in Arabic and 12 in French, while television provided it once a day in each language.

Throughout this period, radio continued to carry a National Service in Arabic and an International Service in French, with 1 hour a day in Italian. Despite their titles, both services were intended largely for Tunisian audiences, although the National Service was relayed to North Africa and Europe on shortwave. Regional studios in Sfax and in Monastir (President Bourguiba's home town)[6] furnished several hours of daily regional news, interviews, and discussions. Television remained one combined service (roughly 25 percent French, 75 percent Arabic) until 1983, when a second TV service came on the air. Such a service had been under discussion since 1978, when the Tunisian Council of Ministers made the decision to create a separate French-language channel, with the support of the French government. The Arabic TV service was able to expand its schedule, and provided approximately 8 hours a day by 1987; the French service was available for approximately 3 hours each evening. Residents of the coastal area running from just north of Tunis to Sousse also could receive Italy's RAI Uno TV signal through an old microwave relay transmitter located near Tunis.

THE FALL OF BOURGUIBA AND THE
RISE OF FUNDAMENTALISM: 1987–PRESENT

On November 7, 1987, a relatively obscure former Army general and Minister of the Interior whom President Bourguiba had appointed as prime minister just a month earlier came on Radio Tunis and announced that a panel of six physicians had determined that Bourguiba had "become totally incapable of fulfilling the duties of the Presidency" (Nelson, 1988, p. xxvi). Zine el Abidine Ben Ali took over the Presidency himself, and pledged that there would be genuine democratic reform.

He faced a situation fraught with difficulties. Democratic reform had been promised often by Bourguiba, but little had come of those promises, and in fact the president appeared to be increasingly Byzantine in his swift appointments and dismissals of cabinet ministers in the years immediately preceding his fall from power. Thus, the populace tended to distrust pledges of reform. Furthermore, the centrist Destourian Socialists were under attack from two ends of the political spectrum: the more "leftist," young, well educated, but underemployed or unemployed city dwellers; and the Islamic fundamentalists on the right, who drew their inspiration from the Ayatollah Khomeini-led Iranian Revolution. The latter were a mixture of young and old, urban and rural, educated and illiterate, and they posed far more of a threat to the established order than did the "leftists." They were far more numerous; they were reasonably united in their opposition to what they saw as the over-Westernization of Tunisia; and they had readily available lines of supply from Tunisia's eastern neighbor, Libya. In fact, the Qaddafi government frequently had used radio to reach Tunisians with messages critical of Bourguiba's allegedly pro-Western stance, and employed it to call for local support for a January 1980 raid carried out on the southern Tunisian city of Gafsa by Tunisian dissidents from Libya (Nelson, 1988, p. 273).[7]

As the Ben Ali government loosened the reins on political dissent and displayed a more open attitude toward religion (including the provision of more broadcast time for religious programming—a scarcer commodity under Bourguiba), various fundamentalist groups took advantage of the newly available channels, albeit mostly through print media or personal appearances: fundamentalist leaders found it difficult to get their more political viewpoints expressed through broadcasting, which allowed readings from the Koran and the transmission of worship services, but little by way of "religious politics." But such groups did succeed in making an issue *of* broadcasting: they called attention to its role as purveyor of Western culture and thus as a threat to the nation's Arab-Islamic character. The second television service was the major object of their attacks; it was almost entirely a relay of Antenne 2 programs from French public television. The Minister of Information responded to those attacks by indicating that "the maturity of the Tunisian people and their attachment to Arab-Islamic authenticity" had protected them from undue French influence during the 75 years of French colonization of Tunisia (Nelson, 1988, p. 252). The subsidization of the relay of Antenne 2 by the French government allowed the Tunisian government to satisfy the more Westernized tastes of some of its citizens at little cost, but the protests were another reminder of the tension that continues to exist between pro-Western and pro–Arab/Islamic viewpoints in Tunisia.

Iraq's invasion of Kuwait in 1990 and the outbreak of the 1991 Gulf War saw fresh manifestations of that tension. Up until those events, the Ben Ali government had continued to exhibit a basically pro-Western foreign policy that followed the same general lines set by Bourguiba. However, Islamic fundamentalists, who saw the Gulf War as a demonstration of Arab pride and power on Saddam Hussein's part, received a great deal of popular support. President Ben Ali was careful to balance his public declarations: condemnation of the allied arms buildup and subsequent invasion, but criticism of Iraq's occupation of Kuwait. Still, criticism of the allies predominated (Riding, 1990, p. 3). RTT regularly showed Iraqi television footage of the war damage inflicted by allied raids, and reported on the numerous pro-Iraq demonstrations taking place around the country.

Even before the war ended, another problem arose. The Islamic fundamentalists had been in the vanguard of the pro-Iraqi demonstrators, and they had made much of the need for Tunisians and other Arabs to distance themselves from Western ways and to achieve a greater sense of Arab and Islamic worth. Part of that could be accomplished through a return to more fundamentalist practices, e.g., use of the *sharia*, or Islamic code of law. Some of their message made its way to the populace through radio and television, thanks to broadcast coverage of demonstrations connected with the war. The government sensed that some of the fundamentalists might seize upon their greater popularity and prominence to make a renewed bid for formal political power. Events in Tunisia's western neighbor, Algeria, already were turning in that direction.

Accordingly, the government cracked down on some of the more prominent fundamentalist groups (Randal, 1991, p. 13A), jailing certain leaders and reducing or eliminating access to media outlets. But the potent issue of "Westernization versus Islamicization" remains, and may be exacerbated in the future through the proposed introduction in Tunisia of satellite-delivered TV services from Europe, through Italy's RAI-TV (Grassi, 1990, p. I-5) or through a proposed (by Canal Plus of France, for summer, 1991) pan-African pay TV network to be called Canal Horizons (Dawtrey, 1991, p. 4, p. 8).

The present radio and television services remain basically what they were in 1987, with no increase in number of transmitters, but a near doubling in power for UHF (French-language television service) TV transmitters. The precise number of radio and television sets in the country is difficult to determine, for reasons noted earlier. The 1991 *World Radio-TV Handbook* indicates nearly 1.7 million radio sets and 650,000 TV sets; a 1990 Country Data Paper prepared by the U.S. Information Service in Tunis lists 4 million radio sets and 3 million TV sets. There does appear to be more emphasis on high-quality production of original Tunisian drama, some of it in serial form. The series *The Spider's Web* (ten 60-minute episodes, scheduled for showing in late 1991/early 1992) centers around a conventional plot: the attempts of a couple to trick a rich man out of his fortune. However, the production features on-location shooting in eight locales scattered around the country, making it something of a travelogue, as well. It required some 90 days of shooting over an eight-month period, making it perhaps the most expensive Tunisian production to date, and leading its director to recommend that future large-scale projects be coproductions with other Maghreb nations or with European countries, possibly with sponsor or advertiser support (Mellah, 1991, pp. 4–11).

Certainly such productions as *The Spider's Web* will help to offset criticisms of an over-Western bent on the part of RTT, although fundamentalists could argue that the plot lines are basically European, that such productions do too little to highlight traditional Islamic values, etc. But they clearly will require a magnitude of investment that is beyond the reach of RTT itself, and European investment almost certainly would strike fundamentalists as a perpetuation of that same overdependency on the West that they so strongly decry.

FINANCING AND GOVERNANCE

Tunisian Radio and Television is a government-operated service and falls under the Ministry of Information. Up until 1980, radio set owners paid an annual license fee of 2 dinars and radio/television set owners a fee of 5 dinars.[8] When the National Assembly discussed the 1980 budget, it mandated that 4 millemes (about one U.S. cent) per unit be added to consumer electricity bills. The amount was not to exceed 1,200 millemes for every two months, and the surtax was expected to raise about 2 million dinars. Since the license fees were producing only 6.43 percent of the RTT budget by 1980 (Houidi and Najar, 1983, p. 145) and cost a certain amount to collect, they were dropped in that year. Since that time, the government has provided almost all of the budgetary support for RTT through an annual appropriation. Advertising was authorized by the Council of Ministers in January 1988, but so far its impact on revenues has been modest.

One consequence of the absence of a strong financial base (the annual operating budget, minus equipment, is about 12 million dinars as of 1991) has been that the long-awaited construction of a new broadcasting headquarters seems no nearer now than it was 25 years ago, when the facilities, dating from 1955, already were inadequate, e.g., three TV studios of modest size for *all* domestic TV production. There also are complaints, well-nigh universal in the field of broadcasting, that administrators take up too much of the budget, and in fact only a little over 10 percent of that budget goes into domestic production (Ben Said, in Najar and Ben Said, 1991, p. 360).

In contrast with most Western European systems of broadcasting, there are no citizen advisory councils or boards, although there is an administrative council comprised of various cabinet ministers, which at least ensures that RTT will know what the government expects of it. There are occasional surveys of amounts and nature of listening and viewing, but very rarely of audience reactions to programming (Houidi and Najar, 1983, pp. 201–2). The successive Directors General of RTT generally have come from within the government; few have had experience with the mass media. Their numbers include a former Director of Political Affairs in the Prime Minister's office, a provincial governor, a Director of Tunis-Afrique Presse, and even an academic (Fethi Houidi) who had co-authored a study of Tunisian mass media before being appointed Director General of RTT in 1988 (but Houidi, too, had occupied certain government posts). A few individuals have served as Director General for a number of years, but most have held the office for no more than a year or two, which has tended to discourage long-term planning.

BROADCASTING AND TUNISIAN DEVELOPMENT

Tunisian broadcasting serves many needs—for entertainment, information, and education. Well over half of the broadcast time for both media is taken up with entertainment, and music plays a major role, even on television, where it appears in variety shows (e.g., Sunday's 4-hour-long *Laou Samatoum*, or *With Your Permission*), shows featuring child entertainers, etc. Information comes primarily in the form of newscasts, analyses, and press roundups, and with a great deal of attention to government leaders; Houidi and Najar have criticized the quality of journalism displayed, on the grounds that "the journalists of the RTT are considered as simply functionaries [of the government]" (Houidi and Najar, 1983, p. 264; translation mine). Information broadcasts take up about 25 percent of the schedule (Najar and Ben Said, 1991, p. 321). Fifteen to 20 percent of the time is devoted to educational material, most of it informal and for adult listeners and viewers.

Each of those three general categories of programming can contain developmental messages, but the second and third serve that purpose far more often than does the first. The messages appear in three general categories: political, economic, and educational.

Political development was part of the mission of Tunisian radio from the first days of independence. The nation was not deeply divided along political lines—indeed, there were no serious challenges to Habib Bourguiba and the Neo-Destour Party, as it was then called—but it was the opinion of Bourguiba that the majority of Tunisian citizens lacked "political awareness," especially in terms of what they should expect of their new government and what parts they themselves should play in that government. Accordingly, not only did Tunisian radio provide accounts of what the government and its leaders were doing; it also prepared programs in which citizens would raise questions and make comments about the government, within reasonable limits. (Certain elements within the Tunisian press have at times been critical of government policies and personalities, although some newspapers and magazines that carried their criticisms too far, in the opinion of the government, have been closed down. The broadcast services have never gone that far.)

But the real star of political broadcasting was President Bourguiba himself. Although he had not used radio often prior to independence (for one thing, he had spent considerable periods of time in jail), he made frequent and effective use of it thereafter. He covered a wide range of topics, from how to treat foreigners who visited the country to why it was no longer necessary or even respectable for women to wear the veil.[9] His manner of speaking was warm, yet direct, and very colorful: in one talk concerning the veil he referred to it as "filthy rag." He seemed often to search for the correct word to catch the precise meaning of what he wanted to convey when he knew it all along. He punctuated his remarks with questions directed to his listeners, discussing their problems in specific enough terms so that he seemed really to know them. He enlisted their help in the task of national development by placing that help in concrete terms and within the realm of possibility. But he also prided himself on his accomplishments, noting that "there is not a Tunisian who does not owe being a free citizen in an independent country to me" (Nelson, 1988, p. xxiv).

As President Bourguiba's health declined in the mid- to late 1960s, he appeared less and less frequently on radio and seldom on television, although his activities, as well as excerpts from his pronouncements, continued to receive full attention on the newscasts of both media.[10] Emergencies of various kinds, e.g., incursions from Libya in the 1980s, usually found him before cameras and microphones, and in one of his last major spontaneous appearances, on January 6, 1984, he called for a restoration of order following riots over price increases for basic foods, and announced the dropping of the increases (Nelson, 1988, p. 229). None of his cabinet ministers or other close political associates appears to have possessed the same charisma where radio broadcasts are concerned, and it may even be that the period of maximum effectiveness for such broadcasts has long since passed. Where the average Tunisian citizen was concerned, radio was a new medium of communication in the late 1950s and early 1960s, and Bourguiba's employment of it was fresh and vital. Now it is an open question as to how long such freshness and vitality can be sustained or whether a "new" political personality could recapture or rekindle the spirit of earlier times.

Bourguiba certainly had not encouraged the formation of opposition parties, but pressures for more freedom of political expression developed during the 1970s, and finally, in the run-up to the November 1981 national elections for the Chamber of Deputies, such parties could and did field candidates, and could claim air time. It was allotted on the basis of 2 minutes of TV time and 3 minutes of radio time for each national district (23 in all) in which a party filed a list of candidates (Nelson, 1988, p. 218). The Destourian Socialist Party swept through the elections, but Tunisians at least had had the opportunity to see and hear individuals whose views were not in perfect accord with Destourian policy.

Economic development has been absent from Tunisian broadcasting in certain forms commonly found in developing nations—e.g., the rural radio forum. However, it has appeared in connection with three sectors of activity that are of considerable importance in the Tunisian economy: family planning, nutrition, and literacy training. Radio has been employed to those ends in numerous developing countries, and Tunisia's use of it in each case can hardly be described as pioneering. Still, formal family planning programs, especially those involving mass media campaigns, are not common in the Arab world, and the initiation of such an effort in Tunisia took a certain amount of courage and resourcefulness. Unfortunately, the effort was not successful and is more interesting in terms of what it tells us about failures than successes.[11]

Discussions about family planning had begun in 1962, and an official, albeit experimental, family planning program was launched in 1964. Several family planning centers were set up around the country, mobile units served more distant centers, and President Bourguiba gave his support to the effort through various speeches and brief remarks, some of them broadcast. In 1969, it was decided that family planning information should be introduced to the primary schools and that television would be the medium through which to do so. The plan called for 10,000 television receivers to be placed in schools throughout the country; a small studio was constructed and a group of Tunisians was sent to France for training in program production and equipment maintenance. (The French government gave the program considerable financial support.) The studio was finally ready in February 1971, but was not inaugurated until May, when 10 television receivers had been installed in classrooms in Tunis only. In the meantime, Tunisian financial commitments to the project had lessened; ministerial commitments were no longer as strong as they had been (partly, it seems, because there were five different ministers of education during the period 1969–1971); and the result was that a projected series of 13 programs emerged as one film and one slide story. The film was incorporated into a television program and was quite enthusiastically received, but the effort stopped at that point.

A nutrition advertising campaign that started in the mid-1970s has enjoyed rather greater success, perhaps because it is less ambitious, perhaps because it does not challenge such deeply held values. It was financed initially through the U.S. Agency for International Development and Tunisia's National Institute of Nutrition (NIN). It limited itself to five basic nutritional themes, e.g., the need to expose infants to sunlight, and condensed the various treatments of each theme into 1- to 2-minute messages. Broadcasts were scheduled three times a day and when both husbands and wives could hear them. A fictional character, "Dr. Hakim" (Hakim means "wise man" in Arabic), presented the messages. An impact study revealed very high recognition of "Dr. Hakim" and his association with advice on nutrition: 88 percent of mothers surveyed could identify him and what he did. Indications of impact on behavior were less clear, but there was a notable increase in use of SAHA, a supplemental food that had been recommended in the broadcasts, and in mothers' self-reports of early exposure of their infants to sunlight. The pilot phase of the campaign ended in 1978, and was then picked up by NIN for continuation (USAID, 1982, pp. 125–26; Smith, 1979).

Tunisia's "literacy through radio and television" efforts also were quite successful, although they were plagued by some of the same problems as was the family planning series. The Tunisian government had launched a literacy campaign in 1966 with the announcement of a series of five-year plans running until 1997. Initial efforts did not involve the broadcast media, but in January 1968 radio and television were employed on an experimental basis for a period of six months, during which time various problems concerning their utilization were discovered, analyzed, and, in some cases, solved. A second and larger experimental effort involving radio and television ran from October 1968 to June 1969. In it, radio and television literacy lessons (the two media essentially duplicated and reinforced one another) were to be followed by people in various circumstances. Some were in highly organized study centers, others were in less formal study centers, and still others followed the lessons at home. The Tunisian Office of Social Education conducted a survey in June 1969 in which it discovered that over 25,000 people had followed the course on a regular basis, almost half of them children of school age. The hour of broadcast—1730—turned out to be unfavorable for the attendance of adults working outside the home, but nearly 9,000 women claimed to have followed the program regularly.

A report made for UNESCO in January 1971 (Allebeck et al., 1971, pp. 41–51) on the literacy series pointed out that the commitment of educational and financial resources to the project by the Tunisian authorities was hardly overwhelming. Budgets were cut back sharply. The presenters themselves often showed up to do the programs at the last minute ("et même plus tard," according to the report) because they were not given release time from their regular teaching jobs. Many of the study centers were not properly staffed since too many facilitators were trained, if at all, only in theoretical aspects of working with the illiterate, and a special series of seminars had to be organized to introduce them to the more practical aspects of this work. Also, the necessary support material did not always reach the centers.

Despite all of those problems and drawbacks, the experiment appears to have been successful and has continued, although not on the massive scale originally envisaged back in 1966. Radio has been made more independent of television, and the special requirements of educating the illiterate have become more clearly understood through a series of research studies conducted by the Economic and Social Research Study Center of the University of Tunis. The virtual collapse of the Tunisian agricultural cooperative scheme at the end of the 1960s was harmful to the literacy training effort, since the latter was closely tied in with the former; but the provision of literacy lessons through radio and television also enabled a large number of Tunisians to follow the lessons on their own, without depending on the study centers that had often been developed in conjunction with the cooperatives.

The past two decades have seen no further broadcast programs introduced that are of the scope or ambition of the three already described. There are regular daily and weekly programs for farmers, women, businessmen, etc., but they generally are brief (5 to 15 minutes) and not coordinated with other media of communication, such as pamphlets or discussion meetings. Furthermore, their effects, derived from assessment of reception to assessment of impact, rarely are measured. It is quite possible that those programs are very successful: most Tunisians appear to be more prepared to consider innovation than are their Maghrebian neighbors; radio and television set ownership is widespread; and the government generally enjoys the confidence of the people. However, more specific indications generally are lacking, aside from anecdotal reports such as an interview with a Tunisian woman in which she stated, "My husband used to say that I was like a chicken with a certain number of eggs, and that I had to lay them. . . . My husband at first didn't know that I had an IUD. I didn't want any more children. My health wouldn't stand it. Now he agrees because they talk about it on the radio" (Huston, 1979, p. 80).

Educational development through broadcasting has been largely confined to adult education. The Ministry of Education appears to have taken relatively little interest in the direct use of radio and television in the classroom, although there was an interesting short-term experiment in 1972 that involved the use of "TV programs of educational interest" from France, Canada, the United States, Sweden, and Niger. In that experiment, the programs, plus introduction and other elements, were copied onto 16 mm film and were shown directly in classrooms if they could not be received directly through transmission of the television signal. Teachers were a bit put off at first by the "unmanageable" nature of student response to the programs (meaning that responses were nowhere near as predictable as they had been for more traditional classroom fare), but the programs appeared to promote a good deal of classroom participation; and some teachers found that the programs sparked fresh student interest in certain subjects (e.g., French, mathematics). The experiment was financed by UNESCO and the French-based Agence de Coopération Culturelle et Téchnique (Egly, 1974). The emphasis on a transnational approach to education should have been especially welcome in Tunisia, given the country's openness to other cultures, but there is no indication that it has been continued in any form, on television at any rate.

There have been a few examples of more or less formal adult education through radio and television, although these have not been tied in with formal credit-granting institutions. Certain series, especially of Tunisian and Arabic culture (music, poetry, etc.), have been offered as self-study courses, and accompanying printed material has been made available for those wishing to purchase it. Tunisia has also participated in the International Radio University, a European-based organization that produces tapes on international topics, predominantly in French, for broadcast.

One might well assume that classroom use of radio and television would be widespread in Tunisia, given the high priority placed on educational development by the government. That it is not could be explained by the aforementioned lack of interest in those media on the part of the Ministry of Education, but this begs the question. Lack of interest may itself be explained by a tendency on the part of the ministry to follow certain of the more traditional French approaches to education, in which the audiovisual media play a very minor role. It may also be due to lack of financial commitment for such activities on the part of the government, perhaps again because the ministry itself sees more pressing needs. There is also little doubt that many teachers, especially in rural areas, feel threatened by educational radio and television, which may present some subjects with greater knowledge or sophistication than the teachers possess. Whatever the reason, efforts in this particular sphere have been modest.[12]

SUMMARY

The Tunisian broadcasting system has been an important element in national development in certain respects, notably political and cultural development, but it is currently underutilized in other respects, notably economic and educational development. The relative quality of Tunisian political and cultural broadcasting should be examined in light of one important factor: the country had strong political and cultural unity at the time of independence that spared Tunisian radio, and subsequently television, the fierce battles that raged over those issues in many developing countries and their broadcast systems. Nevertheless, President Bourguiba's use of broadcasting in his heyday was quite remarkable; and the commitment to broadcasting most facets of Tunisian culture gives Tunisian broadcasting officials justifiable pride.

There is, however, a lack of coverage of *village* culture, especially oral history, which can be quite rich but is in danger of being lost (Dahklia, 1990, pp. 150–53). There also is some question as to whether RTT's policy of using modern classical Arabic in its newscasts is serving the needs of the less well educated members of the audience for television news. A survey conducted by the Ministry of Information in 1977 (N = 100, so the data must be treated with caution) showed a strong majority (90 percent) of the illiterate viewership and 52 percent of the less well educated (primary education) favoring the Tunisian dialect for TV newscasts (Houidi and Najar, 1983, p. 234). Also, the amount of time, money, and effort going into the French-language radio service may be too great given the apparently low level of listenership: a 1977 Ministry of Information survey of *urban* listenership (N = 5,328) showed that only 4 percent of the respondents had listened to the service the preceding day (Houidi and Najar, 1983, p. 213). As formal instruction in French is decreasing, and as rural areas are likely to contain even fewer people who can speak it, one wonders whether it merits the amount of air time it receives.

The low levels of effort in Tunisian economic and educational broadcasting should also be examined in light of certain factors. Two of the major attempts at economic development—family planning and literacy training—were exceptionally ambitious: the first was at the time virtual *terra incognita* for Arab countries, while the second has been one of the most difficult types of developmental broadcasting for any nation to execute successfully. The general lack of in-school educational broadcasting may be due as much to a lack of interest on the part of the Ministry of Education as it is to a lack of interest on the part of broadcasting officials,[13] and interministerial cooperation has not been common in Tunisia. Finally, the strong opposition in rural Tunisia to most collectivization efforts, notably the one launched by Minister of Planning Ahmed ben Saleh in the late 1960s, has had its impact on the few Tunisian attempts to organize broadcast forums of the sort that have been quite successful in many developing countries.

Tunisia's economic poverty must also be taken into account when assessing the uses made of broadcasting for national development. The modest license fees charged to listeners and viewers up until 1980 were inadequate to support an already well-established technical infrastructure, much less an ambitious program of developmental broadcasting. During the 1960s, the country was able to interest certain donor groups in sponsoring a few efforts at developmental broadcasting, but such aid has been harder to come by in more recent decades, perhaps because Tunisia is now considered to be one of the better-off, less problematic (for the West) developing countries.

Regional cooperation might be of some help to Tunisia, and in fact there is an organization that promotes such cooperation: Maghrebvision. Founded in 1970 by Morocco, Algeria, and Tunisia, it features a microwave hookup between the capitals of the three countries. However, most of the material exchanged through the system (labelled "Chaine Maghrebine") or coproduced by its members has been cultural in nature: economic and educational development have received little attention.[14] Tunis also was the new headquarters of the Arab League for a little over a decade following the removal of the League's offices from Cairo as a result of the Egyptian-Israeli Peace Treaty (1979); as such, Tunis also became the headquarters of the Arab States Broadcasting Union (ASBU). That appears to have had no notable impact on Tunisian broadcasting, although Tunisian households with satellite dishes—no more than several thousand—can bring in whatever happens to be available on the jointly operated ARABSAT, as well as the 3-hour nightly TV service of the Chaine Maghrebine.

In sum, the Tunisian approach to broadcasting has been characterized by the usual mixture of successes and failures enjoyed by most developing nations. While broadcasting does not appear to have a high position in the list of national priorities, it has been used with resourcefulness in certain spheres of activity. Its failures could in some cases be considered noble. But if it is to progress, it will require a higher level of financial support; a greater degree of interministerial cooperation; the flexibility to deal with a situation in which there appear to be increasing pressures to assert more strongly Tunisia's Arab-Islamic identity; and a commitment to serving its audience by confronting them with harsh realities at least some of the time. As a May 1991 editorial in *La Presse*'s "Weekend" (TV Guide) put it, "The télé isn't there to embellish the group portrait of society, but rather, so that people may see, mark, identify themselves without distorting prisms, and draw nourishment from a reflection on their lives" (S.B.F., 1991, p. 15).

Part 5
International Radio Broadcasting in Arabic

CHAPTER 20

Broadcasting to the Arab World

THIS IS THE FIFTH in a series of surveys concerning international radio broadcasting to Arabic-speaking countries. The preceding studies were published in Boyd, 1976, 1982, 1983, and 1989. Each study gave historical information for the services; this effort reiterates some earlier findings and adds new information. In some cases, information not previously included has come to light. Since the last survey, several new Arabic services have been started, and transmission hours have been increased for some services and decreased for others. A few broadcasters have stopped providing programming in Arabic. Historically Eastern Europe and what was the Soviet Union have been significant contributors to the number of Arabic hours transmitted to the Middle East. However, the political and economic changes that have taken place in Eastern Europe since 1989 have negatively affected the number of services using Arabic and of hours this region transmits in Arabic. For example, Moscow's Radio Peace and Progress, a long-time Arabic broadcaster, ceased operations on May 31, 1991 (British Broadcasting Corporation, 1991c); not only have Radio Berlin International's (RBI) Arabic broadcasts stopped—RBI went off the air permanently shortly after German reunification. Even with these and other changes, Arabic broadcasting has increased by 8.5 percent since 1988. After English, Arabic is the world's most internationally broadcast language.

Since the last survey, economic and political factors have influenced developments in the Middle East and, consequently, those who transmit radio programs to the Arab world. The two main factors influencing those who transmit in Arabic during this survey period were the August 1990 Iraqi invasion of Kuwait and subsequent Gulf War, as well as the deterioration of the Eastern European countries that had been important Arabic-language broadcasters. There continues to be general political instability in the Middle East.

This instability has been caused by several factors, including continued Palestinian discontent over Israeli occupation of the Golan Heights, the Gaza Strip, and the West Bank. The dramatic reduction during the early 1980s in the worldwide price of crude oil resulted in economic stagnation and budget reductions in the Gulf states. Libyan international terrorism has been met by Western countries' attempts, including the U.S. bombing of Libya, to stop it. The Iran-Iraq War of the 1980s and the U.S. Navy escort of "re-flagged" Kuwaiti tankers in the Gulf intensified worldwide interest in that area. The political turmoil in Lebanon continues, despite the fact that some stability has returned to parts of this war-ravaged country. However, more importantly, the August 2, 1990, Iraqi invasion and subsequent American-led liberation of Kuwait may have permanently altered the political structure of the Arab world.

The purpose of this chapter is to update earlier findings and to continue exploring why and under what conditions countries of various economic, religious, and political orientations believe it important to transmit radio programming to the Arab world.[1] The attention paid to the Arabic-speaking world by broadcasters, discussed in this chapter, may provide a basis for examining the importance attached to the region by the radio program organizers.

AN INTRODUCTION TO TRANSNATIONAL ARABIC RADIO BROADCASTING

Boyd (1986), drawing on earlier work by Boyd and Benzies (1983), identified four reasons why organizations broadcast across borders: (1) to enhance national prestige; (2) to promote national interests; (3) to attempt religious or political indoctrination; and (4) to foster cultural ties. The top nine major international broadcasters in terms of total transmission hours are either single-party states or large Western democracies. Of course, no international broadcaster organizes programming for reception outside the originating country for a single purpose, yet every broadcaster has at least one of the above as a major reason for transmitting. Conversely, the broadcaster assumes that there is at least a potentially receptive audience for transmissions. According to Boyd's (1986) categories of motivations for listening, audiences have more reasons for listening than broadcasters do for providing programming. These reasons are (1) to hear news and information; (2) to be entertained; (3) to learn; (4) to hear religious or political broadcasts; (5) to enhance one's status; (6) to protest; and (7) to pursue a hobby. The fifth reason concerns the status-gaining activity in some cultures—particularly those where illiteracy is high—of being well informed and thus in a position to inform others. As a means of protest, listening to foreign radio is a relatively harmless way of rebelling against one's family or the state when such activity is either discouraged or, in some cases, illegal.

Wood (1979, pp. 117–18) identified six specific reasons for Arabic speakers to tune to foreign programming:

1. There is high appreciation for oral culture in the Arab world.

2. Radio surmounts both the physical and political barriers which hamper the distribution of printed matter, and the obstacle of illiteracy.

3. The historical primacy of external broadcasting has turned listening to foreign stations into a tradition and a habit.

4. There is a saturation of shortwave receivers in most Arab countries.

5. In sharp contrast to countries where the cultural elites have inherited the ex-colonial languages, there is a comparative lack of such linguistically alienated elites in most Arab countries.

6. For technical, political, and geographical reasons, little or no high-frequency jamming is carried out in the Arab countries.

Three additionally important factors influence Arab world radio listening. First, it is convenient for listeners to receive several foreign programs in the Arab world because of the availability of such services on mediumwave frequencies. Second, the credibility and entertainment value of foreign broadcasts make them attractive. A major factor determining whether a foreign service will be listened to in the Arab world is whether broadcasts are receivable on the mediumwave rather than shortwave bands. As discussed later, the two Arab world mediumwave relay sites for the British Broadcasting Corporation (BBC), the Rhodes location of the Voice of America's (VOA) mediumwave transmitter, the Cyprus relay for the French-owned Radio Monte Carlo Middle East (RMCME), and the North African location for French-Moroccan Radio Mediterranean International (RMI) make these services available to listeners on the standard broadcast band, often quite near local stations on the radio dial. This technical advantage allows the foreign broadcaster to appear to be a regional service, rather than having to be found only in the shortwave bands where almost all international radio broadcasting takes place. Third, Arab world radio listeners do not lack receiver access, although the distribution is uneven. The wealthy Gulf states have more radio receivers per 100 inhabitants than poorer countries such as the Sudan, Yemen, or Egypt. The BBC's International Broadcasting and Audience Research unit estimates that at the end of 1990 there were 73.5 million radio receivers in the Arab world, an impressive 26.5 percent increase since 1985. The estimated percentage of radio receivers with shortwave reception capability is high in the Arab world; the lowest percentage (65 percent) was for Tunisia, the highest in Jordan and Bahrain (81 percent) (British Broadcasting Corporation, 1991b).

Arab world states were late in developing both domestic and international radio broadcasting services. Partly as a result of the French and British colonization of the region in the 19th and early 20th centuries, there is a tradition of listening to foreign broadcasts in this highly oral culture. With the exception of the clandestine and pirate stations operating in Lebanon since the beginning of the 1975–1976 Civil War, virtually all of the electronic media in the Arab world are operated by governments. Surveys show that many Arab world radio listeners tune to foreign stations to learn the international perspective on news and current affairs and to hear programming not generally available on government-operated stations.

This chapter approaches the discussion of international broadcasting to the Arab world geographically: individual sections include Western Europe, the Commonwealth of Independent States and Eastern Europe, Asia and the Middle East, the Americas, and Sub-Saharan Africa. Discussed separately are the Christian religious organizations transmitting in Arabic. Broadcasters were asked to supply a current transmission schedule, historical information about programming, and any technical changes (such as new transmitters) that would help radio signals reach the Arab world. Data were gathered through letters sent to every broadcaster with an interest in Arabic in 1974–1975, 1979–1980, 1983, and in 1987–1988. These data were updated in 1991. Editions of the *World Radio-TV Handbook* were invaluable for determining specific program hours, transmitter power, and frequencies. Various issues of the British Broadcasting Corporation Monitoring Service publication *World Broadcasting Information* and the Foreign Broadcast Information Service's *Daily Reports* were helpful in tracking the evolution of the services. An especially valuable source of information was the *BBC World Service and International Competitors Comparative Schedules* (1991c). Carol Forrester, head of the BBC World Service's International Broadcasting and Audience Research Library has been especially helpful in supplying information about the ever-shifting Arabic-language broadcast schedules.

EARLY BROADCASTING TO THE ARAB WORLD

The Arab world was the location of the first effort by the West to broadcast to a developing area for the purpose of attempting to influence people. Beginning in 1934, Italy, through its international radio service, Radio Bari, started broadcasting across the Mediterranean in Arabic

(Radiotelevisione Italiana, 1979). The motivation for this service remains unclear because radio receivers in the Middle East were almost nonexistent at the time; those with receivers needed electricity, then available only in urban areas. In the 1920s and early 1930s, there were a few low-power, privately owned stations in Egypt. The Egyptian government contracted with a British company to start an official radio station in 1934 ("The history of," 1970). The Italian Arabic-language programs had a virtual monopoly on the Middle East frequency spectrum. Looking ahead to future military ventures in North Africa and Ethiopia, Mussolini's Radio Bari broadcasts turned increasingly anti-British just after 1935. This caused some concern on the part of British diplomats serving in Egypt, Palestine, Trans-Jordan, and the Arabian Gulf sheikhdoms, then known as the Trucial States. The British Foreign and Dominions Office was alerted to the potential effects of such broadcasts, but reports from the field generally concluded that the programs were not effective in swaying public opinion (Diplomatic Correspondence, n.d.).

Despite the officially unconcerned, measured British diplomatic response to the Bari broadcasts, reports circulated both unofficially and in the British press that the increasingly anti-British Italian programs found a receptive audience and were effective in promoting Italian interests. Some of these reports came from Arabists who understood the oral culture and the potential power of carefully crafted spoken Arabic delivered to a primarily illiterate audience. Further, some of the more well informed Westerners residing in the Arab world knew about the male custom of frequenting coffeehouses in the evening, drinking coffee and tea, and discussing politics. The following scene described by Rolo (1941, pp. 45–46) is the type of listening pattern about which some in the British government apparently grew increasingly concerned.

> When the day's work was done both the *fellaheen* (peasants) and the city dwellers would betake themselves to their favorite cafes, huddle together under a fuming oil lamp, and stolidly smoking their water pipes play game after game of backgammon until the communal loudspeakers gave forth the voice of the Bari announcer.

By 1937, the British Government realized the potential danger of international armed conflict, particularly in Europe. At the time, the BBC had a monopoly on broadcasting within the United Kingdom. Its external transmissions, known then as the Empire Service, started in 1932 essentially as an extension of the home radio service; the service transmitted only in English and was primarily intended for British citizens residing abroad. It was unclear whether radio broadcasting would play a role in the diplomatic process, but the United Kingdom was studying the possibility of starting foreign-language broadcasts using the model adopted by the Soviet Union,

Germany, and Italy. In 1936, the British Foreign and Dominions Office asked diplomats around the world their reaction to the possibility of beginning BBC foreign-language broadcasts. The results were mixed, but posts in the Middle East were unanimous in recommending that an Arabic service be added (Mansell, 1982). On January 3, 1938, the Empire Service officially started transmitting in its first foreign language, Arabic ("Arabic broadcasts," 1938). This event marked the beginning of the first international radio war over a developing region.

The British had a strong and pervasive political foothold in the Arab world and BBC advisors were employed to help establish the new Egyptian radio service (see Chapter 2, Radio). Once the BBC started its Arabic Service, it determined that it would be of exceptionally high quality; Britain then had the resources, talent, and experience in the Arab world to ensure the goal was met. The BBC hired Egyptian announcers and sought to bring to its London microphones prominent Arab leaders as well as singers and musicians, resulting in what must have been an appealing radio offering. Radio Bari's Arabic broadcasts attempted to meet the British radio challenge by increasing the strident, vituperative nature of their political commentary.

Radio Bari thought it had a major advantage over the BBC. Although no evidence has been found to back the claim, in the mid-1930s Italy reportedly distributed to sympathetic political supporters and to friendly coffeehouse owners free radio receivers tuned only to Bari frequencies. However, by 1938, receivers were becoming more common in urban area homes and public coffeehouses. The so-called Radio War between Britain and Italy was, in fact, only a brief contest for listeners in the Arab world. Lasting from January to April 1938, verbal hostilities ended officially on April 16, 1938, with the signing of the Anglo-Italian Pact (Grandin, 1939). However, Nazi Germany started transmitting in Arabic just as the Pact came into force; Germany thus became an Italian radio surrogate, providing a new programming dimension by the addition of anti-Jewish and anti-Soviet themes. In 1939, both the Soviet Union and France began broadcasting in Arabic. The French, with interests then in North Africa, Lebanon, and Syria, had the advantage of either possessing mediumwave facilities there for local programming or influencing domestic schedules, making possible local relays of Paris-based Arabic programming. The British had a similar advantage with the Palestine Broadcasting Service (PBS) it started in Jerusalem.

It is impossible to assess the impact of the Italian, British, German, and Soviet war years' broadcasts to the Arab world. Their effectiveness is only a matter of speculation, and little of that exists. Audience research, except that done by the major international broadcasters, is still deemphasized in the area. None was done during the 1930s. The beginning of World War II in Europe decreased interest in the Middle East; for those on both sides of the conflict, broadcasting priorities were closer to home.

During the Second World War, the main international broadcasters to the Arab world were Germany and the United Kingdom. It was these two countries that encouraged rather strong and distinctive on-air radio personalities to develop. The Nazi Arabic Service employed an Iraqi by the name of Yunus al-Bahri who may have been the most gifted Arabic-language broadcaster ever to speak from Europe. However, the BBC also had popular announcers during the war. Isa Sabbagh, a Palestinian who later became an American citizen and worked as a foreign service officer for the U.S. Information Agency, was a broadcaster with an Arab world following.

In his early 1950s study, Brunner (1953, p. 150) mentions the importance of the coffeehouse as a place for radio listening, noting that then the coffeehouse was "a center of considerable importance, comparable to the country store of yesteryear in the United States." Surveys indicate that post–World War II Arab world radio listening was still a popular activity. Even in the modern, sophisticated Gulf states, radios are heard in hotel lobbies and in shops. Car radios are standard equipment; many are capable of receiving shortwave transmissions. Just as in the 1930s, particularly in the poorer Arab states, men still pass the evening hours in coffeehouses listening to radio or viewing television.

As the following geographically organized survey shows, international attention continued to focus on the Middle East during the years following World War II, and each event, whether political, military, or economic, has seemed to inspire an increase in the number of Arabic services and transmission hours to the region. There are numerous major post–World War II events that have tended to increase Arabic broadcasts to the Middle East: the departure of Britain from Palestine and the subsequent creation of Israel; the 1956 Suez War; the Arab-Israeli military conflicts of 1967 and 1973; the fourfold increase in the price of oil following the October 1973 war; the mid-1970s beginning of the Lebanese Civil War; Egyptian President Sadat's trip to Jerusalem in 1977 and his subsequent assassination; the 1982 Israeli invasion of Lebanon and the subsequent stationing of U.S. Marines in Beirut; and the August 2, 1990, Iraqi invasion of Kuwait and the resulting Gulf crisis.

WESTERN EUROPE

As Table 20.1 indicates, Western Europe continues to be the leader in Arabic transmission hours. Since 1976, the number of weekly hours during each reporting period has grown steadily, from 225.9 in 1976 to 457.2 in

Table 20.1. Total hours in Arabic per week to the Middle East

Country	Hours Per Week				
	1976	1980	1983	1988	1992
Western Europe					
Austria	a	a	a	a	.80
France					
Radio France Int'l	a	a	a	a	21.00
Radio Monte Carlo M.E	71.6	119.00	145.25	119.00	108.50
Radio Mediterranean	a	a	16.00	126.00	126.00
Great Britain	63.00	63.00	63.00	63.00	74.00
Greece	b	8.00	8.00	2.30	2.30
Italy	12.80	14.00	8.00	10.80	10.80
Malta					
Radio Mediterranean	b	b	7.00	7.00	7.00
Voice of Mediterranean	b	b	b	b	14.00
The Netherlands	28.00	22.10	30.00	19.25	22.00
Spain	6.00	31.50	14.00	14.00	23.00
Switzerland	5.00	3.50	3.50	7.00	7.00
Germany	39.50	32.00	32.00	29.10	40.80
Total Western Europe	**225.90**	**293.10**	**326.75**	**397.45**	**457.20**
The Commonwealth of Independent States and Eastern Europe					
Albania	28.00	21.00	21.00	17.50	14.00
Armenia (Radio Yerevan)	b	b	7.00	3.50	7.00
Azerbaijan (Radio Baku)	b	b	7.00	7.00	7.00
Bulgaria	17.50	21.00	24.50	24.00	24.50
Czechoslovakia	14.00	14.00	14.00	14.00	c
East Germany	49.00	38.00	28.00	28.00	c
Poland	17.50	17.50	21.00	18.60	18.60
Romania	14.00	14.00	14.00	14.00	14.00
Russia					
Radio Moscow	73.50	49.00	52.50	45.50	56.00
Radio Peace and Progress	3.50	3.50	3.50	3.50	c
Tashkent (Radio Tashkent)	b	b	3.50	3.50	7.00
Yugoslavia	7.00	7.00	7.00	7.00	5.25
Total CIS and Eastern Europe	**224.00**	**185.00**	**203.00**	**186.10**	**153.35**
Asia and the Middle East					
Afghanistan	3.50	3.50	3.50	3.50	3.50
Bangladesh	b	3.50	3.50	3.50	3.50
China (People's Republic)	14.00	14.00	21.00	21.00	21.00
China (Republic)	b	14.00	14.00	7.00	7.00
Cyprus	21.00	0.00	0.00	31.50	d
India	17.50	17.50	17.50	22.75	22.75
Indonesia	b	7.00	7.00	7.00	7.00
Iran	84.00	10.50	47.00	66.30	78.75
Japan	3.50	3.50	3.50	7.00	7.00
Korea (North)	14.00	42.00	38.50	23.30	23.30
Korea (South)	7.00	3.50	21.00	15.75	15.75
Malaysia	7.00	10.50	10.50	10.50	10.50

Table 20.1. (continuted)

Country	Hours Per Week				
	1976	1980	1983	1988	1992
Pakistan	10.50	28.00	14.00	14.00	14.00
Sri Lanka	b	0.50	0.50	c	c
Turkey	7.00	7.00	14.00	14.00	56.00
Total Asia and Middle East	89.00	165.00	215.50	243.60	270.05
Americas					
Argentina	b	b	7.00	7.00	5.00
Brazil	b	b	7.00	c	c
Canada	b	b	b	b	6.75
Chile	b	14.00	0.00	c	c
Cuba	14.00	14.00	14.00	14.00	14.00
U.S.A.	49.00	52.50	52.50	66.50	91.00
Venezuela	a	7.00	c	c	c
Total the Americas	63.00	87.50	80.50	84.00	116.75
Sub-Saharan Africa					
Chad	a	a	a	10.50	c
Djibouti	a	a	a	33.00	35.00
Ethiopia	a	7.00	7.00	7.00	7.00
Ghana	10.50	c	c	c	c
Nigeria	7.00	10.50	10.50	10.50	7.00
Senegal	a	1.75	2.30	2.30	c
Somalia	3.50	7.00	7.00	7.00	5.50
Total Sub-Saharan Africa	21.00	26.25	26.80	70.30	54.50
Christian Religious Broadcasters					
AWR	a	a	a	2.25	.50
ELWA	10.50	13.50	14.00	17.50	c
FEBA	a	14.00	17.50	12.00	16.75
HCJB (Ecuador)	a	a	a	a	.50
Trans World Radio	5.30	8.25	9.00	14.50	15.00
Vatican Radio	2.00	3.50	7.00	7.00	8.15
WYFR	7.00	3.50	7.00	7.00	21.00
Total Christian Radio	24.80	42.75	51.00	60.25	61.90
GRAND TOTAL	747.70	799.60	887.40	1041.70	1113.75
Percentage increase over previous surveys		6.9%	10.9%	17.4%	6.9%

Note: Hours of Arabic services extended temporarily resulting from the Iraqi invasion of Kuwait are not included.

a. Did not exist during designated survey period.

b. Not reported in previous surveys.

c. Discontinued operation.

d. For this survey the Arabic broadcasting hours for both the Turkish and Greek portions of Cyprus were not calculated because both areas of the island transmit in Arabic, but this is via the domestic service, primarily for Arabic-speaking tourists.

1992. For most Western European countries, since the 1980s the hours per week have varied only slightly, if at all. The obvious exception is France, the country accounting for the majority of increased hours. This is because French-owned Radio Monte Carlo Middle East (RMCME) serves the Eastern Arab states and Egypt, and a clone operation, Radio Mediterranean International (RMI) or Médi 1, transmits from Morocco for North Africa. Since the late 1980s, Radio France International (RFI) has started an Arabic service.

Located on the fashionable Avenue Raymond Poincaré in downtown Paris is a former apartment building that houses the government-owned media holding corporation SOFIRAD (Boyd and Benzies, 1983; Taquet interview, 1989). From this structure, advertising time is sold to international advertising agencies whose clients want to reach Arab countries. The original idea for what is the undisputed leader for listeners among foreign stations in the Arab world came from former President Charles de Gaulle, who believed that a popular radio service competing with the Voice of America and the BBC would produce closer Arab-French ties ("Analysis/Radio Monte Carlo," 1979). SOFIRAD officials knew that to compete with BBC and VOA would require a powerful Mediterranean-based mediumwave transmitter with a favorable frequency. Such a facility was located on Cyprus where the government had inherited from Britain a frequency formerly used by a privately operated station that ceased operation after the 1956 Suez War; during the war, the station was controlled by British intelligence and armed forces.[2] At first, Radio Monte Carlo Middle East transmissions originated from Monaco, but after the capability became available to link France with the 600,000-kilowatt transmitter on Cyprus, the RMCME studios moved in the mid-1970s to the SOFIRAD building in Paris (Regnier, 1980). The strong mediumwave signal can be heard clearly during the day in the northern part of Egypt, Israel, Jordan, and Syria. After sunset, the station reaches Saudi Arabia and some of the Arabian Gulf states. RMCME tried adding a shortwave frequency after 1985, but that experiment lasted approximately one year (Taquet interview, 1989).

Although RMCME gained some popularity in the first few years of the 1970s, it was the 1973 Middle East War that attracted listeners because of alleged pro-Arab newscasts. However, the uniqueness of the station's service rests with its programming. First, this is a successful commercial station. Radio Monte Carlo Middle East costs the French government nothing—in fact, the station makes a profit. It was especially profitable between the mid-1970s and early 1980s when oil income fueled Arab economies. Second, its popularity is unusual among foreign stations. By combining a mixture of popular French, American, and Arabic music, news, and commentary, the station has attained an enviable position among rival VOA and BBC broadcasts that are less entertainment oriented, and tend to reflect either British or U.S. government policy. Third, RMCME is well connected as a news organization. Rumors continuously circulate—perhaps because they are not discouraged by the station—that the station's extensive network of news stringers have ties to Arab intelligence organizations.

> During the December 1983 siege of Palestinian guerrillas by Syrian troops in Tripoli, Lebanon, Yasser Arafat, the head of the Palestine Liberation Organization, became, in effect, the radio's correspondent. For days, until he left the city, he gave numerous live interviews and conducted his negotiations with the Syrians over the airwaves. (Ibrahim, 1987, p. 13)

RMCME played a major role in covering the November 1979 Mecca Mosque incident, Sadat's assassination, the various hostage-taking incidents in Lebanon, and the Achille Lauro hijacking.

> During the hijacking of the Italian cruise liner Achille Lauro in October, 1985, Palestinian guerrilla leader Abdul Abbas tried frantically to contact his men aboard the ship.
> In a moment of desperation, Abdul Abbas telephoned a number in Paris and, within minutes, his orders had been heard by his men—and by a large audience of startled radio listeners. (Wallace, 1988, p. 1)

The station broadcasting the information was RMCME. Its pro-Arab political orientation favorably influences its popularity—a subject discussed later. Ayish and Hijab's (1988, p. 22) content analysis of foreign radio stations broadcasting to the Arab world indicates RMCME ranked highest with regard to the political content of news: RMCME 62.6 percent; VOA 50 percent; BBC 32 percent; Radio Moscow 30 percent.

I spent several hours with staff and management of the station in September 1989 and January 1992. It seems clear that the station's commercial fortunes have declined since the mid-1980s. According to station management, advertising revenue decreased significantly in the late 1980s primarily because the Saudi Arabian television system started accepting advertising in 1986, thus drawing revenue away from RMCME (Taquet interview, 1989). On the other hand, the French government has apparently decided that RMCME will be its primary Arabic voice. Expansion of the also Paris-based Radio France International Arabic service is not expected (Darwish interview, 1992). Also, SOFIRAD has decided to double the RMCME Cyprus transmitter to 1.2 million watts (Ghoneim interview, 1992).

It would be wrong to call Radio Médi 1 RMCME's sister station, but there are several similarities between them. Both have administrative headquarters in the SOFIRAD building in Paris and their commercial formats are similar. Médi 1, however, services the North African countries with medium-, long-, and shortwave signals from several transmitter locations in Morocco; unlike RMCME, programming on the North African station originates from studios in Tanger. The type of Arabic used by this Morocco-based station is the Western, rather than the Eastern language used for Arab countries from Egypt to Iraq and throughout the Arabian peninsula. Started in 1980 at the request of Morocco's King Hassan to former French President Valéry Giscard d'Estaing, the station is a joint venture between the two governments. As Table 20.1 indicates, the programming hours have grown impressively since the station started, having increased to the point where Médi 1 transmits more weekly hours than does RMCME. In fact, the station accounts for the majority of increased Western European programming hours noted in this survey since 1983. The station's coverage area, and thus its potential audience, increased dramatically in 1983 with the completion of a large multi-transmitter facility in Nador, Morocco ("Trois fois 50," n.d.). The SOFIRAD umbrella has been useful in arranging for RMCME's signal to be relayed throughout the Arab world via a shortwave transmitter at Radio Médi 1's Nador transmission site, thus extending its coverage and influence.

Continuing French interest in the Arab world motivated the official international radio voice of France, Radio France International, to commence Arabic transmissions. The service is still too new to determine whether it has been well received.

Surveys indicate that Radio Monte Carlo Middle East is the most listened to foreign station in the Arab world; the BBC is without question the most credible. (Previously mentioned in this chapter is some of the BBC's early history of broadcasting to the Arab world.) The facts that it is a long-time international broadcaster, that it has two desirable Middle Eastern multi-frequency mediumwave transmitter sites—East Mediterranean Relay on Cyprus and the Eastern Relay on Masirah Island, Oman—plus multiple shortwave services to the area, that its hours are strategically placed throughout the day, and that it has earned almost unmatched credibility in its news programming make the BBC Arabic service a formidable broadcasting force in the Arab world.

When the BBC's Arabic Service started in January 1938 the weekly schedule did not exceed 3 hours. In 1939, weekly hours increased to 7; the service continued to expand until it reached 44 hours per week in 1944. After World War II, the United Kingdom played a crucial role in the Middle East—particularly in the Trucial States, Trans-Jordan, Iraq, the Suez Canal Zone, and Palestine. After Britain left Palestine in 1948, the Arabic schedule decreased to 28 weekly hours by the eve of the 1956 Suez War. As the war started, the BBC increased program hours dramatically to 84 per week, and in the ensuing 11 years until the June 1967 Israeli-Arab war, the weekly schedule remained at 70 hours. Following the practice of increasing international broadcasting hours during times of crisis, the BBC almost doubled its Arabic schedule to 120 hours in the week following the start of the 1967 war. By 1970, the weekly hours returned to 70; in 1976, an economy move required a 1-hour per day reduction in the Arabic program to a weekly 63 hours (Mansell communication, 1975), the schedule until the August 1990 Gulf crisis. Shortly after Iraq invaded Kuwait, the BBC increased the number of daily Arabic hours by 1.5 to 10.5 (Horsnell, 1990). As of 1992 the weekly schedule is 91 hours. Surveys indicate that among the major international services transmitting in Arabic—the Voice of America, BBC, Radio Monte Carlo Middle East, Deutsche Welle, and Radio Moscow—the BBC consistently has had the largest audience. John Tusa, BBC World Service Head, enthusiastically agrees; after extending the Arabic hours during the Gulf crisis he said, "For untold numbers we are a lifeline in a time of crisis. Our Arabic service is the only network giving a full picture of events" (*The Times*, 1990, p. 10).

In 1959, Deutsche Welle (DW), West Germany's official international service, started its first foreign-language service with a weekly Arabic schedule of only 1.75 hours (Wald communication, 1983). Transmission time reached a peak of 39.5 hours per week in 1979, but programming was cut to 32 hours in 1980 and has been reduced further to a weekly 1988 total of 29.1. Surveys indicate that DW is not listened to in the Middle East by a large audience. This is at least in part because Germany has had little impact on the Arab world and because post–World War II Germany has not played an important political role in the area. Also, in the late 1970s DW negotiated both medium- and shortwave transmitter locations in the Mediterranean. The acquisition of the Malta transmitter site was for the purpose of relaying several Cologne-based DW language services, including Arabic. Supposedly this location was to have given DW the same medium-wave advantage as the BBC and VOA. However, it did not work out to be an advantage for the Arabic Service signal. Malta is too far West of the major Arabic-speaking population to reach them with a strong, reliable mediumwave signal, even at night. Further, for a period of time in the early 1980s, DW suffered the embarrassment of having Malta lease to Libya some of the DW transmission time gained in the transmitter agreement.

Radio Nederland (RN) was the first continental European broadcaster to begin a new Arabic service after World War II. Arabic programming started in 1948 after a study by the RN Board of Governors noted that the Dutch had an interest in the Arab world and also because other international broadcasters either had or were starting Arabic transmissions (Helbach communication, 1979). Although an influential international radio broadcaster, RN does not have the same motivations as do other broadcasters for transmitting in Arabic. The Netherlands is, of course, an important country in the international petroleum business, but it has never had a major political or economic interest in the Arab world. Understandably, RN does not have many Arab listeners with its limited transmission schedule and lack of mediumwave transmitters capable of reaching the Middle East. RN's Arabic programming hours have fluctuated since the mid-1970s: 28 hours per week in 1976; 22.1 in 1980; 30 in 1983; 22 in both 1988 and 1992.

The remaining six European countries in this chapter—Austria, Greece, Italy, Malta, Spain, and Switzerland—are minor Arabic broadcasters. Although these states all have a desire to reach Arabic speakers, they have not committed sufficient resources to do so with any significant result. Specifically, their daily schedules are too limited to attract a sizable following.

Austria is the newest Western European Arabic broadcaster. The Austrian international service, ORF, started its modest service in 1989 with less than 1 hour of weekly transmission time.

In 1983, Greece broadcast 8 weekly hours in Arabic, but by 1988, this had decreased to only 2.3 hours per week. The country apparently believes that its proximity to the Arab world and the sizable trade with some Middle Eastern countries require at least a minor presence on the shortwave band. Ironically, the Voice of America's mediumwave transmission site for the Arab world is located on Greek soil.

Italy, the first country to transmit internationally in Arabic, has long since lost that initial importance and interest and, like Greece, features only a few hours of Arabic per week. In 1980, Italy's Arabic service broadcast 14 hours per week, but this was reduced to 8 hours in 1983; in 1988 Italy transmitted Arabic programming for 10.8 hours each week.

Malta's serious interest in international broadcasting dates from an agreement in the 1970s to allow Deutsche Welle to build a relay station there. Libya's relationship with Malta in the late 1970s and early 1980s helped foster that interest. The commercial success the French have had with both RMCME and Médi 1 have prompted the Maltese to examine their geographical position in the Mediterranean with an eye toward commercial broadcasting. In 1982 an agreement was signed between Algeria and Malta to start a station to transmit in English, Arabic, and French (British Broadcasting Corporation, 1983). The result, Radio Mediterranean—no relation to Radio Mediterranean International or Médi 1—as of 1992 transmits in Arabic for 1 hour per day. In the late 1980's yet another station, Voice of the Mediterranean, started with a 14-hour per week service.

Spain's Arabic service began in 1955 (Rico communication, 1983) and has had an erratic operating history. With little motivation for reaching Arabic speakers, Spain's major interest is in the North African Arabic-speaking states, particularly Morocco. Its Arabic schedule was just under 1 hour per day in 1976; this increased to 31.5 per week in 1980, but then decreased to 14 weekly hours in 1983 where it has remained.

Like the Netherlands, Switzerland has no particular political reason for attracting Arabic radio listeners. However, Switzerland is aware of its unique role in the world with regard to its banking institutions and as a headquarters for international organizations. Its Arabic-speaking service started in 1964 and, despite the fact that Swiss Radio International (SRI) does not emerge as a listened-to station on Middle Eastern radio surveys, the Swiss say they receive a large number of letters from Arabic-speaking listeners voicing appreciation. Further, SRI believes that its Arabic programming is "heard increasingly at high official levels" (Frankhauser communication, 1983). No evidence exists to substantiate this belief. In 1983 SRI provided only 30 minutes per day in Arabic; this had doubled to 1 hour per day by 1988, where it remained in 1992.

The newest members of the European Arabic broadcasters' fraternity are France and Austria. For several years, France entertained the idea of starting an Arabic service. When Radio France International (RFI) decided in the early 1980s to expand services, Arabic seemed to be a logical choice. France has, after all, had close relations with the Middle East since the end of World War I. Before the rather modest RFI service started, RMCME was France's Arabic voice.

Finally, the Austrian radio service decided to start an Arabic service to the Middle East on September 24, 1989 (British Broadcasting Corporation, 1989b). That effort, although modest at this point because it is transmitted on Sundays only, is an obvious attempt to strengthen ties with Arabic speakers in the Middle East.

Western Europe is where Arabic international radio broadcasting started, and it is the most important area in terms of weekly transmission hours. In 1992, Western European countries broadcast 443.45 hours per week, 45 hours per week more than in 1988.

THE COMMONWEALTH OF INDEPENDENT STATES AND EASTERN EUROPE

At this writing, the Commonwealth of Independent States—essentially the former Soviet Union—and the Eastern European countries are still reorganizing their political and economic structures. Because the international broadcasting situation in these states is still evolving, it will be several years before new international broadcasting schedules are finalized.

The Commonwealth of Independent States and Eastern Europe is a unique section of this survey because it is the only one where Arabic programming hours have decreased since 1983. The decrease and the occasionally erratic nature of Arabic transmissions from this area since 1976 lend support to the claim that the East European communist countries react primarily in a manner that they believe to be in their best short-term political and military interests.

The Soviet Union started Arabic broadcasts during World War II and until the U.S.S.R. was formally dissolved in January 1991 used five radio services to reach Arabic speakers. The main service, Radio Moscow (RM), operating a multitude of transmitters, is clearly heard in the Arab world on the shortwave band. Wanting to join Britain, France, West Germany, and the United States in providing a mediumwave signal to the Arab world, Radio Moscow does broadcast limited mediumwave transmissions from its own soil. However, listener surveys indicate that the Commonwealth of Independent States is too far from the Middle East to place a reliable mediumwave signal in the area. Surveys also confirm that neither RM nor the other four Soviet services are popular.

At first, wishing to give the appearance of addressing Arabs with many voices, the U.S.S.R. broadcast in Arabic via its Radio Peace and Progress, plus three regional services: Radios Baku, Tashkent, and Yerevan.

Prior to its demise in 1991, Radio Peace and Progress (RPP), "the Voice of Soviet Public Opinion," transmitted in a limited number of languages, including Arabic. Its purpose was to give the impression that the U.S.S.R. had an independent radio voice not controlled by the state. While RPP listed "sponsors" such as the Soviet Peace Committee, the Soviet Women's Committee, and the Soviet Writers' Union (Radio Station Peace and Progress, n.d.), it was, in fact, as government controlled as RM; the service used RM's transmitters and frequencies. One of the reasons it did not appear on audience surveys in the Arab world is the modest 30-minute per day schedule it maintained since 1976. Finally, three regional services from the eastern part of the old Soviet Union feature Arabic transmissions. Radio Baku (7 hours per week), and Radios Tashkent and Yerevan (also with 7 hours per week) complete the regional Arabic-language radio effort.

Although showing decreases in transmission hours, the East European stations have maintained a steady stream of Arabic programming since the 1983 survey. Albania is a country that had decreased Arabic transmissions from 28 weekly hours in 1976 to 21 in both 1980 and 1983; by 1992, the schedule was shortened to 14 hours. Unlike most other East European countries, post–World War II Albania did not become a Soviet-dominated state; after the Chinese revolution in 1949, it maintained close relations with the People's Republic of China and for many years rebroadcast Arabic- and Chinese-language services. Apparently almost without Arabic-speaking listeners, the former Islamic state uses both shortwave and mediumwave facilities for its Arabic Service, but its location is too far away and the competition too overwhelming for the struggling service.

Bulgaria has slightly increased its schedule since 1976 with the 1992 total at 24.5 hours per week. The remaining East European countries became interested in the Arab world, and thus in Arabic broadcasting, after Yugoslav President Tito and President Nasser of Egypt became champions of the nonaligned movement after the 1956 Suez War. In part because of the belief that communism and Islam were incompatible, the Soviet Union and the East European countries had little success in establishing close ties with the Arabs until the Suez invasion. After 1956, Nasser purchased arms from Czechoslovakia and took technical and financial assistance from the Soviet Union in order to build the Aswan Dam. Until the mid-1970s, when Egypt and the United States reestablished diplomatic relations broken during the 1967 war, the Soviet Union was Egypt's principal arms supplier. In 1959, East Germany's Radio Berlin International (RBI) started Arabic broadcasts (Rummelsburg communication, 1975). The East German enthusiasm for Arabic programming peaked in 1976, declining to 38 hours per week in 1980 and 28 hours in 1983. All Radio Berlin International broadcasting stopped shortly after German reunification in 1990. Czechoslovakia maintained its 14 hours per week until it stopped Arabic transmissions altogether following the 1989 move away from the communist government that had dominated the country since the 1940s. Romania has continued its 14 hours per week in Arabic despite the December 1989 government change. Yugoslavia still holds to 1 hour per day in Arabic. The Polish schedule has fluctuated only slightly since 1976, and as of 1992 Poland transmits 18.6 hours per week.

Surveys consistently show the Soviet and East European services are seldom listened to in the Arab world. This is due, at least in part, to the fact that these countries do not have mediumwave facilities close to the Arab world. Also, by most accounts, programming before changes in the Communist states was too dogmatic for the Arabs. One would have had to be an ardent supporter of communism to listen to one of the old U.S.S.R. or East European services regularly when so much high-quality, credible news and entertainment was, and still is, available from other foreign broadcasters.

ASIA AND THE MIDDLE EAST

As of 1992, 14 Asian and Middle Eastern countries broadcast in Arabic to the Middle East, indicating a substantial increase since 1988. Countries in Asia and the Middle East have the same motivations for transmitting to Arabs as do other areas. Yet this region has become increasingly interested in the Arab world because the transmitting states either are Moslem or want to have strong, positive relations with the Arab world because of its importance to their economies.

Iran has had an Arabic service since the inception of external broad-casting. The 1976 total reflects the number of transmitted hours per week prior to the 1979 revolution. The Shah saw himself as the protector of the Gulf and took pains to promote good relations between Iran, populated by those following the Shi'a branch of Islam, and neighboring Sunni-dominated Arab states. Mediumwave transmitters easily reach the Gulf states from across the Persian Gulf; the rest of the Middle East can be reached from shortwave facilities. The dip in Arabic programming from Iran in 1980 and 1983 is explained by the adjustment following the revolution. The upsurge in transmission time since 1983 is due to the increased fighting between Iran and Iraq and the "tanker war" starting in 1986. Iranian Arabic transmission time increased after the August 2, 1990, Iraqi invasion of Kuwait. In the Middle East, the "word war" is often as important as military combat.

For a brief period prior to the 1975–1976 Lebanese Civil War, Cyprus broadcast to Lebanon and Syria in Arabic. After the war started, the Lebanese government lost its monopoly on radio when it could not keep the various military and religious factions from transmitting radio programming. During the 1972 Lebanese elections, several political candidates purchased commercial time on a station in Cyprus (Phipps, 1972). The need for transmissions from Cyprus ceased when the civil war, in effect, decentral-ized the Lebanese radio system. The fact that Cyprus was once an active Arabic broadcaster stems from the island's sizable Arabic-speaking refugee population and the desire to take advantage of its location for commercial broadcasts to Arabic speakers. Now, the island's Arabic radio transmissions are intended primarily for Arabic speakers living there or for visitors from the Middle East. Cyprus is the ideal location for mediumwave transmissions to the Arab world, as both Britain and France have found.

Then British-influenced India claims the distinction of being the first in this area to transmit to the Middle East in Arabic when All India Radio (AIR) started Arabic broadcasts in 1941 (Srivastava communication, 1979). Although India is not a Moslem country, it has a Moslem minority and there are a large number of Indian temporary workers in the Arab world. One of the goals of the Arabic broadcasts is to help build good relations with Arabic speakers with the hope of positively influencing the climate for these temporary workers. For a number of years, India provided 17.5 hours per week in Arabic, but as of 1988 this was increased to 22.75.

North Korea's interest in Arabic is related to two factors: an attempt to counter the growing influence of South Korea in the Arab world—particularly in shipbuilding for Arab countries and construction projects in the Gulf—and reported involvement by North Korea with military training activities for the Palestine Liberation Organization, for

South Yemen, and for Libya. After a modest 14-hour per week schedule in 1976, there was a dramatic increase in programming hours in 1980. There was a slight decrease in 1983 and a further decrease to 23.3 hours in 1988.

The People's Republic of China has provided an external Arabic service since shortly after the 1949 revolution. Until the 1970s, the service provided the type of strident radio rhetoric that made the service a classic radio propaganda operation. However, in post–Mao China, the tone of transmissions has changed considerably, stressing the PRC's interest in the Middle East and its desire to increase trade with the Arab countries.

Turkey and Pakistan have similar interests in maintaining good relations with the Arab states. Both are Moslem countries that have received considerable financial aid from the wealthy Gulf states. These two countries supply personnel to the Gulf states, but Pakistan is by far a larger labor exporter. One result of Turkey's "front line" status during the Gulf crisis is a dramatic increase in Arabic transmission hours. In 1988 Turkey broadcast 14 hours per week in Arabic; by 1992, the weekly schedule had increased to 56. Two more Moslem countries, Afghanistan and Bangladesh, each broadcast only 30 minutes of Arabic per day to an audience too small to appear on known media surveys. Islamic Indonesia and Malaysia, with 7 and 10.5 hours in Arabic per week respectively, have maintained those schedules since 1980.

Japan has a weekly 7-hour Arabic output. This schedule, doubling transmission hours in previous surveys, is in some respects surprisingly small when one considers that Japanese companies have oil operations in the Gulf and supply most of the electronic consumer goods and cars to the area. However, a lack of funds, personnel, and a mediumwave service to the area does not permit more transmission hours (Wada interview, 1991).

Finally, two countries that had little presence in the Arab world, but now see the Arab states, particularly the Gulf countries, as recipients of manufactured goods and expatriate workers are Taiwan and South Korea. South Korea, with 15.75 hours per week, is responsible for a major construction force in the Gulf. Even with the economic situation remaining dull because of low OPEC oil prices, Korea's construction companies are still active in the Arabian Gulf states and consumer goods are almost as pervasive as those from Japan. The Republic of China (Taiwan) with 7 hours per week is very active in trade-related practices in the Arab world.

Three factors—history, trade, and religion—are the major determinants whether a country in this area of the world will transmit in Arabic. Thailand and the Philippines are particularly active in supplying expatriate service-industry workers to the Gulf. Because of this, they are likely future Arabic broadcasters as they attempt to maintain good relations with Arabic speakers.

THE AMERICAS

This geographical area experienced only a slight increase in Arabic hours over the previous survey in 1983. The countries in North and Latin America are a great distance from the Arab world and a strong motivation is required to transmit programming there. Presently, only four countries broadcast to the Middle East in Arabic: the United States, Canada, Cuba, and Argentina. For a brief period, Chile had an Arabic service, as did Brazil and Venezuela. Chile still does not have strong ties to the Arab world or a large immigrant Arab population. Economically, it is unable to justify a large external broadcasting service. Brazil transmitted in Arabic for a brief period when it realized that substantial trade with Arab states could help it economically. In terms of internal support for such an effort, there is a large Arab immigrant population in Brazil, particularly from Lebanon. Venezuela's brief experience with broadcasting in Arabic was surely motivated by its close association with Arab states through its membership in OPEC.

Cuba's Arabic Service has maintained a reliable 14-hour per week service since 1976. Started shortly after the Cuban Revolution, Arabic programming began in 1961 and increased until it reached 14 weekly hours in the late 1970s (Triana communication, 1983). The external service espouses the "export the revolution" goal of the government. Although militarily active mainly in Central America and Africa, Cuba has aided some Middle Eastern terrorist groups and has provided military personnel and advisors to South Yemen. Its radio service is part of that mission.

The major Arabic broadcaster in North America is the Voice of America (VOA). Prior to the formation of the VOA at the outset of World War II, shortwave international broadcasting was done by privately owned commercial stations and networks in the United States. Although directed primarily toward Latin America, one station—WRUL in New York—did experiment with limited Arabic programming in the late 1930s. It was in January 1950 that the VOA first broadcast a 30 minute per day transmission in Arabic from its studios in New York City (*VOA Arabic broadcasts,* n.d.). The 3.5-hour per week schedule continued until 1954 when VOA studios moved to Washington, D.C., enabling several services, including Arabic, to increase transmission hours.

After the 1956 Suez crisis and 1958 Lebanese Civil War, which brought U.S. troops to Lebanon, it became clear to policymakers in Washington that the Arab countries were to be increasingly important to U.S. security interests. A viable VOA Arabic Service became a part of the American presence in the Arab world. Unlike Britain, the United States did not have locations for mediumwave transmitters to reach the Middle East. For several years, the United States operated in the Mediterranean a former

Coast Guard cutter, USS *Courier,* that served as a floating mediumwave relay station for Washington-originated Arabic broadcasts. The ship received shortwave signals from U.S.-based transmitters and then rebroadcast them to the Arab world via its mediumwave facilities. In the meantime, the United States successfully negotiated an agreement with Greece allowing the VOA to construct a multi-transmitter and studio complex on Rhodes, including a powerful mediumwave transmitter to replace the one on *Courier.* In February 1963 the Rhodes site was activated and the relay ship decommissioned. Part of the Arabic service was moved from Washington to Rhodes so that entertainment and some public affairs programming could originate in the Mediterranean. The motivation for this was to obtain good signal quality; it was not until the mid-1970s that satellite circuits became available, thereby enabling the Rhodes mediumwave transmitter to rebroadcast a high-quality signal from Washington (*VOA Arabic broadcasts,* n.d.), rather than one picked up on shortwave and then relayed.

With the introduction of satellite relays, Arabic programming from the United States increased and in the summer of 1977, the Rhodes-based Arabic service closed and moved to Washington, D.C. In 1976, VOA broadcast 49 hours per week in Arabic, increasing to 52.5 hours by 1980; the service was further expanded in the mid-1980s to 66.5 hours per week. This was made possible by increased VOA funding under the Reagan administration. Like the BBC's Arabic Service, the VOA also increased daily Arabic programming hours, in this case to 9.75 following the August 1990 Gulf crisis. In fact, in September 1990 the VOA went to a 24-hour per day English and Arabic broadcasting schedule to the Middle East by using transmitters operated by the U.S. Board for International Broadcasting's Radio Free Europe in Portugal (Marks, 1990).

Following the Iraqi invasion of Kuwait, the Voice of America successfully negotiated an agreement with Bahrain permitting the VOA to install a 50-kilowatt mediumwave transmitter on the island nation located just off the coast of eastern Saudi Arabia. The facility allowed the satellite-fed retransmission of Arabic from VOA in Washington, D.C., that would reach Kuwait and southern Iraq. Rebroadcasts of VOA English started in late January 1991, but because of the Bahrain government's stalling, Arabic was delayed until March—following the Gulf crisis (U.S. Advisory Commission on Public Diplomacy, 1991). This situation highlights some of the frustrations faced by international broadcasters. It is difficult to get a signal—particularly mediumwave signal—to an intended audience. Negotiations with other governments and the relocation of transmission facilities is time-consuming. Often a crisis is over by the time host country negotiations are solved.

Since 1983 there have been programming changes and the service has been reorganized and moved to new offices in the VOA building. As discussed later, the Voice of America's Arabic Service ranks third, behind RMCME and the BBC, in terms of audience size in the Middle East.

The newest North American Arabic service is that of Radio Canada International (RCI). Expanding trade with the Arab world and the increasing size of the Arabic-speaking community in Canada were the two major motivations for this new service. Following on-site training by a member of the BBC Arabic Service in March 1990, the service survived the elimination of several languages because of RCI budget cuts (Familiant communication, 1991). The smaller international broadcasters such as Radio Canada International have adopted a policy of transmitter time-swapping, allowing for example, RCI, Radio Japan, and ORF (Austria), to trade transmission time in order to reach parts of the world in which they are interested, but are otherwise unable to build transmission facilities to reach. RCI reaches the Middle East via shortwave through Austrian transmitters. On September 5, 1991, RCI gained the use of one of the most important mediumwave frequencies in the Middle East when it leased 15 minutes per night, from 2015 to 2030 GMT (immediately following the *Panorama* news program), from Radio Monte Carlo Middle East's transmitter on Cyprus (Tétrault interview, 1990).

SUB-SAHARAN AFRICA

As reported in the 1983 survey, four sub-Saharan countries were then transmitting in Arabic; this number had increased to six by 1988 with the addition of Chad and Djibouti. By 1992, two African states, Chad and Senegal, had stopped Arabic broadcasts.

For countries south of the Sahara, interest in Arabic broadcasting dates from the late 1950s and early 1960s—a time when many African states gained independence from colonial powers. Egyptian President Nasser's expansion of Cairo Radio's international service included several African languages. Some of the target countries reciprocated by broadcasting in Arabic, but not on an impressive scale. Most African states have other, higher priorities than broadcasting internationally in Arabic. For those countries that have Arabic services, reasons include either Islamic orientation or substantial Moslem minorities. In the latter case, this then becomes "national" broadcasting.

Nigeria is an example of a state interested in good relations with the Arab world for political, religious, and economic reasons. Its size and population make it an important African state; it is also an OPEC member. Starting in 1964, Nigeria began transmitting internationally in Arabic (Okesanya communication, 1975). In 1980, the number of weekly hours increased to 10.5 from the previously reported 7. By 1992 the Nigerian

Arabic schedule had returned to 1 hour per day.

Prior to the August 1974 revolution in Ethiopia, which replaced the government of Emperor Haile Selassie with a Marxist regime, the state broadcasting service had only a modest Arabic service, even though an important Arabic broadcaster was headquartered in Ethiopia. Addis Ababa–based Radio Voice of the Gospel (RVOG), the radio service of a West German religious group, featured 20 hours per week of Arabic programming. Known for its credible news, RVOG continued to operate for a short period after the government change, but soon the new leaders nationalized the RVOG transmitters and studios, using them for the state's international broadcasting service. Arabic was reintroduced by the Ethiopian international service in the late 1970s and remains at 7 hours per week, even after the 1991 coup.

Prior to the mid-1980s, Djibouti did not transmit in Arabic, but its Islamic orientation, proximity to the Arab world, and status as an Arab world economic aid recipient apparently persuaded the state to start communicating via international radio with Arabic speakers. The service transmits 35 hours per week.

Chad's most obvious motivation for starting Arabic radio broadcasts was its ongoing military conflict with neighboring Libya. Egypt provided military assistance in the conflict; the Gulf states helped with economic aid. However, military conflicts and economic problems necessitated the closing of the short-lived service.

CHRISTIAN RELIGIOUS BROADCASTERS

Between 1983 and 1988, the total weekly hours of Christian-oriented Arabic programming increased from 51 to 60.25. During that period, an additional United States–based Christian broadcaster—Adventist World Radio—began an Arabic service. Between 1988 and 1992 Heralding Christ Jesus' Blessings (HCJB) began a modest Arabic schedule, but the increase in transmission time for this group of broadcasters increased only slightly.

Religious groups with Arabic broadcasts are well organized, established, multi-language radio broadcasters with various worldwide locations for both studios and transmitters. Most of the broadcasters are American; Far East Broadcasting Association is British; and, of course, Vatican Radio is operated from Vatican City by the Catholic Church. The purpose of programming in Arabic, usually a minor language for all of these services, is generally twofold. First, religious broadcasters wish to reach Christians whose native language is Arabic. Although a minority in the Arab world, Christians are found in Egypt, the Sudan, and some parts of the Levant. Second, and consistent with the mission of Christianity, the broadcasters want to seek converts, admittedly a difficult task. Moslems are tenacious about their religion and are generally suspicious of those who wish to convert them. Surveys indicate that non-Christian Arabic speakers do not seek out Christian religious programming via shortwave radio. With the exception of some research in the 1970s showing that RVOG was listened to in neighboring countries, no known Arab world survey indicates that listeners hear any of the religious broadcasters listed in Table 20.1.

New Jersey–based Trans World Radio (TWR) is probably the world's largest religious international radio broadcaster, and Arabic is an important language to TWR. This is because TWR's founder, Ralph Freed, spent many years in Palestine as a missionary during the 1920s and as a result learned to speak Arabic. This broadcaster has an advantage shared by no other Christian broadcaster—for over a decade it has utilized the same Cyprus-based mediumwave transmitter as Radio Monte Carlo Middle East. The mediumwave signal is heard briefly throughout the Arab world following a break after RMCME's sign-off. From 9 hours per week in 1983, the service had increased to the 1988 total of 14.5 hours. By 1992 TWR had added 30 minutes per week for a total of 15 hours.

ELWA (Eternal Love Winning Africa) broadcast from Monrovia, Liberia, from 1954 until 1990. Before fighting during the Liberian Civil War during 1990–1991 destroyed the ELWA shortwave transmitters (Dexter, 1992), this organization programmed the largest number of Arabic hours of the six Christian broadcasting organizations. Far East Broadcasting Association (FEBA) decreased its Arabic hours from transmitters in the Seychelles since 1983 to 12 per week in 1988. By 1992, the weekly schedule has increased to 16.75. Vatican Radio's Arabic programming is mainly confined to the broadcasting of Catholic Mass, which it does for a total of 1 hour per day.

Family Stations of Oakland, California, has been a long-time domestic religious broadcaster, entering international radio broadcasting in 1974 when it acquired the transmitters of a famous American shortwave station. Originally W1XAL, and then WRUL in New York, the station operated during the 1960s and 1970s under a series of owners, including the Metromedia group, as a commercial English-language service. It was eventually sold because it could not support itself on a commercial basis. Now operating as WYFR, it is the only religious Arabic service transmitting from U.S. soil.

Adventist World Radio (AWR) seems to be experimenting with Arabic. Its 1988 schedule was 2.25 hours per week, but this had decreased to 30 minutes per week in 1992.

The newest Arabic broadcaster is Quito, Ecuador–based HCJB (Heralding Christ Jesus' Blessings), whose total weekly Arabic service is 30 minutes. HCJB, "the first Christian missionary radio station in the world"

(*Heralding Christ Jesus' Blessings*, n.d.) transmits its Arabic programming only two days per week—Saturday and Sunday.

THE ARAB AUDIENCE FOR
FOREIGN RADIO BROADCASTS

Data on international radio listening in the Middle East are available, but their collection is plagued by the type of problems usually associated with doing survey research in the Third World. Further, data are only available from areas that permit survey research to be undertaken on behalf of commercial or governmental clients. Iraq and Libya, for example, have not permitted surveys to be done by Western broadcasters. Syria did not allow an international radio audience survey until 1991. In the conservative Gulf countries such as Saudi Arabia, surveys are permitted only after governmental approval of the questionnaire. It is particularly difficult to gather data on media usage by women in Moslem countries. This is especially so in the Gulf states.

There have been a few academic studies of radio listening and occasionally an Arab Ministry of Information will do a study, but the only reliable data on both domestic and international radio-listening habits come from surveys financed by advertising agencies and commercial broadcasters or from international radio organizations such as the BBC, RMCME, or Voice of America.

A foreign radio-listening research project undertaken in 1943 is both interesting and remarkable in several respects. It was the first attempt to study radio-listening habits in the Arab world. Commissioned in 1943 by the U.S. military as part of an effort to assess public opinion in the Middle East, academics at the American University of Beirut designed and undertook a study of radio listening in Lebanon, Syria, and Palestine. Completed that summer, the survey included 4,427 interviews with Arabs in 15 towns in the three countries; respondents were asked about their listening habits and preferences for the 23 radio stations known to be received in the area. The data yielded several conclusions. First, the majority of listeners said that they listened primarily for world news, followed by "serious music" and religious programs. Second, 87 percent of the radio sets of those interviewed could receive short-, medium-, and long-wave frequencies. Third, the BBC was both the most popular and the most credible foreign station. Fourth, the most listened-to regional station was Radio Cairo (Dodd et al., 1943). With regard to the third and fourth points, the situation has changed little in almost 50 years.

Systematic survey research started in the 1960s, after the major Western broadcasters became more interested in audience statistics, in part as a means of justifying either their existence or the expansion of their services. Commercial stations needed audience size estimates in order to price advertising time. The latter motivation was the reason that Jordan's Hashemite Broadcasting Service undertook a 1965 survey in Saudi Arabia. The Associated Business Consultants (n.d.) survey is particularly important because it was the only known study of radio listening in the kingdom's capital city prior to the introduction of television. The data indicated that Hashemite Radio (Radio Jordan) along with Cairo Radio's Main Service and Egypt's Voice of the Arabs were the most listened-to foreign services. These survey data, however, must be considered in light of the fact that Radio Jordan commissioned the study; at the time, Jordan's transmitters were not powerful enough to reach Riyadh on a reliable basis.

Since the late 1960s, the Arab world has become more important for broadcasters; available listening estimates come from studies they have commissioned as well as from marketing surveys motivated by advertising agencies aware of the potential for product sales in the affluent Gulf region. The following reviews audience data from three Arab world regions: Egypt and the Sudan, the Levant, and the Gulf.

EGYPT AND THE SUDAN

A U.S. Information Agency (USIA) survey of urban Egypt in February and March 1975 indicated that the VOA was the most listened-to international station among Egyptian adults, with 8.5 percent or 735,000 people listening at least once per week. Radio Monte Carlo Middle East was a close second with 8.3 percent, or 717,000; the BBC's audience size was 6.2 percent and Deutsche Welle was 0.2 percent (U.S. Information Agency, 1975). This propensity for the VOA Arabic service is atypical and probably reflects the extremely close relations the United States had in the mid-1970s with the Sadat government.

The international radio-listening situation among urban Egyptians had changed rather markedly by November and December 1982 when USIA commissioned another survey. Data from this study indicate that the most popular stations among regular international radio listeners were RMCME (31.3 percent), Israeli Radio (21.4 percent), BBC (19.4 percent), and the VOA (15.0 percent) (U.S. Information Agency, 1984). The popularity of Israeli radio is explained in part by the fact that Egypt had stopped jamming the station by the time the survey was taken. A BBC study done in Egypt in 1989 noted continued listenership for Israeli broadcasts. BBC "regular audience" estimates in this survey were RMCME (17.7 percent), Radio Israel (13.9 percent), BBC (12.7 percent), and VOA (6.3 percent) (British Broadcasting Corporation, 1989a).

Projecting to the urban population of northern Sudan, 1986 USIA data indicate that the BBC had 2.2 million, Radio Monte Carlo Middle East 1.9 million, and the VOA 385,000 respective listeners (U.S. Information Agency, 1986).

Stated throughout this and other chapters is the obvious fact that international radio broadcasting is much more attractive to listeners during times of crisis. The 1990–1991 Gulf crisis is no exception. A BBC study done in Cairo and Alexandria, Egypt, during the week of August 22, 1990, showed that audiences for foreign broadcasts had increased substantially, but especially for the BBC and Radio Monte Carlo Middle East. The audience for the BBC doubled (British Broadcasting Corporation, 1990b).

THE LEVANT

Data for this geographical area are scarce. Syria did not permit survey research by foreign broadcasters until the Gulf crisis, when the BBC studied listener preferences in Damascus and Aleppo in late February 1991. Survey results indicated that Radio Monte Carlo Middle East was the most listened-to foreign station. The study concluded that the regular audience among those surveyed for RMCME was 32.1 percent, the BBC 15.6 percent, and the VOA 3.6 percent (British Broadcasting Corporation, 1991a).

The Lebanese Civil War and its aftermath created instability and danger sufficient to discourage the most motivated researcher. The exception is the BBC, which did a survey in Beirut during a brief lull in the fighting. Completed in 1984, the survey indicated that residents in the western and eastern sections of Beirut had differing listening preferences for both local and foreign stations. RMCME, with just over 30 percent, ranked first among residents who "usually use" foreign radio; the BBC was the second most popular station with about 20 percent, and the VOA third with about 4 percent (Mytton interview, 1985).

In September 1984, USIA commissioned a survey of 1,250 Jordanian adults to determine radio-listening habits. Among foreign stations, RMCME was estimated to have 966,000 regular listeners; the BBC, VOA, and Deutsche Welle were estimated to have had 818,000, 222,000, and 1,000 respectively (U.S. Information Agency, 1985). Both RMCME and the BBC can be heard reliably in Jordan on mediumwave.

A study commissioned in Amman, Jordan, in November 1990, four months after the Iraqi invasion of Kuwait, documents the popularity of the BBC. Among those listening regularly to foreign radio, the BBC had a regular audience of 47.5 percent, RMCME 35.2 percent, and the VOA 9.9 percent (British Broadcasting Corporation, 1990c).

THE GULF STATES

A November and December 1972 USIA radio survey in Saudi Arabia indicated that the BBC was the most popular foreign service. Among regular Saudi adult listeners to foreign radio (those tuning in at least once per week), the VOA ranked second and Radio Moscow last with only 1 percent of regular listeners (U.S. Information Agency, 1973). A study done in Kuwait between November 1983 and March 1984 showed the importance of foreign stations broadcasting on mediumwave. Among the foreign stations, the BBC was first with 13.5 percent of regular international radio listeners. Radio Monte Carlo Middle East was second with 7.6 percent, followed by the VOA (2.8 percent), and Radio Moscow (0.2 percent) (U.S. Information Agency, 1984). The BBC's credibility has always been high, thus adding to its popularity, but signal strength in the Gulf states because of the Masirah Island (Oman) mediumwave transmitter location provides strong signal coverage all along the Eastern Arabian coast.

Audience surveys since the late 1970s have consistently shown that in Egypt and the countries to the east, Radio Monte Carlo Middle East is the most listened-to foreign station. RMCME's music and news format and its powerful mediumwave signal make it a formidable Arab world radio force. Using BBC survey data that exclude RMCME, *The Economist* notes Arab world preferences for the major foreign broadcasters: Deutsche Welle and Radio Moscow, about 1 percent; the VOA, approximately 5.5 percent; and the BBC about 11 percent of listeners ("Truth is in," 1987). Given the continuation of both medium- and shortwave transmitting patterns, there will be minor changes in station popularity.

In May 1986 the U.S. Information Agency undertook audience surveys in Bahrain and the United Arab Emirates. The results show low levels of interest in the Voice of America's Arabic service—1.8 percent in Bahrain and 0.7 percent in the U.A.E. In Bahrain the BBC claimed 13.2 percent regular listenership for Arabic, 11.7 percent in the U.A.E. Radio Monte Carlo Middle East did rather better in Bahrain than in the U.A.E., with a 4.2 percent regular listenership; in the U.A.E. regular audience was only 2.3 percent (U.S. Information Agency, 1987a). The data illustrate rather clearly the important role mediumwave signal strength plays in attracting audiences. Even after sunset, neither the VOA mediumwave nor RMCME signals from the Mediterranean are effective in reaching beyond the middle of the Arabian peninsula. On the other hand, the farther south one lives, the greater the chances of receiving a reliable BBC signal from Masirah Island, Oman. Perhaps one of the few truths spoken by Libyan leader Qadhafi concerns the BBC's Arabic broadcasts. The *Times Sunday Review* quotes him as saying, "All the Arab radios rave from dawn to dusk but nobody listens because everyone switches to London" (Whittstock, 1992, p. 4).

With regard to listening during the Gulf crisis, BBC data show that the audience for foreign broadcasters had increased significantly during post-invasion weeks. In Saudi Arabia and the U.A.E., foreign listening had increased; in Riyadh the BBC claimed a weekly listenership of 53 percent (British Broadcasting Corporation, 1990b).

CONCLUSION

One indication of the importance a region attaches to the Arab world is the number of hours countries in that area transmit internationally to Arabic speakers. In each of the five surveys completed by this researcher, the total number of Arabic hours has increased over the previous survey, even though individual hours from a number of countries have fluctuated. This increase does not include the temporary increase in broadcast hours from the major Western broadcasters during the Gulf crisis. The grand totals from Table 20.1 show the trend.

Perhaps the question to be asked at this point is whether this trend will continue. Speculation on my part yields a qualified "yes." However, the pace of increase will likely slow to the point that at the time of the next survey three or four years hence, the increase will be small.

The Arab world will continue to be an important political and economic region. The extent to which this is true will depend on military disputes and political clashes there as well as on the international price of oil. There is no doubt that the political and military situation will to some degree dictate whether people will continue listening to external radio broadcasts during times of crisis. Those both broadcasting and listening will be affected by the present reality and the future prospects of international radio broadcasting to the Middle East. Five points are worth considering.

1. *Leisure time and disposable income:* In the more affluent countries of the Arab world, alternative media are increasingly competitors of foreign broadcasts. Audio cassettes and CD players in cars and at home and home videocassette recorders provide high-quality leisure-time alternatives to foreign radio listening.

2. *Improved domestic television and radio broadcasting:* In an effort to win back television viewers from VCRs and to distract radio listeners from regional and foreign stations, several Arab states have increased the number of electronic media outlets and have improved the quality of radio transmission by adding music-oriented stereo FM services. Regardless of the attraction of foreign radio, the sound quality of local FM stereo cannot be matched by either short- or mediumwave broadcasting.

3. *Government-controlled media:* With the exception of post–civil war

Lebanon, all electronic media in the Arab states are government owned. This situation produces a particular type of pro–status quo news and public affairs reporting that usually lacks complete credibility. The tendency on the part of the consumer is to utilize local electronic media to learn about the government's agenda. Regional and non-Arab broadcasts provide more credible international news. Stations such as RMCME and Médi 1 provide the type of music not generally available on local radio stations.

4. *The mediumwave advantage:* The major foreign stations with measurable audiences transmit to the Arab world on mediumwave. The Voice of America, BBC, RMCME, and Médi 1 will not encounter future competition on the mediumwave band for two reasons. First, the medium-wave spectrum in the Arab world is already saturated with high-powered transmitters. Second, Arab countries or neighboring non-Arab states are reluctant to allow any additional foreign radio facilities on their soil. As noted earlier, it took months of negotiations between the U.S. Department of State and Bahrain before this Arab island nation would permit the Voice of America to locate and operate a mediumwave station to rebroadcast VOA Arabic to Kuwait and Iraq. Once the transmitter was operational, Bahrain was reluctant to allow its use. It was after the Gulf War that the transmitter broadcast VOA Arabic (U.S. Advisory Commission on Public Diplomacy, 1991). Relay stations located away from the transmitting country are important to international broadcasters, but they are increasingly seen by states allowing them (Greece, Oman, and Malta) as a sign of cultural and media imperialism.

5. *Direct broadcast satellites:* Future competition for international radio broadcasting may be international television. Already in the Middle East, some homes receive the down-link of Atlanta-based Cable News Network (CNN). The United States, Britain, and the European Community are either experimenting with or studying the possibility of international television in languages other than the official one used domestically. Only the financial and technical constraints await resolution by organizations such as the BBC and VOA that wish to add international video to international audio delivery. However, Arab citizens seem to be the first to innovate DBS television to the Arab world. They are doing it from the West.

London-based Middle East Broadcasting Centre (MBC) is owned by wealthy Arabs, including Walid al-Ibrahim, whose sister is married to Saudi King Fahd. With a format emulating Western-style television, MBC emphasizes news and public affairs programming. Available to dish owners in the Arab world, some non–dish owners can view the service because it is rebroadcast by government channels in Kuwait and Bahrain (Ibrahim, 1992a; Waldman, 1992). The nature of MBC's programming puts it in direct competition with both the government electronic media and international radio broadcasters.

What is unlikely to change in the near future is the long-standing practice of non-Arabs broadcasting to the Middle East or of Arabic speakers to tune to radio broadcasts from outside the Arab world.

CHAPTER 21

International Radio Broadcasting in the Middle East

THERE APPEAR TO BE three factors that determine whether an Arab country broadcasts to listeners outside its own borders. One, hardware—sophisticated and expensive equipment such as directional antennas and powerful medium- and shortwave transmitters—is essential; and not all countries can or will invest sufficient time, personnel, and financial resources. Countries such as Egypt and Saudi Arabia, which differ vastly in their political and cultural orientations, have built impressive production studios and large numbers of medium- and shortwave transmitters. Saudi Arabia can well afford this kind of undertaking. Egypt saw fit after its revolution in 1952 to devote relatively large amounts of its development funds to the construction of a radio system that could reach other countries. Those countries that have built extensive facilities and powerful transmitters have tended to continue using them to reach other Arab countries.

Determination to export political and/or religious philosophies is another important factor that affects whether a country is willing to invest in the effort necessary to reach other Arab countries with a radio service. Egypt, under Nasser, was interested in spreading the message of pan-Arabism; there is some evidence that this effort was at least partially effective. Saudi Arabia believes that its conservative religious (*Wahhabi*) tradition and the presence of the holy cities of Mecca and Medina within its borders obligate it to reach other countries with a reliable radio service. The kingdom, moreover, has a strong political motivation for its regional broadcasting effort. Iraq's Arab Ba'ath Socialist Party seeks to unite all Arab countries into one nation and broadcasts radio programs that attempt to win listeners to this belief. This was particularly true after Egypt signed a peace treaty with Israel and following Saddam Hussein's invasion of Kuwait in August 1990. What was South Yemen also devoted some of its national resources to a radio service that attempted to incite Omanis to overthrow the national government in Oman.

The third factor is affluence, for financial resources determine whether one country is able to broadcast to another. Quite apart from the funds required to acquire the hardware and personnel necessary for such an undertaking, the poorer countries—many of which depend on trade, loans, or grants from the wealthier—feel constrained in this kind of broadcasting and tend to be unaggressive. Examples include the Sudan, Oman, Bahrain, and Tunisia, which have tried to steer a middle course and concentrate on economic development rather than on the export of a particular religious or political philosophy. Conversely, countries that are relatively secure financially, mostly because of a steady income from petroleum exports, have tended to use radio to disseminate their messages, with no fear that economic retaliation will take place. Examples include Libya, Iraq, and, to some extent, Algeria.

Countries that do not meet at least two of these requirements have not become active in broadcasting to other Arab countries. Examples include pre-1975 Lebanon, Jordan, and what was North Yemen.

Radio remains an important medium of communication within the Arab world. It is true that the penetration of television is high in the wealthy Arab countries, but the majority of people in the Arab world still depend on radio as a source of entertainment and information. Although the number of illiterate Arabs is decreasing, the overall rate of illiteracy is very high; Egypt's 70–75 percent illiteracy rate is not unusual in the region.

There have been a series of ongoing as well as short-term radio propaganda campaigns by various Arab governments since the 1950s. Non-Arab observers have often been amazed at the strong rhetoric that is involved in these radio battles. Those who have had some experience with Arab culture and have studied the radio exchanges have observed the apparent inconsistency in people who are so polite in interpersonal situations yet so hostile and vindictive on the radio. Arabs tend to use their language as a substitute for action—particularly physical action. This aspect of Arab culture was much discussed in the West following the 1967 Six-Day War. The Arabs themselves have become particularly sensitive to and increasingly cognizant of this characteristic. In the spring of 1972, a Kuwaiti newspaper printed a cartoon that accurately described thinking at the time. The cartoon showed a large radio receiver made to look like a military tank. The caption, referring to those who threaten war in their radio broadcasts, said, "We will fight you every word of the way."

One of the most important aspects of Arab radio broadcasting is the Arabic language itself—particularly when the subject is politically motivated propaganda. Traditionally, there have been two types of Arabic, classical and colloquial. Classical Arabic is the language of the Koran and is rich in both religious and historical connotations. Colloquial Arabic differs from one country to another and often from one area of a country to another. The spoken dialects are so different that North African Arabic speakers often must converse with peninsular Arabs in classical Arabic or another language. The growth in Arab mass media since the 1950s, however, has greatly enhanced the wider use of yet a third form—neoclassical (or modern standard) Arabic. This is the language of newspapers and the electronic media and is generally understood by the population of the Arab world.

There are certain characteristics of Arabic speakers and of Arabic itself that tend to make this language ideally suited for those who wish to make effective persuasive use of radio for propaganda purposes. In the West it is generally agreed that it is difficult to change public opinion through radio broadcasts; an extensive mass media campaign can only hope to alter the opinion of a small, albeit sometimes important, segment of the population. On the other hand, there remains a general belief in the Arab world that the Arabic language, creatively employed and strongly delivered, will produce the intended reaction among listeners. Of course, the listener to radio broadcasts from other Arab countries must be receptive to efforts to change existing attitudes; but Arabic itself is viewed as an important element in the effectiveness of a propaganda effort. The direct translation of these efforts from Arabic to English does not, of course, communicate the same meaning. Examples are Gamal Abdul Nasser's pre-1967 speeches as well as those of Iraqi President Saddam Hussein following the invasion of Kuwait. Laffin (1975, pp. 81–82) makes the following observations about Arabic and its effect on speakers:

1. To the Arab there may be several truths about the one situation, depending on the type of language he is using.
2. Language is not used to reason, but to persuade.
3. The Arab means what he says at the moment he is saying it. He is neither a vicious nor, usually, a calculating liar but a natural one.
4. The value of words is often assessed by quantity.
5. Words can justify or rationalize anything.

Arabic is not an exact language and much of the responsibility for interpretation is left to the listener. Sharabi (1966, p. 93) observes:

> In political life Arabic is a most effective instrument of influence and persuasion. . . . In public speeches effect is created not so much by reasoning and explication as by repetition and intonation. Indeed, a speaker trying to sway an audience seldom expresses his ideas directly or succinctly; meaning is conveyed rather than directly or precisely expressed, and is always couched in terminology that evokes emotional rather than rational responses.

Shouby (1951, pp. 292–93) discusses the general vagueness of Arabic words and sentences; several circumstances, in his view, may cause this ambiguity of words.

1. They perhaps were never sharply defined when they first came into use, and have been retained without much change.
2. They have gradually been used to denote meanings which were later introduced into Arabic culture, with the result that they now represent not only the original vague and global meaning but also the numerous usages which have accreted to them throughout the centuries.
3. The recent sudden and rapid influx of Western culture into the Arab world has forced writers and thinkers independently to use old words to denote new meanings. The same word may be used to denote one thing by one writer and another by another.
4. A further factor contributing to the vagueness of the Arabic language is the rigidity of Arabic grammar—an extra-complex conglomeration of intricate rules and regulations which certainly restricts the freedom of the Arab thinker. The matter-of-fact acceptance of the vagueness of meaning on the one hand, and the strict insistence on the observance of the rigid grammatical and formal aspects of the language on the other, naturally heightens the only too human tendency to be lax and tolerant.

Arabic, then, is in many ways ideally suited to radio broadcasts specifically designed to influence others because of its rich grammar, repetitive style, and vagueness. The Arabic speaker who seeks to persuade others uses appeals that are more emotional than logical.

VOICE OF THE ARABS

The radio service whose name would literally become a household phrase in the Middle East was started on July 4, 1953 (*The A.R.E. broadcasting in brief,* n.d., p. 3), less than one year after the Egyptian revolution. There is a difference of opinion among Egyptian media observers as to who started the Voice of the Arabs.[1] Although Ahmed Said would become well known as its director and chief announcer, he was not in a position at the time to authorize its beginning. The real power behind the Voice of the Arabs lay with Gamal Abdel Nasser and Mohammed Abdel-Kader Hatem (Annis interview, 1974; Sharf interview, 1974). Dr. Hatem, who would serve Egypt in several information-related capacities including the post of Minister of Information, probably initiated the idea for the service, and Nasser provided enthusiastic support.

Following its 30-minute daily beginning, the service grew at a steady pace, eventually becoming a 24-hour-a-day service. The particular geographical target areas and major subjects for discussion were constantly changing, but it is possible to note trends or general phases. For the first three years, the Voice of the Arabs tended to concentrate its efforts on the various political struggles occurring in the Maghreb. The radio was used to support the cause of French-exiled Sultan Mohammed V in Morocco, as well as for Habib Bourguiba's Neo-Destour party in Tunisia. It gave support also to the Algerian revolution, putting a heavy strain on Egyptian-French relations, and allowed its facilities to be used by Algerian revolutionary leaders who maintained an office in Cairo (Hatem, 1974, p. 167; see also Fanon, 1965, pp. 69–97). From the mid-1950s, Cairo would embrace resident representatives of liberation movements in Africa and the Middle East and would allow—in fact, would encourage—their use of its radio services.

During this early period, the service experimented with various program formats, many of which were eventually utilized in some form as the demand for programs expanded with increased transmission time. The Voice maintained a broad appeal, but it also became regionally oriented during certain periods of the day. Programs were designed for the Gulf states, Lebanon and Syria, and the southern peninsula, Yemen and Aden. Programming consisted of news and commentary, the two often indistinguishable; press reviews from Egyptian papers; speeches; talks by and interviews with various Arab politicians; and dramas with political themes and music. Songs praising Nasser and his accomplishments performed by popular artists such as Abdel Wahhab and the late Um-Kalthoum (Loya, 1962, p. 105) were used both as a propaganda vehicle and as an attraction for "serious" programs scheduled adjacent to the musical programs.

It was the circumstances surrounding Egypt's campaign against the participation of Jordan and Iraq in the Baghdad Pact as well as the events leading to the nationalization of the Suez Canal and the 1956 Suez War that first gave the Voice of the Arabs its rather infamous reputation.[2]

Revolutionary Propagandist

After testing its effectiveness to the West of Egypt during the first three years of broadcasting, the service became increasingly bold in supporting President Nasser's Middle East political aspirations. One reason for the shift in regional emphasis was that Egyptian broadcasts had been significantly strengthened during the three years following the revolution.

Although it is impossible to determine the exact amount of power that the Voice used at any one time as the service could be shifted to any number of transmitters by master control, Egypt's total short- and mediumwave transmission power grew from 72 kilowatts at the beginning of the revolution in 1952 to more than 500 kilowatts by 1956.[3]

It was during the second half of the 1950s that the Voice of the Arabs established itself as an enthusiastic medium for revolutionary propaganda. Under Nasser, Egypt adopted an anti-colonialist, anti-imperialist position, and although anti-Zionist themes were ever present, Egypt turned her attention to other Arab countries. Nasser's stature in the Middle East and Africa increased greatly as the result of a 1954 agreement that he negotiated with Great Britain for the removal of British military forces from the Suez Canal Zone. With this accomplished he set out to rid the rest of the Arab world of Western influence and turned his attention to Iraq and Jordan, respectively a member and a potential member of the Baghdad Pact.[4] For the next three years until the 1958 Iraqi revolution, the Voice of the Arabs waged a propaganda war with varying degrees of intensity against Nuri as-Said, Iraq's pro-West prime minister. The service was also involved with events surrounding the 1958 Lebanese crisis. But it was radio propaganda against Western efforts to include Jordan in the Baghdad Pact that brought to the forefront the effectiveness of Egypt's radio efforts.

What follows is a discussion of radio broadcasts as they relate to specific events in the Middle East. It would be misleading to imply that radio was solely responsible for those events; yet the broadcasts by the Voice of the Arabs did constitute a major part of the entire Egyptian propaganda effort, and there is reason to believe that the radio broadcasts were the most important and influential part of the propaganda campaign. Egyptian newspapers could be banned or censored, activities of Egyptian citizens in other countries could be restricted, but at the time there was no effective deterrent to Egypt's powerful radio transmitters. A deterrent that might have been effective—viable domestic and international radio services—did not exist in any Arab country outside of Egypt until well into the next decade.

Jordan had long been closely associated with Great Britain. British subjects exercised considerable influence over Jordan's Arab Legion in the persons of General John Glubb, a veteran soldier Arabist who had been in Jordan for more than 25 years, and other British military officers. Through a series of particularly vehement radio broadcasts that started in late 1955, Nasser appealed directly to Jordanian citizens to campaign against their country's participation in the Baghdad Pact. The demonstrations that resulted from this campaign gave observers one of the first indications of the broadcasts' effectiveness. The responsibility for demonstrations in remote Jordanian villages was laid directly to the Voice's urgings as they occurred simultaneously with those in the capital (Carruthers, 1956, p. 5). A specific target of the broadcasts from the Voice of the Arabs was General Glubb himself. It was relatively easy to point to Glubb as a foreigner who by nature of his position influenced Jordan's young King Hussein. Although the exact reason for Glubb's dismissal by Hussein on March 1, 1956, is open to speculation, Egyptian radio broadcasts seem to have played a significant part. As one observer noted, "A foreigner [Glubb] is never fully accepted by the Arabs, but the Jordanians had to be reminded of that by the Voice of [Ahmed] Said" (Ellis, 1961, p. 58). General Glubb himself believed that the Voice of the Arabs was partly responsible for Hussein's action: "I think we may say without hesitation that my dismissal was really entirely due to Egyptian propaganda. . . . The radio played a leading part" (Glubb communication, 1973).

The result of the radio broadcasts and Glubb's subsequent dismissal may well have been far-reaching. According to Anthony Nutting, "After the news [of Hussein's action against Glubb] reached London, the Prime Minister [Anthony Eden] declared a personal war on the man whom he held responsible for Glubb's dismissal—Gamal Abdel Nasser" (Nutting, 1967, p. 17). After Nasser nationalized the Suez Canal Company, this personal war probably influenced Britain's decision to join France and Israel in an attack on Egypt that would result in the 1956 Suez War.

By the time that Nasser nationalized the Suez Canal Company in the summer of 1956, he was widely known in the Arab world as a leader to be reckoned with; daily broadcasts from Egypt's increasingly powerful radio transmitters seldom failed to note the stance that Egypt was taking as a "progressive" Arab state. Nasser's accomplishments had been broadcast to every corner of the Arab world, and village peasants—including the heretofore ignored women—found themselves sought after as important members of the listening audience. The Czechoslovakia arms deal, the agreement for the departure of British forces from Egypt, and the Suez Canal nationalization caused some worry among Western powers who were concerned about communist influence and about their own waning prestige in the Middle East. Britain, for one, hoped that its participation with France and Israel in the Suez attack would result in the political end of Gamal Abdel Nasser. Just the opposite happened.

All of these events drew attention to Egypt's radio expansion and the monitoring of Egyptian broadcasts was intensified. Great Britain and France drew up plans that proposed ways to counter these broadcasts. The British took the most drastic measures when, during pre-invasion raids on Egyptian military installations, radio transmitters at the Abu Zabal site near Cairo were bombed. They hoped to silence the Voice of the Arabs as well as to make way for their own station on the island of Cyprus that would propose Nasser's ouster. The British tactics failed for two reasons. The bombing attack was only partly successful: antennae and towers were knocked down, but damage to the equipment was not extensive and engineers soon had other transmitters on the air (El-Kashlan interview, 1974). The British began broadcasting from Cyprus by way of the Near East Broadcasting Station; although owned by a private company, it reportedly had links with British Intelligence. The station, renamed "The Voice of Britain," came on a vacant Egyptian frequency and called on Egyptians to support those who had come to free them from their "mad" leader.[5] The British station was not successful with what it hoped would be a propaganda coup, largely because the station's Arab staff resigned en masse when they realized the new direction the programming had taken.[6]

In addition to raising President Nasser's prestige in the Arab world, the Suez War had a significant effect on Egypt's radio transmission planning. Those responsible saw the need for more transmitters and an emphasis on decentralization of transmitter sites (El-Kashlan interview, 1974).

The three-year radio war against Iraq's Nuri as-Said government, which lasted from 1955 until the summer of 1958, is a further example of Egypt's efforts to promote revolution in another Arab country. When Iraq became a member of the Baghdad Pact, Nasser sought to bring about a reversal of what he saw as a Western attempt to influence Middle Eastern affairs. The main target of the Voice of the Arabs broadcasts was Prime Minister Nuri as-Said. After diplomatic attempts failed to halt the radio attacks, Iraq decided that an offensive strategy would be the best defense; but it was inadequately equipped either to jam or to match Egyptian transmission power. In this connection, Iraq's Prime Minister personally appealed to the American Ambassador in Baghdad for assistance in securing 100-kilowatt medium- and shortwave transmitters that he wished air-shipped in a matter of weeks. Because of bureaucratic inefficiency in Washington, Iraq never got the equipment that it had requested, and instead British transmitters were eventually supplied (Gallman, 1964, pp. 50–57; Eilts interview, 1974). Even with the increased transmission strength and attempts to jam Egyptian broadcasts, the Iraqis clearly remained the underdogs in the radio contest. As Glubb notes, the radio war "illustrated the extraordinary efficacy of Egyptian methods in this form of radio demagogy. Broadcasting indeed appears to be a weapon ideally suited to the Egyptian mentality, with its eloquence, excitability and emotional appeal."[7]

The events surrounding the Suez War brought a brief respite from the radio attacks on Iraq, but by 1957 the Voice of the Arabs was openly calling for the assassination of Prime Minister as-Said and the royal family. "The hearts of the people in Iraq are full of vindictive feelings against the rule of Nuri es-Said and British colonialism. The extermination of the agents of imperialism is the first step towards the extermination of imperialism itself" (BBC, *Summary*, 1958a, p. 2). On July 14, 1958, a military coup overthrew the government and a republic was proclaimed. The bodies of Prime Minister as-Said and King Faisal were dragged through the streets of Baghdad in a particularly gruesome display of anti-Western feeling. After the revolution Ahmed Said, the chief announcer and director of the Voice of the Arabs, received a letter in which was enclosed a piece of Nuri as-Said's finger: it had been sent in appreciation of the support that the Egyptian radio service had given to the revolution (Ellis, 1961, p. 58).

The union of Egypt and Syria in February 1958 into the United Arab Republic brought an expansion of Egypt's radio transmission facilities. Those in Damascus could be added to those in Cairo, resulting in a more powerful Voice of the Arabs. Although the attacks on Iraq temporarily stopped after the July revolution, the attacks turned with renewed enthusiasm against Jordan and Lebanon as well as against the British and American military forces that landed in these countries at the request of the respective governments.

Today America is intervening in the affairs of the Lebanon. America is aggressing against the Lebanon. America is hurling its soldiers into the Lebanon. America is killing free Lebanese. . . . American imperialism has forgotten the utter defeat which was inflicted by Arab nationalism and the whole world against British and French imperialism. (BBC, *Summary*, 1958b, p. 2)

The British and American governments in addition to the United Nations began diplomatic moves intended to cool down the Egyptian radio offensive. U.N. Secretary General Hammarskjold himself attempted to persuade Egyptian officials to tone down the radio broadcasts (Urquhart, 1972, p. 265), but these moves were ineffective in bringing about a change in Egypt's radio attacks. Hammarskjold then decided to appeal directly to Nasser, who, by 1958, brought Egyptian radio more directly under his control when it was shifted from the Ministry of National Guidance to the office of the President ("The history of," 1970). The British and Americans had hinted that their respective withdrawals from Jordan and Lebanon might be stepped up if the Voice of the Arabs would stop the hostile broadcasts. In a meeting with Nasser in Cairo in September 1958, Hammarskjold asked Nasser, "Can we disarm the radio?" Nasser's emphatic refusal to stop the broadcasts provided some insight into his feelings about his radio service: "How can I reach my power base? My power lies with the Arab masses. The only way I can reach my people is by radio. If you ask me for radio disarmament, it means that you are asking me for complete disarmament" (Heikal, 1973, p. 173).

Decline of Impact

After 1958, although the Voice of the Arabs attacks on various Arab leaders continued, relative stability replaced the stormy period that marked Egypt's 1954–1958 consolidation as the leading Pan-Arabic power. Nasser believed that the union with Syria was but the first step to a united Arab world, the center of which would be Cairo. The radio broadcasts of the Voice of the Arabs continued to play an important role in Egyptian efforts to promote President Nasser's call for Arab unity. In this connection, Egypt's transmitter power continued to grow to the point that by 1960 the total medium- and shortwave power was over 1,300 kilowatts, or more than double what it had been four years earlier ("What do you," 1971, p. 76). Some of this new transmitter power was being used to broadcast to African countries south of the Sahara for the specific purpose of supporting liberation struggles.

During the period 1958–1967 there were no spectacular successes such as those that had marked the Voice's previous development. There are several reasons for the Voice's loss of impact. First, audiences of the 1960s were more sophisticated than those of the 1950s; radio was a relatively new phenomenon when the Voice of the Arabs scored its Jordanian and Iraqi successes. As time passed, however, it is likely that listeners became accustomed to Cairo's name-calling, exaggerations, and outright untruths. Other Arab countries also had increased their domestic media services during the 1960s, adding television, for example, and thereby providing competition for the Voice's broadcasts.

Another reason for the Voice's loss of impact was the lack of research by Egyptian media managers. Apparently the only sources of feedback were listener letters and reports from Egyptian diplomatic missions, the latter usually dealing with comments on signal strength rather than listener reactions (H. Shaban interview, 1974; M. Shaban interview, 1974). Those in management positions at the Voice may well have been lulled into a sense of success after 1958, and they appear to have become increasingly out of touch with Arab audiences. The Voice looked for new targets. British forces in the Suez Canal Zone, the Baghdad Pact, General Glubb, and Western intervention in Arab countries had been vulnerable targets; once these were eliminated, the propaganda turned with increasing vehemence against those countries that were termed to be less "progressive" than Egypt, notably Jordan, Saudi Arabia, and the Gulf states. King Faisal of Saudi Arabia was a particularly formidable target as it was he who supported the Royalists in the Yemen War—Nasser's Vietnam.

There had been a period when Saudi Arabia both diplomatically and financially had supported some of Nasser's Middle Eastern policies. The situation changed after King Saud (son of the kingdom's founder) was, in effect, made a figurehead when his brother Faisal became crown prince in 1958 and king in 1964. Saudi Arabia became an example of a "reactionary" regime; and because of its enormous oil wealth, its unevenly distributed revenues, and its close ties with the United States, it was a ready-made target for radio attack from Egypt. A conservative Islamic society that to this day does not allow nightclubs or public cinemas, Saudi Arabia did not have a domestic radio service that could serve the entire country until the mid-1960s. With visits to family and friends being the major social diversion, and with the growing availability of the transistor radio, the Voice of the Arabs was a popular radio service. The Voice took the obvious approach in its campaign against Saudi Arabia: it told the Saudis that their government was tied to the United States and to its oil company, ARAMCO; that the royal family squandered most of the oil revenue; and that Saudi workers were being exploited by imperialist sympathizers.

The Saudi government acted slowly to counter Egypt's radio propaganda. During the early 1960s plans were initiated that would give the kingdom a powerful domestic as well as an international radio service. The country started its own version of the Voice of the Arabs, stressing Saudi Arabia's importance as an Islamic country and as the home of the holy cities of Mecca and Medina. Saudi Arabia was not alone in pointing out that Nasser's army in Yemen was killing Arabs, that Nasser's radio service was meddling in the internal affairs of an independent country, and that perhaps the most important goals should be national development and the Palestine question. The Saudis also took another step that they hoped would, among other things, help divert their citizens' attention from Egyptian radio broadcasts—they started a television system.[8]

While the Voice was popular in Saudi Arabia,[9] the incessant attacks against the kingdom were greeted by some as entertainment rather than as something that was to be taken seriously. The Voice of the Arabs attacks on King Faisal and ranking officials were particularly vicious:

Arabs, is Faysal an Arab or a British King? Arabs, is Faysal a King of the Muslims' Holy Land, or a King of the Jews and the Saxons? Arabs, by God, Arabs: what is the people's verdict, what is God's verdict on such an agent King? We know the verdict and wait for the execution. For the people always convict agents; and always inflict the traitor's destiny on all agents. (BBC, *Summary*, 1967, A6)

However, the broadcasts did not produce the reaction that similar broadcasts had produced in Jordan and Iraq. There were no discernible effects of the radio propaganda on the kingdom's population; but Saudi government officials were concerned about Egyptian media. A facility for jamming Egyptian television broadcasts was built in Jidda in order to interfere with Cairo television signals that travel long distances during the summer months and are regularly received in Jordan, Lebanon, and Syria.

Much of the Voice of the Arabs propaganda directed toward the Arabian peninsula concerned the Yemen War that pitted Egyptian troops—50,000 at one point—against Saudi-supported Yemeni Royalist forces. In this relatively remote and inaccessible country, radio proved to be an efficient means of reaching the people. Ahmed Said, the popular Voice of the Arabs announcer, was given in Yemen the status of President Nasser and Abdul Hakim Amer, the Egyptian Army commander, when his picture was included with Nasser's and Amer's on the cover of student writing tablets.[10] The Yemen propaganda campaign also provides an example of the importance that Nasser placed on reaching the masses directly by radio. Heikal (1973, p. 173) notes, "Following several setbacks [in Yemen] he [Nasser] ordered the distribution of 100,000 transistor radios to the tribes. That connected them to the Voice of the Arabs and it had more effect than a whole division." Voice broadcasts incited revolution in Yemen and probably speeded the withdrawal of British troops from Aden. However, the broadcasts did not achieve their intended effect on all of the Arabian peninsula, as they brought neither victory to Egypt in Yemen nor an end to the Saudi monarchy.

Loss of Credibility

Although the Voice of the Arabs gradually lost its impact during the 1960s, its broadcasts during the early days of the 1967 Middle East War seriously undermined the Voice's credibility. Ahmed Said repeatedly told the Egyptians and others in reach of the Voice's signal that Egypt was winning the war. These claims, which were widely broadcast by other radio stations in the Arab world, only built up the hopes of those who wanted victory. When the reality of defeat became known, the letdown was more complete than it would have been had battle reports been more truthful. One casualty of the June 1967 war was Ahmed Said, who had personally made many of the victory claims and had thus put himself in a vulnerable position. Said had become the brunt of jokes in Cairo as he had become the symbol of Egypt's self-deception, and his eventual dismissal was necessary in order to remove that symbol.[11] Although he undoubtedly had a hand in shaping the Voice's programming, Said did not make the policy decisions; these were made by Nasser himself. Journalist Mustapha Amin (Interview, 1974) states that Nasser even hand-wrote instructions to Said on a day-to-day basis and that the service was a reflection of Nasser's personality.

Conclusion

The Voice had not entirely given up its revolutionary radio propaganda, as evidenced by broadcasts during the late 1960s and early 1970s that encouraged liberation movements in Muscat and Oman;[12] but the 1967 war and the government change after Nasser's death clearly affected the Voice of the Arabs. In an obvious reference to past practices, the service lists as one of its goals the "adher[ence] to the scientific interpretation of language

[and] purif[ication of] that language from repetition, exaggeration, superficiality, and unpreparedness" ("What do you," 1971, p. 69). Missing during the October 1973 war were the Voice's widely distorted claims of victory—even when the Egyptians moved across the Suez Canal during the first days of the conflict. The Voice's calm tone seemed to have a stabilizing effect on the Arabs and instilled in them a sense of pride in Arab accomplishment.

Charles Issawi (1963, p. 217) perhaps best characterized the Voice of the Arabs' pre-1967 period when he observed that it had "to be heard to be believed: for sheer venom, vulgarity and indifference to truth it [had] few equals in the world." In contrast, it is not unusual now to hear Middle Eastern media observers refer to the Voice's broadcasts as "tame" or even "almost unexciting." Given the confidence and economic strength that the Arabs have acquired since October 1973, the Egyptian government is likely to maintain the present programming philosophy rather than return to the pre-1967 days when Nasser personally called the shots.

Although Egypt did not return to the approach taken before 1967 by the Voice of the Arabs, this service and others operated by the Egyptian government have worked since 1975 to counter radio attacks from Libya, Iraq, and other Arab countries that oppose the Sadat-inspired peace agreement with Israel.

It is unlikely that any other Arab radio service can match the attention given to or the alleged successes of the pre-1967 Voice. During the 1970s, there appeared many imitators on Arab radio frequencies who called for revolution or promoted their political philosophy. Listeners became increasingly subjected to a kind of radio service that no longer held their attention. Yet, while there are obvious exceptions, such as Iraq and Libya, emotional appeals to support a particular political party, religious sect, or national leader are heard from the recognized government radio services less often on the whole than in the 1960s. The rise of domestic radio services that cater to the needs of the local populations has made it unnecessary for nationals to tune to radio services of other countries to obtain news and entertainment programming. Television has apparently decreased radio listening—particularly at night. Also, home video recorders among residents of the Gulf area have allowed a further diversion from radio. So many powerful transmitters have become operational in the Arab countries since the late 1960s that finding a clear mediumwave signal at night can be challenging for the most dedicated radio-listening enthusiast. Yet, this situation has not discouraged the continued proliferation of radio services officially identified as being operated by Arab governments; nor has it altered what appears to be a continued interest in unofficial or clandestine radio broadcasting.

CLANDESTINE RADIO IN THE ARAB WORLD

There is no clear definition of clandestine radio broadcasting in the Arab world. Many kinds of unofficial stations operate for various purposes and under different conditions. Some stations operate from within a country or from a neighboring country to support revolutionary activities. Others appear for short periods during armed conflicts. Still others operate intermittently to support a particular political movement. Very few are clandestine in the sense that their location and affiliation are unknown. This is due in part to the fact that even casual listeners know that the stations operate on frequencies that are associated with a country. Each Arab country monitors the official and clandestine radio broadcasts of other Arab countries, and when an unofficial station is identified as hostile to a regime, the government publicizes the supposed location and purpose behind the station. Some countries jam clandestine broadcasts.

Some clandestine broadcasting took place during World War II. Prior to that time, the signals from Italy and Germany, for example, were clearly identified with those countries as the radio programs were intended to promote favorable reactions among Arab listeners toward those countries. One of the first documented users of secret radio transmissions in the Arab world was the United States. A 10-kilowatt transmitter aboard the battleship *Texas*, stationed off the coast of North Africa, broadcast programming on the frequency adjacent to Radio Morocco's, so that the Allied point of view could be heard (Carroll, 1948, p. 37).

There was considerable clandestine radio broadcasting from both the Arab and Jewish sides prior to and during the 1948 Palestine War. The Jews were much more organized in this respect and did most of the broadcasting. Hebrew and Arabic broadcasts were featured by both sides. From the Jewish side, three major clandestine services were active during the 1948 Palestine War. A Haganah station started broadcasting in the 1930s when there were disturbances by those who opposed Jewish immigration to Palestine. Haganah Radio, named after the illegal Jewish military organization, appears to have been the oldest and most well organized of the Jewish clandestine services. Between 1945 and 1948 its Arabic broadcasts increased and at one time were headed by Shaul Bar-Haim, an Iraqi Jew who had immigrated to Palestine (Bar-Haim interview, 1980). Haganah Radio was most active during the months immediately prior to May 1948, when the British officially left the area, thus triggering the first Arab-Israeli war. On May 12, 1948, Haganah Radio announced that it would later become the Voice of Israel, Kol Israel (Foreign Broadcast Information Service, 1948a)—the official name of the Israeli national radio broadcasting service after independence was declared. Another service was operated by the Irgun Zevai Leumi, a terrorist group headed by Menachem

Begin. This station used the name Voice of Fighting Zion to broadcast its own philosophy in the British mandated area (Begin, 1951, pp. 332–35). Finally the Lohame Herut Yisrael, or "Stern Gang," operated a clandestine service that it called Fighters for the Freedom of Israel (Foreign Broadcast Information Service, 1948b). It was for this station that Geula Cohen, who would become an outspoken, right-wing member of Israel's parliament, broadcast. At one point, she was arrested, and later imprisoned, by the British for making illegal broadcasts (Cohen, 1966).

When the various factions of Jews decided to cooperate after the state of Israel was declared in May 1948, most stations amalgamated and became the official government station. It would, however, be inaccurate to leave the reader with the impression that these stations were operated primarily to propagandize Arabic speakers. It is true that Arabic broadcasting increased in 1948, but the initial, and most important, motivation for the stations was to provide Jewish residents with information that each faction believed most helpful to its cause. For the most part the Jewish clandestine stations were anti-British, at least until it was obvious that Mandate government would leave Palestine.

The Palestinian Arabs did not need clandestine stations as much as the Jews did because the radio services of the neighboring countries served as advocates for the Arab side. Although transmitter power was limited, Egypt and Syria appear to have been most involved with Arabic broadcasting to Palestine. One Arab station, Inqza Radio, was operated by the Arab Liberation Army from an undisclosed location. First identified on March 25, 1948 (Foreign Broadcast Information Service, 1948b), broadcasts were lengthened as the May 1948 fighting intensified. Two other Arab stations were active prior to and during the 1948 war. "Saut al-Sawra" (Voice of the Revolution) and "The Secret Jihad" (Holy War) clandestine operations broadcast in several languages, including Hebrew, in support of the Arab side (BBC, *Summary*, 1948, p. 56; BBC, *Summary*, 1947).

SHARQ AL-ADNA

Although the exact beginnings of Britain's Sharq al-Adna (The Near East Arab Broadcasting Station) remain unknown, Hurewitz (1968) said the station started broadcasting from Palestine in 1942. It was probably built by British intelligence interests during the war as part of the Allied radio effort. Soley (1989) noted the connection between a World War II British propaganda operation SO2, which had radio operations in Palestine, and SO2's successor—the famous British Special Operations Executive (SOE) that sponsored both propaganda and resistance operations in Nazi-held areas during the war. Throughout World War II, Palestine was an ideal location for Allied radio transmissions to the Middle East, and southern Europe.

When the British left Palestine in 1948, Sharq al-Adna was moved to then British-controlled Cyprus. At first, the station transmitted its commercial Arabic programs from four shortwave transmitters near Limassol.[13] By 1955 a 100-kilowatt mediumwave transmitter broadcasting on 635 kHz had been added (*World radio handbook*, 1957, p. 88). After the British left Palestine, the station was criticized by the various Jewish political factions as being pro-Arab, specifically pro-King Abdullah of Jordan. Following the peace agreement establishing the boundaries of the State of Israel, the station turned its attention to building what appears to have been an audience big enough to attract advertisers. In many respects, Sharq al-Adna was an early Radio Monte Carlo (Middle East). Most of the production and announcing staff were Palestinians. The British government's association with the station was no secret and Hale (1975, p. 121) in *Radio Power* notes that the Lebanese referred to the station as the "Cavalry of St. George," after a British coin then in circulation that featured the patron saint's image. The exact relationship between the station and the British government until the 1956 Suez War is not clear. Barbara Castle, a prominent British politician, wrote that the station "kept in touch with the Foreign Office and had helped to 'sell' British policy, as well as British exports, in Arab countries—all the more successfully because it was not tied to official directives" (Castle, 1956, p. 832).

As part of the preparations for the 1956 British-French-Israeli invasion of Egypt, the British government decided to take over the station and provide its own alternative to Egypt's Voice of the Arabs, which the British military had failed to eliminate by destroying its transmitters. The commandeering of the studios and transmission facilities of Sharq al-Adna was made easy by the fact that they were adjacent to a military facility near Limassol, Cyprus (Zada, 1979b). Under the direction of an officer attached to the Psychological Warfare Unit of the invasion forces, preparations to broadcast calls to overthrow President Nasser were made. However, the British did not anticipate that the Arab staff would resist such moves and on October 30, 1956, only hours after the station became the "Voice of Britain," the Arab staff resigned en masse. In support of the Arab staff, the British station director resigned too (Zada interview, 1979b). BBC Arabic Service employees who were rushed to the station in an attempt to keep programming going were not able to gain audience respect. Gradually the attacks against Nasser diminished and by March 1957 the station went off the air. The BBC used the frequencies assigned to Sharq al-Adna, but suffered some loss of credibility following the "Voice of Britain" fiasco. After the invasion, the British Foreign Office assumed responsibility for programming the station. Some material supplied by the BBC was relayed over the "Voice of Britain" frequencies along with the obviously pro-British material supplied by the Foreign Office. At times there appeared to be rather obvious inconsistencies between the two different sources of news about events in the Middle East. Attempts after 1957 by non-Arab governments to influence broadcasting in the Arab world have been covert and apparently were better organized and executed than the attempt by the British in October 1956.

CLANDESTINE BROADCASTING: 1960–1980

The following excludes the unofficial stations operating from Lebanon since 1975 that were discussed in Chapter 4, Broadcasting during the Civil War. It also excludes those stations that appear to be clandestine but that use frequencies of Arab countries.

Voice of Arab Syria. First heard on October 26, 1976, the Voice of Arab Syria originated from Iraq (BBC, *Clandestine . . . Middle East*, n.d., p. 2). Syria has consistently jammed the station because of its attacks against Syrian President Assad. When the station first appeared, it devoted considerable time to attacking the Syrian Army's role in the efforts to bring peace to Lebanon. Iraq became the country most active in this kind of broadcasting activity during the 1970s, replacing Egypt as the Arab world's foremost disseminator of virulent radio propaganda. John Cooley (1977, p. 11) observed:

> In tone some of these [Voice of Arab Syria] broadcasts remind some observers of the years before the 1967 Arab-Israeli war when the late Egyptian President Nasser's radio station in Cairo, Voice of the Arabs, broadcast a program called Enemies of God by commentator Ahmed Said. It included attacks on Israel, the United States, and the reactionary Arab regimes like Saudi Arabia, now the target of some rather similar, though less vituperous language from Radio Baghdad.

Voice of the Arabian Peninsula People. Started on May 10, 1973, and last heard on March 25, 1975 (BBC, *Clandestine . . . Middle East,* n.d., p. 2), the Voice of the Arabian Peninsula People was located in Iraq and promoted anti–Saudi Arabian feelings in the Middle East.

Voice of Iraqi Kurdistan. The Voice of Iraqi Kurdistan started transmitting on September 10, 1965, and was last heard on March 16, 1975 (BBC, *Clandestine . . . Middle East,* n.d., p. 3). It broadcast in Arabic and other languages in support of the Kurdish cause.

Mutawakallite Royal Radio. The exact location of Mutawakallite Royal Radio, a Saudi Arabia-sponsored clandestine service, was never learned. It started on October 5, 1962, at the beginning of the civil war in Yemen, and was last heard on May 30, 1970 (BBC, *Clandestine . . . Middle East*, n.d., p. 3).

Free Yemeni South Radio. Free Yemeni South Radio was another broadcasting operation backed by the Saudi Arabian government. The service used Mutawakallite facilities and concentrated on broadcasts against South Yemen. First heard on December 16, 1970, the broadcasts ceased prior to April 1976 (BBC, *Clandestine . . . Middle East*, n.d., p. 3).

Radio Freedom from South Yemen. Radio Freedom from South Yemen began transmitting anti–South Yemen government material in mid-1978 on the same frequencies as Free Yemeni South Radio.

Aden Voice of Oman Revolution. Aden Voice of Oman Revolution uses the radio facilities of South Yemen to broadcast propaganda attacking Oman's Sultan Qaboos. Started in November 1973 as the Voice of the Popular Front for the Liberation of the Arabian Gulf, the station's name was later changed to reflect the aims of the Popular Front for the Liberation of Oman. On November 19, 1976, Aden Radio announced that the program was being discontinued, but it did not stop (BBC, *Clandestine . . . Middle East*, n.d., p. 3). PFLO broadcasting activity intensified after the Iranian Revolution as efforts were increased to prevent British and U.S. military forces from helping Oman protect the Straits of Hormuz. The following is an example of PFLO broadcasting style:

> Brothers, of late the secrets of the game being played by Qabus and some of his advisers have started to come out into the open, especially after most of the Omani citizens in Muscat have noted the intensive visits by the American Ambassador to the regime of Qabus.
>
> While Britain, because of certain exigencies, had to abandon its role in the Gulf region for the benefit of American imperialism, Qabus for his part revealed some months back a letter written in his own hand to the American President, Jimmy Carter, in which he included a tempting offer to the United States. Qabus promised in the letter to compensate America for its losses in Iran by offering extensive facilities and privileges for an American presence in Oman and its territorial waters.
>
> All this is in harmony with what Qabus said some years ago; that he would enter into an alliance with even the Devil if that would protect his regime. (BBC, "Aden Voice of Oman Revolution," 1979)

Voice of Palestine. Voice of Palestine is apparently the only radio service under the complete control of the Palestine Liberation Organization (PLO).

Almost all Arab countries allow broadcasting time to Palestinians for cultural, educational, and information programs. However, the host country usually maintains some control, and when broadcasts are not in accordance with the policy of the country whose studios and transmitters are being used, they have been suspended. The Voice of Palestine started in September 1973 from Syrian territory under the title "Voice of Fatah, Voice of Asifah [The Storm]." On July 13, 1975, the station discontinued broadcasting, but resumed again on September 21, 1975, from somewhere in Lebanon. The loss of Lebanese government authority during the civil war allowed the move to be made. However, according to the BBC Monitoring Service, the station reportedly suspended transmissions on February 20, 1977 (BBC, *Clandestine . . . Palestine,* n.d., p. 1), because of the presence of the Syrian Army in Lebanon. Although the PLO lost its only independent means of radio programming, it still has the use of radio facilities in many other Arab countries.

Voice of the Eritrea Revolution. Another clandestine service financed and equipped by Iraq, the Voice of the Eritrea Revolution started daily broadcasts in August 1976 on four shortwave frequencies. The programs, in Arabic and Tigrigna, feature newscasts and information about military operations supported by Iraq against Ethiopian troops (BBC, "Monitoring," 1979a).

Gafsa Radio. Gafsa Radio broadcasts in Arabic and occasionally in French. Programs last for several hours per day on mediumwave and allow the service, also known as the Voice of the Revolutionary Movement for the Liberation of Tunisia, an opportunity to program material that is hostile to the Tunisian government (BBC, "Gafsa Radio," 1980).

National Radio of the Saharan Arab Democratic Republic. National Radio of the Saharan Arab Democratic Republic, first heard in 1981, broadcasts material hostile to the Moroccan government in Arabic and Spanish on mediumwave (BBC, "National Radio," 1980).

Voice of the Egyptian People. The Voice of the Egyptian People, an unofficial Libyan service, used one shortwave frequency to disseminate material hostile to the Sadat government in Egypt. The station was first heard during the summer of 1979, following the formalization of the Egyptian peace treaty with Israel (BBC, "Monitoring," 1979b).

CLANDESTINE BROADCASTING: 1980–1992

This 12-year period was not a particularly notable one for clandestine broadcasting within the Middle East. While it is true that various stations in Syria, Jordan, and Iraq and some of the private stations in Lebanon supported the *Intifada*, the Palestinian uprising on the Gaza Strip and the West Bank, the type of radio wars among Arab states that took place in the 1960s and 1970s did not occur during this period. The exception to this is, of course, the brisk radio broadcasting activity that took place immediately after the August 2, 1990, Iraqi invasion of Kuwait. For all intents and purposes, the Gulf propaganda radio war ceased after virtually all of Iraq's high-powered medium- and shortwave transmitters were destroyed by U.S.-led air attacks. Until this happened, however, listeners throughout the Middle East were treated to a vast array of vituperative Arabic broadcasts from virtually all sides.

Readers are reminded of how difficult it is to track clandestine radio broadcasts in the Middle East. Unlike some of the rather organized radio efforts of both sides during World War II, Arabic-language stations often change names, frequencies, programming, and hours of operation with neither notification nor an apparent rationale. Especially true of some of the short-lived services, the name of a program has been known to change at the whim of a duty announcer.

The following are selected stations identified and followed by the British Broadcasting Corporation Monitoring Service in Caversham Park, England (British Broadcasting Service, 1990a).

Voice of the Masses. This is one of several radio services from Baghdad that either emerged or were lengthened after the Kuwaiti invasion. For example, beginning on August 29, 1990, this service included *Voice of the Peninsula and Arabian Gulf* that attempted to give the Iraqi position on the invasion. However, this was not a new concept from Baghdad; since 1967, Iraq has transmitted its own form of radio propaganda to the Gulf states under various radio service names, including *Voice of the Arabian Gulf*, *Voice of the Arabian Peninsula*, and *Voice of the Arabian South and Arabian Gulf*.

Voice of the Jihad, Voice of the Holy War from Baghdad. First heard in December, 1990, this English-language service was beamed to India and Pakistan.

Voice of the People of Kurdistan. An anti-Iraq station that broadcast in Bahdinani Kurdish and Arabic, Voice of the People of Kurdistan supported the Patriotic Union of Kurdistan.

Voice of the National Alliance for the Liberation of Syria/Voice of Arab Syria. This service of Republic of Iraq Radio is anti-Syrian, calling for the removal of President Hafez al-Assad.

Voice of the Kurdistan Democratic Party. This was an anti-Iraqi station, probably transmitting from Turkey. It was first reported by the Turkish newspaper *Hurriyet.*

Voice of Iraq. This is a daily anti-Iraq radio service transmitted by Syrian Arab Republic Radio.

Voice of the Libyan People. Supporting the Front for the Salvation of Libya, this service is anti-Qadhafi and has broadcast from the facilities of several countries, including the Sudan, Iraq, and Chad.

Voice of the [Libyan] People. This station supports the Libyan National Movement and is anti-Qadhafi.

Voice of the Mediterranean. A joint Libyan-Maltese service, this station uses the facilities of Deutsche Welle's relay station in Malta. (See Chapter 20.)

Holy Mecca Radio. First heard on August 10, 1990, this was an anti-Saudi Arabian station especially hostile to the Saudi Royal Family. Although the transmitter was believed to be in Iraq, the station claimed to be broadcasting from "the land of Hijaz" (western Saudi Arabia).

Voice of Arab Awakening. This was a service of Republic of Iraq Radio in Arabic to troops of Arab states stationed in Saudi Arabia to support the military buildup in the kingdom against Iraq.

Voice of Peace Republic of Iraq/Voice of Peace from Baghdad. During the 1990–1991 U.S. and British troop concentrations in Saudi Arabia, these English-language broadcasts were attempts to demoralize American troops. Such broadcasts at first received some attention in the American press because they were such a poor attempt to imitate some of the tactics used by "Tokyo Rose" (Japan) and "Lord Haw Haw" (Germany) during World War II. Because these broadcasts were so poorly done, short in duration, and on a shortwave frequency, probably very few troops heard them.

For example, on August 24, 1990, C-SPAN, the U.S. public service television network, played some of the Iraqi broadcasts:

> Your children are waiting for you. Your wife is waiting for you. Your wife has a lover. This is Radio Baghdad, the broadcasting service of the Iraqi

Republic. ("Radio Baghdad in," 1990)

The *Washington Times* reported the following Iraqi broadcast excerpts in a front-page story:

> Remember what the petrol emirs are doing with the American girls. Do you want to defend them?
> Is it in your interests as a civilized person to defend people who are living in the Middle Ages?
> The sand heaps are moving in the Arabian desert, and they swallow many people, and they will swallow you. ("Iraq Jack keeps," 1990, p. 1)

Voice of Free Iraq. Finally, from Saudi Arabia, and with the apparent aid of U.S. psychological warfare experts, there was the Voice of Free Iraq, a station utilizing Iraqi exiles who mimicked the musical theme of Radio Baghdad and called for the ouster of Saddam Hussein. Horwitz suggests that the station, although originating from Saudi Arabia, was the work of the U.S. military or the CIA or both because Voice of Free Iraq broadcasts "fit the pattern of stations in Latin America long suspected of having CIA links" (Horwitz, 1991b, p. A5).

SUMMARY

It is difficult to forecast the future of international broadcasting to and within the Arab world. The 1980s were quite different from the 1960s. All frequencies are very crowded with high-powered medium- and shortwave transmitters. Even the most dedicated and determined listener may have trouble finding a clear signal. The occasional as well as the sophisticated listener in the 1990s is much more aware that Arabic's vagueness tends to breed exaggeration. Also, the focus of international broadcasting within the Arab world has changed dramatically since the 1960s. Egypt no longer has the most powerful transmitters in the Arab world nor the dynamic radio personalities that it had under Nasser. The fact that Egypt has signed a peace treaty with Israel has caused Egypt's stature in the Middle East to change.

For several years, Iraq did replace Egypt as a leading Arab country, and Iraq increased its radio services to other Arab countries with the aim of achieving this goal. However, the entire political situation changed after the Iraqi invasion of Kuwait and the subsequent Gulf War of early 1991.

Another change since the 1960s is that with the increase of government services in many countries—specifically in the Gulf states—Arab listeners no longer need to tune to the transmissions of other Arab countries for news and entertainment. It is widely believed among broadcasters in the

West and in the Arab world that television has decreased interest in radio broadcasts from other countries during evening hours. The growing affluence in some countries has promoted the purchase of high-quality home sound systems. Local FM stereo music has become an attraction for those with sophisticated systems and for owners of portable radios with FM bands.

For those countries and organizations that transmit in Arabic to the Middle East the above observations have some relevance. It cannot be emphasized too strongly that the most important technical advantage that a non-Arab country can have is a strong mediumwave signal to the area. However, more than a technical advantage is needed to attract Arab listeners. Services such as Radio Monte Carlo Middle East, the BBC, and VOA all find an audience because listeners are attracted to broadcasts that fill some need not otherwise satisfied by local or regional services. Canada and Austria, industrialized countries that only started an Arabic service in 1990, were the last hold-outs among the major Western countries that did not broadcast to the Middle East in Arabic.

CHAPTER 22

Arab Broadcasting: Problems

THE PRECEDING CHAPTERS of this study have explored various aspects of Arab world electronic media. They have focused on the problems of individual Arab countries as well as on more broadly defined concerns such as transmitter construction, broadcast rhetoric, and programming: they have sought to delineate the major problems that Arab countries will continue to face in the last decade of this century as changes occur in the Arab systems of broadcasting that will, in turn, affect the communication patterns of the Arab culture. These concluding pages discuss the major problem areas under the headings of cooperation, training, financing, and technology.

COOPERATION

Those who have read much about the Arab world already know that the concept of Arab unity and cooperation is largely a myth. Even many staunch advocates of Arab unity experienced an eye-opening experience on August 2, 1991—the day Iraq invaded Kuwait. Despite religious, linguistic, and other cultural similarities, each nation state in the area has a unique character; usually this character is both defined and promoted by the mass media. Yet, while it is recognized that differences do exist from country to country and region to region, there have been numerous attempts to bring the Arab countries together in order to promote interests common to all. A good deal of this cooperation has been undertaken under the framework of the Arab League, an organization chartered in Egypt following World

War II. The League has had some success in promoting agreements among Arab countries in a range of fields, among them civil aviation, health, education, postal services, and broadcasting. With the League's help (and after several false starts), the Arab States Broadcasting Union (ASBU) was officially formed in 1969, with headquarters in Egypt: full alliance was achieved when Saudi Arabia agreed to join in 1974 (Boyd, 1975b). The Arab States Broadcasting Union meets annually in a member country; the head of the organization, then elected, serves for one year.

ASBU has been successful in varying degrees in promoting news exchanges and cooperative audience research, training, and technical efforts. Perhaps the area of cooperation that held the greatest promise was promoting news exchanges, and the Arab world was divided into areas within which both radio and, more importantly, television news were to be exchanged. But after an initial enthusiastic response among member countries generally, the regional exchanges prospered primarily in the Gulf states: financial, technical, and political matters undermined the experiment. A more successful outcome of the interest in news among Arab countries was an agreement negotiated between ASBU and the European Broadcasting Union (EBU) for daily satellite relay to the Middle East of important North American and European television news stories: this has become an important source of news for those Arab countries that have the capability of receiving the transmissions. Through the ASBU some of the wealthier countries have subsidized the service so that poorer countries are able to take it at little or no cost.

ASBU has been an almost prototypical victim of shifting political priorities in the Arab world. The Arab League headquarters had been located in Egypt since that organization's creation; like most of the other specialized agencies of the League, ASBU was also located in Cairo and was staffed mainly by Egyptian nationals. When Egyptian President Sadat signed the peace agreement with Israel in 1979, there was an immediate attempt among many other Arab countries, headed by Iraq, to isolate Egypt. One action that the then "rejectionist" countries were able to promote was the move of the Arab League headquarters from Cairo to Tunis—and the headquarters of the ASBU were shifted with it, the non-Egyptian staff being permanently moved there. Other Arab League agencies were likewise moved from Cairo to other countries. Egypt responded by freezing all financial assets to League agencies in Cairo and mandating that Egyptians remain in Cairo—continuing work as before, still receiving salary and benefits. Although the Tunis ASBU headquarters under their new Secretary General—Abdallah Chakroun, a Moroccan—was officially recognized as the legitimate one by Arab League supporters, the original ASBU Secretary General, Salah Abdel Kader, kept the Cairo office operating for several years. After the office officially moved to Tunis, some associate members continued to pay annual dues to the Cairo office, thus adding more hard currency, in this case American dollars, to the several million that that office had in the bank (Kader interview, 1979). Before the 1979 relocation, in an attempt to decentralize the administrative functions of ASBU, offices were created in various Arab countries to promote training, technical research and monitoring, and audience research. There arose questions among the Khartoum (Sudan) Technical Center, the Baghdad (Iraq) Research Office, and the Damascus (Syria) Training Center staffs regarding to whom they should report. Indeed, overall confusion and the associated financial problems have stymied the development of the Training Center in Damascus—whose founding director now lives in a small town in the United States—and brought about the closing of the Technical Center in the wake of its frustrated director's resignation (Yousef interview, 1979).

However, ASBU, always weak politically because its administration was possibly too sensitive to the individual broadcasters, is an organization that has outlived its usefulness. Overall, political and economic events have taken over the role of this regional organization. The wealthier states that invested most heavily in ARABSAT are the ones who have reaped the benefits of both its telecommunications potential and information-oriented advantages. Arab states never did need the technical help of ASBU; they hired engineering help from the West. Even the news exchange programs with the West have been pushed aside by the agreements that some countries such as Egypt have made directly with CNN. Only the Iraqis trusted the audience research done by the Baghdad-based ASBU audience research office.

ARABSAT is an organization whose headquarters is in Riyadh, Saudi Arabia; the technical center is located in Tunis. Promoted and heavily financed by the Saudi government during the height of the oil-boom years, the idea was for all Arab states to be linked by satellites owned and controlled by Arabs. From the beginning, the Arab need for ARABSAT was based on the desire to be self sufficient in the satellite field. The Arabs did not want to be completely dependent on INTELSAT for satellite connection.

For the most part, the project was technically successful. Two satellites were launched—one by the United States, the other by a French-backed European space group. Although at first envisioned as a means of linking countries with television and radio programs, ASBU has been unsuccessful in beginning an Arab worldwide television and radio news exchange similar to the one in Europe previously mentioned. Some stories have been exchanged via the satellite, but Arab electronic news tends to reflect the state-operated broadcaster transmitting it. It is almost impossible to imagine Libyan television news stories, for example, being used regularly in the Gulf states. During the eight-year Iraq-Iran war, Iraq regularly used ARABSAT to provide at no cost Arab television stations with film and tape of the fighting—of course, from Iraq's point of view. The result has been further erosion of the effectiveness and credibility of the Arab States Broadcasting Union.

Yet the events surrounding the fragmentation of ASBU since 1979 may ultimately be beneficial. The organization itself has attempted to promote regional and binational cooperation. Probably the best example of this is the continuing effort among Gulf states and North African countries to cooperate in many facets of broadcasting. These regions have achieved what no others have been able to do: undertake some joint television production projects. Even if ASBU becomes a viable, respected organization, the future of cooperation in broadcasting apparently rests primarily with those countries in North Africa and the Gulf that believe it to be in their best interests to cooperate in certain areas.

TRAINING

Broadcasting executives in Arab countries usually state that personnel matters rank high among major concerns. Almost every Arab country has shortages of adequately trained research, production, and technical personnel: though several schools, institutes, and specialized training centers in the Arab world provide education in the field of mass communication, training continues to be largely informal and on-the-job. Egypt has tended to be a leader in several respects. The Egyptian Radio-Television Federation operates both radio and television training centers that attract nationals from other Arab countries, especially for advanced training. The courses through which students progress are very specialized: a student may concentrate on either production or engineering. Common criticisms of the Federation operation are that it is underfunded and that the training is often done in an informal and unstructured manner.[1] Several Egyptian universities also offer courses in mass communication. The courses, unlike those offered by the radio and television institute, are usually theory and policy oriented. The largest communication school in the Arab world is the Faculty of Information at Cairo University that offers undergraduate, M.A., and Ph.D. degrees in broadcasting, print journalism, and advertising and public relations. Thousands of students attend the large lecture sections there, many of them graduate students who are already professionally employed and hope that a graduate degree will benefit their careers.

The American University in Cairo (AUC) offers undergraduate and M.S. degrees in mass communication. The instruction at the American University is in English, although graduates often find employment in the

Arab-language press and radio and television stations.[2] In 1988, AUC started a program under its mass communication department that is unique to the Arab world. The Adham Center for Television Journalism was started by AUC faculty member and former NBC Cairo bureau chief Abdullah Schleifer. The Adham Center—named for the Saudi national who helped finance the project—uses state-of-the-art BetaCam recorders and Sony editing equipment to give students intensive, hands-on experience. The Adham Center operates a small, campus, closed-circuit operation and students have had stories placed on Cable News Network's *World Report*. Egypt and Jordan train adequate numbers of students for themselves in all facets of broadcasting—but then have difficulty retaining them. Many people from those countries are lured by high salaries to wealthier countries, mostly in the Gulf states, that still must import much of their production and technical staffs.

The most ambitious effort by the Arab broadcasters to help train technical and production personnel was promoted under the auspices of ASBU. Recognizing that ASBU could play an important role in the training of broadcasters, the organization decided in the mid-1970s to build a training center where nationals of all Arab countries could be sent for basic as well as advanced study. Originally, the location for the ASBU center was to have been in Amman, Jordan; however, the Jordanian government was unable to provide the necessary land for the facility (Shaar interview, 1979). The Syrian government did provide the needed land, in Damascus, and that city became the location of the ASBU Training Center under the leadership of Khudr Shaar, a former Syrian broadcasting official. Construction on the facility, which includes a dormitory, started in 1977, and in 1980 the building was completed. But—and it is another result of Middle East political tension—the Training Center never received essential equipment. The original funding for the building was gained through ASBU with the hope that funds for equipment would be contributed by the Gulf states, those countries that would most benefit from and could afford the Center's instruction. However, the Gulf states remain hesitant to contribute to the undertaking, primarily because of its location. Gulf broadcasting officials have many reservations about Syria, despite the fact that Syria supported the Gulf states in the 1990–1991 Gulf War. Many Gulf Ministers of Information are concerned that students will be given political instruction along with their broadcast training.

ASBU officials deny that these fears will be realized, but nonetheless the fears persist; and the 1980–1988 war between Iraq and Iran only served to exacerbate them, with Syria supporting Iran while the Gulf states gave tacit political support to Iraq. At one point, the Gulf states considered the possibility of building their own training facility, which, it was reasoned, would mesh well with the other non-ASBU efforts at cooperation that those states had fostered in the broadcasting field. But until a decision is made about the location of a facility, training will continue in the Gulf states, as elsewhere, to be on an informal basis. The expertise of some Egyptian-, Jordanian-, and Western-trained personnel notwithstanding, one of the most pressing problems of Arab broadcasters remains unsolved.

FINANCING

Except for those Arab countries that have become wealthy from petroleum exports, the financing of radio and television broadcasting will continue to be a serious problem. Though many of the less wealthy Arab countries discussed in this study, such as Jordan and the Sudan, realize how important the electronic media have become to the internal and external political process, funds to continue the dissemination of their services have become increasingly scarce in light of national military, education, and health needs. The less financially fortunate countries will have to continue to struggle and to compromise to find funds needed to continue national broadcasting services. The Arab broadcasting organizations that accept advertising are likely to continue to accept it: it yields income, in some cases in essential hard currency. When the Saudi government found itself in some financial difficulty in the mid-1980s, it introduced advertising on its English-language second channel; later advertising was also allowed on the main channel.

More innovative attempts to finance both radio and television services may be found. Several Arab countries, Jordan and Tunisia for example, have adopted the system of financial help for radio and television pioneered by Egypt: it being reasoned that every citizen benefits from broadcasting, a surcharge that goes to the broadcasting authority is added to all electricity bills. But of course in that case, in a developing country where many lower-income people do not own television sets, those who have sets pay an unfairly low share of the burden and those who do not own sets pay an unfairly high one. And as color television equipment ages and must be replaced, and as the demand for more and better-quality local programming increases, additional funds will be even more necessary: the difficulties in raising them both reliably and fairly will remain a major problem for many Arab countries.

TECHNOLOGY

Satellite communications probably has been the technical advance of greatest benefit to Arab broadcasters. During the 1970s, most Arab countries constructed ground stations in order to help provide faster and more reliable telephone and telex communication, and the satellite circuits leased from INTELSAT also brought television signals from Asia, Europe, and North America. Perhaps the most used satellite service is the daily European Broadcasting Union (EBU) news exchange sponsored by ASBU. International sporting events are also popular in Arab countries and some soccer events are taped from the satellite or televised directly. Leased satellite circuits, moreover, make possible an internal distribution of television signals that would otherwise have been almost impossible in those Arab countries with large land masses—Saudi Arabia, Oman, the Sudan, and Algeria. Long distances, rough terrain, and difficult weather conditions make microwave or cable distribution of television programming difficult, and extremely expensive satellites have pushed some of them as much as 10 years ahead of schedule for television signal distribution. Enthusiasm for satellite technology prompted a group of Arab states headed by Saudi Arabia to contract with a French consortium to build and launch a satellite for their exclusive use. Previously mentioned was the system's failure to be a successful distributor of Arab television news. But there is another aspect of ARABSAT that has been a problem, primarily for the smaller, less wealthy states. These countries such as Bahrain already had invested large sums in the construction of stations to receive INTELSAT signals; in most cases, countries built two ground stations, one for the Indian Ocean and one for the Atlantic satellite. In order to participate in ARABSAT, each country had to build yet another ground station at a cost of millions of dollars.

In short, ARABSAT, first envisioned by the Gulf state ministers of information as a means of Arab news and program exchange, has become the Arab equivalent of INTELSAT. Rather than being used primarily for the distribution of broadcast signals, it has become an expensive telecommunications satellite whose primary emphasis, like INTELSAT, is telephony and data transmission.

Direct Broadcast Satellites (DBS)

Each passing decade seems to bring a new potential for the delivery of electronic media. In the 1970s and 1980s, videocassette recorders became attractive for those wishing an alternative to government-run television; in the 1990s the Arab states will be focusing on DBS. Direct satellite reception of television in areas other than North Africa remains limited, but this will surely change. In poorer Arab states, most homes cannot afford the mandatory dish and associated electronic equipment to downlink signals, and legal constraints still limit development in this area. Saudi Arabia, for example, does not allow home satellite receiver ownership, but some members of the royal family and prominent, wealthy Saudis do possess satellite dishes and receivers. Direct satellite broadcasting (DBS) will become more attractive as services become more available. Egypt is using its vast store of films and television programs to start SpaceNet, a satellite-delivered television service. Also, in March 1992 the Middle East Broadcast Centre—a Saudi Arabian-financed, London-based television service—started transmitting daily to the Arab world via a European satellite (Waldman, 1992). In the Gulf, MBC is rebroadcast by stations in Kuwait and Bahrain. Star TV, a Hong Kong-based five-channel satellite television service, reaches most countries on the Arabian peninsula (Schloss interview, 1992).

But earthbound broadcasting technologies also present Arab countries with difficulties and with grounds for confrontation. The rapid growth of super-power mediumwave transmissions has made clear daytime and evening mediumwave reception more difficult—and each new super-power transmitter tends to motivate its neighbors to purchase additional high-power facilities of their own that only make matters worse. The scarcity of mediumwave frequencies is also a serious problem, and even relatively friendly countries—Jordan and Saudi Arabia—have argued over frequency ownership. These problems and the growth in sales of high-quality home sound equipment, especially in the Gulf states, have increased interest in FM transmission. If for no other reason than lack of mediumwave frequencies, the FM spectrum will be the area of important development in the last decade of this century.

But, in the end, such problems as those here summarized are only challenges: they will not deter further development of radio and television systems in the Arab world. The electronic media have become an established part of the political and cultural process. Whatever political and cultural changes occur, then, in the 1990s—and however rapidly and dramatically they occur—Arab broadcasting will continue to be an integral part of the busy scene.

Notes

CHAPTER 1

1. In the late 1970s, the Arab ministers of information met and decided to standardize the name of their ministries. Prior to this action many were named Ministry of National Guidance, which, at least in English, had a harsh ring to it.

2. Hard currencies are those that are internationally recognized and traded. Arab currencies such as the Egyptian and Sudanese pound are basically worthless outside of those countries.

CHAPTER 2

1. For additional information see Part 5.

2. There are several sources that discuss Egyptian print journalism history. Consult, for example, Alrnaney, 1972, pp. 34–38; Nasser, 1979, 1990.

3. The name of the BBC's Arabic-language magazine is *Hunna London*, "Here is" or "This is" London.

4. This study notes results of various research efforts by the U.S. International Communication Agency to determine radio and other media habits. The agency does not undertake data collection itself but contracts with survey research organizations to do surveys based on a questionnaire design prepared by USICA. Radio surveys undertaken in the Middle East during the 1970s were often done on a shared-cost basis with the BBC, which in turn had some say in the questionnaire design. Associated Business Consultants (ABC) of Beirut, Lebanon, did several of the surveys in the early 1970s. There was some concern about the reliability of ABC, and the Lebanese civil war interrupted its activities. Most of the survey work in the Arab world is now done by Middle East Marketing Research Bureau of Nicosia, Cyprus. It was this organization that did the fieldwork for the multi-country 1977 and 1979 McCann Middle East Media Studies ("VOA-CAAP audience estimate for Kuwait 1974," 1975, p. 10).

5. This date is much celebrated in Egypt because it is the date, three days after the revolution started, that King Farouk was exiled.

6. A 1958 study suggests that the mass media, particularly radio, had an effect on rural villages. See Hirabayashi and Khatib, 1958, pp. 357–63.

7. The daily schedule for Egypt's two television channels and the European Program is published in *The Egyptian Gazette*, a daily Egyptian English-language newspaper.

8. For a comprehensive discussion of Palestine radio broadcasts, see Browne, 1975, pp. 133–50.

9. I first observed Egyptian television in 1964, and later monitored it during a one-month residence in August 1974 and a nine-month residence from September 1976 to June 1977.

10. The Arab League Boycott Office is located in Damascus, Syria. It attempts to ban foreign companies from doing business in Arab countries that either trade with or have a

strong presence—such as a manufacturing capability—in Israel.

11. The ban stopped Arab countries from purchasing new equipment from RCA, although Saudi Arabia did buy an entire television station for the Eastern Province from RCA after the boycott was announced. Arab countries that have operating RCA transmitters must still purchase spare parts from the company. However, most RCA studio equipment in the Arab world has been replaced with non-RCA equipment purchased from the United States, Europe, and Japan.

12. The boycott organizers were interested in distinguishing between the Egyptian people and the Egyptian government. Those Arab world television officials who supported the boycott did not consider programs produced outside of Egypt with Egyptian talent subject to it.

CHAPTER 3

1. I inspected the devastated studio building on February 3, 1977.

2. For details of the attempted coup, see "Nimeiry's justice," 1976, pp. 36–37.

CHAPTER 4

1. I observed the procedure while at the Télé-Orient studios, Beirut, Lebanon, April 3, 1972. For example of censorship on Lebanese television, see Browne, 1975a, pp. 695–98.

2. I spent November 13, 1979, at the station. Even though the Ministry of Information at the time did not officially recognize the station, most taxi drivers knew its location; permission to visit it was granted by the Program Director, a former CLT employee, after the Ministry of Information informally arranged the contact.

CHAPTER 9

1. Technical and other information about radio studios and equipment was provided by staff engineers at the complex on January 16, 1980.

CHAPTER 10

1. I was the American announcer.

2. The U.S. Air Force established a television station in Libya at Wheelus Air Force Base that broadcast its first program on December 22, 1954. See *USAFE television story*, 1955, p. 1.

3. Shobaili, 1972. Dr. Shobaili attempted to obtain clarification of the incident from the Minister of Information, who, at that time, was Deputy Minister of the Interior. The minister declined to clarify the story, stating that he thought it best not to resurrect the incident. Various inaccurate accounts are available. See, for example, *The Economist*, 1965, p. 742, and Walpole et al., 1971, pp. 185–86.

4. For a discussion of the French effort to have other countries adopt the SECAM system, see Crane, 1979.

5. Programs concerning the mosque incident were seen by Americans and Saudis interviewed by me. I viewed the tapes produced after the incident on December 29, 1979, at the Dammam, Saudi Arabia, television station.

CHAPTER 16

1. On October 5, 1988, crowds of unemployed young Algerians and high school students

demonstrated in Algiers in protest against unemployment, the high cost of living, the housing shortage, and the unequal distribution of wealth. As the protests persisted, the army was called in, and the soldiers were given orders to shoot at the crowds. Between 300 and 500 young people were killed. Many observers have pointed out that the events played an important role in influencing the drafting of the 1989 Constitution, which formally ushered in a multi-party political system. Among the newly formed parties, the FIS (Front Islamique du Salut) or the Islamic Salvation Front, has emerged as the main opposition party to have seriously challenged the FLN. Indeed, in the first round of the legislative elections in December 1991, the FIS won a landslide victory, which would assure the Islamists the majority in the Algerian parliament if the second round of elections were held. However, as of this writing (January 1992), President Benjedid Chadli has resigned from his post and a military junta has taken over the government in a coup which appears to have been organized in order to stop the second round of elections and thus to prevent the FIS from gaining power. The situation remains uncertain at this point, and the key question is what will happen to the democratic process which started only a couple of years ago. The future of Algeria will very much depend on whether the desire for democracy will prove to be stronger than the force of the army or the radicalism of the FIS.

2. State socialism refers to the type of planned economics found in former Eastern bloc countries and other socialist nations like Cuba and North Korea. Socialism under "state socialism" is defined by the party in power as a system of social and economic organization meant to reduce capitalist exploitation and distribute the country's wealth more equally among the various social groups. The economy under this system is planned by the state, leaving very little room for private initiative.

3. For a valuable overview of the movement of decentralization and the opening to private investments in the audiovisual industry, see Mostefaoui, 1988.

4. According to the Algerian Director of Programming, whom I interviewed in Cannes in April 1989, Algerian television imports 65 percent of its programming from, in order of importance, the United States, the United Kingdom, Canada, France, and Egypt.

CHAPTER 18

1. Until it stopped broadcasting in April 1981, the station was one of so-called French peripheral stations, an American-style commercial outlet like Europe No. l, Radio Luxembourg (RTL), or Radio Monte Carlo (RMC)—stations whose transmitters were just outside the French borders in Saar, Luxembourg, and Monaco.

2. It may also reflect the fact that 150,000 foreigners live in Morocco, many of them French citizens, and that tourism is a major industry.

3. It is not easy to be precise about Moroccan programs, for the RTM is so discreet that newspapers, whether in French or Arabic, do not publish listings (Pigé, 1966, p. 93). That is still true for radio.

4. Approximately 85 percent to 90 percent of the population is of Berber descent, half of them having been arabified. Because it is the religious and the unifying national language, Arabic is gradually displacing the three native tongues.

5. In 1971 that meant 32 percent of urban households and 97 percent of villages.

6. The company that used to hold the French State's shares in the so-called peripheral stations like RTL and Europe 1. By 1991, it was involved in running RMC, RMC Middle East, Africa No. 1, Radio Caribbean Internationale, and Médi 1.

7. A (mainly agribusiness) conglomerate with a turnover of $1 billion which is controlled by the royal family and presided over by the king's son-in-law.

8. This was evident as early as 1963, when, to prepare for the December referendum on the Constitution, the government had 4,000 television sets distributed to cafés, hotels, and other public places.

9. A July 1974 survey showed peak viewing time was 2100 to 2330, with a maximum between 2130 and 2300. See *Lamaliff*, 1977.

10. For a historical survey, see Boyd, 1976, pp. 183–96.

CHAPTER 19

1. *Tunisia: The Political Economy of Reform* (Zartman, 1991) provides several interesting reflections on political reform in post-Bourguiba Tunisia, as well as on the growth and diversity of fundamentalist movements; see especially Chs. 1 (Zartman), 2 (Waltz), and 10 (Magnuson).

2. I can recall several conversations with Tunisian businessmen and government officials in the course of which those feelings and desires were disclosed during the latter part of my service in Tunisia with the U.S. Information Agency (1960–1963).

3. Not all of the time in the intervening years was spent in merely contemplating television. Training of television personnel had begun in the early 1960s, and a small practice studio was set up in 1963. Experimental broadcasts, both in Arabic and French, began in early 1966 (Houidi and Najar, 1983, pp. 114–22).

4. Akrout, 1966, p. 64. There was a considerable French role in the development of Tunisian television, including assistance with preliminary audience surveys and the dispatching of a team of 27 experts, in August 1965, to help prepare Tunisian staff to operate the new service (Hirsch, 1968, pp. 10–12).

5. This and other official figures on sets in use, from 1966 to the present, are drawn from the yearly statistical charts on radio and television licenses as they appear annually in the *EBU Review*, generally in the March or May issue. One must bear in mind that, in any country where there are license fees or taxes on sets, as was (license fees)/is (taxes) true for Tunisia, there will also be a certain degree of evasion of payment and black market trade in illicit receivers. It is impossible to judge the extent of this trade in Tunisia.

6. The Monastir station came on the air in 1971. That its value is more symbolic than real may be indicated by a 1978 study ($N = 8{,}571$) conducted through the Ministry of Information, in which there was no measurable listenership for Radio Monastir, even in its own geographical region! Radio Sfax, on the other hand, was mentioned by 65 percent of the survey sample in its region as listened to daily or nearly every day (Houidi and Najar, 1983, p. 219).

7. The Libyan broadcasts continued for some time after the January incursion. A station calling itself Radio Free Gafsa and broadcasting from Tripoli, Libya, continued to call for Bourguiba's overthrow during the next few months, despite attempts of the Arab League to moderate the dispute between the countries ("Tunisia," 1980, p. 30264).

8. Statistics from *EBU Review*, March 1980, p. 45. Because of conditions noted in note 5 above and because transistor radios are especially easy to smuggle, it is presumed and even acknowledged by Tunisian officials that the number of undeclared radio sets may be considerable.

9. See Duvignaud, 1970, *passim*, especially p. 291, for some interesting observations on Bourguiba's "national development" speeches and the role of radio in bringing them to the nation. Duvignaud is somewhat critical of the government and, by implication, of Bourguiba for having aroused a number of false hopes by the broadcast of these speeches. Bourguiba's use of radio and television has not been the subject of scholarly analysis, but something of his background and his approach to working with the Tunisian people is shown in Knapp, 1970, Ch. 8. This book, though dated, is an excellent introduction to the country. Considerably drier in style but more up to date is Nelson, 1988. Also, Bourguiba's speeches from time to time touched directly upon the role of the media in national development. For example, in an April 1974 speech, he talked about the dissolution of moral values through "the texts of songs, which, on the whole, support base instincts" (*Interstages*, October 1979, p. 6).

10. One example of a different mode of conveying the President's words and thoughts to

the nation was a radio series entitled "With the Great Struggler" (1969), which featured excerpts from past speeches by Bourguiba and which was designed to give Tunisians, especially younger ones, a better sense of the history of the national movement ("Radio Tunis in Arabic," 3 July 1969, cited in *BCC Summary of World Broadcasts*, ME/W527/B1, July 11, 1969).

11. See Mahjoub, 1976, pp. 217–30. For a more detailed account of some of the problems and successes in Tunisia's overall family planning effort during the 1960s, see Lapham, 1970, pp. 241–53, and Huston, 1979, *passim*.

12. An elaborate plan for the expansion of educational broadcasting in Tunisia was prepared in 1971 by a joint team from UNESCO and the Swedish International Development Authority (SIDA). It called for the expenditure of several million dollars for the creation and equipping of new studios and for increased production and distribution of television receivers (Tunisia assembles receivers from parts supplied by European firms, thus making it possible to offer the public relatively low-priced sets), etc. The plan was not put into operation for reasons unknown to me. See Allebeck et al., 1971, pp. 85–151, for an outline of this plan.

13. There also appears to be a tendency on the part of Tunisian broadcast officials to view radio and television first and foremost in terms of political and cultural broadcasting. This may be something of a legacy from the French, whose broadcast system emphasizes the same things: most Tunisian broadcast staff who receive overseas training do so in France, which helps to perpetuate the tradition. Also, cultural broadcasting is a relatively "safe" (politically) area, compared with economic or educational broadcasting.

14. The early years of Maghrebvision are described in El Shafei, 1974, pp. 26–30, and in Houidi and Najar, 1983, pp. 184–94.

CHAPTER 20

1. Excluded from this survey are the Arabic Services of Israel. The problem is in distinguishing between Arabic broadcasts intended for its own Arabic-speaking citizens and programming for listeners in the occupied territories: Golan Heights, the Gaza Strip, and Jordan's West Bank.

2. As Britain, France, and Israel invaded Egypt to take control of the Suez Canal, Sharq al-Adna (the Middle East Arab Broadcasting Station), a British-owned, Cyprus-based commercial station, started transmitting anti-Nasser programming. As the invasion started, the station was taken over by the British military on Cyprus, who set programming policy for the subsequent months. For additional details, see Boyd, 1982; Soley and Nichols, 1987.

Many in the BBC are still unhappy with the scenario immediately preceding RMCME's agreement with the Cypriot government to use the former British frequency. Apparently the British Foreign Office sent a diplomat to Cyprus after independence with the aim of negotiating several agreements. The BBC had asked that the Sharq al-Adna frequency be at the top of the list. Somehow, the diplomat or his staff got the order of the items on the list reversed. The frequency was relegated to the bottom of the list and was subsequently leased to France for RMCME.

CHAPTER 21

1. Portions of this section were first published in *Journalism Quarterly*, and appear here, with permission, re-edited. See Boyd, 1975b, pp. 645–53.

2. The Voice was not the sole Egyptian radio service that could be heard in the Middle East. Radio Cairo, which is sometimes confused with the Voice by expert and casual listeners alike, is the main Egyptian domestic service and also can be heard in most other Arab countries. The confusion stems partially from the fact that Cairo is the city of origin for all of

Egypt's national and international radio services. Although Radio Cairo's mediumwave signal is powerful, it was not originally intended for international consumption as was the Voice's, and each service has always had a separate staff. But Radio Cairo's news and commentary, in fact its entire programming tone, have not been inconsistent with those of the Voice of the Arabs.

3. "What do you," 1971, p. 76. In the early part of 1956, some Western powers became concerned about the reach of Egyptian broadcasts, and in that year the American Central Intelligence Agency sponsored a survey that concluded that Cairo's broadcasts were heard from Morocco to Iraq (Copeland, 1969, p. 247).

4. The Baghdad Pact became METO (Middle East Treaty Organization) and then CENTO (Central Treaty Organization). Iraq was the only Arab Middle East country to join and her membership ended with the 1958 Iraq revolution.

5. Nutting, 1972, p. 174. There were other clandestine radio stations that broadcast to Egypt during this period. Although most were located in other Middle Eastern countries, one operated by an exiled Egyptian transmitted from France.

6. The BBC was concerned about the Cyprus station because it was feared that the station, which also relayed the BBC Arabic service, would damage the BBC's credibility.

7. John Bagot Glubb, 1959, p. 330. One of the techniques that the Voice of the Arabs employed was the derogatory reference to Arab leaders to whom Egypt was opposed. For example, Nuri es-Said was "Traitor Nuri"; King Faisal of Saudi Arabia was the "Bearded Bigot"; and King Hussein of Jordan was "Son of Zain"—a good example of how Egyptians effectively use Arabic to convey subtle meanings. "Son of Zain" is a derogatory phrase that implies that Hussein's mother was not married.

8. I was an employee of both the Saudi Arabian and the U.S. governments during the planning and construction of the television system.

9. Associated Business Consultants, n.d., pp. 8–10. The survey indicated that the Voice of the Arabs was the third most popular radio service (following the local service and the BBC) among those listeners surveyed. But when combined, the Voice of the Arabs, Radio Cairo, and Middle East Radio—the three Egyptian radio services that could be received in Riyadh—ranked second in popularity.

10. Kandil, 1974. It was apparently in Yemen that the now famous story about a man who wanted to purchase a "Voice of the Arabs radio" originated. The customer entered a radio shop asking for such a radio and the clever merchant told him that he would have one for him if he returned at 1900, a time when he knew the Voice would be broadcasting. The man returned at the appointed time to find the radio he had requested.

11. Reportedly, Saudi Arabia's late King Faisal demanded Said's ouster during the Khartoum Summit following the 1967 war, making it a precondition to the granting of financial aid to Egypt. What more likely happened was that Said was sacrificed by Nasser—like the lamb before the arrival of the honored guest.

12. These broadcasts may have been motivated in part by a desire to show the competition—a revolutionary-oriented station near or in Aden—that it still retained some revolutionary zeal.

13. Early station program schedules and transmission frequencies supplied by the BBC External Broadcasting Audience Research Office. See BBC Monitoring Service reports entitled *Cyprus Station: Sharq al-Adna*, dated June 28, 1948; March 20, 1952; and April 1, 1954.

CHAPTER 22

1. I lectured at the institute in 1977 and 1987.

2. I taught at both Cairo University and the American University during the 1976–1977 academic year under the sponsorship of the Fulbright Program, and I lectured at Cairo University and the American University in Cairo in 1987 and 1990.

Bibliography

REFERENCES

Abderahim, M. (1978). *L'Information audiovisuelle au Maroc: Aspects et politique de développement*. Unpublished master's thesis, Institut français de presse, Paris, France.

_____. (1982). *La RTM, essai de monographie*. Unpublished doctoral dissertation (Communication Sciences), Université de Paris-2.

Abu-Argoub, I. A. (1988). Historical, political, and technical development of ARABSAT. Unpublished doctoral dissertation, Northwestern University, Evanston, Ill.

Abu Bakr, Y., Labib, S., and Kandil, H. (1983). *Development of communication in the Arab States: Needs and priorities*. Paris: UNESCO.

Abu-Lughod, I. (1963). The mass media and Egyptian village life. *Social Forces*, pp. 97–104.

Abu-Nasr. (1971). *A history of the Maghrib*. Cambridge: Cambridge University Press.

Abzinada, Z. A. (1988). *The diffusion and uses of videocassette recorders among adult members of an extended community in the Kingdom of Saudi Arabia*. Unpublished doctoral dissertation, The Ohio State University, Columbus, Ohio.

Adams, J. B. (1964, Spring/Summer). Problems of communication in the Arab world. *Arab Journal*, pp. 83–88.

Ads go on Saudi tv. (1986, January 13). *The Oman Daily Observer*, p. 9.

Advertising rates and general conditions effective April 1, 1980. (n.d.). Doha, Qatar: Ministry of Information.

Adwan, N. (n.d.). M.A. thesis. (In Arabic. Translated in Cairo, Egypt, by Sami Aziz.) Unpublished master's thesis, Université de droit, d'economie et de sciences sociales de Paris, Paris, France.

_____. (1985, April). *Research on video programs in Iraq, Kuwait, and Qatar*. Arab Center for Audience Researches. Baghdad, Iraq.

Africa Research Bulletin. (1985, February 28). *22*(1), 7,593–94.

After heeding calls to turn on Saddam, Shiites feel betrayed. (1991, December 26). *Wall Street Journal*, pp. A1, A5.

Agha, O. H. (1978). The role of mass communication in interstate conflict: The Arab Israeli war of October 6, 1973. *Gazette*, *24*(3), 181–95.

Akol, J. (1979). Interview with Ahmed Abdel Rahman. *Sudanow*, October.

Akrout, H. (1966, November). Television service inaugurated in Tunisia. *EBU Review*, p. 100B.

al-Deen, H. S. (1990, November). *Western media effects on middle eastern society.* Paper presented at the meeting of the Speech Communication Association, Chicago, Ill.

Alexander, Y. (1973). *The role of communications in the Middle East conflict: Ideological and religious aspects.* New York: Praeger.

Algérie Actualité. (1986, February 27–March 5).

al-Ghassani, A. (1974). The necessity of establishing the national democratic mass media in the Arab countries of the non-capitalist way of development. In *The contribution of the development of consciousness in a changing world.* Leipzig, East Germany.

al-Lawzi, S. (1980, January 11). Interview with Amir Fahd. *Al Hawadith.* Translated by Foreign Broadcast Information Service, London.

Allebeck, S. S., Errahmani, A. B., and Ouldali, B. (1971). Radio-television educative en Tunesie. Mission Report ED/FT/o13 Rev. Paris: UNESCO.

Allen, E. (1963, April 30). Report on the establishment of television broadcast service in Saudi Arabia. Mimeo.

al-Makaty, S. S. (1990). *The function of establishing a private commercial broadcasting system in the context of a totally controlled broadcasting system: The case of Saudi Arabia, as perceived by Saudi students in the United States.* Unpublished master's thesis, Michigan State University, East Lansing, Mich.

Almaney, A. (1972). Government control of the press in the United Arab Republic. *Journalism Quarterly, 49*(2), 340–48.

Al-Mu'ti, A. (1980). Egyptian broadcasting: Content analysis. *The Jerusalem Quarterly,* 110–14.

Al-Oofy, A. (1986). *The impact of the videocassette recorder on young Saudi television-viewing habits and life style.* Unpublished master's thesis, Michigan State University, East Lansing, Mich.

Al-Soze, A. A. (1963). Factors influencing public opinion formation in Iraq. Master's thesis, University of Wisconsin.

al-Yusuf, A. (1989). *Commercial advertising in Saudi Arabia: A content analysis.* Unpublished master's thesis, Florida State University, Tallahassee, Fla.

Amin, H., and Boyd, D. (1991, May). *The impact of the home videocassette recorder on Egyptian film and television consumption patterns.* Paper presented at the meeting of the International Communication Association, Boston, Mass.

Amt, W. (1987). ARABSAT: A regional approach to telecommunications. *Development Communications Report,* p. 15.

Analysis/Radio Monte Carlo. (1979, June–August). How to reach the Arabs from a station in France. *Campaign Mid-East.*

Andoni, L. (1991, February 25). Iraqis caught in propaganda war. *The Christian Science Monitor,* p. 4.

Arabic broadcasts from London. (1938, January 13). *Great Britain and the East.*

Arab States Broadcasting Union. (1969, July 22). The United Arab Republic: TV. Cairo, Egypt: ASBU. Mimeographed.

Arab station vying with Christians. (1984, April 4). *New York Times,* p. 36.

Arabs try to tone down news agency furore. (1976, February 5). *The Christian Science Monitor.*

Arab world to get first commercial tv. (1959). *Broadcasting,* June 29, p. 84.

Aramco tv on the air. (1963, May). *Aramco World Magazine*, pp. 3–7.

Aramco World Magazine. (1979, November/December). Houston, Tex.: Arabian American Oil Company.

The A.R.E. broadcasting in brief. (n.d.). Cairo: Egyptian Radio-Television Federation. Mimeographed.

ASBU Review. (1975, April). Recommendations of the eighth meeting of the permanent program committee, pp. 16–28.

_____. (1979, January). News, pp. 34–35.

Asi, M., and Boyd, D. A. (1989, May). *Transnational radio listening among Saudi Arabian university students*. Paper presented at the meeting of the International Communication Association, San Francisco, Calif.

Associated Business Consultants, Ltd. (1972, February). A t.v. and radio survey in Jordan.

_____. (1978, May–June). *Extracts of a media audience survey*. Beirut, Lebanon.

_____. (n.d.). A seven-day media effectiveness survey conducted on behalf of the Hashemite broadcasting service in the city of Riyadh. Beirut, Lebanon.

Associated Business Consultants/RTV International. (n.d.). *Recent RTV contracts*. Beirut, Lebanon. Mimeographed.

Audience, penetration and listenership of pan Arab commercial radio stations in Jordan—Saudi Arabia—Kuwait—U.A.E./Oman. (1979). Table no. 1 only, supplied by SOMERA MMEMS.

Ayish, M. I. (1990). Media access in the third world: A case study of a Jordanian radio program. *Gazette*. 45, 173–87.

Ayish, M, and Hijab, I. (1988). International broadcasting in Arabic: A comparative exploratory study of RMCME, VOA, BBC and RM. *Abhath Al-Yarmouk*, (Yarmouk University, Jordan, Humanities and Social Science Series) 4, 15–26.

Badran, B. A. R. (1991). Christian broadcasting in the eastern Mediterranean: The case of Middle East Television. *Gazette*, 47(1), 47–53.

Baker, R. W. (1974, January–February). Egypt in shadows. American *Behavioral Scientist 17*, 393–423.

Baker, S. (1989). The tale of ARABSAT. *Cable and Satellite Europe*, pp. 58–63.

Bakhaider, B. (1981). *The impact of the videocassette recorder on Saudi Arabian television and society*. Unpublished master's thesis, San Diego State University, San Diego, Calif.

Barbour, N. (1951). Broadcasting to the Arab world. *Middle East Journal*, (Winter), 60.

Barghouti, S. M. (1974). The role of communication in Jordan's rural development. *Journalism Quarterly*, 51(3), 418–24.

Batson, L. D. (1930). *Radio markets of the world*. U.S. Department of Commerce Trade Promotional Series No. 109. Washington, D.C.: Government Printing Office.

Battling radios vie for Arabs' ears. (1957, March 16). *Business Week*, p. 48.

Bearman, J. (1986). *Qadhafi's Libya*. London: Zed Books.

Begin, M. (1951). *The revolt*. New York: Nash Publishing Company.

Benoist-Mechin, J. (1958). *Arabian destiny*. Translated by D. Weaver. Fairlawn, N.J.: Essential Books, Inc.

Binder, D. (1980, June 29). United States concedes it is behind anti-Khomeini broadcasts. *New York Times*, p. 3.

Bookmiller, K. N., and Bookmiller, R. J. (1990). Palestinian radio and the intefada. *Journal of Palestine Studies, 19*(4), 96–105.

Boyd, D. A. (1971). Saudi Arabian television. *Journal of Broadcasting, 15*(1), 73–78.

_____. (1972). *An historical and descriptive analysis of the evolution and development of Saudi Arabian television: 1963–1972.* Ph.D. dissertation, University of Minnesota, Minneapolis, Minn.

_____. (1973). The story of radio in Saudi Arabia. *Public Telecommunications Review, 1*(2) (October), 53–60.

_____. (1975a). The Arab States Broadcasting Union. *Journal of Broadcasting 19*(3), 311–20.

_____. (1975b). Development of Egypt's radio: "Voice of the Arabs" under Nasser. *Journalism Quarterly, 52*(4), 645–53.

_____. (1976). International broadcasting in Arabic to the Middle East and North Africa. *Gazette, 22*(3), 183–96.

_____. (1977). Egyptian radio: Tool of political and national development. *Journalism Monographs*, p. 48.

_____. (1978). A q-analysis of mass media usage by Egyptian elites. *Journalism Quarterly, 55*(3), 501–7, 539.

_____. (1980). Saudi Arabian broadcasting: Radio and television in a wealthy Islamic state. *Middle East Review, 12*(4)/*13*(1), 20–27.

_____. (1982). *Broadcasting in the Arab world: A survey of radio and television in the Middle East.* 1st ed. Philadelphia: Temple University Press.

_____. (1983). Cross-cultural international broadcasting in Arabic. *Gazette, 32*(3), 143–68.

_____. (1985). The Janus effect? Imported television entertainment programming in developing countries. *Critical Studies in Mass Communication, 1*, 379–91.

_____. (1985). VCRs in the developing countries: An Arab case study. *Media Development, 32*(1), 5–7.

_____. (1986). International radio broadcasting: Technical developments and listening patterns in the developing world. *Space Communication and Broadcasting, 4*(1), 25–32.

_____. (1989). International broadcasting to the Arab world: Cultural, economic and political motivations for transnational radio communication, *Gazette, 44*(2), 107–27.

_____. (1991). Lebanese broadcasting: Unofficial electronic media during a prolonged civil war. *Journal of Broadcasting and Electronic Media, 35*(3), 269–87.

Boyd, D. A., and Asi, M. (1991). Transnational radio listening among Saudi Arabian university students. *Journalism Quarterly, 68*, 211–15.

Boyd, D. A., and Benzies, J. Y. (1983). SOFIRAD: France's international commercial media empire. *Journal of Communication, 33*, 56–69.

Boyd, D. A., and Kushner, J. (1979). Media habits of Egyptian gatekeepers. *Gazette, 25*(2), 106–13.

Boyd, D. A., and Najai, A. M. (1984). Adolescent television viewing in Saudi Arabia. *Journalism Quarterly, 61*(2), 295–301, 351.

Boyd, D. A., and Straubhaar, J. D. (1985). The developmental impact of the home videocassette recorder in the third world. *Journal of Broadcasting and Electronic*

Media, 29(1), 5–21.

Boyd, D. A., Straubhaar, J. D., and Lent, J. A. (1989). *Videocassette recorders in the third world*. New York: Longman.

Brahini, M. (1989). *Audiovisuel et vidéo au Maroc*. Unpublished doctoral dissertation (Communication Sciences), Université de Paris-2, Paris.

Brewer, S. P. (1958, September 6). Lebanese rebels close radios: Business in the capital improves. *New York Times*, pp. 1, 2.

Briggs, A. (1965). *The golden age of wireless*. London: Oxford University Press.

British Broadcasting Corporation. (n.d.). *Clandestine and unofficial broadcasts*. Reference WBI/5 and 6.

_____. (n.d.). *Clandestine and unofficial broadcasts*. Reference WBI/5 and 7.

_____. (n.d.). *Clandestine and unofficial broadcasts*. Reference ME/5515/A/1 and WBI/20.

_____. (n.d.). *Clandestine and unofficial broadcasts*. Reference ME/5520/A/2 and WBI/21.

_____. (n.d.). *Clandestine and unofficial broadcasts*, Part 4, *Middle East*. Reference ME/5158/i; ME/5388/i; WBI/51.

_____. (n.d.). *Clandestine and unofficial broadcasts: Middle East*. Caversham Park, Reading, England.

_____. (n.d.). *Clandestine and unofficial broadcasts: Palestine*. Caversham Park, Reading, England.

_____. (n.d). Monitoring service report no. 129/78.

_____. (1947). *Summary of world broadcasts*. Monitoring report. December 7.

_____. (1948). *Summary of world broadcasts*, no. 36, Part 3, February 5.

_____. (1948, 1952, 1954). *Cyprus station: Sharq al-Adna*. June 28, March 20, and April 1.

_____. (1958a). *Summary of world broadcasts*, no. 539, May 2.

_____. (1958b). *Summary of world broadcasts*, no. 603, July 17.

_____. (1967). *Summary of world broadcasts*, no. 2460, May 9.

_____. (1969). *Summary of world broadcasts*, ME/W527/B/1, July.

_____. (1979a). Monitoring service report no. 92/79, July.

_____. (1979b). Monitoring service report no. 121/79, September.

_____. (1979c). Aden Voice of Oman revolution. 1545 GMT, August 25.

_____. (1979d). *BBC handbook 1980*. London: British Broadcasting Corporation.

_____. (1980a, February). Gafsa radio. BBC Monitoring Service.

_____. (1980b, February). National radio of the Saharan Arab Democratic Republic. London: Author.

_____. (1983, January 18). *Summary of world broadcasts*. ME/W1219/B/1. London: Author.

_____. (1987). *BBC annual report and handbook*. London: Author.

_____. (1988, September 30). *Clandestine and unofficial broadcasts*. Part E1., ME/0270.

_____. (1989a). *1989 survey in Egypt*. London: International Broadcasting and Audience Research.

_____. (1989b). *Summary of world broadcasts*. No. 39/1989. London: Author.

_____. (1990a, December 6). *Clandestine and unofficial broadcasts*. Caversham Park, Reading, England.

_____. (1990b, August). *Crisis listening in the U.A.E. and Egypt*. London: International Broadcasting and Audience Research.

_____. (1990c, November). *Crisis Listening in Amman*. London: International Broadcasting and Audience Research.

_____. (1991a, February). *The BBC in Syria: survey in Damascus and Aleppo during the Gulf War*. London: International Broadcasting and Audience Research.

_____. (1991b, June). *World radio and television receivers*. London: International Broadcasting and Audience Research.

_____. (1991c, Summer). *BBC World Service and international competitors comparative schedules*. London: International Broadcasting and Audience Research.

British Colonial Office. (1960, July). Sound and television broadcasting in the overseas territories. The Information Department, Colonial Office.

Broadcasting from Jerusalem. (1935, 17 August). *Wireless World*, p. 128.

Browne, D. R. (1975a). Television and national stabilization: The Lebanese experience. *Journalism Quarterly 52*, 692–98.

_____. (1975b). The voices of Palestine: A broadcasting house divided. *The Middle East Journal, 29*, 133–50.

_____. (1980). The media of the Arab world and matters of style. *Middle East Review 12* (4) (Summer) and *13*(1), 11–19.

Brunner, E. des. (1953). Rural communications behavior and attitudes in the Middle East. *Rural Sociology, 18*, 149–55.

Carroll, W. (1948). *Persuade or perish*. Boston: Houghton Mifflin Company.

Carruthers, O. (1956, January 15). "Voice of Arabs" stirs Mideast. *New York Times*, p. 5.

Castle, B. (1956, December 29). The fiasco of Sharq al-Adna. *The New Statesman and Nation*, p. 832.

Cawston, R. (1963). Television—A world picture. In *The eighth art: Twenty-five views of tv today*. New York: Holt Rinehart and Winston.

Celarie, A. (1962). La radiodiffusion harmonisee au service du developpement. *Les cahiers africains*, p. 6.

CENTO. (1971). *CENTO seminar on management and training in television and radio broadcasting*. Tehran, November 4–8. Ankara: CENTO.

Chakroun, A. (1975). Broadcasting cooperation between Moslem countries. *EBU Review,* 26(November), 14–17.

_____. (1979, July). Cinquante années de radiodiffusion au Maroc. *Revue de l'UER*, pp. 12–20.

Channel 3 program schedule: January 9–15, 1991. (1991, January). ARAMCO Television. Dhahran, Saudi Arabia: ARAMCO.

Cheriet, A. (1970). *Circulaire no. 2/dg*. RTA. September 25.

Chevaldonné, F. (1981). *La communication inégale. L'accès aux medias dans les campagnes algériennes*. Paris: CNRS.

_____. (1988). *Lunées industrielles: les médias dans le monde arabe*. Aix-en-Provence: Edisud.

Christie, J., Moody, P., and Boyd, D. (1985, March–April). ARABSAT: The impact. *ARAMCO World*, pp. 18–23.

Clark, B. (1959). The B.B.C.'s external service. *International Affairs, 35*(2), 170–80.

CLT program schedule. (1972, April 1). Supplied by CLT, Beirut, Lebanon.

Cobbs, E. (1984). Broadcasting hope to the Middle East. *Focus*, pp. 9–10.

Codding, G. (1959). *Broadcasting without barriers*. New York: UNESCO.

Cohen, G. (1966). *Woman of violence: Memoirs of a young terrorist*. London: Rupert Hart-Davis.

Continental Electronics. (1979, January). Broadcast transmitter customer list.

Cooley, J. K. (1977, January 11). A propaganda war rages on Mideast radio. *Christian Science Monitor*.

_____. (1982). *Libyan sandstorm*. New York: Holt, Rinehart and Winston.

Copeland, M. (1969). *The game of nations*. New York: Simon and Schuster.

Crane, R. J. (1979, April 10). *The politics of international standards: France and the color tv war*. Norwood, N.J.: Ablex Publishing Corporation.

Cycle of programs. (1989). Doha, Qatar: Ministry of Information, Department of Program Control.

Dahklia, J. (1990). *L'oubli de la cité*. Paris: Éditions de la Découverte.

Dajani, K. F. (1979). Egypt's role as a major media producer, supplier and distributor to the Arab world: A historical-descriptive study. Unpublished doctoral dissertation, Temple University, Philadelphia, Pa.

_____. (1980). Egypt: Film center of the Arab world. *Middle East Review, 12*(4)/*13*(1), 28–33.

Dajani, N. H. (1971). The press in Lebanon. *Gazette, 17*, 152–74.

_____. (1973). Media exposure and mobility in Lebanon. *Journalism Quarterly*, (50), 297–305.

_____. (1979). *Lebanon*. London: International Institute of Communications.

Dakhakhni, M. (1976, October 3). Television: Three for the dustbin. *The Egyptian Gazette*, p. 2.

Davis, J. (1988). *Libyan politics: Tribe and revolution, an account of the Zuwaya and their government*. Berkeley: University of California Press.

Dawtrey, A. (1991, January 16). African pay net launches in Senegal. *The Hollywood Reporter*, pp. 4, 8.

De-Borchgrave, A. (1974, April 1). Egypt's anti-Nasser campaign. *Newsweek*, pp. 42–43.

Deeb, M. (1990). New thinking in Libya. *Current History, 89*, 149–52.

Delcourt, X. (1978, July 9–10). Le transistor des veillées paysannes. *Le Monde*, p. 42.

de Onis, J. (1975, March 27). Saudis bury Faisal and hail Khalid. *New York Times*, pp. 1, 3.

Department of Information and Cultural Affairs. (1976). *The human march in the Libyan Arab Republic*. Tripoli: Ministry of Foreign Affairs.

Dexter, G. (1992, January). Dx'ing Africa's hot spots. *Popular Communications*, pp. 16–19.

Diplomatic Correspondence FO 395/663 and 395/557–60, File 2. (n.d.). Commonwealth and Foreign Office Archives. London: United Kingdom.

Dizard, W. P. (1966). *Television: A world view*. Syracuse, N.Y.: Syracuse University Press.

Dodd, Khuri, Rustum, Jurdak, Badr, Najjar, and Haddad. (1943, September). *A pioneer radio poll in Lebanon, Syria, and Palestine*. Beirut, Lebanon: American University of Beirut.

Dodd, P. (1968). Youth and women's emancipation in the United Arab Republic. *Middle East Journal, 22,* 159–72.

Dubai radio and colour television program schedule. (1980). January 1–March 31.

Duvignaud, J. (1970). *Charge at Shebika.* New York: Vintage Books.

EBU Review. (1980, March). *31*(2), 45.

The Economist. (1965, November 13). Faisal the fabian, p. 742.

Eddy, W. (1963). King ibn Sa'ud: "Our faith and your iron." *Middle East Journal 17*(3), 257–63.

Eggerman, M. (1992, December). BBC doubles daily audience in Saudi Arabia, *ARC News,* p. 1.

Egly, M. (1974). Etude de la réception transnationale d'émissions de télévision educative. Paris: Agence de Coopération Culturelle et Technique.

Egyptian Radio and Television Union. (1988). Cairo: Author.

Egyptian Radio and TV Union in brief: 1986/1987. (1987). Cairo: Egyptian Radio and Television Union.

Egyptian Radio and TV Union yearbook. (1986). Cairo: Egyptian Radio and Television Union.

Egyptian Radio-Television Federation. Rate card for 1979. Cairo, Egypt.

Egyptian teletext. (1992). *Espace,* p. 7.

Eilts, H. (1971). Social revolution in Saudi Arabia, Part II. *Parameters,* (Summer), pp. 22–33.

El Fathaly, O. I., Palmer, M., and Chackerian, R. (1977). *Political development and bureaucracy in Libya.* Lexington, Mass.: Lexington Books.

Elgabri, A. Z. (1972, November). Maghrebvision. Aims and present state of television cooperation between Tunisia, Algeria, and Morocco. *EBU Review,* pp. 39–42.

_____. (1974). The Maghreb. In S. W. Head (ed.), *Broadcasting in Africa: A continental survey of radio and television.* Philadelphia: Temple University Press.

El-Hammali, A. A. (1980). *Modernization trends in Libya.* Unpublished doctoral dissertation, University of Pittsburgh, Pittsburgh, Pa.

El-Harouni, Y. (1973, April). Mass media in Egypt and their role in simplifying sciences. *ASBU Review,* pp. 10–22.

El Jerary, A. T. (1981). *The design of a mass media training program: The formulation of a paradigm for the developing nations with particular application to the Libyan example.* Unpublished doctoral dissertation, University of Wisconsin, Madison.

El-Khatib, M. F., and Hirabayashi, G. K. (1958). Communication and political awareness in the villages of Egypt. *Public Opinion Quarterly, 22,* 357–63.

Ellis, W. S. (1961, June). Nasser's other voice. *Harper's Magazine,* p. 58.

El Moudjahid. (1987, January 20).

El Shafei, el M. (1974, January). Maghreb-vision: An experiment in tv cooperation between Tunisia, Algeria and Morocco. *ASBU Review,* pp. 26–30.

El-Shaked, M. (1973, October). Qatar radio enters its sixth year. *ASBU Review,* pp. 1–2.

El-Shenaway, W. (1970, December). An educational television pilot project in Cairo. *Educational Broadcasting International, 4,* 301–04.

El-Sherif, M. (1980, March). The Arab attitude to mass media. *Intermedia 8*(2)(March), 28–29.

El-Zilitni, A. M. (1981). *Literacy in Libya: A feasibility study.* Unpublished doctoral dissertation, Ohio State University, Columbus.

England in Egypt. (1935, January 4), *Wireless World*, p. 15.

Extracts from pan Arab media survey, 1978: Saudi Arabia. (1978). Pan Arab Computer Center Information Systems.

Facts about Iftah Ya Simsim. Furnished by the Arabian Gulf States Joint Program Production Institution, Kuwait.

Fanon, F. (1965). *A dying colonialism.* (Translated by H. Chevalier.) New York: Grove Press.

Farley, R. (1971). *Planning for development in Libya.* New York: Praeger Publishers.

Farrag, M. Y. (1965). *The postrevolutionary development of international broadcasts in the United Arab Republic.* Unpublished master's thesis, Stanford University, Stanford, Calif.

Fattah-Allah, A. (1991). *La régionalisation radiophonique au Maroc.* Unpublished doctoral dissertation (Communication Sciences), Université de Paris-2, Paris.

Finance gap short-circuits ARABSAT. (1985, February 15). *Middle East Economic Digest*, p. 22.

First, R. (1974). *Libya: The elusive revolution.* Middlesex: Penguin Books.

Five year plan allocation up by 2 percent. (1976, January 30). *Middle East Economic Digest*, p. 22.

Flint, J. (1989). Black hole of Beirut. *Gannett Center Journal, 3*(4), 65–73.

_____. (1990, March 18). Beirut. *Observer* (London), p. 17.

FM station gaining popularity. (1988, February). *Arab Ad*, p. 28.

Foote, J. S., and Amin, H. (1992, August). *Global TV news in developing countries: CNN's expansion to Egypt.* Paper presented at the meeting of Association for Education in Journalism and Mass Communication, Montreal, Canada.

Foreign Broadcast Information Service. (1979). Monitoring Report.

Foreign Broadcast Information Service, European Section. (1948a). Report 311.

_____. (1948b). Report 314.

Fourth cycle JTV. Supplied by Jordan Television Commercial Department.

Free China Weekly. (1979, July 15). Taipei, Riyadh pledge cooperation. 20(27).

Freed, P. E. (1979). *Towers to eternity: Reaching the unreached.* Nashville, Tenn.: Sceptre Books.

Freed, R. (1972). *Reaching Arabs for Christ.* Chatham, N.J.: Trans World Radio.

French swap arms for hostages, a la Ollie. (1987, December 14). *U.S. News and World Report*, p. 17.

Friedman, T. L. (1989). *From Beirut to Jerusalem.* New York: Farrar, Straus, and Giroux.

Frost, J. M. (Ed.). (1970). *WRTH (world radio-tv handbook).* New York: Billboard Publications.

_____. (Ed.). (1980). *WRTH (world radio-tv handbook).* New York: Billboard Publications.

Gadaffi to purge news and secret service. (1989, January 18). *The Times* (London), p. 7.

Gallagher, M. (1985). *Becoming aware: Human rights and the family.* Paris: UNESCO.

Gallman, W. J. (1964). *Iraq under General Nuri.* Baltimore: The Johns Hopkins

Press.

Gartley, J. (1980). Broadcasting in Libya. *Middle East Review 12*(4)/*13*(1), 34–39.

Gavin, R. J. (1975). *Aden under British rule*. New York: Harper and Row, Publishers.

Geertz, C. (1975). *The interpretation of cultures*. New York: Basic Books.

Glubb, J. B. (1959). *Britain and the Arabs*. London: Hodder and Stoughton.

Goldman, K. (1992, June 24). Saudi-controlled firm wins bidding for troubled United Press International. *Wall Street Journal*, p. B10.

Grandin, T. (1939). The political use of radio. *Geneva Studies*, *10*(3), 50–55.

_____. (1971). *The political use of radio*. New York: New York Times Books.

Green, T. (1974). Egypt. In S. W. Head (ed.), *Broadcasting in Africa: A continental survey of radio and television*. Philadelphia: Temple University Press.

Grassi, G. (1990, September 25). RAI-TV planning Arab link-up, *The Hollywood Reporter*, p. I-5.

Gress, L. (1973, September 3). Jordan television: The first 5 years. *EBU Review*, pp. 30–31.

Grille des programmes. (1980, January). Radio Monte Carlo Moyen Orient. SOMERA.

Guide to broadcasting stations. (1970). London: Iliffe Books.

Gulf Daily News. (1979, December 4), p. 6.

Gulf Mirror. (1980a, January 12–18). TV and tape may blank out screens. (Kuwait) p. 3.

_____. (1980b, January 12–18), pp. 16, 17.

Hale, J. (1975). *Radio power: Propaganda and international broadcasting*. Philadelphia: Temple University Press.

Harik, I. F. (1971). Opinion leaders and the mass media in rural Egypt: A reconsideration of the two-step flow of communications hypothesis. *American Political Science Review*, *65*, 731–40.

Harris, L. C. (1986). *Libya: Qadhafi's revolution and the modern state*. Boulder, Colo.: Westview Press.

Harris wins $5.2 million Egyptian radio contract. (1979, March 19). Melbourne, Fla.: Harris Corporation Public Relations Department.

Hashemite Broadcasting Service. (n.d.) *History of the Hashemite Broadcasting Service*.

Hatem, M. A.-K. (1974). *Information and the Arab cause*. London: Longmans Group.

Head, S. W. (1962). The NAEB goes to the Sudan. *The NAEB Journal 21*(2), 48–53.

_____. (1974). *Broadcasting in Africa: A continental survey of radio and television*. Philadelphia: Temple University Press.

Heikal, M. (1973). *The Cairo Documents*. New York: Doubleday and Company.

Heralding Christ Jesus' Blessings. (n.d.). Opa Locka, Fla.: HCJB.

High Adventure Broadcasting Network. (n.d.). *Information summary*, p. 2.

Hijazi, I. A. (1985, October 18). 5 reported dead in a Lebanon raid. *New York Times*, p. A12.

Hilleson, S. (1941, July). Broadcasting to the near East. *Royal Central Asian Journal*, 27, part III, 340–48.

Hirabayashi, G. K., and El Khatib, M. F. (1958). Communication and political awareness in the villages of Egypt. *Public Opinion Quarterly 22*(3), 357–63.

Hirsch, M.-L. (1968, January). Professional solidarity expressed in concrete terms. *EBU Review*, p. 107B.

The history of the U.A.R. radio since its establishment in 1934 until now. (1970a, August). *Arab Broadcasts*, translated by F. Barrada, pp. 63–70.

Holden, D. (1966). *Farewell to Arabia*. London: Faber and Faber.

Horsnell, M. (1990, August 20). World service gives listeners a radio lifeline. *The Times* (London), p. 4.

Horwitz, T. (1990, September 4). Embargo's noose still isn't strangling life in teeming Baghdad. *Wall Street Journal*, pp. A1, 10.

_____. (1991a, May 2). With Gulf War over, Saudi fundamentalists reassert themselves. *New York Times*, pp. A1, A17.

_____. (1991b, December 26). Forgotten rebels: After heeding calls to turn on Saddam, Shiites feel betrayed. *Wall Street Journal*, pp. A1, A5.

Hottinger, A. (1984, June). Personality cult and party in Iraq. *Swiss Review of International Affairs*, *12*, 12–15.

Houidi, F., and Najar, R. (1983). *Presse, radio et télévision en Tunisie*. Tunis: Maison tunisienne de l'édition.

Hurewitz, J. C. (1968). *The struggle for Palestine*. New York: Greenwood Press.

Hussein, S. (1977). *Democracy is a comprehensive view of life*. Republic of Iraq Documentary Series No. 61. Baghdad, Iraq: Ministry of Information.

Huston, P. (1979). *Third world women speak out*. New York: Praeger.

Ibrahim, Y. M. (1987, January 29). French-owned station sways mideastern governments; Yasser Arafat's bulletins. *Wall Street Journal*, pp. 1, 13.

_____. (1992a, March 4). TV is beamed at Arabs. The Arabs beam back. *New York Times*, p. A4.

_____. (1992b, June 29). Saudis pursue media acquisitions, gaining influence in the Arab world. *New York Times*, p. D8.

International Press Institute. (1954). *The news from the Middle East*. Zurich: IPI. Reprinted by Arno Press, 1972.

Interstages. (1979, October). L'enjeu socio-culturel du cinéma en Tunisie. P. 107.

Iraq Jack keeps GIs laughing. (1990, August 23). *The Washington Times*, p. A1.

Issawi, C. (1963). *Egypt in revolution: An economic analysis*. London: Oxford University Press.

Jamming ends. (1987, July 17). *The Times* (London), p. 10.

Jarrar, F. A. (1970). *Television in Jordan*. Amman, Jordan: Jordan Television Corporation.

Jeune Afrique. (1990, June 11).

Jibril, M. (1977, April). Le marasme télévisé. *Lamalif*, *87*, 26–34.

Johansen, O. L. (Ed.). (1955). *WRTH (world radio-tv handbook)*. Copenhagen: Johansen.

Jordan Television Engineering Department. (1979, October). Television transmitter locations and power. Amman, Jordan.

Jordan television foreign program, JTV 6. Fourth cycle television schedule. Supplied by Jordan Television Commercial Department.

Journal Officiel. (1963, August 1). Décrêt No. 63.684.

_____. (1964, June 27). *150*, Loi no. 64-621.

Kader, S. A. (1976, January). Role of radio and television in strengthening Afro-

Arab ties. *ASBU Review*, pp. 5–12.

Kahn, R. A. (1967). *Radio Cairo and Egyptian foreign policy, 1956–1959.* Unpublished Ph.D. dissertation, University of Michigan, Ann Arbor, Mich.

Kallati, I. (1973). La politique marocaine de l'information face au développement. Paris: Institut français de presse.

Katz, E. (1971, June). Television comes to the Middle East. *Trans-Action,* pp. 42–50.

_____. (1977). Can authentic cultures service new media? *Journal of Communication,* 27(2), 113–121.

_____. (1979). Cultural continuity and change: Role of the media. In K. Nordenstreng and H. Schiller, (eds.), *National Sovereignty and International Communication,* Norwood, N.J.: Ablex.

Katz, E., and Wedell, G. (1977). *Broadcasting in the third world.* Cambridge, Mass.: Harvard University Press.

Keith, A. N. (1965). *Children of Allah.* Boston: Little, Brown and Company.

Khadduri, M. (1969). *Republican Iraq.* London: Oxford University Press.

Khader, B. (1987). Libyan oil and money. In B. Khader and B. El-Wifati (eds.), *The economic development of Libya,* London: Croom Helm, pp. 195–212.

Khaldun, B. (1973, April). Educational programmes in the Algerian radio and tv. *ASBU Review,* pp. 5–9.

Khoury, C. (1976, March 28). The Lebanese radio and television stations present: The reluctant partisans. *Monday Morning,* pp. 40–44.

King, J. (1991, August 3). *Iftah Ya SimSim.* ABC Evening News. New York.

Kingdom of Saudi Arabia Central Planning Organization. (1970). Development plan 1390 A.H. Riyadh: Author.

Knapp, W. (1970). *Tunisia: Land and people.* New York: Walker and Company.

Knowing the job. (1980, January 29). *Egyptian Gazette,* p. 2.

Koppes, C. R. (1976). Captain Mahan, General Gordon and the origins of the term "Middle East." *Middle Eastern Studies,* 12(1), 95–98.

Kuwait television schedule for first quarter. (1980). Supplied by Ministry of Information.

Labaki, G. T. (1986, December). On the air! The rise of private radio and television stations in Lebanon. *Lebanon Monitor,* 2(1), pp. 1, 2, and 8.

Labib, S. (1972, July). TV in the culture struggle. *ASBU Review,* pp. 43–52.

Lacheraf, M. (1965). *L'algérie: Nation et société.* Paris: Maspero.

Laffin, J. (1975). *The Arab mind considered.* New York: Taplinger Publishing Company.

L'Algérie Contemporaine. Gouverneur général de l'Algérie, Service d'Information. (1954). Paris: Coulouma.

Lamalif. (1977, April). P. 87.

_____. (1979, February). P. 104

Lamb, D. (1988). *The Arabs: Journeys beyond the mirage.* New York: Vantage Books.

Lamrhili, A. El K. (1980, June). Information ou debilisation. *Al Asas 20.*

Lapham, R. J. (1970, May). Family planning and fertility in Tunisia. *Demography* 7(2), 241–53.

LBC 1987 commercial spots break record. (1988, February). *Arab Ad,* p. 28.

LE 1.45 m modern tv studio opened. (1974, August 7). *Egyptian Gazette,* p. 1.

Lebanon's tower of babel. (1987, July 27). *Al-Forsan* (The Leaders), p. 47.

Le Matin (du Sahara). (1980a, June 2).

_____. (1980b, July 27).

_____. (1990, November 9).

Le Monde Economique. (1956, June). Tunisia faces the future. Special Issue, p. 196.

Lerner, D. (1958). *The passing of traditional society: Modernizing the Middle East.* New York: The Free Press.

Lewis, P. (1991, July 28). As life improves in Baghdad, Hussein government digs in, *New York Times,* pp. A1, A8.

Libya extends cultural revolution to broadcasting. (1973, June 4). *New York Times,* p. 3.

Libya, now 17, gets TV. (1968, December 25). *New York Times,* p. 38.

In Libya, wary middle class endures. (1987, April 21). *New York Times,* p. 3.

Libyans televise corruption trials. (1980, April 18). *London Times,* p. 8.

Lichty, L. W. (1970) *World and international broadcasting: A bibliography.* Washington: Association for Professional Broadcasting Education.

Lorimor, E. S., and Dunn, S. W. (1968–1969). Use of the mass media in Egypt. *Public Opinion Quarterly, 32,* 680–87.

Loya, A. (1962). Radio propaganda of the United Arab Republic—An analysis. *Middle Eastern Affairs, 13*(4), 98–110.

McDaniel, D. (1980). Some notes on political broadcasting in the Arab world. *Middle East Review, 12*(4)*/13*(1), 5–10.

MacDonald, C. A. (1977). Radio Bari: Italian wireless propaganda in the Middle East and British countermeasures 1934–1938. *Middle Eastern Studies 13,* 195–205.

McEwen, A. (1988, September 2). Malta and Libyans end visas and start joint broadcasting. *London Times,* p. 7.

Mackenzie, A. J. (1938). *Propaganda boom.* London: John Gifford.

McKenzie, V. (1940). *Here lies Goebbels.* London: Michael Joseph.

McLachlan, K. (1987). The Libyan south: Background to current developments and future outlook. In B. Khader and B. El-Wifati (eds.), *The economic development of Libya,* pp. 37–57. London: Croom Helm.

Macro, E. (1968). *Yemen and the Western world.* New York: Praeger.

Madanat, N. (1976). *The story of Jordan television.* Amman, Jordan, 8 August. Mimeographed.

The Maghreb at a glance. (1990, May 9). *Variety,* p. 53.

Mahamdi, Y. (1989). Tradition, "national" culture and television in Algeria. *Media Development, 2,* 28–31.

Mahjoub, E. M. (1976). The role of the change agent. In *Change in Tunisia,* Albany: State University of New York Press.

Mansell, G. (1982). *Let truth be told.* London: Weidenfeld and Nicolson.

Marks, J. (1990, September 7). *Gulf crisis report.* Hilversum, The Netherlands.

Mellah, M. (1991, May 25). En Couverture. *Le Renouveau* (Tunis) Magazine (TV Guide), No. 167, pp. 4–7.

Merdad, A. S. (1987). *A comparative analytical study of the Arabian Gulf broadcasting systems: The foreign contextual television penetration.* M.A. thesis, Michigan State University, East Lansing, Mich.

Metwally, E. A. (n.d.). *Historical survey of the Egyptian broadcast with background of pre-revolution period.* Cairo: Egyptian Radio-Television Federation. Mimeographed.

The Middle East and North Africa. (1980). London: Europa Publications.

Middle East Economic Digest. (1976, January 30). *20*(5).

The Middle East connection. (1980, November 3). *Video Week*, p. 4.

Middle East television program schedule. (1990, March 7). Virginia Beach, Va.: Christian Broadcasting Network.

Ministry of Information and Culture. (1971). *Sudan today.* Nairobi, Kenya: University Press of Africa.

_____. (1979, March 17). Sudan refutes Libyan and Syrian distorted news reporting. *Newsletter*, 2, p. 4.

Mirshak, M. (1972, April 13). Mother hen government: Farid Salman's campaign for press freedom. *The Daily Star* (Beirut), p. 7.

Mohamed, S. K. (1965). A plan for the alleviation of illiteracy through the use of television in the United Arab Republic. Unpublished master's thesis, Boston University.

Mostefaoui, B. (1988). Tendances actuelles de l'audiovisuel en Algérie: A propos de brèches dans le monopole de l'état. In F. Chevaldonné (ed.), *Lunes industrielles: Les médias dans le monde arabe.* Aix-en-Provence: Edisud.

_____. (1990, February, March, and May). La télévision au Maghreb, *Tribune d'octobre.*

Mowlana, H. (1971). Mass media systems and communication behavior. In *The Middle East: A handbook.* London: Anthony Blond.

_____. (1974). Mass communication elites and national systems in the Middle East. In *The contribution of the mass media to the development of consciousness in a changing world.* Leipzig, East Germany.

_____. (1976). Trends in Middle Eastern societies. In *Mass Communication Policies in Changing Cultures.* New York: John Wiley.

The murder of King Faisal. (1975, April 7). *Newsweek*, pp. 21–23.

Nadir, M. J. Minister Plenipotentiary, Embassy of Saudi Arabia. (1971). The modernization of Saudi Arabia. Talk given at Morgan State College, Baltimore, March 2.

Najar, R., and Ben Said, K. (1991). *Les télévisions du monde.* Tunis: Maison Tunisienne de l'Édition (Z).

Nallino, C. A. (1939). *Raccolta di scritti, Vol. I: L'Arabia Sa'udiana.* Rome: Instituto per l'Oriente.

Nasser, G. A. (1955). *Egypt's liberation: The philosophy of revolution.* Washington, D.C.: Public Affairs Press.

Nasser, M. K. (1979). *Press, politics and power: Egypt's Heikal and Al-Ahram.* Ames, Iowa: Iowa State University Press.

_____. (1990). Egyptian mass media under Nasser and Sadat: Two models of press management and control. *Journalism Monographs, (124).*

Nassr, B. E. (1963, June 10). TV in Egypt. *Broadcasting*, pp. 86–87.

Nelson, H. D. et al. (1979). *Libya: A country study.* Washington, D.C.: Government Printing Office.

Nelson, H. D. et al. (1988). *Tunisia: A country study.* Washington, D.C.: U.S. Government Printing Office.

New hours of overseas transmission on shortwave by radio Lebanon. (1972).

Supplied by Radio Lebanon Department of International Programs, April 1.

News. (1979, January). *ASBU Review*, pp. 34–35.

Nimeiry's justice. (1976, August, 16). *Newsweek*, pp. 36–37.

1978 yearbook of international trade statistics. (1979). New York: United Nations.

Novotay, J. (1976). Sudan rural television project. Pictorial brief. Rome: FAO.

Nutting, A. (1967). *No end of a lesson.* New York: Clarkson N. Potter.

_____. (1972). *Nasser.* New York: E. P. Dutton and Company.

Nyrop, R. F. et al. (1977). *Area handbook for the Yemens.* Washington, D.C.: Government Printing Office.

Oman colour television: TV transmitters in operation. (n.d.). Supplied by Ministry of Information, Muscat, Oman.

Oman television schedule: January 1 to March 31, 1980. (n.d.). Supplied by Ministry of Information. In English and Arabic.

Organ, J. (1990, August 13). *Radio Canada International news release.* Montreal: Radio Canada International.

ORTF '73. (1973). Paris: Presses Pocket.

Osterhaus, W. E. (1979). *Tele-Liban 1979: An evaluation with some recommendations.* October. Photocopy.

Ottaway, D., and Ottaway, M. (1970). *Algeria: The politics of a socialist revolution.* Berkeley: University of California Press.

Palestine calling. (1936, May 1). *Wireless World,* p. 424.

Palestine Department of Posts and Telegraphs annual report, 1935. (1935). Jerusalem.

Palestine Department of Posts and Telegraphs annual report, 1936. (1936). Jerusalem.

Pan Arab Computer Center. (1978, December). *Extracts from pan Arab media survey 1978: Saudi Arabia.* Kuwait City: Kuwait.

Pan Arab Research Center. (1982a, October). *Kuwait media survey.* Kuwait: PARC.

_____. (1982b, November). *Basic media survey, Saudi Arabia.* Kuwait: PARC.

Partner, P. (1988). *Arab voices: The BBC Arabic service 1938–1988.* London: BBC External Services.

Pawlouschek, A. (1991, March–April). Arabvision—A new player in the world of news exchange. *Intermedia. 19*(2), 34–36.

Peace ship broadcasts to Arabs and the Israelis. (1973, May 24). *New York Times.*

Peled, T., and Katz, E. (1974). Media functions in wartime: The Israel home front in October 1973. In J. G. Blumler and E. Katz (eds.), *The uses of mass communications.* Beverly Hills, Calif.: Sage Publications.

Penrose, E., and Penrose, E. F. (1978). *Iraq: International relations and national development.* London: Ernest Benn; Boulder, Colo.: Westview Press.

Persian Gulf to get more tv. (1991, November 6). *Wall Street Journal,* p. A10.

Philby, H. St. J. (1952). *Arabian jubilee.* London: Robert Hale.

_____. (1955). *Sa'udi Arabia.* London: Ernest Benn.

Phipps, K. (1972, April 10). The stranglehold of radio Lebanon. *The Daily Star* (Beirut), pp. 4, 5.

Pigé, F. (1966). *Radiodiffusion et télévision au Maghreb.* Paris: Fondation nationale des sciences politiques.

Present-day Iraqi culture. (1970). Baghdad, Iraq: Ministry of Culture and Information.

La Presse. (1962). Les projets gouvernementaux. Tunis, October 16, p. 2.

Qaddafi fails to make live appearance after bombing. (1986, June 12). *New York Times*, p. 11.

Qadhafi, M. (1976). *The green book.* Tripoli: Public Establishment for Publishing, Advertising, and Distribution.

Rachty, G., and Sabat, K. *Importation of films for cinema and television in Egypt.* Paris: UNESCO.

Radio and colour television advertising rates effective January, 1980. Dubai.

Radio Baghdad in English. (1990, August 24). C-SPAN Television. Washington, D.C.: C-SPAN.

Radio Bahrain commercial rate card number 5. Provided by Radio Bahrain.

Radio Corporation of America. (1969, June 27). *Summary report of propagation and coverage as related to Dammam, Saudi Arabia tv station.* Livorno, Italy.

Radio France Internationale. (1991). *Répertoire de l'information en Afrique et dans l'Océan Indien.* Paris: Radio France.

Radio Jordan English service. (1979). Schedule for July, August, September.

Radio Jordan frequency schedule. (1979, June 1). Amman, Jordan: Hashemite Broadcasting Service, Engineering Services Department.

Radio Qatar from Doha. (1986, January). Doha, Qatar: Ministry of Information, Department of Broadcasting.

Radio schedule. (1991, September 23). *Times of Oman*, p. 8.

Radio station peace and progress. (n.d.).

Ragheb, M. E., and Haddad, Y. (1979). *A pilot study on the opinions of certain categories of citizens of the establishment of a second television channel (1978).* Kuwait: Ministry of Information.

Randall, J. (1991, June 30). Tunisian crackdown targets Islamic fundamentalists. *Minneapolis Star-Tribune* (from *Washington Post*), p. 13A.

Rand McNally illustrated world atlas. (1975). New York: Rand McNally.

Rawya, A. (1965). A historical and cultural analysis of broadcasting in the United Arab Republic 1932–1962. M.A. thesis, San Francisco State College.

Recommendations of the eighth meeting of the permanent program committee. (1975, April). *ASBU Review*, pp. 16–28.

Report on the Near East farm broadcasting seminar. (1963). Cairo, March 2–April 5. Rome: FAO.

Republic of Algeria. (1970, 1974, 1978). *Plan quadriennial 1970–1973; Plan quadriennial 1974–1977; Plan quadriennial 1978–1981.* Algiers: Secrétariat d'Etat au Plan.

Republic of Tunisia: A communications factbook. (1964). Report R-87-64, June. Washington, D.C.: U.S. Information Agency.

Revolution Africaine. (1979, January 31).

Revue de l'UER. (1979, July).

Richardson, D. R. (1979, July 23). Malta: The rock that may trip Qadhafi. *U.S. News and World Report*, pp. 40–41.

Riding, A. (1990, October 20). Tunisians, in search of roots, turn toward Iraq. *The New York Times*, p. 4.

Rolo, C. J. (1941). *Radio goes to war.* New York: G. P. Putnam's Sons.

Rubin, B. (1975–1976). The media and the Middle East. *Middle East Review* (Winter), pp. 28–32.

Rubin, R. (1973). Israel's foreign information program. *Gazette 19*, 65–78.

Rugh, W. A. (1975). Arab media and politics during the October war. *The Middle East Journal, 29*, 310–28.

_____. (1979). *The Arab press: News media and political process in the Arab world.* Syracuse, N.Y.: Syracuse University Press.

_____. (1980). Saudi mass media and society in the Faisal era. In W. A. Beling (ed.), *King Faisal and the modernization of Saudi Arabia.* Boulder, Colo.: Westview Press.

Said, E. *Qatar broadcasting service: 1980/1981.* (n.d.). Qatar: Ministry of Information.

Saudi Arabia: No singing or dancing. (1992, February). *Index on Censorship*, p. 22.

Saudi Arabia: The impact of the Gulf crisis on the press. (1990). *Intermedia, 18*(6), 7.

Saudi Arabian broadcasting: A synopsis. (1980). Supplied by the Office of the Assistant Deputy Minister for Radio and TV, Riyadh, Saudi Arabia.

Saudi Arabian television: A synopsis. (n.d.). Supplied by the Office of the Assistant Deputy Minister for Radio and Television, Riyadh, Saudi Arabia.

S.B.F. (1991, May 26). Pluralité. *La Presse* (Tunis) Weekend (TV Guide), No. 190, p. 15.

Schmidt, D. A. (1961, July 17). Kassim dedicates radio station, first of Soviet's Iraqi projects. *New York Times*, p. 7.

Schmidt, W. E. (1991, August 18). Cairo's rule on tape and video: Copy it and sell it. *New York Times*, pp. 1, 9.

Sennitt, A. G. (1991). *World radio-TV handbook.* New York: Billboard Publications.

Shalaby, A. A. (1979). The Arab world: An eligible case for collective self-reliance. In *International foundation for developmental alternatives, dossier 10*, pp. 3–11.

Sharabi, H. (1966). *Nationalism and revolution in the Arab world.* Princeton, N.J.: D. Van Nostrand Company.

Shobaili, A. S. (1971). A historical and analytical study of broadcasting and press in Saudi Arabia. Unpublished doctoral dissertation, The Ohio State University, Columbus, Ohio.

Shouby, E. (1951). The influence of the Arabic language on the psychology of the Arabs. *Middle East Journal, 5*(3).

Shummo, A. (1977). Communication delivery services in developing nations. Paper delivered at International Institute of Communications Conference, Washington, D.C.

Smith, A. (1973). *The shadow in the cave: The broadcaster, the audience and the state.* London: Allen and Unwin.

Smith, R. M. (1974, January–February). Censorship in the Middle East. *Columbia Journalism Review*, pp. 43–49.

Smith, W. A. (1979). Dr. Hakim: A new voice in the village. Washington, D.C.: Academy for Educational Development.

Soley, L. C. (1989). *Radio warfare: OSS and CIA subversive propaganda.* New York: Praeger.

Soley, L. C., and Nichols, J. S. (1987). *Clandestine radio broadcasting: A study of revolutionary and counterrevolutionary electronic communication.* New York: Praeger.

Sound on television broadcasting in the overseas territories, handbook 1960. (1960).

London, England: Information Department, Colonial Office.

Souriau, C. (1975). La Libye moderne. In *La Libye nouvelle: rupture et continuité*. Paris: Centre de Recherches et d'Etudes sur les Sociétés Méditerranéennes.

Special Committee for the UN/Libyan Institute for Radio and Wire and Wireless Communications. (1971). Operational plan (draft). In Arabic.

Spotlight: The Maghreb. (1990, May 9). *Variety*, p. 41.

State of Qatar: Qatar t.v. (n.d.). Doha, Qatar: Ministry of Information.

Stolz, J. (1983). Les algériens regardent Dallas. In *Les nouvelles chaînes. Techniques modernes de la télécommunication et le tiers monde: Pièges et Promesses*. Paris: PUF.

Straubhaar, J. D., and Boyd, D. A. (1989). Adoption and use of videocassette recorders in the third world. In J. L. Salvaggio and J. Bryant (eds.), *Media use in the information age: Emerging patterns of adoption and consumer use*, pp. 163–178. Hillsdale: N.J.: Lawrence Erlbaum Associates.

Studio One and Studio Two program guide. (1990, July–December). Dhahran, Saudi Arabia: ARAMCO.

Sudan Echo. (1965, July 6). Radio and television advertising in the Sudan.

Sudanow. (1979a, October). Radio, p. 70.

———. (1979b, October). Television, pp. 69–70.

Sudan Television. (n.d.). Extension of television service—Sudan centralized regional rural tv programmes project, 1978–1980. Khartoum, Sudan.

———. (n.d.). The first survey of television: 1968–1969. In Arabic. Translated portions provided by U.S. Information Agency, Khartoum Office.

SUNA-Daily Bulletin. (1979, October 10). On the Iraqi News Agency allegations. 3180, p. 7.

Syrian Television schedule. (1979). Supplied by Syrian Television.

Tanner, H. (1975, September 12). Egyptian takeover of voice of Palestine broadcasts is indicated. *New York Times*, p. 3.

Tawffik, T. (1980). Television in Egypt. Paper delivered at Annenberg School of Communications World Communication Conference, Philadelphia, Pa.

Telecommunications—MEED special report. *Middle East Economic Digest*.

Tele-Orient program schedule. (1972, April 3–9). Supplied by Tele-Orient, Beirut, Lebanon.

La télévision étraugère. (1990, July 4). *Almaghrib*, p. 7.

Television schedule. (1991, September 17). *Al Watan* (Oman), p. 3.

Television's 12,000. (1977, April 7). *Egyptian Gazette*, p. 2.

Terrorists blow up pro-Christian tv station in south Lebanon. (1983, August 3). *Variety*, p. 57.

Text of the presidential decree on the law concerning the establishment of the Egyptian Radio-Television Federation. (1970, August). *Arab Broadcasts*, translated by F. Barrada, pp. 50–51.

Thieves who steal your tv shows. (1980, September 9). *Nottingham Evening Post*, p. 9C.

Thomas, R. (1972). *Broadcasting and democracy in France*. London: Bradford University Press.

The Times. (London). (1990, September 5). P. 10.

Tracy, W. (1979, September–October). Sesame opens. *Aramco World Magazine*. pp.

9–17.

Trois fois 50 métres plus haut que la tour Eiffel. (n.d.). *Médi 1 votre média pour le Maghreb*. Paris: Radio Méditerrané International, p. 10.

Truth is in the air. (1987, June 6). *The Economist*, pp. 19–20, 22.

Tunisia. *Kessing's contemporary archives*, May 23, 1980. P. 30264.

Tunisia: A country study. (1979). Washington, D.C.: U.S. Government Printing Office.

TV. (1990, January 8). *Daily Gulf Times*, p. 4.

TV employees banned from private work. (1976, November 29). *Egyptian Gazette*, p. l.

TV in the Gulf states. (1979). Riyadh, Saudi Arabia: Gulfvision.

TV today. (1991, September 18). *Gulf Times Tabloid*, p. 2.

UNESCO. (1949). *Press, film, radio*. Paris: UNESCO.

_____. (1951). *Press, film, radio*. Paris: UNESCO.

_____. (1965). *World radio and television*. Paris: UNESCO.

_____. (1973). *Management and planning of new systems of communication: conclusions drawn from an inventory of communication resources in Tunisia*. Paris: UNESCO.

_____. (1975). *Arab states media innovation system*. Paris: UNESCO.

UNESCO statistical yearbook 1977. (1978). Paris: UNESCO.

United Nations statistical yearbook 1978. (1979). New York: United Nations.

United States Advisory Commission on Public Diplomacy. (1991). *1991 report*. Washington, D.C.: Author.

United States Agency for International Development (USAID). (1982). *Project profiles*. Washington, D.C.: Clearinghouse on Development Communication.

United States Department of State. (1964). Saudi Arabia, establishment of television system in Saudi Arabia. *United States treaties and other international agreements*. Washington, D.C.: U.S. Government Printing Office.

United States Information Agency (USIA). (1960, July 1). *International radio broadcasting in the United Arab Republic*. Research Note 32-60.

_____. (1961, August 10). *UAR reorganizes and increases its international radio broadcasting services*. Research Note 21-61.

_____. 1975a. "VOA-CAAP audience estimate for Kuwait 1974." Research Report E-7-75, June 16.

_____. (1975b, December 16). *VOA audience estimate for Israel 1974*. E-15-75.

_____. (1984, December 18). *Radio Baghdad, BBC and Saudi radio leading foreign stations in Kuwait; VOA tenth*. Washington, D.C.: Office of Research, Research Memorandum.

_____. (1985, May 7). *Israeli and Syrian radios have most Jordanian listeners; VOA ninth with 10.8 percent rating*. Washington, D.C.: Office of Research, Research Memorandum.

_____. (1986, October). *Egyptian stations have largest foreign radio audiences in northern Sudan*. Washington, D.C.: Office of Research, Research Report R-22-86.

_____. (1987a, March). *VOA behind other international broadcasters in Bahrain and the United Arab Emirates*. Washington, D.C.: U.S. Information Agency.

_____. (1987b, July 31). *VOA reaches one in eight better educated adults in Saudi*

Arabian cities; Radio Monte Carlo most popular. Washington, D.C.: U.S. Information Agency.

_____. (1991, February 14). *Foreign radio listening rates high in four Arab gulf nations; VOA increases audience during crisis.* Washington, D.C.: U.S. Information Office of Research.

_____. Office of Research. (1973, August 30). *Media habits of priority groups in Saudi Arabia—Part II: Appendix.* Research Report R-20-73A, Washington, D.C.

_____. Office of Research. (1975, June 16). *VOA-CAAP audience estimate for Kuwait 1974.* Research Report E-7-75, 16 June.

_____. Office of Research and Analysis. (1961, August 8). *UAR broadcasting.* Research Note 19-61.

_____. Office of Research and Assessment. (1974, March 27). *Media habits and VOA listening among priority audiences in Bahrain.* Research Report R-1-74.

United States International Communication Agency (USICA), Office of Research and Evaluation. (1978a, August 16). *Listening to international radio stations, including VOA, and perceptions and interests of radio listeners in urban Sudan.* Research Report E-17-78.

_____. (1978b, September 12). *Listening to international radio stations, including VOA, and perceptions and interests of radio audiences in urban Jordan.* Research Report E-20-78.

_____. (1978c, October 6). *Listening to international radio stations, including VOA, and listener reactions and program interests in urban Egypt (1977).* Research Report E-23-78.

Urquhart, B. (1972). *Hammarskjold.* New York: Alfred A. Knopf.

USAFE television story. (1955, December 13). From the files of the Office of Information for the Armed Forces, OASD (M&RA). Washington, D.C.: Department of Defense.

Vatin, J-C. (1974). *L'Algérie politique: Histoire et société.* Paris: Armand Colin.

VHF television assignments obtained for Aden at the African VHF/UHF broadcasting conference, Geneva, 1963. (n.d.). Document written by British authorities.

VOA Arabic broadcasts—Yesterday and today. (n.d.). Washington, D.C.: VOA Arabic Service.

Voice of America. (1991, February 26). *VOA broadcasting initiatives in the Middle East.* Washington, D.C.: Voice of America.

Voice of venom. (1958, March). *Time,* pp. 28–30.

Voss, H. (1962). *Rundfunk und fernsehen in Afrika.* Koln: Verlag/Deutscher Wirtschaftsdienst, GmbH.

Waldman, P. (1991, October 22). Syrians have a way of recalling the war of 1973 as a big win. *Wall Street Journal,* pp. A1, 13.

_____. (1992, March 5). Western-style news, entertainment is dished out to Arab viewers via MBC. *Wall Street Journal,* p. A12.

Wallace, C. (1988, January 7). Radio: Town crier of the Arab world. *Los Angeles Times,* pp. 1, 12, 13.

Walpole, N. C. et al. (1971). *Area handbook for Saudi Arabia.* Washington, D.C.: U.S. Government Printing Office.

Watson, P. S. (1965). *Operation report,* Jidda, Saudi Arabia: NBCI.

What do you know about Egyptian broadcasting? (1971, July). *Arab Broadcasts,* translated by F. Yousef, pp. 63–77.

Whittstock, M. (1992, January 25). Broadcasting the world to a captive audience. *Times Sunday Review*, pp. 4, 5.

Wilbur, D. N. (1969). *United Arab Republic: Egypt*. New Haven, Conn.: Hraf Press.

Williams, K. (1933). *Ibn Sa'ud: The puritan king of Arabia*. London: Jonathan Cape.

Wood, J. (1991, July/August). Desert sounds: International broadcasting in the Arab world. *IEE Review*, pp. 275–80.

Wood, R. E. (1979). Language choice in transnational radio broadcasting. *Journal of Communication, 29*(2), 112–23.

World Bank. (1989). *World development report, 1989*. New York: Oxford University Press.

World Bank atlas, 1978. (1978). Washington, D.C.: World Bank.

World radio handbook. (1957). Copenhagen, Denmark: Lindorffsalle Hellerup.

World radio tv handbook. (1991). Amsterdam, The Netherlands: Billboard.

Wren, C. S. (1980, August 15). Lebanese hills echoing with gospel tunes. *New York Times*, p. A10.

WYFR international program schedule. (1979). 2 September–3 November.

Ysami, S.-L-A'. (1977). *The Ba'ath party: The period of its foundation (1940–1949)*. Baghdad, Iraq: Ministry of Information and Culture.

Zakya, D. (1979, February). Le véritable débat sur l'information. *Lamalif*, p. 104.

Zartman, I. W. (1991). *Tunisia: The political economy of reform*. Boulder, Colo.: Lynn Rienner Publications.

Zimmerman, J. (1973–1974). Radio propaganda in the Arab-Israeli war 1948. *Wiener Library Bulletin, 30/31*, 2–8.

PERSONAL COMMUNICATIONS

Abdu, Mohammed. (1979, October 29). Acting Chief Radio and Television Engineer, Egyptian Radio-Television Federation. Personal interview. Cairo, Egypt.

Abdullah, Tawffik. (1979, October 26). Controller, Commercial Section, Egyptian Radio-Television Federation. Personal interview. Cairo, Egypt.

Abonaja, Abdulaziz S. (1991, January 1). General Manager, Second Saudi Arabian Television Channel. Personal interview. Riyadh, Saudi Arabia.

Adrian, Otto. (1975, August 29). Head, English Language Broadcasts, Radio Prague. Personal communication. Prague, Czechoslovakia.

Adwan, Nawaf. (1980, January 17). Director, Arab States Broadcasting Union Center for Radio and Television Research. Personal interview. Baghdad, Iraq.

Ahmed, Hassan. (1980, January 7). Radio Controller General, Radio Dubai. Personal interview. Dubai, U.A.E.

Al-Fieli, Rida. (1980, January 16). Director, Kuwait Television. Personal interview. Kuwait City, Kuwait.

Ali, Jawad. (1980, January 19). Director, Iraqi Radio Broadcasting. Personal interview. Baghdad, Iraq.

Al-Mowaled, Fawzia. (1974, August 10). Director, People's Program. Personal interview. Cairo, Egypt.

Al-Muhaiteeb, Ahmad A. (1990, December 30). Manager, Saudi ARAMCO Television, Personal interview. Dhahran, Saudi Arabia.

Al-Najai, Ali. (1983, August 25). General Supervisor, Second Television Channel. Personal communication. Riyadh, Saudi Arabia.

_____. (1991, January 1). Deputy Minister of Information for Broadcasting. Personal interview. Riyadh, Saudi Arabia.

Al-Sharif, Essam. (1979, November 7). Director, Commercial Sector, Syrian Television. Personal interview. Damascus, Syria.

Al-Warthan, Othman M. (1979, December 29). Manager, Dammam Television Station. Personal interview. Dammam, Saudi Arabia.

Al Yusuf, Ibrahim. (1980, January 15). Director General, The Arabian Gulf States Joint Program Production Institution. Personal interview. Kuwait City.

Amin, Hussein. (1991, August 9). Associate Professor, Hilwan University and Advisor, Egyptian Television. Personal interview. Boston, Massachusetts.

Amin, Hussein, (1992, May 1). Associate Professor, Hilwan University and Advisor, Egyptian Television. Personal communication. Cairo, Egypt.

Amin, Mustapha. (1974, August 12). Editor, Al-Akbar Al-Youm. Personal interview. Cairo, Egypt.

Amoako, Ayo. (1975, April 24). Head of Management Services, Nigerian Broadcasting Corporation. Personal communication. Lagos, Nigeria.

Annis, Ahmed. (1974, August 12). Under Secretary for External Information and Official Egyptian Government Spokesman. Personal interview. Cairo, Egypt.

Ashfoura, Osama. (1979, November 4). Director of Engineering, Hashemite Broadcasting Service. Personal interview. Amman, Jordan.

Ashworth, Anthony. (1980, January 9). Advisor to Minister of Information. Personal interview. Muscat, Oman.

Bang, Hans. (1979, October 29). Agency for International Development. Personal interview. Cairo, Egypt.

Bar-Haim, Shaul. (1980, January 26). Advisor, Israeli Broadcasting Authority. Former Director of Arabic Broadcasts, Voice of Israel. Personal interview. Jerusalem.

Bellatt, Fouad. (1979, November 8). Director General, Syrian Radio and Television. Personal interview. Damascus, Syria.

Bolbois, Henri. (1975, April 17). Office of the Director General, Radio Monte Carlo. Personal communication, transmitting "Note sur la 'Societe Monegasque d'Exploitation et d'Etudes de Radiodiffusion.' " Monte Carlo, Monaco.

Butt, Shamsuddin. (1975, August 1). Controller, External Services, Pakistan Broadcasting Corporation. Personal communication. Rawalpindi, Pakistan.

Choi, Chang Hoon. (1979, June 30). Chief, Overseas English Broadcasting Division, Radio Korea. Personal communication. Seoul, Korea.

Corcoran, Marilyn. (1980, January 27). International Business Associates. Personal interview. Cairo, Egypt.

Darwish, Naboul. (1992, January 8). Director, Arabic Service, Radio France International. Personal interview. Paris, France.

Edison, Edward. (1979, August 28). Hammett and Edison, Incorporated. Personal communication. San Francisco, California.

Edwards, Jim. (1979, August 22). Public Information Office, ELWA. Personal communication. Monrovia, Liberia.

Eilts, Hermann Frederick. (1974, July 27). Former U.S. Ambassador to Egypt. Personal interview. Cairo, Egypt.

El-Kashlan, El-Garhi. (1974, August 10). Chairman, Broadcast Engineering Section, Egyptian Radio-Television Federation. Personal interview. Cairo, Egypt.

ElSheki, Saleh Ahmed. (1975, June/July). Director of Public Affairs, PRBC. Personal interviews. Tripoli, Libya.

ElShweikh, Rashid Tawfik. (1980, May, June, July, August). PRBC Staff member. Personal interviews. Athens, Ohio.

Fakery, Mohammed. (1980, January 24). Chief of Planning and Projects, Ministry of Information. Personal interview. Baghdad, Iraq.

Familiant, Allan. (1991, May 21). Acting Director, Radio Canada International. Personal communication. Washington, D.C.

Frackiewicz, Zdzislaw. (1979, October 12). Editor, Polskie Radio. Personal communication. Warsaw, Poland.

Frankhauser, W. (1983, January 25). Press Officer, Swiss Radio International. Personal communication. Bern. Switzerland.

Ghoneim, Magdi. (1992, January 7/8). Director of Communication, Radio Monte Carlo Middle East. Personal interviews. Paris, France.

Glubb, Lieutenant General Sir John. (1973, April 17). Personal communication. Sussex, England.

Gustafsson, Bengt. (1979, September 17). Director, Radio Sweden. Personal communication. Stockholm, Sweden.

Haffar, Awater. (1979, November 7). Director, Public Relations, Syrian Radio and Television. Personal interview. Damascus, Syria.

Hamilton, George. (1972, May 24). Vice-president, RTV International. Personal interview. Beirut, Lebanon.

Hart, Parker T. (1970, December 23). President, Middle East Institute. Personal communication. Washington, D.C.

Helbach, J. C. Weltcamp. (1979, September 8). External Relations Department, Radio Nederland. Personal communication. Hilversum, Holland.

Hellyer, Peter. (1980, January 9 and 10). Advisor, Foreign Language broadcasting, U.A.E. Radio. Personal interviews. Abu Dhabi.

Helwani, Ahmed. (1977, March 3). Director General, Syrian Radio and Television. Personal interview. Damascus, Syria.

Hijab, Abdul Salam. (1979, November 7). News Director, Syrian Television. Personal interview. Damascus, Syria.

Hopkins, Arthur H. (1975, April 15). Voice of America Public Information Officer. Personal communication. Washington, D.C.

Ibrahim, Mohammad. (1980, October 16). Acting Director, Qatar Television. Personal communication. Doha, Qatar.

Ismail, Salal. (1980, January 16). Assistant Director Kuwait Radio and Director of Foreign Programs. Personal interview. Kuwait City, Kuwait.

Jarrar, Farouk. (1979, November 5). Program Director, Jordan Television. Personal interview. Amman, Jordan.

Kader, Salah Abdel. (1979, October 27). Secretary General, Arab States Broadcasting Union. Personal interview. Cairo, Egypt.

Kandil, Hamdy. (1974, August 14). Radio-TV Expert, UNESCO. Personal interview. Cairo, Egypt.

Karkoush, Antone. (1979, November 8). Deputy Chief Engineer, Syrian Radio and Television. Personal interview. Damascus, Syria.

Kazmi, M. A. (1979, July 17). Controller, External Services, Pakistan Broadcasting Corporation. Personal communication. Islamabad, Pakistan.

Khoury, Ibrahim. (1979, November 13). Program Director, The Voice of Lebanon. Personal interview. Ashrafieh, Beirut, Lebanon.

King, Everett L., Jr. (1979, July 18). Manager, International Marketing, Continental Electronics. Personal communication. Dallas, Texas.

Kouhakja, Mickel. (1979, November 7). Director Arabic Service, Syrian Radio. Personal interview. Damascus, Syria.

Mahrns, Abdel Moez A. (1974, August 11). General Controller of Research and Statistics Egyptian Radio-Television Federation. Personal interview. Cairo, Egypt.

Mansell, G. E. H. (1975, May 1). Managing Director, BBC External Broadcasting. Personal communication with attachments. London, England.

_____. (1979, July 16). Deputy Director-General and Managing Director, External Broadcasting, British Broadcasting Corporation. Personal communication, with "The Arabic Service Over Forty Years." London, England.

Megri, Abdullah. (1975, June, July). Director of Programming, PRBC. Personal interviews. Tripoli, Libya.

Minette, William E. (1961, October 30). Commercial Manager, Hashemite Broadcasting Service. Personal letter to Chester T. Davis, Reports Officer, USOM. Amman, Jordan.

Monsour, Abdul Aziz. (1980, January 16). Director, Kuwait Radio. Personal interview. Kuwait City, Kuwait.

Mubarak, Abdul Hadi. (1980, January 8). Director of Radio Programs, U.A.E. Radio. Personal interview. Abu Dhabi.

Mytton, Graham. (1985, March 21). Head International Broadcasting and Audience Research, BBC World Service. Personal interview. London.

Najai, Ali M. (1983, August 25). General Supervisor, Second Channel, Saudi Television. Personal communication. Riyadh.

Nasser, Salah Bin. (1980, January 3). Assistant Deputy Minister for Radio and Television, Ministry of Information. Personal interview. Riyadh, Saudi Arabia.

Nawwab, Ismail. (1979, December 29). Director ARAMCO Public Relations Department. Personal interview. Dhahran, Saudi Arabia.

Odeh, Adnan Abu. (1977, March 9). Minister of Information. Personal interview. Amman, Jordan.

Odeh, Adnan Abu. (1979, November 5). Minister of Information. Personal interview. Amman, Jordan.

Okesanya, Ayo. (1975, April 24). Head of Management Services, Nigerian Broadcasting Corporation. Personal communication. Lagos, Nigeria.

Oun, Amer Salem. (1975, June, July). Director of Planning and Training, PRBC. Personal interviews. Athens, Ohio.

_____. (1976, December). Director of Planning and Training, PRBC. Personal interviews. Tripoli, Libya.

Patel, Adi. (1980, October 14). Instructional Resources Center, University of Delaware. Personal interview. Newark, Delaware. (Mr. Patel was employed by Aden television prior to the country's independence.)

Radio Station Peace and Progress. (1975, December 22). Personal communication. Moscow, U.S.S.R.

Radiotelevisione Italiana. (1979, October 19). Il Segretario di Radazione, Direzione Servizi Giornalistici e Programmi per l'Estero. Personal communication. Rome, Italy.

Radio Vaticana. (1975, July 13). Propaganda Office. Personal communication. Citta del Vaticano.

Radiotelevisione Italiana. (1979, October 19). Il Segretario di Radazione, Direzione Servizi Giornalistici e Programmi per l'Estero. Personal communication. Rome, Italy.

Rahman, Hassan Ahmed Abdel. (1979a, October 21). Director General, Sudan Television. Personal interview. Khartoum, Sudan.

_____. (1979b, October 22). Personal interview. Khartoum, Sudan.

Rahman, Samiha Abdul. (1974, August 7). Director of Television Programming, Egyptian Radio-Television Federation. Personal interview. Cairo, Egypt.

Ramsay, John M. (1979, September 12). Operations Manager, Radio Canada International. Personal communication. Montreal, Canada.

Regnier, Jean Pierre. (1980, February 1). Commercial and Marketing Manager, Radio Monte Carlo Middle East. Personal interview. Paris, France.

Reichard, Herbert. (1979, August 13; September 11). Chief of Near and Middle East Department, Deutsche Welle. Personal communications. Koln, Germany.

Rico, Julio. (1983, May 31). Director, Radio Exterior de Espana. Personal communication. Madrid, Spain.

Rizk, Charles. (1979, November 12). President, Tele-Liban. Personal interview. Beirut, Lebanon.

Robertson, Lewis. (1980, January 7). General Manager, Dubai Television. Personal interview. Dubai, U.A.E.

Rugh, Andrea B. (1980, January 23). Personal interview. Cairo, Egypt.

Rummelsburg, David. (1975, April 10). Radio Berlin International. Personal communication. Berlin, German Democratic Republic.

Rushty, Ali. (1979, October 29). Director of International and Foreign Language Broadcasting, Egyptian Radio-Television Federation. Personal interview. Cairo, Egypt.

Salheen, Mohammed. (1977, February 2). Director General of Radio Broadcasting, Ministry of Information. Personal interview. Khartoum, Sudan.

Schloss, Peter. (1992, June 12). General Counsel, Star TV. Personal interview. Hong Kong.

Shaar, Khudr. (1979, November 7). Director, Arab States Broadcasting Union Training Center. Personal interview. Damascus, Syria.

Shaban, Hassan. (1974, August 8). Director General for Planning and Research, Radio-TV Federation. Personal interview. Cairo, Egypt.

Shaban, Mohammed. (1974, August 14). Chairman, Egyptian Radio Broadcasting, Egyptian Radio-Television Federation. Personal interview. Cairo, Egypt.

Sharf, Mohammed. (1974, August 6). Director General for Foreign-Language Programming Egyptian Radio-Television Federation. Personal interview. Cairo, Egypt.

Shaw, Indris Ahmad. (1975, April 16). Head, Overseas Service, Radio Television Malaysia. Personal communication. Kuala Lumpur, Malaysia.

Shobaili, Abdulrahman S. (1972, May 20). Director General of Television. Personal interview. Riyadh, Saudi Arabia.

Shummo, Ali. (1979, October 21). Minister of State for Youth and Sports, former Minister of Information. Personal interview. Khartoum, Sudan.

Simon, Andrew. (1990, March 23). Executive Director, Radio Canada International. Personal interview. Montreal, Canada.

Siyabi, Salam. (1980, January 9). Director General of Radio and Television Broadcasting. Personal interview. Muscat, Oman.

Skowrowski, Michael B. (1979, December 29). Chief Engineer, ARAMCO Radio and Television Personal interview. Dhahran, Saudi Arabia.

Sobh, Massoud. (1972, April 3). Tele-Orient. Personal interview. Beirut, Lebanon.

Srivastava, G. P. L. (1979, June 28). External Services Division, All India Radio. Personal communication. New Delhi, India.

Stepanova, Eugenia. (1975, May 29). North American Service Radio Moscow. Personal communication. Moscow, U.S.S.R.

_____. (1979, July 19). Personal communication. Moscow, U.S.S.R.

Suliman, Ahmed. (1980, January 13). Manager, Radio Bahrain. Personal interview. Manama, Bahrain.

Sweiden, Mohamed Saleh. (1979, December). Director, Overseas Broadcasting, The Voice of Friendship and Solidarity. Personal communication. Valletta, Malta.

_____. (1980, January 2). Director, Overseas Broadcasting, The Voice of Friendship and Solidarity. Personal communication. Tripoli, Libya.

Tabori, Eli. (1982, March 24). Deputy Director, Economic Development, Israeli Ministry of Foreign Affairs. Personal interview. Salzburg, Austria.

Taquet, Jacques. (1989, September 9). Director General, Radio Monte Carlo Middle East. Personal interview. Paris, France.

Tawffik, Tomader. (1980, May 13). Director, Egyptian Television. Personal interview. Philadelphia, Pennsylvania.

Tétrault, Roger. (1990, March 22). Chief, Arabic Service, Radio Canada International. Personal interview. Montreal, Canada.

Thiik, Ambrose Riny. (1979, September 12). Regional Minister of Information, Southern Region, Sudan. Personal interview. London, England.

Triana, Maria. (1983, June 3). Head of Correspondence Department, Radio Habana Cuba. Personal communication. Habana, Cuba.

Tuch, Hans. (1979, July 27). Acting Director, Voice of America. Personal communication. Washington, D.C.

Wada, Ryochi. (1991, June 17). Director, Arabic Service, Radio Japan. Personal interview. Tokyo, Japan.

Wald, Peter. (1983, March 16). DW Office of Information. Personal communication. Cologne, Germany.

Warugaba, Cosma. (1979, August 30). Deputy Director of Broadcasting and Television. Personal communication. Kampala, Uganda.

West, Harold. (1972, March 28). Chief of Construction Division, U.S. Army Corps of Engineers. Personal interview. Livorno, Italy.

Yasmie, Walid. (1979, November 12). Manager, Tele-Management. Personal interview. Beirut, Lebanon.

Yousef, Abdul Amir. (1980, January 19). Director, Iraqi Television. Personal interview. Baghdad, Iraq.

Yousef, Ahmed. (1979, October 24). Director, Arab States Broadcasting Union Technical Center. Personal interview. Khartoum, Sudan.

Zada, Jawad. (1979a, November 4). Director, Radio Jordan, English Service. Personal interview. Amman, Jordan.

_____. (1979b, November 5). Director, Radio Jordan, English Service. Personal interview. Amman, Jordan.

Index

Aden Voice of the Oman Revolution, 329
Adventist World Radio, 230
Advertising
  in the Arab world, 340
  in Bahrain, 173–174, 176
  in Egypt, 16, 25–26, 45–46, 47–48
  in Jordan, 94–95, 96, 100, 104, 106
  in Kuwait, 134
  in Lebanon, 70, 72, 73, 74, 75, 79, 80,
    81, 83
  in Morocco, 243, 251, 255
  in Qatar, 181
  in Saudi Arabia, 152, 156–158
  in the Sudan, 65
  in Syria, 90–91
  in Yemen, 112
Agency for International Development
    (AID)
  loans to Egyptian Radio-Television
    Federation, 37 (*Table 2.4*)
  loan to Egypt, 36
  and RTV, 96
  in the Sudan, 56–57
AJL-TV, 146
al-Bahri, Yunus, 287
Algeria, 203–220
  financing of broadcasting in, 207, 209,
    211, 213–214, 216, 217
  set ownership in, 205, 216
  use of ARABSAT, 217, 219
Algeria, radio in
  Emissions des Langues Arabe et Kabyle
    (ELAK), 205–206
  establishment of national service
    (RTA), 207
  first broadcasts of, by French, 205
  foreign-language services, 216
Algeria, television in
  first broadcasts of, 206
  set ownership, 216

Tipaza Audiovisuel, 215
  Western programming and, 206, 218
American Broadcasting Company (ABC),
    73
Arabian Gulf, definition of, 115–116
Arabian Gulf Production Company, 187,
    188, 189
Arabian Gulf states. *See* Gulf states.
Arabian Gulf States Joint Program Pro-
    duction Institution, 198
Arabic language, 313–315, 333
Arab League Boycott Office
  circumvention of, by Egypt, 42
  circumvention of, by Saudi Arabia, 150
  RCA, 42, 87–88, 150
Arab Maghreb Union (UMA), 219
ARABSAT, 9, 52, 217, 219, 233, 278, 337–
    338, 341
Arab States Broadcasting Union (ASBU),
    101, 197, 216, 253, 278, 336–339
Arab world
  definition of, 3
  financing of broadcasting in, 340
  set ownership in, 11, 283–284
ARAMCO
  broadcasting in Eastern province of
    Saudi Arabia, 140
  dual color systems (PAL, NTSC), 163
  dual language broadcasts of, 146
  early television station, 38, 146
  program subtitling in Lebanon, 41
  radio services of, 163–164
  television program censorship and, 163
  television services of, 162, 163
Associated Business Consultants (ABC).
    See RTV International.
Audience research
  on the Arab audience for foreign radio
    broadcasts, 305
  in Bahrain, 174, 308

Audience research (*continued*)
  on BBC programs, 132–133, 293, 306,
    307, 308
  in Egypt, 43, 54, 306, 307
  after the Gulf War, 293
  in Jordan, 22, 95, 99–100, 105–106, 307
  in Kuwait, 22, 132, 133
  in Lebanon, 78, 305, 307
  in Libya, 233–234, 235
  in Morocco, 250, 254–255
  in Palestine, 305
  reasons for lack of, 54, 166
  on RMC programs, 307, 308
  in Saudi Arabia, 22, 166–169, 306, 308,
    309
  in the Sudan, 60–61, 66, 307
  in Syria, 305, 307
  in the United Arab Emirates, 308, 309
  on VOA programs, 307, 308
AVCO, 151

Bahrain, 172–176
  importance of Saudi Arabian market to
    broadcasting in, 173
  set ownership in, 172
Bahrain, radio in
  first broadcasts of, 172–173
  popularity of in Kuwait, 133; in Saudi
    Arabia, 168
  use of foreign personnel in, 173
Bahrain, television in, first broadcasts of,
    174
BETA, 151
British Broadcasting Corporation (BBC),
    5
  Arabic Service, 286, 292–293
  Empire Service, 285–286
  first foreign-language broadcast of, 286
  jamming by Iraq, 125
  personnel in Aden, 111
  popularity of
    in Egypt, 307
    in Jordan, 99–100
    in Lebanon, 305
    in Libya, 234
    in Palestine, 305;
    in Saudi Arabia, 168, 169
    in the Sudan, 61
    in Syria, 305
  relay
    on Bahrain television, 176

    from Masirah Is. (Oman), 191–192
    from South Yemen, 110–111
  sponsoring research, 166, 307
Broadcasting, educational/instructional
  in Algeria, 217, 218, 219
  in Egypt, 24, 39, 42
  in the Gulf states, 195, 198–199
  in Iraq, 127–128
  in Kuwait, 131, 136
  in Lebanon, 72, 74
  in Libya, 231, 234
  in Morocco, 259
  in Oman, 193
  in Qatar, 178, 179, 180
  in Saudi Arabia, 160, 169
  in the Sudan, 58, 61, 62
  in Tunisia, 264, 265–266, 271, 273–276,
    277
  in the United Arab Emirates, 184, 185,
    186, 189
Broadcasting equipment suppliers
  Ampex, to Iraq, 122
  Cable and Wireless, to Yemen, 110
  Continental Electronics
    to Egypt, 35
    to Jordan, 98
    to Saudi Arabia, 142
  GTE, to Algeria, 211
  Harris Corporation
    to Egypt, 36
    to Saudi Arabia/ARAMCO, 163
  ITT, to Saudi Arabia, 39
  Marconi
    to Egypt, 17
    to Jordan, 100
    to Kuwait, 134
    to Saudi Arabia, 138
    to Yemen, 112
  Mitsubishi, to Algeria, 211
  Philips, to the Sudan, 57
  Pye
    to Iraq, 126
    to Yemen, 112
  RCA
    to Algeria, 213
    to Egypt, 38
    to Saudi Arabia, 139, 150
    to Syria, 87
  RTF, to Algeria, 206
  Schlumberger, to Kuwait, 132
  Soviet Union and East European coun-
    tries

to Egypt, 34–35
to Iraq, 121–122
to South Yemen, 111
to the Sudan, 57
to Syria, 86
Télécommunications Radioélectriques
    et Téléphoniques (TRT), to Alge-
    ria, 209
Telefunken, to Saudi Arabia, 138
Tesla
    to the Sudan, 57
    to Syria, 86
Thomson-CSF
    to Iraq, 125
    to Kuwait, 134
Broadcasting in Arabic from non-Arab
    countries, 3 (*Table 2.2*)

Cable News Network International
    (CNNI), 52, 105, 176
Censorship
    of news
        in Lebanon, 74
        in Morocco, 256
    of television programs, 10
        by ARAMCO, 163
        in Libya, 232
        in Saudi Arabia, 158–160
        in the Sudan, 64
Central Intelligence Agency (CIA)
    and RTV International, 95–96, 175
    use of Egyptian transmitters, 36
Clandestine radio broadcasting
    to the Arab world, 284
    in Egypt, 27
    in Iraq, 121, 124
    in Lebanon, 69–70
    in the Middle East, 324, 325–326, 328–
        333
    in Yemen, 112
Continental Electronics, 35, 98–99, 142
Culture, oral, 4, 5, 20, 254, 277, 283, 284,
    285
Cyprus, 3, 34, 48, 71, 96, 110, 166, 174,
    283, 290, 291, 292, 298, 302, 304, 318,
    319, 327

Deutsche Welle (Voice of Germany), 5
    Arabic Service, 293
    transmitters in Malta, 230

Direct Broadcast Satellite (DBS) transmis-
    sion, 8, 341–342, 310
    in the Gulf, 171
Dubai, 186–189
    Arabian Gulf Production Company,
        187, 188, 189
Dubai, radio in
    domestic, Arabic Service, 188
    foreign-language program, English
        Service, 188–189
    use of foreign personnel, 187
Dubai, television in
    Arabian Gulf Production Company,
        187, 188, 189
    first broadcasts of, 186
    Program One (Arabic), 187
    Program Two (English), 187–188
    use of foreign personnel, 187

Egypt, 15–54
    set ownership in, 15, 52–53
Egypt, radio in
    beamed services of, 29–34
    broadcasting facilities of, 20–21, 34–37
    domestic and regional services
        Alexandria Local Service, 23
        Communication Network, 34
        Cultural Network, 33
        European Program, 26–27
        Holy Koran Broadcast, 26
        Local Network, 33
        Main Network, 33
        Main Program (Radio Cairo), 21–22,
            30
        Middle East Program, 24–26, 133,
            168, 174
        Musical Program, 27
        Overseas Network, 34
        Palestine Broadcast, 27–28
        People's Program 23–24
        Quran Network, 33
        Second Program, 23
        Sudan Program, 22–23
        Voice of the Arabs, 28–29, 34, 94,
            111, 121, 140, 168, 225, 315–324
        Youth Broadcast, 26
    foreign-language services, 29–34 (*Table
        2.1*)
    Marconi contract and, 17, 18
    military importance of, 320, 323
    transmission power of, 35–37 (*Table 2.3*)

Egypt, television in
  advertising revenues of, 45–46
  contemporary programming, 49
  coverage of Nasser, 41, 42
  coverage of Sadat, 42
  criticism of, 49–50
  Egyptian feature films and, 40
  financing of, 48
  first broadcasts of, 38
  foreign programs, 41–42
  news, 40–41
  programs for export, 46–47
  services of
    Main Program, 38–39, 48–49
    Second Program, 38, 49
    Third Channel, 50
    Third Program, 38
Egyptian-Israeli Peace Treaty (1979), 10,
    16, 28, 30, 47, 50, 119, 124, 188, 278,
    313, 324, 333
Egyptian Radio-Television Federation
  establishment of, 43
  financing of, 48
  training facilities for, 338
European Broadcasting Union (EBU),
    196, 216, 253, 336, 341
  news feeds by satellite
    to Jordan, 101, 103
    to Oman, 193
    to Qatar, 180
    to the Sudan, 64
    to Syria, 89
    to the United Arab Emirates, 184

Fighters for the Freedom of Israel (Pales-
    tine), 326
FM, 6, 7, 70, 97, 98, 116, 131, 132, 145,
    146, 163, 164, 178, 179, 184, 186, 188,
    196, 228, 230, 240, 244, 248 (*Table
    18.2*), 259, 309, 334, 342
Free Lebanon Radio, 77
Free Radio of the Voice of South Leba-
    non, 77
Free Voice of Iran (Egypt), 36
Free Yemeni South Radio, 329

Gafsa Radio, 330
Gulf states, Arabian, 115–199
  television (Gulfvision) in, 197–198
Gulf War, 268, 281, 282, 287, 298, 309,

310, 333, 339
Gulfvision, 197–198

Haganah Radio (Palestine), 325
Holy Mecca Radio, 332
Home video recorders, 8, 164–166
HZ-22-TV (ARAMCO TV), 146, 162

Iftah Ya Simsim
  criticism of, 199
  production of, 198–199
    in Kuwait, 134
    in Qatar, 180
    in the United Arab Emirates, 184
Inqza Radio (Palestine), 326
INTELSAT
  in Algeria, 211
  and Arab broadcasting, 9, 341
  in Jordan, 101
  in Libya, 233
  in Morocco, 246, 253
  at O.A.U. Conference (the Sudan), 63
International Religious Broadcasters
    (Christian), 303–305
  Adventist World Radio (AWR), 303,
    304
  Eternal Love Winning Africa (ELWA),
    304
  Far East Broadcasting Association, 303,
    304
  Heralding Christ Jesus' Blessings
    (HCJB), 303, 304–305
  Radio Voice of the Gospel (RVOG),
    61, 303, 304
  Trans World Radio (TWR), 304
  Vatican Radio, 303
  WYFR (W1XAL, WRUL), 304
International Telecommunications Union
    (ITU), 99
  study by, in Saudi Arabia, 142
International/transnational broadcasting,
    definition of, 6
Intifada, 92, 331
Iraq, 119–129
  set ownership in, 120
Iraq, radio in
  destruction of transmitters during Gulf
    War, 125
  domestic and regional services of
    Kurdish Program, 120–121, 124

Main Program, 123, 133
Palestine Program, 123–124
Voice of the Masses, 123–124
first broadcasts of, 120
foreign-language and beamed programs,
    123, 124–125
King Ghazi as broadcaster, 120
Mother of All Battles Radio, 125
USSR help, 121–122
Iraq, television in
as first Arab world government station,
    126
political trials, 126
political use of, 128, 129
Western programming and, 127
Israeli Broadcasting Service, 99

Jamming
in the Arab world, 283
by Egypt, 306
by Iraq
    Voice of the Arabs, 319
    in war, 125
by Lebanon (Lebanese political broad-
    casts from Cyprus), 71
by Libya (BBC), 234
by Saudi Arabia
    Egyptian television broadcasts, 149,
        322
    Mecca Mosque takeover broadcasts,
        168, 170
Jordan, 92–106
broadcasting to Israel, 104–105
financing of broadcasting in, 106
set ownership in, 92
Jordan, radio in
domestic and regional services
    English Service (Radio Jordan), 97–
        98
    FM Stereo Service, 98
    Main Arabic Program, 97
first broadcasts of, 93
foreign-language programming in, 97–
    98, 104
Hashemite Broadcasting Service (HBS),
    93, 168
impact of 1970 Civil War on, 101
Israeli audience of, 104–105
Palestine Broadcasting Service (PBS),
    93, 286
Jordan, television in

early broadcasts of, 101
financing of, 102, 106
Hebrew news, 105
impact of 1970 Civil War on, 101
imported programs, 103–104
Jordan Television Corporation, 100
production of programs for export, 102
RTV involvement in, 95–96
subtitling, 103

Kuwait, 130–136
financing of broadcasting in, 134
set ownership in, 130
Kuwait, radio in
domestic and regional services
    English Program, 131
    FM Music Program, 132
    Koran Program, 132
    Main Program, 131
    Second Program, 131
first broadcasts of, 131
foreign-language programming on, 131,
    132
impact of Gulf War on, 133
Kuwait, television in
destruction of studio facilities during
    Gulf War, 52, 136
early broadcasts of, 133–134
financing of, 134
imported programs, 135
production of *Iftah Ya Simsim*, 134, 136
services of
    Main Channel (KTV One), 135
    Second Channel (KTV Two), 135
subtitling, 134

Lebanon, 68–83
set ownership in, 69
Lebanon, radio in
Amsheet transmitter, 72
broadcasting facilities, 69–70
clandestine, 76–79
first broadcasts of, 69
government control of, 69–70
impact of 1958 Civil War on, 69
impact of 1975 Civil War on, 70
Voice of Lebanon, 77, 78–79
Lebanon, television in
Advision, 73
American Broadcasting Company
    (ABC), 73

Lebanon, television in (*continued*)
  Christian takeover of, 76
  Compagnie de Télévision du Liban et
    du Proche-Orient (Télé-Orient),
    73, 74, 76, 79, 81
  La Compagnie Libanaise de Télévision
    (CLT), 72, 73, 74
  impact of civil war on, 75
  Lebanese Broadcasting Corporation
    (LBC), 81
  Middle East Television, 82
  Moslem takeover of, 75–76
  Rizk brothers, 73, 80, 81
  SOFIRAD, 73, 80
  Télé-Liban, 80–81
  Télé-Management, 74, 81
  Thomson (British), 73
  Time-Life Corporation, 73
  use of foreign programming on, 74
  Varitel, 80
Libya, 221–237
  establishment of People's Revolutionary
    Broadcasting Co. (PRBC), 227
  financing of broadcasting in, 227, 236
  set ownership in, 222, 223, 233
  training of broadcasting personnel, 228
  use of foreign personnel, 228
Libya, radio in
  anti-Bourguiba broadcasts, 268
  domestic and regional services of
    Holy Quran Program, 229
    National Service, 228
  early broadcasts of, 223
  foreign-language programming and,
    229, 230–231
  international services of
    Voice of the Great Homeland, 229
    Voice of the Mediterranean, 230
  use of Deutsche Welle transmitters on
    Malta, 229–231
Libya, television in
  first broadcasts of, 224
  Western programming and, 232

Maghrebvision (Chaine Maghrebine)
  in Algeria, 209, 217, 218–219
  in Libya, 233
  in Morocco, 253
  in Tunisia, 278
Mecca mosque takeover, 5, 155, 158, 161,
    168, 170, 291

Middle East, definition of, 3
Middle East Broadcasting Centre (MBC),
    52, 168, 171, 310–311, 342
Middle East War (1967) (Six-Day War),
    29, 92, 287, 313
  impact of, on Egyptian broadcasting,
    29, 41
  impact of, on Jordanian broadcasting,
    96–97
Middle East War (1973) (Yom Kippur), 5,
    30, 142, 287, 290, 324
  impact of, on Egyptian television, 44–45
  impact of, on Saudi Arabian radio,
    141–142
Morocco, 238–260
  establishment of Radiodiffusion-Televi-
    sion Marocaine (RTM), 242
  financing of broadcasting in, 242–243
  set ownership in, 239, 254
Morocco, radio in
  domestic and regional services of
    Berber Service, 240, 244, 253, 254
    International Network, 244, 245, 254
    National Network, 244–245, 253, 254
  first broadcasts of, 239–240
  foreign-language services of, 240
  imported programming, 245
  transmitters, 247–248 (*Table 18.2*)
Morocco, television in
  contract to TELMA, 241
  criticism of, 255–256
  early broadcasts of 241–242, 246
  imported programming, 251
Mutawakallite Royal Radio, 329

Nasser, Gamal Abdel. *See* Political phi-
    losophy, of Nasser
National Broadcasting Company Interna-
    tional (NBCI), 147, 149, 153, 154
National Radio of the Saharan Arab
    Democratic Republic, 330
News agencies
  Libya (JANA), 235–236
  Middle East (MENA), 40
  Morocco (MAP), 253
  the Sudan (SUNA), 60
  Syria, 89
  Tunisia (TAP), 264
News protocol, 40–41
Northern Stations Project, 98–99, 142, 149
NTSC Color System, 163, 165

Oman, 190–194
  financing of broadcasting in, 192
  internal distribution of broadcasting by
    INTELSAT, 192
  set ownership in, 190, 193–194
Oman, radio in
  English Service, 191
  first broadcasts of, 191
  Masirah Island relay transmitter, 191–
    192
  use of foreign personnel, 191
Oman, television in
  first broadcasts of, 192
  use of Egyptian programming by, 192–
    193
  use of Jordanian personnel by, 102, 192
Operation Desert Storm/Desert Shield, 6,
    138, 157, 163
Over-the-horizon propagation (tunneling)
  in the Arabian Gulf, 6, 116–117, 180,
    196
  in Bahrain, from Iraq, 127
  in Israel, from Egypt, 6, 52
  in Jordan, from Egypt, 52
  in Kuwait
    from Iraq, 127
    from Qatar, 180
  in Lebanon, from Egypt, 6, 52
  in Saudi Arabia
    from Egypt, 52, 149, 322
    from Gulf states, 162
    from Kuwait, 134
  in Syria, from Egypt, 6
  in the United Arab Emirates, from
    Qatar, 180

Palestine broadcasting
  in Egypt, 27–28
  in Iraq, 123–124
  in Syria, 329–330
Palestine Broadcasting Service (PBS), 93,
    286
Palestine War (1948), 19, 325
Personnel
  artistic
    in Egypt, 15–16, 17
    in Gulf states, 117
  production
    in Egypt, 16, 39
    Jordanian export of, 102–103, 195
    in Qatar, 181

technical
  availability of, in Egypt, 41
  expatriate, use of, 7, 16
  Jordanian export of, 102–103
  Omani use of, 102, 192
  training of, 10–11
Phase Alternating Line (PAL) system, 6
  adoption of
    by Algeria, 211
    by ARAMCO, 163
    by Bahrain, 174
    by Dubai, 187
    by Jordan, 102
    by Kuwait, 134
    by Oman, 192
    by Qatar, 179–180
    by the Sudan, 62
    by the United Arab Emirates, 184
    by Yemen, 109
  recommendation of, to Saudi Arabia,
    151
Political philosophy
  of Ba'ath, 84, 89, 119, 125, 313
  of Benjedid, 212
  of Boumedienne, 208
  of Bourguiba, 264–265, 267–268
  of Nasser, 20, 28, 29, 312
  of Qadhafi, 225, 226, 236
Program content research, 244, 248–250

Qatar, 177–181
  set ownership in, 177
Qatar, radio in
  domestic and regional programs in
    Arabic Programs, 178
    English Services, 178–179
    Urdu Programs, 178
  motivation for starting broadcasting
    service, 178
Qatar, television in
  financing of, 181
  first broadcasts of, 179
  programming, 180–181
  use of foreign personnel, 181

Radio Africa, 241
Radio Africa Maghreb, 241
Radio Africa Tanger, 241
Radio Andorre, 241
Radio Baghdad, 133
Radio Bahrain, 133, 173, 174

Radio Baku, 296
Radio Bari, 93, 284–286
Radio Berlin International, 281, 197
Radio Cairo, 21–22, 30, 94, 108, 133, 168, 305
Radio Canada International (RCI), 302
Radio Damascus (Main Program), 85–86, 99
Radio Dersa Tetuan, 241,
Radiodiffusion Télévision Française (RTF), 206–207
Radio France International (RFI), 290, 292, 295
Radio Freedom from South Yemen, 329
Radio Free Iraq, 121
Radio Hodeida, 109
Radio Inter Africa, 241
Radio Kuwait, 168
Radio Lebanon, 70
Radio Libya, 223
Radio Maroc, 240
Radio Mediterranean (Malta), 294
Radio Méditerranée Internationale (RMI), 250, 288 (Table 20.1), 290, 291–292
Radio Monte Carlo Middle East (RMC), 5, 61, 98, 133, 156, 168, 174, 288 (Table 20.1), 290–292
Radio Moscow, 296
Radio Nederland, 293–294
Radio of Free and Unified Lebanon, 77
Radio Oman, 191
Radio Omdurman, 58
Radio Pan American, 241
Radio Peace and Progress (Voice of Soviet Public Opinion), 281, 296
Radio San'a, 109
Radio Taiz, 109
Radio Tanger, 241, 250
Radio Tanger International, 241
Radio Tashkent, 296
Radio Tunis, 263, 264
Radio Voice of the Gospel (RVOG), 61, 303, 304
Radio Yerevan, 296
RTV International
   in Bahrain, 174–175
   in Jordan, 95–96, 101

Sabbagh, Issa, 287
Said, Ahmed, 29, 315, 318, 320, 323

loss of credibility, 323
period of success, 29
Saudi Arabia, 137–171
   set ownership in, 167–168
Saudi Arabia, radio in
   domestic and regional services
      European Service, 144–145
      General Program, 143
      Holy Koran Broadcast, 143–144
   foreign-language and beamed programs, 143, 144
   during Gulf War, 145
   jamming by Iraq, 125
   Northern Stations Project, 98–99, 142, 149
   use of foreign personnel, 143
Saudi Arabia, television in
   financing of, 150
   first broadcasts of, 147
   King Faisal's death and, 148–149
   Kuwait television availability in, 150
   and Mecca mosque takeover, 161
   motivation for introduction of, 146, 322
   operation and maintenance contracts
      AVCO, 151
      BETA, 151
      NBCI, 147, 149, 153, 154
   opposition to, 147–149
   training of personnel, 150
   transmission on both PAL and SECAM systems, 151
   Western programming and, 155, 163
Secret Jihad (Palestine), 326
Sequential Color and Memory (SECAM) system, 6, 165
   adoption of
      by Egypt, 44–45, 48
      by Iraq, 127
      by Libya, 232
      by Saudi Arabia, 151
      by Syria, 88
   evaluation of, by Algeria, 211
Sesame Street. See Iftah Ya Simsim
Sharq al-Adna, 326–328
   in South Yemen, 110
Six-Day War. See Middle East War (1967)
SOFIRAD, 73, 250, 251, 290, 292
The Sudan, 55–67
   financing of broadcasting in, 64, 65
   set ownership in, 55
The Sudan, radio in
   damage to, in attempted 1976 coup, 58

domestic and regional services
 Juba Local Service, 59
 Koranic Station, 59
 National Program (Radio Omdur-
 man), 58
 National Unity Radio, 59
 Voice of the Sudanese Nation, 59
The Sudan, television in
 aid to, from West Germany, 61
 news, 64
 programming, 63–64
Sudan Domestic Satellite (SUDOSAT)
 System, 63
Sudan Rural Television Project, 62
Suez War (1956), 110, 111, 287, 290, 316,
 318, 319, 327
 invasion of Egypt, 34
Syracuse University, 94–95
Syria, 84–91
 early broadcasting in, 85
 effects of union with Egypt on broadcasting in, 85
 set ownership in, 84
Syria, radio in
 domestic and regional services
 Main Program (Radio Damascus),
 95–96, 99
 Voice of the People, 86–87
 first broadcasts of, 85
 foreign-language and beamed services,
 85–86
Syria, television in
 contract with RCA, 87
 financing of, 90
 first broadcasts of, 87

Television operation and maintenance
 contracts, in Saudi Arabia
 AVCO, 151
 BETA, 151
 NBCI, 147, 149, 153, 154
Television receive-only equipment
 (TVRO), 8, 211
Transistor radios, 4
 low cost of, 7
 military value of, 323
Transliteration of Arabic, x–xi
Tunisia, 261–278
 financing of broadcasting in, 264, 270–
 271
 set ownership in, 262, 269

Tunisia, radio in
 domestic and regional services, 267, 269
 early broadcasts of, 263, 265
 International Service, 267, 269
Tunisia, television in, first broadcast of,
 265
Tunneling. *See* Over-the-horizon propagation

United Arab Emirates (U.A.E.), 182–189.
 See also Dubai
 set ownership in, 182
United Arab Emirates, radio in
 domestic and regional services, 183
 first broadcasts of, 183
 foreign-language services, 183–184
United Arab Emirates, television in, first
 broadcast of, 184
United Press International (UPI), 171
USSR/East European countries
 aid to the Sudan, 56–57
 in Egypt, 34–35
 estrangement from the Sudan, 57
United States Army Corps of Engineers
 (COE)
 and RTV, 95–96
 in Saudi Arabia, 141, 142, 147, 149, 150,
 153
United States Federal Communications
 Commission (FCC), 147
United States Information Agency
 (USIA), and audience research
 in Bahrain, 308
 in Egypt, 306
 in Kuwait, 132, 308
 in Saudi Arabia, 167–168, 169, 308
United States International Communication Agency (USICA)
 aid to Lebanon, 80
 aid to Syria, 88
 support for Egypt, 37

Videocassette recorders (VCRs), 8, 51,
 117, 164–165, 170–171, 235
Videocassettes
 Death of a Princess, 166
 first appearance of, in Saudi Arabia,
 165
 in Gulf states, 117–118, 196
 in Saudi Arabia, 164–166, 170

Voice of America, 5, 300–302
  and Iraq, 121, 125, 129
  popularity in Saudi Arabia, 168
  and the Sudan, 61
  transmitter on Bahrain, 175, 301
  use of Tangiers transmitters, 241
Voice of Arab Awakening (Iraq), 332
Voice of Arabism (Lebanon), 77
Voice of Arab Lebanon (Lebanon), 77
Voice of Arab Revolution (Lebanon), 77
Voice of Arab Syria (Iraq), 328, 332
Voice of Arab Syria/National Alliance for
  the Liberation of Syria (Iraq), 332
Voice of Britain (Cyprus), 319, 327–328
Voice of Cairo (Egypt), 46–47
Voice of Egyptian People (Libya), 330
Voice of Egypt of Arabism (Iraq), 124
Voice of Eritrea Revolution (Iraq), 330
Voice of Fatah/Asifah (Syria), 330
Voice of Fighting Zion (Palestine), 326
Voice of Free Iraq (Saudi Arabia), 333
Voice of Friendship and Solidarity (Lib-
  ya), 230
Voice of Germany (Deutsche Welle), 293
Voice of Hope (Lebanon), 78
Voice of Iraq (Syria), 332
Voice of Iraqi Kurdistan, 328
Voice of Islam (Saudi Arabia), 141, 143,
  149
Voice of Israel (Palestine), 325
Voice of Lebanon (Lebanon), 77, 78
Voice of One Lebanon (Lebanon), 77
Voice of Palestine (Syria/Lebanon), 329
Voice of Peace Republic of Iraq/Voice of
  Peace from Baghdad (Iraq), 332
Voice of Soviet Public Opinion (Radio
  Peace and Progress) (USSR), 296
Voice of the Arabian Peninsula People
  (Iraq), 328
Voice of the Arabs (Egypt), 28–29, 94,
  111, 121, 315–324
  attacks on Iraqi Prime Minister as-Said,
    121, 317, 319
  attacks on Jordan and Glubb, 317, 318
  attacks on Saudi Royal family, 140, 322
  influence on Qadhafi, 225
  popularity in Saudi Arabia, 168

Voice of the Great Homeland (Libya),
  229
Voice of the Jihad/Voice of the Holy War
  from Baghdad (Iraq), 331
Voice of the Kurdistan Democratic Party
  (Turkey), 332
Voice of the Libyan People (the Sudan,
  Iraq, Chad), 332
Voice of the Masses (Iraq), 123–124, 331
Voice of the Mediterranean (Libya, Mal-
  ta), 230, 294, 332
Voice of the People (Syria), 86–87
Voice of the People of Kurdistan, 331
Voice of the People's Resistance (Leba-
  non), 77
Voice of the Revolution (Palestine), 326
Voice of the Sudanese Nation (the Su-
  dan), 59

Wheelus Air Force Base, early television
  station, 37–38, 224

Yemen, 107–118
  set ownership in, 107
Yemen, North (Yemen Arab Republic),
  107–109
Yemen, North, radio in
  broadcasts from Egypt and Saudi Ara-
    bia, 108
  effect of 1962 military coup on, 108–109
  influence of Egyptian radio on, 108
Yemen, North, television in
  first broadcasts of, 109
  use of imported programs by, 109
Yemen, South (People's Democratic Republic of Yemen), 110–113
Yemen, South, radio in
  anti-Oman broadcasts, 191, 194
  assistance from USSR/East European
    nations, 111
  clandestine Saudi Arabian broadcasts
    112
  first broadcasts of, 110
Yemen, South, television in
  commercial advertising and, 112
  first broadcasts of, 112